The Dutch Sherlock: Forty Years of Detective Work

In loving memory of Co van Ledden Hulsebosch Junior.

And in honor of the entire van Ledden Hulsebosch family for supporting the Co van Ledden Hulsebosch Center and for looking after the heritage and legacy of their famous great-grandfather and ancestor, the founding father of forensic science in the Netherlands, our own Dutch Sherlock Holmes—Co van Ledden Hulsebosch.

The Dutch Sherlock:
Forty Years of Detective Work

By the Famous Dutch Forensic Pioneer
Co van Ledden Hulsebosch

Maurice Aalders en Arian van Asten (red.)

Routledge
Taylor & Francis Group

LONDON AND NEW YORK

The publication of this book is made possible by the Co van Ledden Hulsebosch Center, Netherlands Center for Forensic Science and Medicine.

We thank Evelien Witte van der Veer, Jasmijn Boonacker, and Inge van der Bijl of Amsterdam University Press for supporting the realization of this special project, for developing the business case, and for proposing the book title.

First published in 2024 by Amsterdam University Press Ltd.

Published 2025 by Routledge
4 Park Square, Milton Park, Abingdon, Oxon OX14 4RN
605 Third Avenue, New York, NY 10158

Routledge is an imprint of the Taylor & Francis Group, an informa business

© Authors / Taylor & Francis Group 2024

All rights reserved. No part of this book may be reprinted or reproduced or utilised in any form or by any electronic, mechanical, or other means, now known or hereafter invented, including photocopying and recording, or in any information storage or retrieval system, without permission in writing from the publishers.

Trademark notice: Product or corporate names may be trademarks or registered trademarks, and are used only for identification and explanation without intent to infringe.

ISBN: 9789048565627 (pbk)
ISBN: 9781003705888 (ebk)
NUR 686 | 910

Cover illustration: with images from iStock.
Cover design: Rouwhorst + Van Roon, inspired by the original design from 1946 (public domain)

DOI: 10.5117/9789048565627

Every effort has been made to obtain permission to use all copyrighted illustrations reproduced in this book. Nonetheless, whosoever believes to have rights to this material is advised to contact the publisher.

For Product Safety Concerns and Information please contact our EU representative:
GPSR@taylorandfrancis.com
Taylor & Francis Verlag GmbH, Kaufingerstraße 24, 80331 München, Germany

Table of Contents

Introduction	7
About the Author: The Work and Life of Co van Ledden Hulsebosch	11
About the Translation and the Use of ChatGPT	15
About the Authors of the Epilogues	17

Forty Years of Detective Work by Co van Ledden Hulsebosch

Foreword	31
Introduction	33
1. My First Expertise	35
2. Treasure Hunt in the Ashes in a Stove	39
3. As an Expert for the Court in Ghent	45
4. Disappearance of a Batch of Diamonds	54
5. Peculiar Traces of Dust	60
6. Rice Powder	63
7. Sixty-seven Thousand Guilders in Securities Recovered	66
8. The Murder of the Notary C. S. in Gorinchem	69
9. A Political Attack?	75
10. Murder in the Celebesstraat	83
11. Theft at a Bank Solved by a Police Dog	86
12. He Had the Silent Witness "in Hand"	91
13. The Murder of the Cat Farmer	94
14. Shoe Wax	103
15. Amateur Snapshots as Evidence	108
16. "Visiting Cards"!	112
17. One Hair Made the Difference	119
18. Murder or Suicide?	123
19. Petty Thief	126
20. Simulated Robbery	130
21. Who Bears the Cost of the Damage?	135
22. Poison!	142
23. How the Mysterious Thefts in Professor Saltet's Laboratory Were Solved	158
24. A Lame Student Joke, for Which Heavy Penalties Were Paid	163
25. The Dishonest Postal Worker	167
26. How the First Lamp for Ultraviolet Ray Investigation Came to Our Country	172
27. The Treacherous Glass Splinter	182

28. The Corpse in the Suitcase	185
29. The Severed Head of a Woman	191
30. Dust Provided the Evidence	195
31. Assisting Criminal Justice in Belgium	198
32. The Anonymous Letter	201
33. Fine Sleuthing by Dogs!	203
34. The Murder of Tania Schovers	210
35. Bombs	216
36. Cigarettes with Water Damage	226
37. Ill-fated Bloodstains	229
38. Arsonists	235
39. To Whom Does This Pocketknife Belong? Whose Key Chain Is This?	245
40. The Pickpocket	248
41. He Had It in Writing	252
42. A Burglar with ... a Brain	257
43. The Evidence-Providing Phonograph Cylinder	260
44. Restoration and Reconstruction of Documents	266
45. Charred Papers	274
46. Emergency Relief	278
47. Yellow Powder	282
48. "*Souches*," or Physical Fits	287
49. What One Little Blood Spatter Proved	294
50. How the Stolen Jewels Were Recovered	299
51. Counterfeiters	305
52. The Clever Swindler	310
53. Faked or Actual Theft of Mail	315
Epilogue	321

Introduction

During the annual symposium on October 26, 2023, the Co van Ledden Hulsebosch Center (CLHC), celebrated its tenth anniversary. Ten years earlier, on September 13, 2013, the Netherlands Forensic Institute (NFI), and the Faculteit der Natuurwetenschappen, Wiskunde en Informatica (FNWI, Faculty of Science) and the Academic Medical Center (AMC) of the University of Amsterdam (UvA) signed a collaboration agreement that marked the start of the CLHC, the first forensic expert and academic network organization in the Netherlands. In preparation for this official start, the name of the center was being discussed and explored by those involved in the initiative. The first name suggested was the "Amsterdam Center for Forensic Science (ACFS)," concise, functional, yielding an attractive abbreviation, but, on the other hand, not very inspirational. Professor Rick van Rijn, forensic (pediatric) radiologist, then came up with the idea to name the center after the famous Dutch and Amsterdam-based forensic pioneer Co van Ledden Hulsebosch, who developed and successfully introduced forensic science into criminal investigations in the Netherlands. This idea quickly got broad support, but it also raised several questions. Were relatives of Co van Ledden Hulsebosch still alive? If so, were they aware of the forensic legacy of their famous ancestor and would they agree to the use of the family name for the new center? After some searching (a well-developed skill for most people involved in the forensic science field), the CLHC associates came into contact with the van Ledden Hulsebosch family and specifically the grandson, Co van Ledden Hulsebosch Junior, who happened to be named after of his famous grandfather. Already retired and at a respectable age, Co Junior turned out to be a very energetic and enthusiastic man with a vivid memory of the great crime and justice stories that his famous grandfather told him when he was a young boy. He had also actively been maintaining records, documents, and artifacts related to the forensic career of his grandfather. He quickly consulted with the van Ledden Hulsebosch family and all the members gave their permission to link their family name to the forensic academic center that was going to be established. And things did not stop there! Co Junior became fully engaged and started to attend the annual symposium, even if it meant that he had to travel from far. During the symposia he was always very visible and approachable, he spoke to the younger generations of forensic scientists and the students of the MSc in forensic science program at the UvA.

He also on several occasions contributed with expositions on the work and life of Co van Ledden Hulsebosch. Together with the CLHC scientists and experts, he contributed to the development of the historical page on the CLHC website.[1] It

---

[1] https://www.clhc.nl/about-clhc/on-co-van-ledden-hulsebosch.html.

Co van Ledden Hulsebosch Junior (middle) with CLHC directors Maurice Aalders (right) and Arian van Asten (left) at the inaugural event of the Co van Ledden Hulsebosch Center on September 13, 2013.

Co van Ledden Hulsebosch Junior with a special exhibition on the work and life of his famous grandfather at the CLHC Annual Symposium in October 2018 at Amsterdam Science Park.

was also Co Junior who scanned the *Veertig Jaren Speurderswerk* (Forty years of detective work) memoirs, allowing those not in possession of a printed copy to read it electronically by downloading the pdf files from the CLHC website. Unfortunately, Co Junior did not live to see the realization of this book, the English translation of these memoirs with views and reflections from several Dutch forensic experts and scientists. He would have undoubtedly loved and supported it! Co Junior passed away early 2020 at the respectable age of 86. We still think and talk about him often here at the Co van Ledden Hulsebosch Center. We dedicate this book to him and the van Ledden Hulsebosch family and we hope that with this English edition we have made a small but valuable contribution to the conservation and dissemination of the fascinating history of forensic science in the Netherlands.

Maurice Aalders and Arian van Asten

January 2024, Amsterdam

About the Author: The Work and Life of Co van Ledden Hulsebosch

Christiaan Jacobus (Co) van Ledden Hulsebosch was born in Amsterdam on March 20, 1877. He studied pharmacy at the University of Amsterdam, obtained his pharmacist's license in 1902, and subsequently started working at his father's pharmacy at Nieuwendijk 17 in the city of his birth. Co's father had conducted basic forensic research on behalf of the police and judicial authorities for some time. His son soon became fascinated with this special task of his father and decided to explore the realm of forensic science further. His career in the field of scientific police research started on March 9, 1902, when his father was summoned to help the Alkmaar police force with the investigation of an alleged sexual assault. With his father attending a conference in Brussels, Co traveled to Alkmaar in his place and successfully solved the first in a long series of cases through the analysis of "silent witnesses" left at the crime scene. The use of "silent witnesses," physical (trace) evidence, such as cigarette butts, blood spatters, burnt matchsticks, fingerprints, and so on, was still relatively uncommon in those days. Most cases were solved on the basis of witness statements and the interrogation of suspects.

In addition to carefully assessing these traces and the criminalistic evaluation of their relevance, Co van Ledden Hulsebosch also experimented with chemical

Co van Ledden Hulsebosch investigating and casting a shoe mark at a crime scene in 1937.

The forensic laboratory of Co van Ledden Hulsebosch at Nieuwendijk 17 in the city center of Amsterdam in the beginning of the 20th century.

methods in order to improve trace visibility and developed chemical analysis techniques for the assessment of suspicious substances. An excellent example would be the use of ultraviolet fluorescence in the identification and analysis of "Flecke und Spuren von Sperma, Harn, Weißfluß, Schweiß und Blutserum" ("sperm, urine, white discharge, sweat and blood serum stains and traces") all of which "deutlich aufleuchten" ("clearly illuminate"). He personally obtained the required UV lamp from Marie Curie herself. In 1914, he established the very first school for scientific police investigation with the "science of forensics" as its core subject. Two years later, he became the official chemist of the Amsterdam Police. In 1923, he was appointed as private lecturer at the University of Amsterdam, where he taught the "science of criminal investigation."

Despite preferring to work on forensic cases in the privacy and calm of his laboratory in Amsterdam ("The Workshop," as he called it), Co van Ledden Hulsebosch provided assistance on cases in both the Netherlands and abroad. In 1929, he cofounded the Académie Internationale de Criminalistique (International Academy of Criminalistics) in Lausanne, Switzerland. At that time he was an established forensic police expert both nationally and internationally. In the Netherlands he became somewhat of a science celebrity and he was often interviewed by journalists

Co van Ledden Hulsebosch at work in his laboratory (nicknamed "The Workshop").

The front cover of the popular memoirs of Co van Ledden Hulsebosch entitled Veertig Jaren Speurderswerk *(Forty years of detective work).*

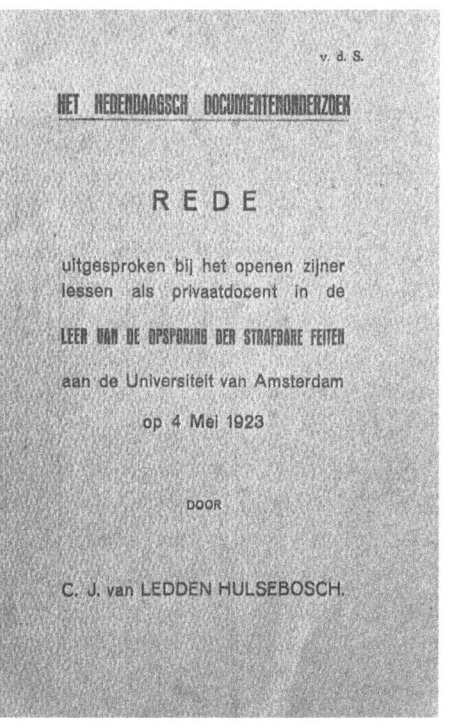

The front cover of the acceptance speech of Co van Ledden Hulsebosch in celebration of his appointment as scholar in forensic science at the University of Amsterdam (1923).

Co van Ledden Hulsebosch teaching forensic science to Dutch police officers from Indonesia in 1921.

and articles on his work appeared in local and national newspapers. Radio interviews were even recorded in his laboratory where he talked about the methods he applied to solve famous cases. In light of the substantial public interest, he wrote his memoirs, entitled *Veertig Jaren Speurderswerk* (Forty years of detective work), of which the first edition was officially released shortly after the end of the Second World War in 1947. This book, containing a substantial collection of case stories, was a great success, and was eventually produced in five editions.

For his outstanding contributions to science and criminal justice, Co van Ledden Hulsebosch was appointed Officer in the Order of Orange-Nassau, a high Dutch royal commendation, and was awarded the Officer's Cross in the Belgian Order of Leopold II. In later life, he suffered from poor health and several illnesses. Co van Ledden Hulsebosch died in Amsterdam on April 18, 1952, at a relatively young age of seventy-five.

About the Translation and the Use of ChatGPT

For years prior to the publication of this book, Dutch forensic scientists and experts involved in the Co van Ledden Hulsebosch Center contemplated the English translation of the memoirs of Co van Ledden Hulsebosch, *Veertig Jaren Speurderswerk* (Forty years of detective work). Such a translation was also requested internationally, especially by forensic scientists from the United States. At the time, the idea could not be followed up due to the lack of funds to pay for the translation of a complete book of 260 pages and excessive time needed for forensic experts to carefully check and edit the translation to make sure that the correct forensic scientific terminology and reasoning was preserved. Like so many other fields and applications, these restrictions suddenly and dramatically disappeared with OpenAI's launch of ChatGPT (Chat Generative Pre-trained Transformer) at the end of 2022. One of the many features of ChatGPT includes its outstanding ability to translate texts from and into English. Because of the way the artificial intelligence (AI) model has been trained, translations are surprisingly accurate and often directly in the correct jargon for a given field of interest. After some tests, forensic scientists at the Co van Ledden Hulsebosch Center (CLHC) came to the conclusion that ChatGPT was quite able to translate the old-fashioned, traditional Dutch text of Co van Ledden Hulsebosch into English. Chapter translations only required a few corrections by an experienced forensic scientist who needed to carefully read the AI-generated result. Instead of days, a single chapter in the memoirs could now accurately be translated in a few hours. With the use of the free version of ChatGPT (model 3.5), several forensic scientists and experts from the CLHC network joined forces to translate the memoirs of our own Dutch Sherlock Holmes. Every translation has been carefully checked and, if needed, improved by a Dutch scientist with the required forensic expertise and knowledge to ensure a correct translation. Occasionally, notes have been added to further explain typical (old-fashioned) Dutch phrasing or to provide some additional information on an area or location. In addition, after reading the chapter and overseeing the translation, each contemporary forensic expert also wrote a short epilogue (or prologue) to review the case context, discuss criminalistic reasoning, and/or provide the reader with a view of how such investigations are conducted in state-of-the-art forensic laboratories today. Although the availability and use of ChatGPT has been elemental in the realization of the translation of the memoirs of Co van Ledden Hulsebosch, it should be noted that ultimately the responsibility for the English text sits with the forensic experts who have checked the translations and have added the epilogues.

About the Authors of the Epilogues

The following forensic scientists and experts have overseen the translation and have included their own thoughts regarding the chapter material in the epilogues.

Maurice Aalders is a professor of forensic biophysics at Amsterdam University Medical Center (Amsterdam UMC). His research bridges the fields of physics, chemistry, biology, medicine, and forensic science, focusing on developing and applying innovative optical and other scientific techniques in forensic and medical practices. The research group has a broad scope which includes research on the aging of bruises and bloodstains, estimating the postmortem interval through body cooling, analyzing bloodstain patterns, and enhancing spectral processing with advanced light transport modeling. This work is conducted in partnership with the Netherlands Forensic Institute and the Dutch Police. Alongside Arian van Asten, he leads the Co van Ledden Hulsebosch Center, where about 30-40 PhD students conduct forensic research. The center also organizes symposiums and lectures. Maurice has published over 120 peer-reviewed articles, teaches biomedical optics to physics students, and various physics topics for students in forensic science and medicine. **Maurice Aalders has overseen the translation and wrote the epilogues of chapters 16, 26, and 45.**

Arian van Asten is professor of forensic analytical chemistry and on-scene chemical analysis at the University of Amsterdam (UvA). Together with Maurice Aalders, he leads the Co van Ledden Hulsebosch Center (CLHC) and he is also the scientific director of the MSc in forensic science program at the UvA. His research interests include the chemical analysis of drugs of abuse, explosives and chemical warfare agents, the chemical profiling of forensic trace evidence, chemical imaging in forensic science, the forensic use of multidimensional chromatography, and the implementation of data science methods in forensic chemistry for intelligence purposes. He has (co)authored over 80 scientific papers on (forensic) analytical chemistry, has published the academic educational book *Chemical Analysis for Forensic Evidence* (2022), and is a member of the editorial board of the scientific journal *Forensic Chemistry*. He was the scientific director of the 2012 European Academy of Forensic Science (EAFS) conference in The Hague and was a member of the scientific board of the 2022 EAFS conference

in Stockholm, Sweden. **Arian van Asten has overseen the translation and wrote the epilogues of Chapters 14, 20, 38, and 47.**

Charles Berger is principal scientist at the Netherlands Forensic Institute (NFI) and professor of criminalistics at Leiden University. He specializes in subjects such as evidence interpretation and inference (logic, probability). At the NFI he is active in a number of areas such as education, R&D strategy, and his own research about which he publishes internationally (https://charles-berger.com). He supports the NFI experts, advises the directors, and guards the scientific quality. He is also involved in promoting logically correct  reasoning and concluding, introducing more objective methods, and going to activity level. For such improvements it is essential to explain them as often and as well as possible to all the stakeholders in the criminal justice system. Charles is a member of the ISO technical committee that developed the upcoming ISO-21043 Forensic Sciences standard and was lead editor of Part 4: Interpretation. **Charles Berger has overseen the translation and wrote the epilogues of Chapters 2, 13, 25, and 44.**

Maarten Blom is a lecturer in the MSc in forensic science program at the University of Amsterdam (UvA). He became intrigued by the field of forensic science during postdoctoral work on the analysis of trace amounts of steroid hormones, when his laboratory became involved in the investigation of a sports doping case. Following up on this experience, he joined the Netherlands Forensic Institute in 2004 as a reporting officer in DNA evidence and later as a coordinator for research and development. In 2009 he started as a forensic  consultant and became involved in lecturing forensics at the Avans University of Applied Sciences. He joined the forensic science service provider Verilabs to conduct DNA analysis for the police and prosecution and DNA kinship analysis. In 2015 he started as lecturer at UvA's forensic science program. Although originally trained as forensic DNA scientist, his interest is much broader and is also built on a background in analytical chemistry and on experience with case assessment and interpretation (CAI) as a forensic consultant and lecturer. The courses he teaches reflect this broad interest—they cover DNA statistics, criminalistics applied to forensic chemistry, and the chain of evidence, where the focus is on CAI, forensic reporting, and testimony in court. Besides his forensic interests, Blom is passionate about reading and writing, he published a debut novel and he is working on his next work of fiction. **Maarten Blom has overseen the translation and wrote the epilogues of Chapters 8, 15, 22, and 40.**

ABOUT THE AUTHORS OF THE EPILOGUES

Jos Brouwers is a professor of analysis techniques in the life sciences at Avans University of Applied Sciences. His forensic interests revolve around chemical profiling, such as analyzing human hair to determine lifestyle markers, and profiling plant metabolites that remain during cocaine purification to reveal geographical locations and trafficking routes. Combating the illegal dumping of drug waste has recently emerged as a new and significant topic. His group has a solid foundation in bioinformatics and analysis of  big data, produced mainly by high-resolution accurate mass spectrometry and nanopore sequencing. **Jos Brouwers has overseen the translation and wrote the epilogues of Chapters 5 and 39.**

Brigitte Bruijns is a senior researcher within the Technologies for Criminal Investigations research group at Saxion University of Applied Sciences and the Politieacademie (Police Academy) in the Netherlands, leading the microfluidic devices research line. She is one of the coordinators of the Co van Ledden Hulsebosch Center (CLHC). She obtained her PhD at the University of Twente in which she combined microfluidic devices with forensic applications. Throughout her (academic) career she has combined various disciplines,  including forensic science, analytical chemistry, nanotechnology, microfluidics, and (bio)chemistry. She organized several international forensic symposia and is member of the board of the Analytical Chemistry section (KNCV) and the East region (KIVI). She has (co)authored several scientific (review) papers on microfluidics and forensics and has been invited to be the guest editor of a special issue on "advanced analysis and sensing at the (crime) scene or location of interest" of *Sensors* (from MDPI, a publisher of open-access scientific journals). **Brigitte Bruijns has overseen the translation and wrote the epilogues of chapters 6, 7, 18, 31, and 36.**

Gareth R. Davies is a world renowned isotope geochemist who leads a multidisciplinary team at the Vrije Universiteit Amsterdam (VU Amsterdam). He became professor in petrology (formation of rocks and minerals) in 2004 and built up the Geology and Geochemistry group from three to twelve academic staff. His career developed from an initial focus on the Earth's interior processes to also include innovative applications in planetary science, archaeology, cultural heritage, and forensic science. Career highlights  include a ~€15M ERC Synergy grant and a €5M national research infrastructure grant to upgrade the national isotope geochemistry facility. **Gareth R. Davies has collaborated in the translation and epilogue of Chapter 27.**

Zeno Geradts is a professor by special appointment in forensic data science and is also a senior forensic scientist at the Netherlands Forensic Institute. Together with Marcel Worring, he is director of the AI4Forensics Lab of Netherland's National Innovation Center for Artificial Intelligence (ICAI). His research interests are multimedia analysis, deepfake analysis, biometric comparison of images, camera identification, and applying artificial intelligence in forensic databases. He (co)authored over a hundred papers  on forensic science, and also coedited *Artificial Intelligence (AI) in Forensic Sciences* (coeditor Katrin Franke, 2023). He is past president of the American Academy of Forensic Sciences, and he received the Distinguished Forensic Scientist award from the European Network of Forensic Science Institutes (ENFSI) in 2012. He is also chair of the Forensic IT working group of ENFSI. **Zeno Geradts has overseen the translation and wrote the epilogue of Chapter 53.**

Paul van den Hoven, a forensic investigator at the Netherlands Forensic Institute (NFI) since 1990, has forensic knot analysis among his areas of expertise. Previously, he worked as an expert in fibers and textiles, and later as forensic trace and bloodstain pattern analysis expert in the CSI team of the NFI. Currently he is a bloodstain pattern expert. Over time, he has gained extensive experience in this niche field of knot and binding analysis. **Paul van den Hoven has overseen the translation and wrote the epilogue of Chapter 50.**

After earning a PhD and short academic career in physical chemistry, **Mattijs Koeberg** started his forensic career in 2006 as a forensic expert and technical lead in the Explosions and Explosive group of the Netherlands Forensic Institute (NFI). In this role he was involved in national and international forensic explosives investigations, including large scale explosion investigations in Lebanon and the Malaysia Airlines Flight 17 (MH17) investigation. Furthermore, he was, among other roles, a steering committee member and  the chair of the Explosives Working Group of the European Network of Forensic Science Institutes (ENFSI), and part of the NFI's Chemical, Biological, Radiological, and Nuclear (CBRN) team. He organized the combined International Symposium on the Analysis and Detections of Explosives/Forensic International Network for Explosives Investigation (ISADE/FINEX) in 2013. In 2016 he transitioned to management within the NFI, where he was a team manager and interim team manager of several teams, acted as policy advisor at the Nationaal Coördinator Terrorismebestrijding en Veiligheid (NCTV, National Coordinator for Security and Counterterrorism), and has been the NFI strategic innovation advisor since 2022. **Mattijs Koeberg has overseen the translation and wrote the epilogues of chapters 9, 30, and 35.**

Bas Kokshoorn is a principal scientist at the Netherlands Forensic Institute (NFI) and is currently appointed professor in forensic trace dynamics at the Amsterdam University of Applied Sciences. Kokshoorn started his career at the NFI in 2008 and since then has submitted over a thousand reports on forensic biology examinations and interpretations to the Dutch criminal justice system, as well as to international tribunals and other jurisdictions in continental Europe, the UK, and Australia. His research interests are in forensic evidence interpretation and, in particular, in the dynamics of biological traces and other particulate evidence. He (co)authored dozens of publications on these topics, both peer-reviewed scientific papers and publications aimed at forensic professionals and the legal community. Together with Professor Duncan Taylor (Flinders University and Forensic Science South Australia), he published *Forensic DNA Trace Evidence Interpretation: Activity Level Propositions and Likelihood Ratios* (2023), a handbook on activity level evaluative reporting of biological traces. **Bas Kokshoorn has overseen the translation and wrote the epilogues of chapters 1, 3, 23, 37, and 42.**

Ate Kloosterman, born in 1951, is renowned for his contributions to forensic DNA technology in the Netherlands. After earning a degree in biochemistry from Utrecht University in 1976, he began his career at the Central Laboratory of the National Blood Transfusion Centre (Sanquin) in Amsterdam, focusing on blood group serology and immunoglobulin allotyping. In 1979, he joined the Netherlands Forensic Institute (NFI), playing a key role in implementing forensic DNA technology. He earned his PhD with honors in 2002 from the University of Santiago de Compostela, Spain, for his thesis on DNA polymorphisms in forensic science. Kloosterman has served as an expert witness in over

250 high-profile court cases, including those at the International Criminal Court in The Hague. Since 2005, he has taught in the MSc in forensic science program at the University of Amsterdam (UvA), where he developed courses and supervised PhD students. In 2018, during the celebration in honor of his retirement, Ate was honoured as a Knight in the Order of the Dutch Lion. After his official retirement in 2018, Ate continued working part-time at the UvA and the NFI (until 2021). **Ate Kloosterman has overseen the translation and wrote the epilogue of Chapter 17.**

Jaap Knotter is a *lector* (full professor) in technologies for criminal investigations at Saxion University of Applied Sciences and the Politieacademie (Police Academy) in the Netherlands. His focus is on promoting investigative practice through applied scientific research. Knotter studied sociology at the University of Amsterdam (UvA), where he received his doctorate in criminology, specializing in the field of kidnapping and hostage situations. During his career he has fulfilled various roles within criminal law. Besides  his academic career, Knotter has worked for the National Police. He started in 1996 as a police officer on the street and also held several positions concerning criminal investigations. During his police career he was a member of the special police team responsible for hostage and kidnapping situations. Knotter's goal is to continue bridging the gap between academia and investigative practice, improving the effectiveness and efficiency of criminal investigations through technological advancements, and preparing future law enforcement professionals for the challenges of the 21st century. **Jaap Knotter has overseen the translation and wrote the epilogue of Chapter 34.**

Shortly after finishing his MSc in analytical chemistry, **Jan de Koeijer** joined the Netherlands Forensic Institute in 1992 as the team leader for document and fingerprint examination and forensic photography. Between 1992 and 2011 he worked in case investigations as both an expert in document examination as well as glass examination. Since 2011, his focus has been on the interdisciplinary aspects of forensic casework. He became the team leader of the Interdisciplinair Forensisch Onderzoek (IDFO, Interdisciplinary Forensic  Research team) and has been involved in combining forensic evidence in criminal cases. In addition to casework, de Koeijer is currently primarily engaged in the theoretically aspects of combining evidence and in optimizing the format in which this is reported. He also educates partners in the criminal justice system about the importance of evaluating findings at the activity level, the impact thereof on laboratory and crime scene forensic investigations, and the combination of forensic evidence in criminal cases. **Jan de Koeijer has overseen the translation and wrote the epilogue of Chapter 28.**

Lisette Kootker is an assistant professor in the Department of Earth Sciences at the Vrije Universiteit Amsterdam (VU Amsterdam). She completed a MSc in geoarchaeology at the VU Amsterdam and holds a PgDip in osteoarchaeology (Bournemouth University, UK). Her prize-winning PhD work focused on the implementation of strontium isotope geochemistry in Dutch archaeological research. Subsequently, she has been utilizing radiogenic and stable isotope systems (Sr-Pb-O-H-C-H) in both archaeological and  forensic contexts, with the aim of elucidating dietary and mobility patterns. Her research pursuits extend to the isotopic characterization of natural archaeological and modern landscapes (isoscapes), alongside investigating the impact of diagenesis on tissue isotopic integrity within forensic settings. Actively engaged in actualistic taphonomic experiments, she collaborates with the Forensic Anthropology Research Facility at Texas State University and the Amsterdam Research Initiative for Subsurface Taphonomy and Anthropology (ARISTA). Her isotope research aids in the identification process of unidentified victims in both cold case and recent forensic investigations, collaborating closely with the Netherlands Forensic Institute and various international law enforcement agencies. She is a VU Amsterdam coordinator at the Co van Ledden Hulsebosch Center (CLHC). **Lisette Kootker has overseen the translation of Chapter 27 and cowrote the epilogue of this chapter with Gareth R. Davies.**

Ruben Kranenburg works as lead specialist in forensic analytical chemistry at the National Expertise and Operations unit of the Netherlands Police. Additionally, he is research associate at the Van 't Hoff Institute for Molecular Sciences of the University of Amsterdam. His research focuses on the identification of illicit drugs, on-scene identification, and remote forensic solutions. He started at the Netherlands Police in 2009, became a forensic reporting officer at the Amsterdam narcotics  laboratory in 2011, and was the quality manager when this laboratory received its ISO 17025 accreditation in 2013. Between 2019 and 2023, he combined his role at the police with a part-time PhD trajectory on illicit drug identification at the University of Amsterdam. Prior to his time at the police, he worked for seven years in various nonforensic laboratory positions, gaining experience in analysis, method development, and validation for GC- and LC-based analytical techniques, mass spectrometry, and sample prep in the environmental trace analysis field. **Ruben Kranenburg has overseen the translation and wrote the epilogues of Chapters 21 and 24.**

Josita Limborgh started as a fingerprint expert at the Netherlands Forensic Institute (NFI) in 1990. Since the establishment of the crime scene investigation team of the NFI in 2005, she has been a member of this team, serving as both a forensic trace and bloodstain pattern analysis expert. The investigations conducted by this team at the crime scene are accredited according to ISO 17020 standards in 2018. Josita has examined both national and international high-profile crime scenes. In recent years, the focus of the  investigation has been on bloodstain pattern analysis at both the crime scene and on pieces of evidence at the NFI. **Josita Limborgh has overseen the translation and wrote the epilogue of Chapter 49.**

Christianne de Poot is professor of forensic science at the Amsterdam University of Applied Sciences and the Politieacademie (Police Academy) in the Netherlands and professor of criminalistics at the Vrije Universiteit Amsterdam (VU Amsterdam). She leads the forensic science research program at these institutions. De Poot studied linguistics and psychology and obtained her PhD in 1996 from the VU Amsterdam. She specializes in conducting and supervising experimental and empirical research in the field of criminal  investigation, investigation methods, crime reconstruction, criminalistics, and crime phenomena. Her research focuses on the impact of societal and technological developments on criminal phenomena and criminal investigations, and on the role of human perception, interpretation, communication, and decision-making in criminal justice processes. De Poot is a member of the Board of Court Experts; a member of the steering committee of the Co van Ledden Hulsebosch Center; a member of the advisory board of the MSc in forensic science program at the University of Amsterdam, and a member of the advisory board of the Taskforce for Applied Research SIA of the Nederlandse Organisatie voor Wetenschappelijk Onderzoek (NWO, Dutch Research Council). **Christianne de Poot has overseen the translation and wrote the epilogue of Chapter 11.**

ABOUT THE AUTHORS OF THE EPILOGUES

Eva de Rijke works as a lab manager in the soil and environmental chemistry laboratories of the Institute for Biodiversity and Ecosystem Dynamics (IBED) at the University of Amsterdam (UvA). She is an analytical chemist who obtained her PhD at the Vrije Universiteit Amsterdam (VU Amsterdam) and worked over ten years as a scientist/project leader in both government and industrial R&D in the area of food quality and safety, before returning to green forensics and environmental chemistry research at UvA.
She has broad (hands-on) knowledge of a variety of analytical techniques such as LC-(HR)MS and GC-(IR)MS, but also spectroscopic techniques such as NMR, UV and fluorescence detection, to determine, e.g., environmental contaminants, taste/odor compounds, additives, and (veterinary) drugs. Apart from being a coordinator for the Co van Ledden Hulsebosch Center, she is a board member of the Benelux Association for Stable Isotope Scientists (BASIS) and organizes yearly spring meetings. Furthermore she has been on the board of the Nederlandse Vereniging voor Massaspectrometrie (NVMS, Dutch Society for Mass Spectrometry) for six years and is responsible for the program of the annual spring and fall meetings and the international symposium held every two years at Rolduc Abbey, in Kerkrade, the Netherlands. She was also a member of the local organizing committee of the International Mass Spectrometry Conference in Maastricht in 2022 and responsible for the program (under the theme "mass spectrometry across disciplines"), including the sessions on homeland security, explosives and environmental monitoring, forensic sciences, cultural heritage and conservation science, environmental mass spectrometry, and Earth and space mass spectrometry. **Eva de Rijke has overseen the translation and wrote the epilogue of Chapter 12.**

Rick van Rijn graduated as a medical doctor from the Erasmus Medical University Rotterdam in 1994 and he obtained his PhD at the same university in 1998. In 2002 he finished his training as a radiologist at the Erasmus Medical Center, Rotterdam, and the Academic Medical Center, Amsterdam. Since 2003 he has worked as a pediatric radiologist at the Emma Children's Hospital of the Amsterdam University Medical Center (Amsterdam UMC). Since 2010 he has also held a part-time position at the department of Forensic
Medicine, Netherlands Forensic Institute. In June 2014 he was appointed as professor of forensic radiology with an emphasis on forensic pediatric radiology. He is a founding member of the Dutch Expertise Centre for Child Abuse (DECCA) and has held/holds several positions in professional societies, amongst others chair of

the International Society of Forensic Radiology and Imaging, chair of the scientific committee of the Forensisch Medisch Genootschap (FMG, Dutch Forensic Medical Society), and general secretary of the European Society of Paediatric Radiology. Besides his clinical work he is involved in scientific research, mainly in the field of imaging of child abuse and imaging in rhabdomyosarcoma. He has published more than 250 peer-reviewed publications, many on child abuse imaging, wrote a book on forensic aspects of pediatric fractures, edited two books on pediatric radiology, and written several book chapters. He is an editorial board member of *European Radiology*, *Pediatric Radiology*, the *Journal of Forensic Radiology and Imaging*, and the *British Journal of Radiology*. A detailed curriculum vitae can be found on LinkedIn (https://www.linkedin.com/in/rickrvanrijn/). **Rick van Rijn has overseen the translation of the foreword, introduction, and epilogue and also looked after the translation of Chapters 10 and 19 and wrote the epilogue of Chapter 48.**

Adee Schoon began her work with police human scent dogs in the Netherlands in 1991 and obtained her PhD in 1997. Since then, her work has included research projects in explosive, drug, biological fluids, human remains, electronic storage devices, corrosion, cancer, and wildlife detection, puppy selection and training programs, and teaching about odors, scent perception, learning, and training. She publishes regularly and participates in a number of international governmental working groups/organizations on detection  dogs. In 2010, she left Leiden University and started Animal Detection Consultancy, with a mission to use, improve, and expand the olfactory detection capabilities of animal/handler teams through focused research, training, and advice, primarily in the field of human security and welfare. She published her ideas in *Training Dogs to Use Their Nose: A Blueprint* in 2021 to commemorate her 30 years of experience. **Adee Schoon has overseen the translation and wrote the prologue of Chapter 33.**

Titia Sijen has led the Research & Development team of the department Human Biological Traces at the Netherlands Forensic Institute since 2007. The main research themes in the team are interpretation of complex DNA profiles, RNA profiling, mitochondrial DNA analysis, and application of massively parallel sequencing for forensic purposes. Besides technological improvements, much effort is spent on developing interpretation strategies, validation, and implementation for forensic casework. Sijen is also a professor by special  appointment of forensic human biology at the University of Amsterdam (UvA). **Titia Sijen has overseen the translation and wrote the epilogues of Chapters 4, 41, and 46.**

About the Authors of the Epilogues

Pernette Verschure is professor of functional epigenome dynamics and holds the chair of the Molecular & Cellular Epigenetics group at both the Swammerdam Institute for Life Sciences (SILS) within the Faculteit der Natuurwetenschappen, Wiskunde en Informatica (FNWI, Faculty of Science) at the University of Amsterdam (UvA) and the Medical Biochemistry Department of the University Medical Centers. Her research is centered on the dynamics and heterogeneity of epigenome functioning, particularly on applied (biomedical) studies. Verschure coordinated an EU H2020 Innovative training network and served as workgroup leader for a COST Action. Currently, she coordinates an international consortium developing sustained epigenetic reprogramming as a key technology addressing significant societal challenges, including age-related diseases, which is funded by the Knowledge and Innovation Covenant (KIC) of the Nederlandse Organisatie voor Wetenschappelijk Onderzoek (NWO, Dutch Research Council). Verschure serves as associate editor for Epigenetic Communications and the Journal of Histochemistry & Cytochemistry. She also serves as SILS coordinator of the Co van Ledden Hulsebosch Center. Verschure is actively involved as lecturer/coordinator and member of the curriculum committee in various BSc and MSc courses in the Faculteit der Natuurwetenschappen, Wiskunde en Informatica (FNWI, Faculty of Science) of the University of Amsterdam (UvA) and she served as chair of the examination committee of the MSc in forensic sciences at the Faculty of Science. **Pernette Verschure has overseen the translation and wrote the epilogue of Chapter 52.**

David L. van der Vloed (MSc) has been a forensic speech researcher at the Netherlands Forensic Institute (NFI) since 2009 and has a background in phonetics and sociolinguistics. He has worked on hundreds of voice comparison cases in over fourteen years. In addition to using auditory and linguistic methods to do comparison, he has broad experience with the use of software-based automatic speaker recognition. He performed validation research on those methods, which resulted in implementation of automatic speaker recognition in NFI casework in 2019. **David van der Vloed has overseen the translation and wrote the epilogue of Chapter 43.**

Forty Years of Detective Work by Co van Ledden Hulsebosch

Foreword

By the Honorable Mr. H. A. Wassenbergh, prosecutor at the Amsterdam District Court

In response to the kind request of the publishers to write a few words on the occasion of the publication of some memories from the illustrious career of our great police expert, Co van Ledden Hulsebosch, entitled *Veertig Jaren Speurderswerk* (Forty years of detective work), I first and foremost want to express my gratitude to the author for his decision to share some of his experiences, which undoubtedly will reach a wide readership. The more knowledgeable readers will eagerly and with great interest delve into the contents of these memoirs. For anyone else who picks up this book, reading it will provide a pleasant diversion. However, both categories will come to admire the man who, sometimes in an almost miraculous way and at other times seemingly effortlessly, managed to unmask criminals or, even more importantly, conclusively prove that a suspect against whom serious allegations were raised could not possibly be guilty. For many years, in my capacity as a prosecutor at the Amsterdam District Court, I regularly called upon Co van Ledden Hulsebosch for assistance in serious crimes, and on numerous occasions I saw him in action at the scene of the crime. Indeed, it is then that detective work takes place, meaning that traces are sought that may lead to the identification of the perpetrator. This is a task that requires a sharp intellect, keen powers of observation, and a solid scientific foundation. It is gratifying to note that many members of our excellent Amsterdam police force possess these qualities and capabilities to a great extent. However, the fortunate combination of all these requirements is particularly evident in our great police expert, van Ledden Hulsebosch, which makes him stand out as the *primus inter pares*.

It is commendable that the author has succeeded in avoiding the excessive use of the word "I" when writing these sketches, which is a very difficult task for someone whose personal involvement plays such a prominent role in his experiences being published. This is especially noteworthy because van Ledden Hulsebosch could have often said: "I came, I saw, I conquered." The author would risk losing one of the noblest human virtues, modesty, if I were to further praise him. As a remedy against this danger, it should be mentioned that van Ledden Hulsebosch did not always succeed, that he sometimes made mistakes, and even once committed a significant act of carelessness that almost cost him his life. This was the occasion when he took a time bomb that had been found—which he deemed harmless—under his arm and calmly walked away with it. Shortly after he had set it down somewhere, it exploded.

On behalf of the judiciary and police, and certainly on behalf of the future readers of *Veertig Jaren Speurderswerk* (Forty years of detective work), I would like to conclude this foreword by wishing Co van Ledden Hulsebosch many more years of vitality, so that he may continue to offer his great talents and experience for the benefit of the general interest, if called upon to do so. Additionally, I hope that in the not-too-distant future, he will surprise us once again with a sequel to this entertaining and delightful literary work.

Amsterdam, summer 1945.

Translation by Rick van Rijn with the use of ChatGPT.

Introduction

The scientific art of investigation has always enjoyed significant interest, not only from those who had to process its results in the rendering of judgments but—perhaps even more so!—from the general public. This latter group, often infatuated with mostly bland detective stories written by countless beginners attempting to emulate Arthur Conan Doyle, never truly understood the art of investigation. When questioning a witness, it is essential to fully understand the language spoken by that witness. If the witness speaks a foreign language, the interrogator would do well to enlist the help of a skilled interpreter, as otherwise, they run the risk of recording "statements" from the witness that the latter never intended to make. Hans Gross, a former professor at the University of Graz, was the first to establish the field of criminalistics on a solid foundation. He emphasized the great importance of the "silent witnesses" who always tell the truth (which cannot always be claimed of living witnesses!) but cautioned against hasty interrogations of these silent witnesses. "If you do not fully understand their language, do not venture into an interrogation but instead leave it to an 'interpreter'!" By this, Gross meant that in such cases, the assistance of an expert should be sought, someone who understands the language of those silent witnesses and can interpret their revelations accurately.

The purpose of criminalistics is to thoroughly study the various types of traces—the silent witnesses—in order to draw conclusions from their presence, location, characteristics, etc., that would contribute to the "reconstruction of the criminal act." Thus, the "scientific art of investigation" must derive its data from the traces at the scene of the crime (or from the traces of the crime on the body or clothing of the perpetrator), construct them, and make deductions, thereby obtaining a comprehensive understanding of the committed crime. The authors of detective novels worked in precisely the opposite manner and wrote their books—so to speak—from back to front. Hence, when Conan Doyle was urgently summoned one night from his bed and asked to participate in the investigation of a murder case, his candid response was, "I cannot! I write my books in such a way that I first work out the solution and then go back, progressing further each time until I have arrived at the very beginning of everything ... the crime itself!" The scientific investigator must truly deduce everything he observes.

At the urging of some friends, I compiled a series of cases that I handled in my career since 1902. These are separate sketches, without frills, each one dealing with a particular case, while I have added a couple of sketches that I prepared over the years for a feuilleton or a lecture. Gratefully, I acknowledge the valuable assistance of my friend K. H. Broekhoff, who willingly agreed to undertake the revision and provide a few "minor touches," as he modestly referred to them!

Amsterdam, summer 1945

C. J. van Ledden Hulsebosch

Translation by Rick van Rijn with the use of ChatGPT.

1. My First Expertise

It was a sunny Sunday in March, in 1902. My father had gone to Brussels for a conference. After spending the morning doing some microscopy work (preparing for my doctoral examination in pharmacy!), I planned to use the afternoon for a bike ride. But then, the doorbell rang, and a telegram addressed to my father was delivered. The message read: "On behalf of the Justice Department, I request you to come here immediately in connection with an investigation into sexual offense—Police Commissioner De Lange, Alkmaar."

   I hurried to the telegraph office with the intention of informing the gentlemen that my father was abroad and couldn't come. However, I discovered that on Sunday afternoons, there was no way to send a telegram to Alkmaar. What to do now….? I didn't dare to put the matter aside, so I thought it best to seek advice from the public prosecutor, Mr. Von Baumhamer, whom I had already met. He had visited us several times out of interest in my father's work, and we had often stood together in the laboratory, observing my father's work. However, when I went to his house on Vossiusstraat, I was informed that he was out. I decided to go to the substitute public prosecutor, Mr. Baart de la Faille, who lived a little further down the same street. Luckily, he was at home! After showing him the telegram and asking what I should do, his laconic response was, "Young man, if your father is not here, then you go instead!" I wasn't sure if I understood him correctly, so I politely pointed out that I was still a student and had not graduated yet, as I was still preparing for my doctoral examination. "That is less relevant; we do not ask for titles but for suitability, common sense, and investigative instinct. Someone who holds a pharmacy diploma but lacks the rest is worth less to us than someone who has been observing and assisting his father in this kind of work behind the scenes for some time. So, gather what you need and go to Alkmaar in place of your father!" To be honest, I found it quite daunting, but I had to obey.

   I thought it best to get a business card with a few words of "introduction" on it to ensure that I wouldn't be suspected of taking over my father's work without proper authorization. And, of course, Mr. Baart de la Faille provided me with one. At home, I quickly gathered some instruments, packed them with the microscope in its case, and took the first available train to Alkmaar. It is difficult to describe my state of mind at that moment. On the one hand, I felt proud that the public prosecutor deemed me worthy to follow in my father's footsteps, and I felt hugely distinguished going on this mission as an expert. On the other hand, I couldn't shake the feeling of fear that I might not do well due to my limited experience. Performing my own independent investigation is quite different from merely observing someone else doing it!

I will never forget the experience of entering the old building that housed the police station. I walked in with a microscope case in one hand and a small suitcase with other instruments in the other. Soon, a somewhat stern voice asked, "Who are you, and what do you want here?" When I mentioned my name and tried to explain why I was there instead of my father, I wasn't given much time to speak, and someone interrupted with the very accurate comment, "We had meant your father, of course!" At that point I presented the business card prepared by Mr. Baart de la Faille, which seemed to shed some light on the situation. With a "Well, well, now, please have a seat over there!" I was shown a chair against the wall of the room, while a few gentlemen were engaged in a lively conversation about "the case" about three meters away from me.

I will spare the reader the details of that unsavory incident—they are irrelevant—but a couple of circumstances that I will never forget are worth mentioning. They gave me the first clue in the right direction. There were two key witnesses who had almost caught the culprit red-handed in the forest where the crime had taken place. Both declared that there was a black book cloth[2] lying on the damp forest ground. However, there was a fundamental disagreement between these undoubtedly credible individuals regarding whether the black side of the cloth was facing up or down. One asserted with great certainty that the black side was up, while the other, under oath, insisted that the white side was facing up. It's no wonder that the servants of Lady Justice sought to ascertain, even in this minor aspect of the investigation, which of these "key witnesses" could be so confidently mistaken and yet still swear to the accuracy of their testimony!

And so, at that moment when I made my joyous entrance, a few gentlemen stood around the table with the book cloth on it. The examining magistrate, the prosecutor, the police commissioner, a doctor, and the clerk—they all pondered the issue and arguments were presented from both sides about the white and black sides of the cloth. It was picked up several times to be thoroughly examined from all angles. At one point, I was struck by the tone in which my involvement in the decision on the matter was brought up. "But we have our expert here," one said, which perhaps gave a somewhat sarcastic impression of me. I will never forget how that remark brought that small four-letter word to my lips and how much effort it took to keep it "inside." In certain circumstances, it is so difficult for a beginner to keep their mouth shut and give full attention to the matter at hand without being

---

2 In the original Dutch text, the exhibit is described as a *"boekenzeiltje."* Today this is not a common object. Ellen van Schie, curator of the Meermanno Book Museum in The Hague described the exhibit as follows: "In the first half of the 20th century, it was customary for schoolchildren to take their schoolbooks to school without a bag. Often, the books were held together by a strap or band. However, when it rained, the books would get wet. To prevent this, a cloth that was waxed or lacquered on the outside was folded around the books" (personal communication). Here we translated *"boekenzeiltje"* as "book cloth."

distracted by sensitivities. So, I focused on examining the book cloth! Then came the question from the old examining magistrate for criminal cases, Mr. Lagerwey: "Tell me, young man, what do you suppose?" and, perhaps still influenced by the way I was involved in the investigation, I replied curtly, "I don't need to suppose anything here because I can prove that the cloth was lying with the black side down and the white side up." And, of course, I had to provide him with that proof.

"When"—this was roughly my reasoning—"a cloth is placed on the damp forest ground with the black lacquered side facing up, undoubtedly the underlying white fabric side will absorb water from the ground. I admit that indeed there are several wet spots found on the white side of the cloth, but I emphasize that these spots are not as irregular in shape as may be initially assumed. They are all figures defined by segments of circles; here and there, a perfectly round wet spot, elsewhere, stains formed by numerous partially overlapping circles. And if the gentlemen now—just like earlier—examine the cloth against the light, they will be able to see how precisely the holes in the black lacquer, where the cloth is "transparent," form the centers of all those circles of moisture. If the cloth had been lying on the white side, the water from the ground would never have magically formed circles around the holes so accurately. No—precisely because the cloth was on the black side, the moisture from the forest ground could only penetrate through those holes in the fabric, where it then spread in all directions with almost equal speed. That's how the circular wet spots were formed. Therefore, the cloth must have been lying on the black lacquered side."

When I was about to return to my seat, the examining magistrate asked me to "stay there." The ice was broken … I had made my entrance. Mr. Lagerwey, my first client, a sympathetic figure whom I still see before me, apparently enjoyed my performance and instructed me to come back the next day to further examine a number of "traces" such as hairs, stains, and particles of dust for comparative analysis. I had success and the unforgettable pleasure of working together with that magistrate in the following days, which I can confidently say was mutually satisfying. That's how I experienced great satisfaction with my debut, and when the memory of this first expertise came back to me later, the famous words always came to mind: "From Alkmaar, the victory began!"

Epilogue by Bas Kokshoorn: Demonstrable Forensic Expertise and Competency

Co van Ledden Hulsebosch is the original Dutch forensic Renaissance man. Throughout the book we learn that he addressed forensic aspects of cases that cover what today we consider the domains of forensic biology, chemistry, physics, medicine, toxicology, and legal psychology. Over the last century, these domains developed into a large number of distinct forensic disciplines, each with their own areas of expertise. This is also reflected by the foundation of the Dutch forensic laboratory in 1948 (only three years after this book was initially published) as well as the Dutch laboratory for forensic pathology in 1951. Both institutes merged into the Netherlands Forensic Institute (NFI) in 1999.

The NFI is an independently funded agency of the Ministry of Justice and Security in the Netherlands. With approximately six hundred FTEs (full-time equivalents), the institute currently hosts over thirty areas of forensic expertise, ranging from pathology, toxicology, archaeology, to forensic statistics, digital forensics, chemistry, and DNA. With the development of these fields, increasing attention has been given to quality assurance and control, including training and certification of forensic experts. Generally they are recruited from diverse academic backgrounds. These may be "classical" fields of science (e.g., biology, mathematics, physics, etc.) but increasingly we see alumni of the forensic science courses at Dutch universities take up such positions. Currently there are academic forensic programs in the Netherlands, including dedicated forensic bachelor degree training at the Amsterdam University of Applied Sciences and Saxion University of Applied Sciences, as well as an MA in forensic science program at the University of Amsterdam (UvA). Regardless of their academic background, all forensic experts at the NFI receive in-house training and competency testing before being allowed to sign forensic reports. This competency is examined by a certification committee composed of an external expert in the respective field, a senior prosecutor, and a principal scientist of the NFI. Recertification takes place every five years, in which the expert needs to demonstrate their continuous professional development. In 2010 the Nederlands Register Gerechtelijk Deskundigen (NRGD, Netherlands Register for Court Experts) was founded as an independent statutory organization. Its purpose is to facilitate quality assurance in forensic science across forensic institutes, but primarily to set standards for fields of expertise and perform competency testing of forensic scientists against these standards. From the original Renaissance man in Amsterdam, to a single governmental institute, to the current situation of the NFI, a number of police laboratories, and (semi-)private and commercial organizations providing forensic services, the NRGD has an increasingly crucial role in competency testing and certification of Dutch forensic experts.

2. Treasure Hunt in the Ashes in a Stove

"There is a plain little man asking to see you," said one of my servants, when one morning, during my consulting hours, between visits, I packed a fresh pipe. "Let him come in!" I said, curious to know what news this visitor would bring.

This was during the war years from 1914 to 1918, when so many raw materials and products were scarce—and for many ordinary people not available at all, so that they had to make what they needed themselves. With slow strides, head bent forward, and something sad in his features, a little man, about forty-five, entered, repeating his request to be allowed to deprive me of my precious time for a few moments. I had him take a seat, and the first thing I received was a tin cigarette case, which he placed before me on the table. My visitor opened it silently, lips pressed together, as if to restrain himself from an outburst of grief. Not a word passed his lips at first. In the now-opened box, I saw a dirty, muddy black mass. The silence lasted (to be frank) a very long time, so I asked him what it was. Slowly his lips parted and, with a look that seemed ominous to me for a moment, he answered: "Money, banknotes!"

I must confess that at first I feared I was dealing with a madman (I had had a mental patient at my office before, and it was difficult to politely persuade him to leave), but the man's calm, sad expression filled me with pity. Perhaps he was a poor soul in the midst of a human tragedy, and I just had to make it easy for him to explain to me—piecemeal, if necessary—how he needed my help. With a great deal of patience, I was told the following story, jolting and jabbering:

> For many years I have worked in the upholstery business, using a lot of passementerie. In recent times this has become so scarce that my competitors and I have run aground, because we can no longer buy this simple but nevertheless essential material for finishing our work, unless we are willing to pay fabulous prices for it. So my brother-in-law and I, through the mediation of an acquaintance, considered having a machine shipped from Germany—at least, if we could obtain money for it!—which would then not only enable us to manufacture our supplies ourselves, but also to find a market for our products in competing companies. Together we were able to raise a capital of three hundred guilders, but it did not look like we would be able to buy the machine required for that amount. It cost more than two thousand guilders, including freight and customs duties! But behold, we found a philanthropist, who lent us two thousand guilders on our honest faces and, overjoyed, I ordered the machine, which is due here in a few weeks.
>
> Lacking a safe, I stored this business capital, which I kept in the form of banknotes, in an empty tin paint box, from which the tubes of hardened paint could be discarded, and that paint box stood behind a row of books in my cupboard in the

living room. Only my wife knew that this was where my treasure was hidden. Last Sunday was a beautiful, sunny April day, so we decided to go for a walk. Before closing the house, I took out the paint box out of its hiding spot. I did not want to leave it in the cupboard, in case some thief came into the house and dumped the cupboard's contents across the floor. No, it was better to put the box in the stove. No burglar would look for money in there! And so I placed the box on top of the burnt-out, cold remains of coal in the cylindrical stove—you know, one of those loose cylinders, surrounded by a mantle, which together stand on a pivot and can be turned into the mantelpiece or in front of it.

When we came home from our walk, the weather had changed somewhat. The sun had gone behind the clouds and we had both even gotten chilled, such that my wife noticed that after arriving home, as I was standing in front of the window facing the street, I was rubbing my hands to make the blood flow a bit faster in them. That good woman, with the best of intentions to make me more comfortable and warmer, ran to the kitchen, got some peat, some bits of wood, and the petroleum can; put all the fuel in the little stove, poured a dash of petroleum over it, and set fire to it. I heard the flame sucked into the chimney! Then suddenly it dawned on me that my money—my benefactor's money—was about to become prey to the flames. More shouting than asking, I expressed my fear to my wife and she—laconic and calmly—asked, "But surely you put that money back in the closet a long time ago?" I was too stunned with fright to think properly. My wife's question even prompted me to go and search in the closet, to see whether I had put it back there, only to come to the conclusion, when I found nothing there, that my money was rapidly turning to ashes.

In my nervousness I lifted the cylindrical part of the stove with two floor mats and ran with it to the kitchen, a flame from the pipe outlet nearly setting my hair on fire. To the kitchen sink! My wife turned on the water tap and I turned the stove upside down over the sink, first dropping the burning logs and peat. They were still burning and were gradually extinguished by the jet of water. But, oh, what a disaster! My paint box, cracked open by the heat, fell into the sink with its brightly burning paper contents, and—as if that wasn't bad enough, the heavy iron grate from the stove plopped on top of it, easily crushing the charred remains of the banknotes, and as an apotheosis, the contents of the ashtray fell over all that, so that the sink drain, clogged, no longer let anything through and the water tap had to be turned off. I was unable to speak a single word. I felt as if I had received a sledgehammer blow to the head and fell down in a chair in the living room in despair, crying like a child. My wife—awfully calm—came in a moment later and tried to console me with, "Well, nothing can be changed now, it just happened…. We have to resign ourselves to it!" But what I had to do about my moneylender, about my partner, whose little savings were in it, too, and about the machine manufacturer, who perhaps had already sent the goods ... she didn't tell me that! I was not able to eat a crumb for the rest of Sunday. My wife cleaned up the mess in the kitchen. She scooped the larger pieces out of the sink to dump them in the waste bin standing on the back porch and rinsed away the rest of the residue from the sink with lots of water. Then came Monday morning. I had had a miserable night. I was continually tormented by the thought of how to tell my moneylender and my brother-in-law about the disaster. Around ten o'clock this morning I first went to my benefactor A. and told him with a trembling voice what had happened. The words were stuck in my throat every time, sir!

When Mr. A. had heard my explanation, he asked where most of the remains of the stove had gone. "In the waste bin," I replied. He then asked me if it was still there, or if the garbage man had already emptied it. I could answer that in our street the garbage man comes on Tuesdays, Thursdays, and Saturdays to collect garbage, so the bucket and its contents were still there. "Thank goodness!" exclaimed Mr. A. suddenly. "Don't throw it away! The police chemist lives on the Nieuwendijk and he will undoubtedly be able to recognize and photograph the remains of the banknotes—insofar as they are still in the dirty mess in the waste bin—and ... I don't rule out the possibility that some of the money will be recovered that way. So go over there!"

And so you see me here, sir, with a cigarette case full of muck from the waste bin as a sample. The rest I can bring you, too, of course, but I just wanted to show you a sample first.

So much for the man's story. He had told me everything nervously and I felt deeply sorry for the simple good man, whom I did not even dare to answer with a heartfelt "Yes!" when he asked me whether I could give him hope that he might recover his money. I could do no more than promise him to do my best to help him.

After only a few hours he telephoned me to inquire if perhaps I had any good news. Oh, what a strange idea this man had of the laborious work I had undertaken. I really didn't know yet which way to go with this dirty mess, this chaos of coal residue, ash, charcoal, peat residue, and fragments of unrecognizable black charred paper! Evening after evening, I spent all my free time on this puzzle, having first of all transferred the contents of the cigarette case into a bowl of water, with the heavier mineral matter from the stove ash collecting at the bottom, while the lighter pieces of charred wood and charred paper tended to drift more, or float on the surface. The wood remains I could easily remove with tweezers; the pieces of charred paper were first "fished out" with a miniature fish scoop made from a small piece of fine copper mesh and transferred to a bowl of clean water for initial inspection.

The man had spoken of banknotes, but there was no evidence of their origin in these charred remnants of paper. Presumably I was dealing with charred banknotes, but they could just as easily be the remnants of charred love letters! Even with other catastrophes, identifying marks often remain, which are easier to discern on the surface of the charred fragments. Possibly nothing was discernible here due to the presence of a covering layer of petroleum soot, which had deposited itself all around from the sooty flames of the oil used. I had rinsed off a few black fragments of burnt paper and dried them carefully, then secured them to a clean glass pane with an extremely small drop of celluloid varnish. This was placed vertically against the wall and one of my cameras was pointed with its "eye" at it. Different plate types were tried and different light sources alternately cast their glow over the mysterious black fragments, and in each shot a dead, black object was represented by the plate, without any particular detail being visible that could reveal what kind of paper the fragments had originally been part of. Thus I had already "wasted" several evenings with these fruitless experiments, and yet I did not give up!

One evening I went back to my photographic laboratory, "adjusted" again to the—increasingly irritating!—black fragments and put my thirteenth photographic plate in the cassette. Yet another exposure method, yet another light filter in front of the camera lens. After the exposure I took the cassette to the darkroom to develop the plate, and imagine my joy when I clearly saw the drawing of one of the corner medallions of a two-hundred-guilder banknote! The number "200" was neatly there, surrounded by the peculiar wavy line, as they appeared on the banknotes of that period! Now I had figured it out! In succession I could now clean a number of larger and smaller fragments of charred paper, dry them and place them in front of the lens, in order to discover by means of exploratory photography what kind of "drawing" or "inscription" had been on them. In fact, this last expression is less correct: it was still there.... It's just that our eye could not discern it and only this special photographic plate, under the special conditions of exposure and use of light filters, was able to perceive and reveal all that! I thus completed some photos and then stopped working for a while. Would the Nederlandsche Bank issue new bills for such "snapshots"? Would it be satisfied with that? And how about the number of similar bills?

I went to the Rokin, where I was kindly received by the head of the banknote department, who could not make a decision about this matter on his own, but asked me to be patient for a few days in order to discuss this important matter with the management of the Nederlandsche Bank, which would decide at its meeting. After an inquiry had been made on their part into the circumstances under which the lot had burned and into the person affected by the disaster, I was informed that an exception would be made for this special case and—in view of my person and the full confidence placed in me by them as well—that they would refund to the person affected those bank bills whose identity I would be able to ascertain by the method I had already followed.

I resumed my search. As I noted before, this all took place at the time when we still had the yellow twenty-five-guilder bills, the green forty-guilder bills, the purple sixty-guilder bills, and the white bills of higher values (hundred, two hundred, three hundred guilders). All these had the value in numerals in each of the four corners, surrounded by an ornament of curved, band-shaped frames. In the middle of the banknotes the value was indicated in capital letters in full. Now, the peculiarity was that the model of these last letters was different for each kind of bill; in the letters of the sixty-guilder bill there were even in the thick parts small widenings, within which, very small, the number "60" was written; by no means everyone's eye had fallen upon this peculiarity—not even in the banking world, where hundreds of bills slipped through their fingers daily! So first of all I made a "sample card," containing the various types of bills. The management of the Nederlandsche Bank was again helpful in this, by giving me one bill of each kind as a "sample." The reader must understand; these were "samples without value" because a punching machine had punched out the numbers while—just to be sure!—the word "worthless" had been punched through the bill with large perforation holes. But for my research these "worthless" banknotes were quite sufficient to study the fonts and so much more. If I now saw capital letters on a picture of a black piece of charred mass, e.g., "NDE"—then I soon knew whether these letters had belonged to "HONDERD," "TWEEHONDERD" or "DRIEHONDERD," because all these denominations, as said, were indicated with totally different fonts.

New questions soon arose in my mind: if I take the letters "ONDE" from a photo, taken from a hundred-guilder bill—and in another photo the letters "GULD"—also taken from a hundred-guilder bill, this proves the existence of only a single hundred-guilder bill: after all, both fragments could have come from the same burned bill. How do I manage to save as much as possible for my little customer? And then I felt that I had to take care that no pieces crumbled any further than they already had! So I found, e.g., the letters "GULD" from a two-hundred-guilder banknote, and in another picture the letters "DEN" from a similar banknote. Had one dot been broken off the last-mentioned charred piece and the letter D detached from it, the Nederlandsche Bank would have rightly observed that the pieces, one with "GULD" on it and the other with "EN" on it, could have come from one and the same banknote. That single letter "D" before the letters "EN" proved that this fragment had to come from a second two-hundred-guilder bill!

So, finally, I arrived with my photos and with my list of the "real, new" bills to be issued. I remember that entire meeting like yesterday. I submitted thirteen photos with the number "40" surrounded by curved frames, taken from corner medallions of bills of that value. They made the calculation: "For this you will get back four bills of forty guilders; to each bill there are four medallions—since you had twelve, you will get three bills and the thirteenth picture entitles you to a fourth bill of forty guilders." "And yet I put it to you that I should receive thirteen forty-guilder bills for these thirteen photos!" I remarked, laughing, adding the following explanation: "I have thoroughly studied the figures on the various bills according to their shape. There are indeed four corner medallions on a single note, but the curved lines wind themselves in different ways around the larger digits of the number "40." In three of these frames it runs with a curved line around the "nose" of the "4"—in the case of the medallion from the lower-left corner of the note, however, there is a protruding angle in the frame just opposite this "nose." It seems as if two angular figures are looking at each other in a hostile way. I repeat that this typical shape is found only on the medallion of the lower-left corner—not on any of the three other medallions. I now show you how all my pictures in question show the forms described…. They are therefore all photographs of bottom-left corners of as many forty-guilder banknotes!" And—with the remark, "You have indeed studied our bills even more attentively than we have done ourselves"—they added thirteen forty-guilder banknotes to the list!

Thus we gradually added everything up … to a total of 1,450 guilders. That was all I had been able to get out of the "mud." It was at least two-thirds of what had been stored in the paint box! And after the gloomy mood in which my little man had been in the first few days after the disaster, his face brightened considerably when I was able to inform him that because of my photos he would be reimbursed 66 percent of what he had lost by the Nederlandsche Bank.

Epilogue by Charles Berger

A paper by Donald Doud in 1953 describes a number of methods in use for the decipherment of charred and burnt papers[3] at that time. Many of them were developed during World War II, proving their usefulness on many occasions. Van Ledden Hulsebosch was working on it one world war earlier, and was probably inspired by some of the work of the Austrian forensic pioneer Hans Gross (1847–1915). Gross had done quite a bit of work on the topic, usually in criminal cases where the culprits had intended to destroy evidence of their crime by burning documents. Fixing the charred fragments on a glass plate was certainly part of Gross's method, and maybe van Ledden Hulsebosch used infrared light, but we can't be sure what he really did, because—even nearly thirty years later—he was not giving us the full details in this story.

See Figure 1 (in the insert section) for a color illustration of the type of currency that Co van Ledden Hulsebosch was working on in this case.

---

3   D. Doud, "Charred Documents, Their Handling and Decipherment: A Summary of Available Methods for Treating Burnt Papers," *Journal of Criminal Law and Criminology* 43 (1953), 812–826.

3. As an Expert for the Court in Ghent

When in any legal proceeding an opposing expert raises objections to the report submitted by the expert of the public prosecutor's office, it is very easy to see that opposing expert as someone who, with "apparent motives," is trying to throw a spanner in the works. It is not surprising, then, that all too often the attitude of the bench towards such individuals is somewhat less "favorable"—which I regret! Considering that all the work of experts is "human work" in which mistakes can be made, an open ear must be given to those who—with full conviction—wish to present a different opinion from that of the prosecuting experts.

I must admit that there have been instances where individuals appeared in the courtroom—presented by the defense lawyer as "expert witnesses"—whose expertise could raise serious doubts. Although there have been cases in which a counter-expert appeared who was "paid so well by the defense lawyer" that they were willing to question the report and put doubt in the judges minds,… generalizations should certainly not be made. In the few instances where I raised my voice against a submitted expert report out of conviction, I fully claimed recognition of my opinion and attentive consideration of my objections. I do not know how many times I—especially from external sources, where a local expert had submitted a report *pro justitia* (for the sake of the law)—was asked to come and challenge that report, to unravel it … perhaps to secure the client's freedom! I always made as my first demand that I would have full access to all the case files, in order to then, after forming my own opinion, decide whether, in my opinion, the submitted report was correct (in which case my assistance could hardly be counted on) or whether I was convinced that based on the grounds set out in the report in question, such a far-reaching final conclusion should not be drawn. But … those latter cases have indeed been rare.

Of one of them, I may tell you a few things here. Now, in the spring of 1933, lawyer v. L. from Ghent asked me when I could make myself available for a meeting regarding an urgent matter. On the evening of that day, my visitor was already with me, requesting my help and assistance in the criminal case against his client who—he assured me—was completely innocent. I then heard approximately the following: In the village of E., the dowager d. C. lived with her two youngest daughters in an old castle. Her eldest daughter, who was married, lived in Knocke, her eldest son was in charge of a monastery, and her youngest son—to the distress of the entire family—had detached himself from everything and had a "relationship" with a Protestant girl whom he would gladly marry … if it were not for the strong opposition from the whole family. The family went even further and no longer allowed him into the castle.

The aforementioned young man felt deeply offended to be treated as if he were the biggest scoundrel, while he only wanted to assert his rights as an honest person, even though he deeply loved a girl who did not profess his family's religion. He urged his eldest sister in Knocke and her husband several times to persuade their mother to change her mind, which might still have been successful—a mother's heart always has its soft spot—but the younger unmarried resident sisters repeatedly thwarted his plans, which he found terribly painful, rejected as he was by his mother. If only he could meet her alone, without those sisters present.... However, that was far from easy to do.

Nevertheless, he made an attempt. One summer evening, he snuck onto the grounds of the castle like a thief. To avoid making a crunching noise on the gravel, he made his way through tall shrubs, along the garden soil by the footpath, until he could distinguish his mother's face through one of the windows. He stared at her, hoping that she might meet his gaze, in which case he would have asked her to come outside for a moment to listen to him, but his sisters were always around their mother. Sadly, he retreated and went home, to a house a few kilometers outside the village, in another municipality, where he had taken up residence with the woman he desired to call his wife. It was a charming, small villa with a garage for his two-seater car. A few weeks had passed since this fruitless journey to the castle. Jacques—that was our friend's name—decided one evening to drive with his "wifey" to Knocke again, to once more seek the intervention of his eldest sister and put an end to the continuous disharmonious torment to the family.

That evening, it happened.... Shortly after midnight, a distinct smell of fire was detected in the castle. Soon, everyone was awakened from their initial sleep. The fire brigade was alerted by telephone and arrived quickly. Upon initial investigation, it became clear that arson must be at play here: in one of the fuel cellars—the one for firewood—old rags and pieces of paper soaked in flammable liquid had been placed among the stacked blocks, which were then ignited. Due to the doors and windows being closed, the fire soon lacked oxygen and naturally diminished in size, preventing it from having more severe consequences than the burning of old wood and parts of an overhead beam.

It was quickly apparent how the perpetrator must have entered. There was a round chute, approximately sixty centimeters in diameter, running from the courtyard next to the side wall of the castle down to the coal cellar. This chute was used for pouring coal. From above, an iron lid covered the chute and a bracket with an eye and a padlock ensured it was properly sealed. Just two days earlier, fifty hectoliters of anthracite had been delivered and poured through that chute into the cellar, where a few workers had shoveled the coal aside into a shed. At the base of the chute there was still a dusty mess made of fine grit. Thus, the situation was quickly assessed once the work to extinguish the fire was done.

There had to be malicious intent—undoubtedly revenge at play. The perpetrator was clearly well aware of the situation. Apparently, they knew that the padlock on the mentioned lid was easy to force open, making it effortless to access the cellars through the chute.

Sadly, but truthfully, when asked by the police if anyone had any suspicions, it was immediately claimed by the daughters of the occupant: "Jacques did this." And the mother did not deny this accusation! The distance to Jacques's villa was not great, especially for a car, so the gendarmes arrived there within moments and loudly demanded the immediate opening of the front door, waking up the couple who had just fallen asleep after the journey from Knocke to home. Although both of them assured, individually, that they had gone to Knocke together, left there late in the evening, stopped to assist with a breakdown at a specific location along the way, and, upon arriving home, went straight to bed.

Not a shred of their stories was believed, and Jacques had to prepare himself to follow the gendarmes to the house of detention as a suspect. The policemen could verify that the engine of the car was still slightly warm—naturally from the last trip to the village of E., where the car would have waited next to the castle grounds, allowing the arsonist to quickly make their escape after committing the act ... and so on and so forth. But no proper investigation was conducted on "silent witnesses." Did the man own overalls? Yes, they had been in the possession of the laundress for a few days—it could be verified! And he did not possess a second pair of overalls? He was instructed to put on his suit, which seemed to have just been taken off and hung over a chair, and then accompany them. And he complied ... for several months of preventive custody!

The morning following the night of the fire, the police returned to conduct further investigations. How satisfied they were when a footprint and impression in the garden soil were found among the rhododendron bushes. Without wasting time, they brought plaster to make a cast of it according to the rules of the art. It wasn't much; the heel was barely discernible, but the sole left a clear imprint and showed up well on the plaster cast. Jacques's inexpensive—factory-made—shoes, which had been confiscated, were handed over by the prosecution to an expert in Brussels, along with the aforementioned plaster cast, with the instruction to determine whether the footprint in the garden soil could have been made by one of the suspect's shoes. (How unfortunate that nobody considered that sliding down and coming back up through that blackened coal chute would likely result in the complete destruction of clothing and create unmistakable traces of that journey. Successful searches for blackened garments were not conducted in J.'s wardrobe or elsewhere in the house. Later, it was simply assumed that the blackened clothing had been energetically cleaned or concealed before going to bed.)

From the outset, the case looked very bad for the defendant, even though there were ultimately only suspicions and one "clue," namely the report of the expert who categorically declared that the footprint, from which the plaster cast had been made, must have been caused by the right shoe of J., which exhibit was now presented as evidence in court! And even though the defense lawyer emphatically pointed out that hundreds of thousands of shoes of the same model and size were in use, and provided testimony from one of the castle servants indicating that Jacques had secretly walked alongside the footpath across the garden grounds two weeks before the fire, Jacques was sentenced to a lengthy prison term.

It will be clear to everyone that his defense lawyer immediately appealed. He searched again for means to plead his client's innocence, the fact that the precise time of his departure from Knocke on that fateful evening could not be pinpointed to the minute, combined with the fact that taking the detour to drive home via the ancestral castle—even if driven a bit faster—made little difference "on the clock." All of this played against Jacques, and the testimony of his life partner was summarily dismissed! That's when Mr. v. L. from Ghent—an acquaintance of mine and of the defense lawyer, as it happens—had the idea to seek my assistance in Amsterdam. He had attended one of the lectures I had given in one of the beautiful halls of the Court of Appeals in Ghent, and he had a strong hope that, now that it was firmly established for him that Jacques was innocent, a skilled expert from Amsterdam could prove that innocence using scientific methods.

And so, he sat in my office in my home, providing the entire account and then answering various questions. But what about the plaster cast that matched the shoes belonging to the defendant? Yes, the lawyer could not provide an expert opinion on that matter, but it was simply impossible because Jacques was innocent! After extensive discussion, it was decided that I would come to Ghent on Thursday, provided that the public prosecutor approved of me independently examining the pieces of evidence at the Registry, about which I would receive further notice. Permission was immediately granted by the attorney general, who, along with the members of the Court of Appeals (Cour d'Assises), had also attended my presentation with demonstrations and had retained such vivid memories that he was willing to offer me the opportunity, "in the interest of truth," to form an opinion on the "evidence" held at the Registry. The trip on that Thursday to the beautiful Palace of Justice in Ghent was marked by the motto "La vérité est en marche!" ("Truth is on the march!").

All the officials, from the porter to the public prosecutor and the officials at the Registry—indicating that they recognized me and had held pleasant memories of the lecture I had given—were highly curious about the role that I would fulfill in the much-discussed case before the Court of Appeals. Everyone was convinced that even the public prosecutor had done everything to assist in serving the truth and to be of service to the counter-expert in every way. The officials at the Registry had been given a special assignment to assist that Dutch expert in every possible way. But how would the latter fare against the evidence presented by his Brussels colleague, and in the face of no one yet stepping forward to save the accused, whom the court had already convicted? First and foremost, I had the relevant plaster cast of the footprint with the suspect's shoes in front of me. I carefully examined it with my stereomicroscope for a considerable amount of time, comparing it to the report of my Brussels colleague to verify if I had sufficient grounds to draw such far-reaching conclusions. At my request, one of the detectives retrieved a quantity of garden soil from the castle garden, from the place where the footprint was found under the rhododendron bushes, and a duly sworn official report was drawn up upon its handover.

And so, I returned to Amsterdam in the evening, with the bag of garden soil and a mass of new impressions. The next few days I devoted entirely to experiments where I—considering they were control tests—pressed a child's shoe into containers of soil under different conditions, etc., in order to create plaster casts of them, neatly numbered to precisely know which casts were mentioned in my report. It became an extensive report, which I put in writing—in duplicate, namely one for the Court of Appeals and one for lawyer v. L. Five days after my examination at the Registry, on the following Tuesday morning, I had to be present at the hearing in Ghent. Since it seemed more convenient to me, I traveled to Antwerp the previous evening and so had enough time to go to the intended location the next day.

When entering the courthouse, the porter quickly noticed me. "On behalf of the president of the Court of Appeals, I must ask you, sir, to come to the gentlemen's dressing room behind the courtroom—I'll guide you there," he said … and soon I was led into a room along the wall of which each magistrate had his own wardrobe. They were in the process of getting dressed; the president and the prosecutor-general were putting on bright red robes, in places adorned with white fur, the lawyers and the clerk were wearing black robes, also adorned with white fur trim. Each pinned the large crosses of their acquired knighthoods on their chests, after which each wound a wide ribbon, several meters in width and in the national colors, around their hips, letting it hang down with a large bow at the side. What a contrast to the simplicity with which the gentlemen are dressed behind the green table during a trial in our country!

Once the hearing had begun—without my presence!—all the other witnesses were questioned first, so it took quite a while before it was my turn. But I certainly wasn't bored. I had a good view of a busy intersection through an open window and, besides, didn't I have my professional journals with me, as is my custom? Finally, I heard my name being called, and I soon stood before the president, who—just like in our country—began with the customary questions about my name, age, profession, and place of residence. Then I was explicitly asked about my religion, in relation to the oath I would take! Depending on whether one is Catholic, Protestant, or Jewish, the first, second, or third formula is recited, to be repeated by the witness. And all oath formulas (of considerable length, which I estimated to be at around a hundred words) were laid out in front of the president in both Flemish and French. Depending on one's nationality and faith, the appropriate formula was selected and read aloud, typically three or four words at a time, which had to be repeated before the next set was recited!

After taking the oath, the president said, "Now go ten meters backward and take a seat in that large chair, then clearly and slowly explain to the jury members what you know about this case." Behind me was a large space, at the rear of which stood the aforementioned large armchair. Once seated there, I had two long benches to my left, along the wall of the room, resembling the benches for the elders in a church. The twelve jury members sat there, displaying a wide range of types at a glance. And opposite those jury benches, to my right, were two long benches. The two lawyers of the defendant sat in the front, while behind them sat the defendant—or as they were still called there, the "accused"—flanked by two gendarmes. I then spoke clearly and, above all, slowly, aiming to minimize any disruptive differences that still exist between Flemish and Dutch. I began by asking the gentlemen to please indicate if my words were not fully understood. What I had to tell them was roughly as follows:

> At the Registry, I first compared the plaster cast with the right shoe of the defendant. This shoe is by no means anything remarkable but rather a factory-made shoe of a common model and size, worn by thousands. It lacks distinctive wear marks or other identifying elements such as rubber heels or sole protectors. The plaster cast shows nothing measurable from the heel. Only the sole allows for comparison and, as I mentioned earlier, it reveals very few specific characteristics. Although I can boast of over thirty years of experience in criminal investigations, I consider it my duty to declare that I would hesitate to declare the plaster cast—or rather the footprint—as identical to the shoe based on these few points of general resemblance. However, gentlemen—even if you may be inclined to place more trust in your Belgian expert in this regard, given that he deems there to be sufficient points of similarity—still, I insist that this does not in any way prove the defendant's guilt!
>
> Regarding the shoes: With the help of my stereoscopic microscope (the so-called binocular) I carefully examined both shoes, not only the surfaces of the soles but also every other part and searched for traces of anthracite. The fact that all that searching was in vain, the fact that not a single shining particle of anthracite is present anywhere, in any of the small cavities of the soles, near the lace holes,

or elsewhere, speaks volumes! If someone slid down the coal chute and walked through that cellar covered in fine coal dust, they must have carried so much of that black powder in the pores of their soles that numerous particles would still be found today. Ordinary foot wiping, no matter how vigorously performed, would be insufficient to remove all the black dust from the deeper crevices of the soles. Hence, I dare to declare here: he who walked in that coal cellar could not have worn these shoes, gentlemen!

Now, one more remark about that plaster cast. You have all held it in your hands and examined it attentively, as did my esteemed colleague. However, I do question whether you also noticed what struck me as extremely remarkable about that plaster cast. Look at the sole surface of this plaster cast; there are three small raised areas, resembling cut pills lying on the surface. These caught my particular attention. Last Thursday, thanks to the kind assistance of the Registry officials, I took a quantity of the aforementioned garden soil from the castle to my laboratory and conducted experiments with a small children's shoe. Here you can see plaster casts of footprints made with this shoe in the aforementioned garden soil. These plaster casts show smooth, even sole surfaces. Now, I also have a plaster cast of a children's shoe impression that exhibits the exact same half-pill shapes on the sole. May I explain to you how they were formed? They were created by a few raindrops that fell into the footprint before I made the plaster cast of it! And thus, I can explain to you that the incriminated footprint with its three little bumps on the forefoot surface (which were naturally small indentations in the original print) was also formed by the same number of raindrops before the police filled it with plaster. But then, gentlemen, I hereby present you with an authentic statement from the Meteorological Institute in Brussels, which conclusively establishes that it did not rain on the night of the fire at the castle. The last rain occurred two days prior. Therefore, if the plaster cast made by the police unequivocally confirms that raindrops fell into that footprint, it can be deduced that it was a track already imprinted in the ground prior to the incident—and it is entirely plausible, as the defendant admits, that he walked along those rhododendrons when he attempted to meet his mother two weeks before the fire. I have spoken!

There was a moment of silence. Then the president asked my colleague from Brussels what he had to say about this, and I eagerly awaited his response with utmost interest. It wasn't much! I heard him say, quite literally, while his facial expressions and gestures suggested a hint of contempt, "Ah, Monsieur le Président, ce ne sont que des expériences au laboratoire!" ("Ah, Mr. President, they are merely laboratory experiments!") There were many more speeches from the public prosecutor and the defense, but I did not listen. When I was allowed to leave, I took the next train to Amsterdam to be home that evening. The following day, I received a telegram from the defense attorney, Mr. v. L., informing me that the jury had unanimously decided on an early verdict and had requested an exoneration. The majority of the court had agreed!

Epilogue by Bas Kokshoorn: Standardization, Harmonization, and International Cooperation

International cooperation in forensic science is not a recent development. Together with colleagues from France, Germany, Switzerland, and Austria, the Amsterdam-based forensic scientist Co van Ledden Hulsebosch founded (and was the first president of) the Académie Internationale de Criminalistique (International Academy of Criminology) in 1929. The academy (and its journal, the *Revue internationale de criminalistique*) was disbanded in 1939. International collaboration in the forensic sciences really took off after World War II. With the advent of different areas of forensic expertise, numerous international professional bodies were founded. Examples of this are the International Society for Forensic Genetics (ISFG) for forensic biologists, founded in 1968, or the International Association of Forensic Toxicologists (TIAFT), founded in 1963. Many such organizations set standards for their field, driving standardization in the application of forensic science to casework practice across laboratories and jurisdictions. Overarching forensic organizations also provide a framework to standardize within field of forensic science, but also to harmonize between those fields.

Many of these organization have a geographical scope. Examples of such organizations are the European Network of Forensic Science Institutes (ENFSI) in Europe, the American Academy of Forensic Sciences (AAFS) and the Organization of Scientific Area Committees (OSAC) in the United States, and the National Institute of Forensic Science (NIFS) in Australia and New Zealand. ENFSI, for instance, provides general forensic guidance on quality assurance and control, but—through seventeen domain-specific working groups—also standards that are specific to areas of expertise like DNA, explosives, handwriting, crime scenes, etc. Beyond setting standards, national and international bodies also provide opportunities for training and professional development. An example of such an international organization is the Chartered Society of Forensic Sciences (CSFS), founded in 1959 in the United Kingdom. This society, which is globally active today, provides opportunities for the professional development of its members. It also provides accreditation of forensic science education programs against its educational quality standards. In the Netherlands the forensic science program of the Amsterdam University of Applied Sciences is currently accredited by the CSFS.

While the expert from Brussels exclaimed, "Ah, Mr. President, they are merely laboratory experiments!," nowadays the need for research and innovation in the forensic sciences is generally accepted. In this sense, with his research-minded approach, Co van Ledden Hulsebosch clearly was ahead of its time. The current (inter)national professional organizations also stimulate and drive research and innovation in the forensic sciences. They do this by providing funding opportunities to researchers and by setting the agenda for critical innovation needs. The Co van Ledden Hulsebosch Center plays a crucial role in this, for instance, by having drafted (together with the Netherlands Forensic Institute) the first Dutch national forensic research agenda in 2023.

4. Disappearance of a Batch of Diamonds

The brothers X, diamond merchants, had offices in Amsterdam and Antwerp. Depending on where the demand was greater, they brought "good" batches, i.e., precious goods, to either Amsterdam or Antwerp for trading. The elder brother usually stayed in Amsterdam, while the younger one traveled back and forth. In the Amsterdam office, the old bookkeeper Y had been in the service of the brothers X for many years and had become the confidant of both partners. Almost all significant transactions were executed together with him. For him, there were practically no secrets in the office.

For a limited time, they had a batch of splendid goods on hand—a collection of water-clear diamonds representing a wholesale value of around a hundred thousand guilders. At that moment, the demand was considered greater in Belgium, so they decided to bring these diamonds to the Antwerp exchange. One might think it was simple to take them to Belgium; import duties were not levied on cut diamonds, so there was no obstacle in that regard. However, a concern was that X Junior, who was fond of "Wein, Weib, und Gesang,"[4] would arrive in Antwerp in the evening, a time when the banks and safe deposit facilities were closed, and so would have to carry the precious goods with him all evening. This was deemed unsafe by both partners. Therefore, it was preferable to send the valuable stones as a registered item to Antwerp in the early afternoon, addressed to "Mister X Junior, Diamant Exchange, Antwerp."

After admiring the batches once more, X Senior and the bookkeeper Y began packing. A cardboard box of the usual model was filled with folded papers containing the diamonds. Then, a tough piece of tough blue linen paper, resembling an open envelope with four flaps, was placed over the cardboard box and subsequently sealed. The oldest partner, assisted by the bookkeeper, performed this task. First, he wrote the address on the package while Y lit a piece of candle to warm the sealing wax. Together, they sealed the package; one applied the portions of melted sealing wax to the seams, while the other pressed X Senior's seal ring into it. A few moments later, the bookkeeper took the package, which had been left on the table, to the nearby auxiliary post office and handed his boss the receipt upon return. Everything had gone smoothly up to this point.

The next afternoon, the mailman who had to deliver the package to the Antwerp Diamond Exchange came to X Junior and had him sign a receipt. All the wax seals were externally intact. X Junior, amidst a group of other diamond traders, loudly called everyone closer to see the extraordinarily beautiful goods that had arrived

---

4   Wine, women, and song.

from Amsterdam in this package. With all eyes on the package, X Junior tore open the blue paper and pulled out the cardboard box to reveal ... to everyone's surprise, a piece of paper containing not diamonds but a bunch of shiny bicycle ball bearings! Good heavens!

His first move was to the telegraph office to inform his brother of the theft. Though the insurance company, covering all shipments properly posted as a registered item, would likely fully compensate for the loss, it was still a shock! After X Senior received the telegram reporting that the package had been opened—fortunately in front of so many witnesses!—and contained worthless bicycle ball bearings instead of diamonds, he first called the insurance company to inform them of what had happened.

Then he went to the police, who referred him to the commissioner of the Pietershal station, Mr. Heeroma, who had gained a certain reputation for investigating postal crimes. Recognizing the importance of the case, they entrusted him with the investigation of postal crimes; he usually succeeded in solving more than others! A few moments later, X Senior was admitted to the room of that shrewd investigator, to whom he gave a detailed account of everything related to packing, sending, and opening the package after its receipt. Silently, the commissioner listened to the entire account, his probing gaze uninterrupted by the "complainant." When it was over, he nodded slightly and asked his visitor to go to a nearby room for a few moments because he needed to have a brief conversation with someone else.

When he was alone in his room, the commissioner called me by phone, told me what it was about, and expressed his wish for me to hear the whole story as inconspicuously as possible. I was to walk directly to his room and sit at a separate table by the window, where I would pretend to be interested in browsing through an old case file that lay there, but in reality, I would lend a keen ear to X Senior's renewed report. And so that's what happened. I nodded a greeting and took a seat at the table by the window. In the middle of the room, armed with pen and paper, the commissioner heard the report again. When the last sentence was put on paper, and the complete report was read to him, X Senior signed the report and left.

"Well, what do you think of that?" the commissioner asked, and from my look, he could already tell that I did not trust the case at all. I had also noticed that there were exceptionally good witnesses, both in closing and posting the package, and in opening it in Antwerp. That, in itself, seemed suspicious to me, and involuntarily I remarked, "How unfortunate that the package is in Antwerp; I would have liked to examine it closely to find out what that silent witness has to tell me!" (As shown in the telegrams received from the Antwerp Police, they had already deposited the opened package at the Registry of the Antwerp Court.) I also pointed out that, as an expert of the Amsterdam Police, I considered my territory for investigations limited to the city limits. Without a special assignment that included the freedom to cover travel and accommodation costs abroad, it seemed unlikely that I could examine the package. "I can find a solution to that!" the commissioner said. Soon, he had sought telephonic contact with one of the directors of the firm who had taken out insurance for the transport of the diamonds. He learned that X Senior not only reported the disappearance of the diamonds but also inquired about when he could come to collect his hundred thousand guilders! Needless to say, the mood of that insurer can be imagined. Understanding that a prompt and thorough investigation could be of great value to his company, he immediately gave "full authority" to let me go to Antwerp with the task of thoroughly investigating the case and providing a written report to the insurance company. I accepted the assignment on the condition that I could also reserve the full freedom to inform the results of my expertise to the public prosecutor, against which there was naturally no objection from that side.

So I went to Antwerp in the evening, where I arrived too late to do anything for my investigation on that day. The next morning, at the opening of the offices, I went to the examining magistrate in the Palace of Justice, to whom I had handed my business card, and who immediately declared on the most benevolent terms that he would help me. I got my hands on the package, which, as I later discovered, had already been inspected by one of the police officers, Mr. Ernest Goddefroy, and could spend the whole day in a free room next to that of the said magistrate for my investigation.

It is unnecessary and unprofitable to mention all the details here that taught me that the package had been closed only once and not opened and resealed in the meantime. It is sufficient to state that I came to the fullest conviction that this package contained bicycle ball bearings when it was handed over to the post and not diamonds. How I knew that is less relevant here. Unable to make the necessary photographic recordings of the flaps and other parts of the package, I had no choice but to use my modest talents in drawing to make sketches to explain my findings in the forthcoming report. It was somewhat satisfying to me when, while packing my papers and heading to the examining magistrate to return the package, the aforementioned police officer came in: he had heard about my arrival and its purpose, wanted to meet me, and was particularly curious about my final conclusion. When I told him, he pulled out a copy of the preliminary report that he had submitted to his chief after a thorough study of the *corpus delicti*; it turned out that we both had come to the same result. That same evening, I returned to Amsterdam and drafted a preliminary police report in a very shortened form, containing almost exclusively the final result of my findings. I immediately sent it to the public prosecutor as requested. This prompted the prosecutor to request a search warrant from the court, for both the firm's office and the private residences of the X brothers, which was granted.

Still, it remained a mystery how it was possible that the accountant Y, a respectable figure, could insist that he had seen the diamonds in the package, and moreover, he himself had handed the package to the post! I wanted to clarify this obscure point. I interrogated the accountant again about everything that happened during the packing and sealing of the package. It had already caught my attention that X Senior, whose signet ring was to be used for making the seven wax seals, had handed this ring to his accountant with the instruction to press it into the wax, which he—X Senior—would smear or let drip onto the package. I wondered why X Senior did not keep the ring in his own hand and let his accountant handle the application of wax. Reflecting on this, I gradually came to see. I asked the accountant to seal another package with me in exactly the same way as he had done with his employer. He neatly pushed the ring, which he had placed on the top of his index finger, into the wax whenever I applied a bit of it to the covering of our "trial package." When this package was "sealed" and I received Y's assurance that it had gone "perfectly the same" as with the specific package, I had already seen it. For me, the problem was solved!

I just needed to learn more from the accountant—there had to be something missing from his account of "the packaging," probably something he considered of minor importance but was crucial for my reconstruction. Once again, I had him recount how the diamonds were placed in the package and how immediately the paper was wrapped around the box of precious stones. X Senior then wrote the address, and the package was sealed together with Y. And then … yes, what happened then, at that moment when the sealing was finished? Did Y immediately go to the post office? No … now Y perfectly remembered the interlude that had occurred at that moment. X Junior had come in to get travel money for his trip to Antwerp. He had, while talking to his brother, approached a wall cabinet containing a box of cigars and taken a handful of cigars from it, saying that he could use them for the journey. X Senior had pretended to be angry and played along, only to suddenly say to Y, "Well, you can also take a cigar from the box." X Senior was sitting at the table, next to the just-sealed package.

At that moment, it must have happened: the swapping of the package with diamonds for a completely similar package containing bicycle ball bearings. That's why X Senior was in charge of the stick of wax. He had to ensure that the same number of wax seals—seven—would be applied to the diamond package and that the same hand, that of X Senior, wrote the address of his brother in Antwerp. And where did I find support for this reasoning? The trial package that I had "sealed" together with Y showed—as expected—the monograms all in the same position, Y had not taken the signet ring off his index finger and had pressed it into the wax in the same position every time. But with the package that I had inspected in Antwerp, the package with the bicycle ball bearings, it was different! The wax seals on it showed the monograms (from the same signet ring!) in different positions—a consequence of the fact that, during the sealing of that package, X (Senior or Junior, that was never clarified!) repeatedly laid the ring aside to apply a new dab of wax to the package, then took the ring back into his hand, without thinking to bring the ring into the same position for each seal.

The certainty which of the two brothers had pulled off the trick could never be established, so the public prosecutor could not initiate a prosecution. However, everyone felt that an attempt had been made to defraud the insurance company—that was accepted as a given and affected the civil procedure that the X brothers initiated against the insurance company. Meanwhile, X Senior made a "mediation proposal" to the insurance company, naming a lower amount with which they would be satisfied—which was naturally rejected! The brothers X then appointed a lawyer to present an "expert" who came to testify that no one could know that the package that had been delivered to the post office had bicycle ball bearings in it! Such statements could have been obtained from thousands of others as well. On the other hand, they had my statements and those of Mr. Goddefroy, which was deemed sufficient! The case was lost by the diamond merchants; they received not a single cent in "compensation"—but still had to pay all the costs of the procedure!

Epilogue by Titia Sijen

Even though the diamond merchants lost the case and did not receive insurance money, the public prosecutor had to abandon prosecution as "the certainty which of the two brothers had pulled off the trick could never be established." This reminds me of forensic cases with DNA evidence for a suspect that is part of an identical (monozygotic) twin: since both brothers or sisters have the same DNA profile, the court cannot be certain who committed the crime (unless one of the two has a very clear alibi) and so nobody is convicted. This can be quite frustrating, of course, but occurs regularly as the Dutch DNA database for criminal cases carries hundreds of monozygotic twins. This is to be expected as approximately one in 400 births involves a monozygotic twin and the number of persons in the DNA database approaches 400,000. But are monozygotic twins fully identical? They do not have the same fingerprints! And in 2014, German scientists discovered that twin pairs carry a handful somatic mutations that can be found by "deep sequencing" ("sequencing" refers to reading the bases of the genome, "deep" refers to an in-depth analysis with many readings for each position in the genome). The basis is that genetic mutations can occur from the first cell division in a developing embryo and that a mutation may occur only in one of the twins. By sequencing the full genome of reference material (a blood or saliva sample) of both twins, these mutations can be found after which the evidentiary trace can be examined for those few positions in the genome at which the individuals differ: does the sequence match individual one or two? The process of analyzing the full genome of both individuals is costly and requires hefty bio-informatics, but sequencing costs have been diminishing over time.

In 2022, this method was applied in a Dutch sexual assault case involving a 76-years old victim. The evidentiary traces were challenging as they did not only contain cell material matching the suspect (the twins) but also the victim. The brothers were found to have genetic differences at a handful of sites in their genomes. Depending on when a mutation occurs in relation to the twinning event (the splitting into two embryos) it can be that a mutation resides in only one of the two brothers (the mutation happened after twinning) or that the mutation is present in both brothers but at a very different frequency (the mutation happened before twinning and one brother received more cells with the mutation than the other brother). We regarded both types of mutations and substantiated it with statistical calculations. It led to the conviction of one of the brothers: the brother who was the actual suspect based on non-DNA evidence in the case but who had tried to frame his twin brother by stating it was not him, but his brother.

5. Peculiar Traces of Dust

In one of the neighborhoods north of the IJ,[5] where many "common" people reside, a housewife left her home for a few hours one day to bring her husband, who was working elsewhere, his meal and to run a few errands in the city. In the late afternoon, she returned home and made the sad discovery that someone had been in her home and stolen some items. She was missing a nickel watch with a chain that had hung from a hook against the wall above the bed, as well as six imitation silver spoons.

She immediately alerted the police, who, treating the matter as a major bank theft, conducted a proper investigation. They sent a detective who, at the end of his inquiries, could find nothing more than a dent, likely from a knee impression, on the canvas covering a couch. Presumably, the unknown visitor had shown interest in what was in a cardboard box placed at the back of the couch, leaning against the wall. However, it only contained some old, worn-out gramophone records. While bending to look into the box, the unknown person had pressed a dent into the canvas, presumably with one of their knees. The canvas, which had been properly waxed, showed faint dusty lines, evidently left by the knee, resembling traces of a pair of corduroy trousers. So, there was dust on the front of those trousers. This was all the detective had found.

This circumstance, coupled with the consideration that he didn't know how to preserve said dusty lines for later examination, led to a request for my assistance. The central investigative forensic photography department also didn't know the best way to photograph those faint, barely "speaking" lines of dust on the shiny surface of the couch canvas. Thus, I headed to the specified address, where I found the detective with the still quite nervous resident. He pointed out the line traces, which he believed to be the only clue, and invited me (as many of my former students did!) to think out loud during my examination. People gladly followed my thought process when making deductions! Naturally, I complied with that request.

Since January 1914 I have been engaged with the task of instructing the police in the "scientific art of investigation." I always considered it a pleasant duty to share my knowledge with my students and former students as much as possible. Putting words into action, the "report" went something like this: "First, let's take a general impression: it looks simple here but neat; everything is clean ... except for this canvas cover on the couch with some dust on it." Here I was suddenly interrupted in my train of thought by the lady, who interjected with regretful envy: "That's from that scoundrel, sir, who stole things here!" "Oh," I continued, "is that so? Then I'm particularly interested in the nature of that dust; let's try to find out what kind

---

5   The body of water at Amsterdam's waterfront.

of particles and crumbs are in there. I'll take a postcard and collect a quantity of particles the size of sand grains with it, to examine them with a magnifying glass."

I quickly realized I was dealing with dried mortar or cement. Now the question was: fresh or old? The answer to this question would determine whether the person who undoubtedly pressed the dent into the canvas while bending over out of curiosity for the box of gramophone records was involved in construction or demolition. My tobacco pipe was still lit (a fatal habit, having a warm pipe in my mouth throughout the day!), so I put a few crumbs of that mortar on the glowing tobacco in my pipe and immediately held a piece of cold glass above it at an oblique angle; in the absence of anything else, I used one of my spectacle lenses for this. I saw no condensation spot. Apparently, there was little to no water in the mortar ... so, a demolisher.

My eye caught one extra-large grain of mortar. It had something more to say and it spoke: "I am much larger than the other grains; I would have fallen off the man's coat more easily than the finer particles and wouldn't be here if he had come from Buiksloot[6]—if so, I would have fallen from his clothing much earlier. I lie right here because he carried me from a nearby demolition site over a short distance."

Once again, the resident interrupted me with her remark: "Next door, at the neighbors, they're working in the basement. They're making a passage to the basement of the neighboring house and they've been hacking away all morning." The message I gave to the detective was, therefore: Find out which mason is working two houses away, making a passage from one basement to another. He will be wearing corduroy trousers with an elongated stain on one of the knees. Bring him to the police station at the Adelaarsweg and let me know. It had just passed twelve o'clock; the workers had interrupted their work for the noon break. We did the same. When I was done with my coffee, I received a phone call to inform me that the concerned friend was eagerly awaiting my arrival at the station!

In the afternoon, I visited the mason, who sat looking genuinely innocent and played dumb. After the usual questions about his name, age, etc., for the purpose of drawing up my official report, I invited him to take off his trousers. Alternately, the surfaces of the trouser legs at knee height were laid flat on a piece of "foil" (which is a paper spread with a sticky layer of gelatin, feeling like hectograph material). A gentle tapping on the fabric caused whatever dust particles were still in the trousers at that spot to adhere to the sticky layer of the foil. Remarkably, the shape of the copied dust stain perfectly matched that of the canvas covering the couch.

To the shock and dismay of the duty sergeant, I confiscated the man's trousers as evidence. The detainee remained at the station without pants. And his better half, seriously objecting to handing over the Sunday trousers to the police, claiming that

---

6   Formerly a village, now a neighborhood of Amsterdam.

they were too good to be "smoothed out" in a detainee cell, didn't understand the tricky situation she put the aforementioned sergeant in. Without pants, the man couldn't be brought before the public prosecutor! Fortunately, the station had a so-called drowning victim's suit available, and the mason soon looked presentable again!

Just as I had returned to my laboratory and was busy documenting my findings, the phone rang again. The police from the Adelaarsweg station informed me that our friend, apparently realizing the hopelessness of his situation, had decided to confess everything!

Epilogue by Jos Brouwers

In this specific investigation, Co van Ledden Hulsebosch addresses the questions whether there has been contact between a given pair of trousers and a couch, and if there is a match between debris at different locations, more specifically, does the age of the debris samples match? Undoubtedly, he would have liked to make use of all the modern techniques available to contemporary forensic investigators for this purpose. At the same time, we must acknowledge that these new (costly) techniques are unlikely to be quickly deployed in simple home thefts, as described in this case. Especially when the loot consists only of a nickel watch and "imitation silver"(!) spoons. It is remarkable how he, using only his pipe and sharp logic, assesses the origin, transfer, and aging of traces.

What makes this chapter exceptional is the exception to the rule that forensic investigation has become easier over time. Co van Ledden Hulsebosch's clever trick to determine the age of cement with his pipe would not be as effective today. In almost every country, laws are in effect prohibiting smoking in the workplace and indoors, stifling Co van Ledden Hulsebosch's quick solution. It raises the question of what would have prevailed in the mind of Co van Ledden Hulsebosch in this era: his respect for legislation and authority or the urge of an unconventional researcher to quickly solve the case. In any case, this chapter contributes to the stereotypical image of a gifted investigator who, in the tradition of Maigret and Holmes, thoughtfully pulling on his pipe, effortlessly brings seemingly unsolvable cases to a successful conclusion.

6. Rice Powder

The police from the Marnixstraat police station—better known as the "Raampoort bureau"—once called upon my assistance for the following issue: A widower—a chunky man in his fifties—had made plans to remarry. His chosen one, who found their current residence—an upstairs apartment on the Nassaukade—somewhat inconvenient, had insisted on making some alterations to the rooms and attic before their marriage could take place.

Once all of that was completed, they went to City Hall and then embarked on a modest honeymoon trip. Now—fate or misfortune?—would have it that on the evening of their return, two burglars happened to be inspecting their house. Suspecting trouble and sensing the arrival of the occupants, the unwelcome guests had to act quickly. One of them managed to discreetly flee to the attic, where he temporarily hid behind a stack of suitcases, baskets, and crates. The other one couldn't make it upstairs and found himself compelled to hide in the bedroom ... under the conjugal bed! Fortunately for him, the bed had rather high legs, allowing him to quickly conceal himself. The residents did not notice the presence of the "intruders." They were in no hurry at all and continued chatting for a while ... even after the bedroom was occupied. It was only when the man under the bed received a convincing signal in the form of their calm breathing, that he deemed it an opportune moment to leave. At the same time, the man in the attic had decided to attempt a discreet exit. Carrying his shoes in his hands, he descended the attic stairs in his socks, but, oh, how creaky several of the steps were! As expected, the occupant heard the noise, realized there was trouble, jumped out of bed, and hurried to the hallway. From there, he had just enough time to witness someone storming down the stairs ahead of him, opening the front door, and running outside. Even though the man was in his pajamas, he rushed downstairs as fast as he could, he couldn't determine the direction in which the uninvited visitor had escaped.

While he looked around for a police officer (who adhered faithfully to the rule that the more you need one, the less likely you are to find one!), the following drama unfolded in the bedroom: the man crawling from under the bed clearly assessed the situation and realized it was necessary for him to gather his belongings before the police arrived. Very calmly, cautiously, and quietly, he slid out from under the bed with reptilian movements, hoping to leave the bride unaware of his departure. But it didn't go as planned! The young woman immediately sensed that "something was alive" under her bed—she didn't know what, but she definitely had to leave the bedroom immediately! She swung her legs out of bed when ... oh, horror! Suddenly, she placed the sole of her foot onto the stubbly beard on the face of the man who was creeping forward. She couldn't proceed any further and crawled back into bed, screaming loudly. This was the signal for the "crawling" man to hurry. He sprung out from under the bed, grabbed the woman tightly by the throat, almost choking her, and snapped, "Make a sound and I'll kill you." The terrified woman chose the most sensible course of action and remained silent!

While she rubbed her sore neck and assessed the situation, she noticed the burglar running out of the bedroom and descending the stairs in leaps. The husband stood by the front door … would he be able to catch the charging man? The savage assailant collided forcefully with the man, pushing him with his elbows against his chest, causing his head to smack against the door frame (and making him to see stars!). However, he couldn't get a grip on the intruder, and this one also escaped! But the resident had observed the burglar closely and somewhat recognized him. The only question was: Where had he seen that face before? He racked his strained brain for quite some time before exclaiming, "Eureka!" There was no doubt about it: it was the guy who had brought timber for the carpenter when the rooms in the attic were being remodeled. It couldn't be anyone else! He rarely managed to get dressed as quickly as he did at that moment and hurried to the nearest police station to report the incident. Thanks to the identification of the second guest, the police apprehended the two culprits a few hours later.

Once I became aware of the situation, I deemed it important, in this particular case, to collect the dirt from under their nails to gain some insight into the nature of the substance gathered there. Although there were some minor difficulties in collecting the nail dirt from these two guests, it was successful, and I received it neatly, folded in separate pieces of paper, labeled with the names of the "interested parties," at my laboratory, exactly according to my instructions.

The black and gray crumbs were soaked in water in shallow glass evaporating dishes and prepared for microscopic examination. It yielded interesting results: the nail dirt from the guy who had been under the bed contained traces of *poudre de riz* (rice powder), among other things. It could have easily ended up under his nails when he gripped the lady's neck so forcefully! However, the powder wasn't composed exclusively of rice flour (despite what the name suggests!). I also found another type of powder, which made me wonder, "Could it be that the lady uses a mixture of cosmetic powders?" The investigators conducted further research and confirmed my suspicion. One powder, with a delightful fragrance, was a bit expensive, so she had mixed it with a cheaper substitute. The detective brought me a small sample he had taken from her powder box. Its composition perfectly matched what I had found in the nail dirt of my customer. Subsequently, a conviction followed.

Epilogue by Brigitte Bruijns

For this epilogue I also made use of the fantastic capabilities of ChatGPT, since I needed some inspiration. I gave the following task to ChatGPT: "I need to write an epilogue for the following story. I would like to focus on the fact that in the story a match is made, but only on the level of the same product. Nowadays evidence analysis is done on the level of individualization, so emphasize this classification versus individualization research. The epilogue should be at max half A4 in length." This was the answer (a bit adapted by myself):

> Our story illuminates a time when evidence analysis operated on the grounds of general matches, where commonalities, even if superficial, sufficed. But as we fast-forward to today's landscape of forensic investigation, a new era emerges. A meticulous focus on individualization has dawned, where every fragment holds a unique story. Nowadays, the spotlight is cast upon the intricacies of individualization—a meticulous journey from generality to specificity. The art of evidence analysis has evolved from making mere connections to crafting narratives from the tiniest details. A world where the batch of makeup powder, once deemed identical, now bears its own fingerprint. Nowadays, in our journey, we celebrate not just a match, but the pursuit of precision, the quest for certainty that rests within the folds of every fragment. As we close this chapter, we embrace the future, where every trace tells a tale of its own, and classification stands as a testament to the ever-evolving artistry of science.

7. Sixty-seven Thousand Guilders in Securities Recovered

It was during the war years 1914 to 1918 that the number of "property crimes" seemed to be increasing rather than decreasing. One evening, I received a telegram from the examining magistrate of the Heerenveen district, instructing me to come to him the next day in because of a report concerning a theft of sixty-seven thousand guilders in securities from a farm in Sondel.

It was still a short hour's drive from the station before we reached a hamlet and arrived at the farmhouse, where the military police and the National Police made it clear that something extraordinary must have happened there. The resident—the farmer v. d. G.—walked around in despair, wringing his hands, half-mad, repeatedly shouting that anyone who caught the thief with his securities could expect a reward of two thousand guilders. My client briefly informed me of the following: v. d. G. had moved here exactly a week ago; hence, the contents had not yet been properly arranged, and the safe was still in the hallway, about a meter from the front door, against the wall. When v. d. G. opened the safe last night, he discovered to his horror that almost all his valuable papers were missing. Only Russian and Austrian shares had been left behind!

Suspicions had arisen against two Belgian internees who had been quartered with the previous occupants of this property and must have known the layout of the house inside out—perhaps were even in possession of duplicate keys for the front or back door! The police had already set out to track down those Belgians ... maybe they were already "incarcerated." The farmer explained various possibilities of how the perpetrator(s) could have entered his house, but my investigation did not lead me to support any of those hypotheses.

I had the safe opened and noticed what a remarkable antique this safe was! To make one of the lion's heads on the front of the door move sideways, revealing the keyhole, you had to press a button upward next to one of the front paws. To turn the key in the lock, you had to press a second button simultaneously! And the thieves were supposed to know this secret?! I was by no means inclined to go in this direction, so I inquired whether there were multiple keys for this lock. Yes, there was another duplicate in one of the drawers of an old desk, and v. d. G. wanted to fetch it for me immediately. I prohibited him from touching that key—he should only point it out to me. I carefully took the duplicate key from the mentioned drawer, inspected the various parts of the key with a magnifying glass. I discovered so many dust particles on it and on the outer edge of the teeth as well as a uniform, thin layer of rust, that I could express my conviction that the safe had not been opened recently with that duplicate key. In that case, it would have had to be done with the man's regular key. He kept it under his pillow at night.

The farmer's wife walked through the hallway from time to time, and I noticed how her figure left no doubt that the stork would visit this farmhouse within the foreseeable future. It is known how some women, during pregnancy, show more or less strong tendencies toward kleptomania. I deemed it necessary to make my opinion known to the examining magistrate, leaving it up to him whether the arrival of a physician was desirable to examine her, possibly physically, considering the chance that she hid the securities under her clothes. However, this magistrate wanted nothing to do with it and declared himself to be convinced that the stolen securities were far away. I, however, assured him that, in my opinion, the securities were all still under "this roof," and it was therefore necessary to search and find them.

The conviction with which I expressed this opinion led to the acceptance of my proposal to search every nook and cranny of the house. That meant something! Oh, what a mess! In the attic, there was a stack of small carpets, bedspreads, floor mats, etc., about a meter high; around it stood about ten large copper kettles—those old-fashioned ones, with a flap on the spout opening, and most of the inventoried items were scattered across the floors!

While the examining magistrate and the public prosecutor began to search upstairs in the house—moving everything from its place—I wanted to examine the inside of the safe for the possible presence of strange fingerprints (the outside seemed to have only the fingerprints of the farmer and his wife). I invited v. d. G. to open the safe for me, which he couldn't do because the door was alarmingly jammed. Although my client initially seemed reluctant to have a blacksmith summoned from a nearby village, I insisted on having the safe opened for me. One of the military policemen then drove to the nearest town, Balk, to fetch a blacksmith. He knocked and banged and managed to open the door. After that, I could examine the interior of the safe at ease.

The others were all rummaging upstairs in the house. On the top shelf lay some Russian and Austrian shares and on the bottom were a few irrelevant trinkets. I noticed that the safe was high at the back, so I directed the light from my lantern upwards into the safe, while using a small mirror, which served as a "spy," to look up into the safe. There, my gaze encountered a small, triangular, white object—a piece of paper. To better examine it, I sat with my back against the open safe, tilted my head back onto the "Russians and Austrians," and then saw that the ceiling of the safe was not horizontal but inclined upward. Risking my fingernails, I placed my fingertips next to the aforementioned triangular piece of paper, which turned out to consist of several layers, pulled ... and with a lot of noise, the true top shelf fell down ... right into place. There on the shelf were the "missing" securities! During the move, a few days earlier, the safe had been transported on a farm wagon. During that trip the upper iron support plate had bumped into the top part of the safe and had become jammed there, with a triangular point of one of the folded pieces in between. It had stayed there when the safe was placed in the new house. The fact that v. d. G. himself had made the distinction between the valuable and worthless papers (which he had placed separately on a lower shelf), led to only the former "disappearing"!

I called "Eureka!" upstairs—the members of the judiciary came down; v. d. G., who was standing next to the safe, initially showed surprise, then became somewhat angry and asked me in a reproachful tone where I had gotten the securities from. Laughing, I told him that I had conjured them and asked him in connection with that if he happened to have another empty safe!

The mission was over—the car brought us back to Heerenveen soon after. My clerk, who had to carry the bags, asked me quietly if v. d. G. had kept his word and paid out the promised reward when he got his securities back. But this "decent farmer" emphasized emphatically that the reward had been offered for the one who apprehended the thief with the loot, so the reward would not be paid out now—since there had been no theft!

Nevertheless, I went home satisfied!

Epilogue by Brigitte Bruijns

In the world of magic, the art of making someone disappear inside an apparently empty box has long captivated audiences. While the illusion seems to defy logic, a forensic perspective can unveil the secrets behind this classic trick. The magician invites an assistant into a conspicuously small box, closing the door, and within seconds, the box appears empty. Forensically speaking, this act requires a masterful understanding of misdirection, hidden compartments, and impeccable timing. Misdirection is paramount in the magician's arsenal, diverting attention away from the actual method. This mirrors the forensic concept of countering biases and anticipating potential misdirection during investigations.

In the realm of forensics, misdirection parallels the artful diversion of attention seen in magic tricks. Forensic investigators encounter the challenge of navigating through potential biases, expectations, and preconceptions that may cloud the interpretation of evidence. Much like a magician adeptly directs an audience's focus away from the true workings of a trick, forensic analysts must remain vigilant to counteract cognitive biases and ensure a neutral examination of facts. The ability to recognize and mitigate misdirection in forensic analysis is essential, allowing investigators to unveil the genuine narratives hidden within the complexities of a case. With some credit to ChatGPT ;).

8. The Murder of the Notary C. S. in Gorinchem

One Thursday evening in November 1931, after giving a lecture at the night school in Veendam, I traveled back home the following day by the morning train. At least, so was my plan! Engrossed in my magazines, I noticed that we had reached Amersfoort and I was wandering whether the time had come to have a coffee. The train stopped. I placed my magazines next to me on the seat (my only fellow passenger was sitting diagonally opposite me in the corner of the compartment) when someone passing through the aisle called out my name. I responded immediately and learned that the public prosecutor in Dordrecht had requested my "arrest" via radio broadcast in connection with a murder committed in Gorinchem, for which he sought my assistance. Having learned from my home that I was traveling by train from Veendam to Amsterdam, he had now made an appeal to the radio listeners to quickly direct my route to Gorinchem.

I bought a ticket via Kesteren to Gorinchem, exchanging the unused part of my ticket from Veendam to Amsterdam, telegraphed to Gorinchem that I had been "tracked down" and was on my way, also informing my home that I had set out on a different course. I arrived in Gorinchem around three o'clock after a stopover in Kesteren (long enough for a lunch break), where the police commissioner had one of his men pick me up and escort me to the notary's house, where a dense crowd of curious onlookers filled the street in front of the door. I found the examining magistrate with his clerk and the public prosecutor, as well as the police commissioner, while the oldest clerk of the murdered notary provided various pieces of information.

It was unfortunate that I—so entirely unprepared—had no tools with me. My heavy handbag contained only the slides from the previous evening! My first task was to call Amsterdam to instruct one of my assistants to immediately bring "the" case, containing the various devices and equipment for the initial on-site investigation, to me. Meanwhile, I received the unofficial assignment for the investigation in this obscure case, in which I was promised the assistance of Police Inspector Tas from Rotterdam (who was on his way!), who would help with the technical part—making a photographic record and gathering fingerprints.

It had been a "hit," as we call it. In the front room—the notary's private office—stood a pedestal desk in the middle. Behind it, an office chair. Between the latter and the fireplace, lying on its back, was the dead body, the head of which showed numerous wounds and bloodstains. It had evidently struck against the mantelpiece during the fall and broken pieces of marble off of it, one of which was lying on the floor in front of the niche, while other pieces of the marble ornament were next to the upper body, which was partially stretched out behind the gas heater in the niche. The clerk told me how around five thousand guilders had been taken from a banknote pouch in the safe and referred to the whole incident as a great mystery.

While trying to suppress my desire for the tools that were being brought from Amsterdam, I nevertheless paid full attention to everything around me. My gaze swept over the desk at which the deceased had apparently been working until the last moment (he lay with his fountain pen still in his hand!) and then over the victim, whose clothing also displayed many bloodstains. After a few moments, I had to complain that there was too much noise around me from talking people and an almost permanently ringing telephone, so I had to state plainly that I could not work under such circumstances. It had to be understood that I had to exert maximum mental effort to make the necessary deductions from what I could observe.

The telephone was disconnected and the talking bystanders sought another room for their discussions, and I was alone … alone with the deceased and his surroundings, where the silent witnesses had so much to tell me. Only the clerk would have some information to give me. I had already understood that I had to look among the acquaintances of the deceased for his murderer and now asked the clerk to search through the correspondence of the last two or three weeks for letters that could be related to a certain member of the clientele who might be in a "particular mood." I also instructed him that the search should first focus on someone whose name began with S.

The public prosecutor, interested in what I had observed and put together, asked me what conclusions I had already drawn. I replied that the notary had received someone in his office in the late hours of the previous evening, whose name had been noted on the weekly calendar page lying on the desk in front of him before or during the visit. Subsequently, the visitor, undoubtedly also the person who murdered the notary, had found it necessary to tear off that page, covering the days of the current week, from that calendar block, apparently resting his left hand near the perforation on the back of the previous weeks' pages, while the right hand tore the page of the current week, with the note, from it. On the back of the "previous week," there was a dirty imprint of the left hand, which seemed doubtful to me whether it could contribute much to the identity investigation, but the page of the future week, containing only a single note, allowed me to perceive a very faint impression on the "Thursday" in the paper surface, caused by a strongly written pencil note in the box of this week's Thursday. And therein I found a strong capital letter S. Would the name starting with an S have prompted the murderer to remove precisely that page from the calendar?

It was somewhat heartening when the notary clerk, based on his investigations in the incoming and outgoing letters of the last two weeks, came to explain to me that a certain S. from Woerden, belonging to the clientele of this notary office, had behaved so badly lately that the notary had recently had to rebuke him in very strong terms and had to warn him that the authorities would receive a complaint if S. did not return the funds he had managed to get from the notary under false pretences within a week. Would he know more about the murder?

On this Friday, I worked all day in the house of the murder to shed light on the dark case that had taken place between half-past seven and half-past eight the night before. In the meantime, I had asked the police commissioner to send someone to Woerden to find out where the aforementioned S. had been last night, and one of his detectives had immediately left for Woerden, where he—as I later learned—found S.'s house closed up. S. appeared to be on the move!

However, I had more secrets to uncover. I studied the bloodstains. Sitting calmly next to the body, I examined all the larger and smaller bloodstains, smears, drops, and splashes, asking myself what could be read in them. At one point, I could declare: "That blood there ... the culprit lost it! So he was also injured!" My audience looked at me incredulously. How could I assert that so decisively? And yet it was simple ... if you knew how! The victim had lost a lot of blood—from several wounds to the back of the head and from a couple of scratches on the face. I found bloodstains on numerous objects around the body. While inventorying the various bloodstains, I also examined some bloodstains on both trouser legs below knee height. At that moment, I noticed that these were perfectly round! Therefore, they could not possibly have come from the victim's wounds. Falling blood drops from his wounds would have at most caused elongated streaks on the trouser legs, while the existing traces were perfectly round, droplet stains created by vertically falling droplets on the horizontally stretched trouser leg—so that blood had to be from someone else ... from the perpetrator!

After establishing this point, I felt the necessity to find out which part of the perpetrator's body had been injured. Outside the room where the drama had taken place, the long, narrow side corridor leading to the back of the house and the kitchen showed some bloodstains that had fallen to the side of the corridor on the marble floor. This could indicate that the injury was to one of the hands. Going to the kitchen, most of the drops were on the right side, while sporadic blood drops were found on the left side of the corridor. Perhaps this indicated that the right hand had been injured. Going to the tap, the perpetrator had bled more than when he walked back through the corridor after refreshing himself with cold water. Both the tap and the handle on the safe showed bloodstains. I asked to be kept informed of everything the detective sent to Woerden found out and planned to personally go there to carry out further independent investigation as soon as I learned that S. had been found with a fresh injury to one of his hands.

The next day passed. In the morning, the prosector from Leiden—my old friend Hulst—performed the autopsy. In the afternoon, my colleague Tas and I collected as much evidence for fingerprint examination as possible, and in the evening we packed our bags in order to be back home before the end of the day. In Rotterdam, we said goodbye to each other ... not suspecting that we would meet again in Woerden a few hours later! I had arrived home with my assistant Viëtor a little after ten. He was busy unpacking the bags and bringing everything that was suitable for further examination to my private laboratory. Within a quarter of an hour the telephone rang, and I learned that S. and his wife had been arrested in Woerden after returning from Rotterdam, where they had made lavish purchases for Saint Nicholas's Day. I also learned that S. had a bandage on the tip of his right index finger.

My mind was made up. There were no more trains to Woerden, so I ordered a car and instructed them to ensure the driver was "fresh" ... it could be a late night. At eleven o'clock the car arrived, and we drove to quiet Woerden, where most of the residents were already asleep! It was a little past midnight when our car stopped in front of the small police station in Woerden. In the police officers' room I found a screaming woman—S.'s wife, who was being held flat on a mattress by three officers in a hysterical fit and was shouting at the top of her voice to the whole neighborhood. In the nearby room were the mayor of Woerden, the police inspector, the detective from Gorinchem, and S., a terrible stuttering bundle of nerves about thirty years old. On a nearby table, everything that the couple had bought in Rotterdam was laid out, including the straw suitcase in which it had all been packed, including many sweets and trinkets for the children and the adults ... even a nicely prepared chicken, as if straight from the poultry shop! He tried to make everything sound very reasonable but had a long way to go due to his stuttering, as he took ten times as long to get through each sentence as a regular person!

When examining his injured finger, I was told that he had injured it in the chain of his bicycle—but the time he mentioned for this incident did not match the freshness of the injury! When I asked him if he knew the notary C. S., he admitted that he did, even though it had been a very long time since he had any contact with this magistrate. I pointed out to him that I had seen the letter he had written to the notary himself a few days earlier, as well as a copy of the reply sent to him. He looked surprised because I seemed to be so well informed. I told him outright that I was suspicious and expressed the desire to take a look inside his house. Before I knew it, S. suddenly blurted out, "Y... y... y... you c... c... c... can!" After which I invited the mayor, who had witnessed our conversation and had thus heard that the resident had unequivocally allowed me to look around in his house, to accompany me to his home.

The house had recently been disconnected from the municipal electricity service due to unpaid bills, so the mayor asked the director of this branch of the service for help and to set up an emergency connection for our searchlights. With his help we soon had an abundance of light in the various rooms of S.'s house, where every nook and cranny could be examined.

As the situation stood (I had only just raised serious suspicions against S.), we only had permission from the occupant to "look around" in his house—and certainly not to damage its contents. Later, it turned out that the wife of S. had hidden a large part of the stolen money in one of the mattresses; we did not find that during this superficial house search! However, in the utility room, I found a striped sports shirt hanging behind the door, of which the left sleeve near the cuff was damp, undoubtedly a result of only partially successful washing attempts to remove fresh bloodstains that had landed on that sleeve. Naturally, I confiscated that shirt and found fresh bloodstains near the button closure during a thorough examination in my laboratory. S. could not provide a satisfactory explanation for those bloodstains either!

On Sunday morning at eight o'clock, we returned to the laboratory in our car and I calculated that I had been working nonstop for exactly twenty-four hours ... without taking any breaks except for quick meals! On Monday, the police commissioner in Gorinchem subjected S. to a lengthy interrogation, and he called me in the evening—at five o'clock—to express his opinion that S. was not the perpetrator, which I had to immediately contradict. This led to a new interrogation, presumably in stronger terms, and half an hour later, the telephone rang again: "Intercommunal government call, with Gorinchem!" ... and the commissioner informed me with satisfaction that S. had finally admitted, swayed by the evidence material I presented, to having struck the notary to the ground and, after he had fallen against the marble fireplace and trying to get up, a few extra blows had led to his swift death! He also confessed to the theft and explained that he had hidden the stolen money in the mattress.

Epilogue by Maarten Blom: Crime Scene Management

This is a marvelous story full of details that may strike us as reminders of a nostalgic past, with long train journeys, communication by telegram and radio broadcast, and an indispensable suitcase delivered to the forensic scientist through a valet service. Those were the days! On the other hand, everything appears to function swiftly and effectively, an impression that is enhanced by the sweeping style of the author. Next to his remarkable pace and dedication (working for twenty-four hours without a break or sleep), van Ledden Hulsebosch also displays a rather modern approach to crime scene investigation.

His first action after accepting the appointment is to arrange the assistance of a photographer to record the crime scene. Upon arrival he takes immediate action to preserve the scene and removes potentially disturbing influences. He has the telephone disconnected and sends everybody away. Even though the author emphasizes that this is meant to benefit his thought processes, it appears to me that it also serves to maximize the quality of his observations. And it is precisely the way that van Ledden Hulsebosch describes his observations that strike me as modern. He tries to establish the potential value of the evidence considering the relevant information that is available to him. He seems to recognize the distinction between source and activity level in the interpretation of evidence. The left palm print is too "dirty" to be useful for establishing identity, but helps to shed light on some of the relevant activities at the crime scene, not to mention noticing the torn page from the calendar.

The bloodstain pattern analysis is described in relatively few words, but I am sure this must have taken up most of the time that van Ledden Hulsebosch spent at the notary's office. The way it is described is kind of intriguing. Working without any of the modern sophisticated tools, van Ledden Hulsebosch's line of reasoning demonstrates some awareness of the complexities and pitfalls that are still associated to bloodstain pattern classification today. He meanders around two components that partly overlap: the assessment of the observable characteristics of the pattern ("perfectly round"); and the opinion about the event(s) that gave rise to those observable characteristics ("vertically falling droplets" that could not be from the victim).[7] He meticulously follows up on the assumption of a wounded perpetrator and considers two-way transfer (both from perpetrator to victim and from victim to perpetrator) when searching the house of S.

Nowadays, DNA analysis of the bloodstains on the trouser of the victim and on the striped shirt found in the house of S would be high on the priority list. Apart from the fact that such analysis was not available at the time, the power of van Ledden Hulsebosch's account of his investigation is such that it leads to a confession, at which point the story ends. A remarkable account of a forensic examination in investigative mode, as we would label it today. Off course we might argue that the tale lacks any consideration of alternative explanations for the observations on the crime scene. But then we must consider that this story about a murder investigation is in fact a story, conceived to entertain and impress the reader. It wouldn't be interesting if everything did not fit so well. Nevertheless, I am almost certain that van Ledden Hulsebosch did consider alternative scenarios—in his mind, if not in the story.

---

7   Adapted from: M. C. Taylor and N. K. P. Osboe, "Letter to the Editor—A Contribution to Contextual Information Management in Bloodstain Pattern Analysis: Preliminary Idea for a Two-Step Method of Analysis," *Journal of Forensic Sciences* 63(1) (2018), 341.

9. A Political Attack?

On a late summer evening in the small provincial town of M., a quiet atmosphere befitting the approaching midnight hour prevailed on one of the country boulevards. Most of the inhabitants had already gone to bed and the sound of the footsteps of a single pedestrian across the street was hollow. Suddenly a bang as of a cannon made all quiet fade away.

Immediately following that bang were clinking shards of glass and shouts of "Fire!" It was soon noticed that from one of the narrow, old houses on the Singel, one of the many buildings that have known "better times," smoke and flames found their way out of a cellar door that had been blown outwards. At the front wall above it, almost all of the glass panes had been shattered by the violence of the explosion that had taken place and had ended up in shards in front of the building. A few hikers saw how a young man of about twenty years of age, heavily distressed, rushed out of the house into the street. He quickly got rid of a blue smock, which had caught fire at the back, and with his torso bared, seriously injured by fire, was taken by passersby to the doctor, who deemed immediate hospitalization necessary.

The fire department soon mastered the fire, which was confined to the basement area. It had only slightly affected the ceiling of the cellar and the beams underneath. The explosion had worse consequences above. The floorboards of the ground floor had been lifted up here and there, whereby they, half turned on their axis, had come to lie upside down, with their nails facing up, on the beams. Higher up in the building, where there were small bedrooms, shards of broken household goods were silent witnesses to the force of the explosion.

The boy, who had suffered ugly burns to the face and back, explained during his first interrogation how, unable to sleep because of the heat in the house, he had walked down the street and heard a suspicious noise coming from the cellar. As he wanted to know if there was anything suspicious going on, he went in. It was completely dark there when, coming from the garden room, he entered the room through a small corridor and passed the cellar door. He lit a match and—when he saw nothing unusual by its light—threw the nearly burnt match on the stone ground next to him. At that moment everything around him had suddenly gone on fire and an ear-splitting bang had startled him violently. Feeling that his blue smock, which he was wearing as the only covering for his torso, was on fire from behind. Fleeing into the street, he had taken off the smock and thrown it on the ground, where passersby extinguished it, picked it up, and handed it to the policeman. The boy was hospitalized. The next day he was subjected to a new interrogation, during which identical statements were made as the previous evening.

While people were looking for an explanation for this strange explosion, a lot of talk soon circulated. The fact that the local section of the Arbeiders Jeugd Centrale (AJC) had its permanent meeting place in a spacious back room in the same building on the Singel, and prints relating to the association were hung on the front of the house, soon led to a vague assumption in the neighborhood, which was immediately expressed in the press as a "well-founded" suspicion that a "bomb" had been planted in the cellar on the part of the communists. Was this a purely political matter? The Justice Department, which was immediately informed of the event, ordered the basement room to be kept under permanent police surveillance until it could take stock of the situation with the assistance of an expert. A telegram from the chief criminal judge called me to the "scene of the crime", where I was ordered to investigate the cause of explosion and the fire in the basement. The boy's condition in the hospital was such that the attending physician preferred him not to have visitors for the first few days. Thus, I had no opportunity to question the only witness who had been in the room during the explosion and who, if questioned, might still be able to point out important points, so that I had no choice but to search for "silent witnesses" on the spot, hoping that they could bring me the light in the darkness I was looking for.

There was a chaotic commotion in the cellar. The plank door, which had been pushed out of its frame, had been put back in place provisionally. A connecting door—never used—which once might have given access to the cellar of the adjoining building (now housing a store selling porcelain, pottery, and household goods), turned out to have been forced outward into the other cellar by air pressure, knocking over—as I heard during the investigation—a large shelf containing an entire stock of crockery, etc., breaking everything! (The fire insurance company ignored the harm done to the poor shopkeeper at the time since the damage was not the result of a fire but of an explosion! Convenient, isn't it? This kind of thing made people suspicious so that they hardly knew whom to contact for help and assistance before committing to an insurance company! From what I hear, those conditions are now much improved).

One of the police officers, who had been there first after the discovery of the fire, filled me in as much as possible. He told me, among other things, that one of the many "interested parties" who had been watching the work to put out the fire had boasted of having a very acute sense of smell and declared that he had smelled "gunpowder fumes"—which indeed could support the *on-dit* (rumor) involving an attack by a bomb with a hellish machine.

After first getting a general impression of the situation in the entire area, I began the special investigation in the basement, where, of course, question number one was whether there was evidence of a bomb or gunpowder attack (in whatever form). I considered that certain combustion products—such as gunpowder or many other explosive substances of similar character—could entirely or partially dissolve in water that has condensed on cold walls. On one side of the cellar the wall was covered with old-fashioned square, glazed tiles. There was a residue deposited on those tiles—richly mixed with "dirt particles"! I rubbed them with clean cotton wool plugs, which were slightly moistened, and transferred them into a well-sealed bottle in my suitcase. I can state right away that I examined the cotton wool balls in my laboratory using every conceivable method to identify any possible decomposition products, but I could not find any positive indications. The complete absence of traces of nitrite and sulfite convinced me that gunpowder was not present at all. Anyway, the smell of gunpowder is so familiar, that it was difficult to accept that in the event of a gunpowder explosion—in which case a lot of gunpowder fumes would have been produced—that the sense of smell of only one person would have been affected. No, all those who had rushed to the scene after the explosion and saw smoke pouring out of the cellar would have had to recognize the smoke as coming from gunpowder. In this case the assertion of this one person was not supported by anyone!

Even though it was rather dark down there, my "light box" once again proved its worth. A reel on which fifty meters of rubber cable are wound ensured that the powerful nitraphot lamp brought a sea of light into the cellar, enabling the deepest nooks and crannies to be searched. When faced with such riddles, the outsider may think that one is working according to a certain scheme or program to find the solution. Nothing could be further from the truth. I never know beforehand which larger or smaller object, or which position or color of a certain part has something to tell as a "silent witness." And so it has always been my habit in such cases to let my gaze calmly pass over everything and anything, taking account of its presence and location—in short, of everything that can be observed in the things I see. Sometimes an object can tell me something because of the place where it is located; at other times something can be deduced from the fact that a certain object is in a local state, from which it can be determined that certain influences (heat as well as otherwise) have made themselves felt from a certain direction. One simply does not know in advance which pieces of the contents of such a space, as silent witnesses, have something to tell. One has to look at them—that is the whole point!

And so I sat myself down on an old chair without a seat, on which I had placed a lid of an old chest, requested all interested parties who were present, both members of the police and residents (the latter were there at the request of the police, in order to be able to answer any questions I might have), to leave me alone with my assistant for a while. I then let my gaze slowly travel along the walls, ceiling and floor, and then inspect the wooden objects (old chairs, a three-legged table, coffin planks, carpenter's waste, etc.) to discover "whether they had something to say."

Let me now describe to the reader in a few sentences how the room was arranged. When one passed the threshold of the cellar door from the back of the house through a small corridor, there was a mass of firewood on the left, held together by a couple of old doors, which made this corner of the cellar into a sort of sheep pen, since they were laid out on their sides on the stone floor. As I said, there was a lot of waste from carpenters' workshops among the firewood, such as small pieces of beam, baseboards, beading, floorboards, slats, etc. Now, if you let your gaze wander from this firewood further along the left wall towards the street, you first saw the door pushed away, lying backwards in a sort of gate in the stone wall. Behind it all the porcelain and pottery lay in ruins! Near that door hung from a nail a very old and worn-out man's vest, frayed and dirty. Continuing on our way, we came to the street door, which the police had provisionally reattached to the frame of the lower façade. To its right was a part of a rubble wall, against which a bunch of old frayed ship's rope hung from one of the beams. Against the right wall was some old garbage, which played no role in my construction. Nearer to us, also against the right wall, stood a bicycle, in front of which, flat on the ground, lay a ten-step ladder, almost parallel to the front of the "sheep pen," which I have just described. Between the ladder and the front bulkhead of the wood storage room only a narrow path of the cellar floor remained ... and on it stood an empty gasoline can. No, it was not empty: it contained a small amount of water for extinguishing fires. Nevertheless, the smell of gasoline could still be detected. I was told that this partially filled can was always in the cellar. The gasoline was used for repairing bicycle tires.

Now I had special reasons, first of all, to subject that old vest and that piece of old rope to an "interrogation." I picked them up one by one and inspected them carefully with the loupe, a small magnifying glass. Both witnesses told me that the charred ends found on the very finest protuberances of threads and fiber bundles owed their origin to the fact that they had been exposed very, very briefly—perhaps only a small part, a fortieth or a fiftieth part, of a second!—to a large flame. The very fact that those two objects themselves had not burned, but that the presence of fire at the scene had only scorched those fine protrusions, proved to me that that fire could only have been in contact with them for an extremely short period—and only the flames of an explosion is of such short duration. It usually fills the entire room, to the extreme corners, in that short period of time, leaving the traces of its presence only on the ends of the finest fibers and hairs, which are then, by that momentary flame, slightly scorched, sometimes charred.

Having found no decomposition products of certain explosive substances used in bombs, it was obvious to ask which substances that do not leave any residue after decomposition could be considered, and—in view of the empty gasoline can—this was the first thing on my mind! When gasoline is poured out, the most volatile parts of the liquid soon evaporate and the resulting gaseous substances mix very easily with the air to form a more or less explosive gas mixture—the same, which, prepared in the right proportions, is ignited in the engines of our automobiles! The obvious assumption was that gasoline had been poured out here—undoubtedly "to start a fire"—and that, after part of it had turned to gas, a match had been lit, which ignited the explosive gas mixture that had just been discussed, after which the flame of the explosion in turn had ignited the gasoline, which was still present as a liquid.

Thus was I faced with a further question: Where was this gasoline poured out? Will I find other indications that a flammable liquid was poured? In the "sheep pen" the top pieces of wood had burned—not fiercely—and yet above it the wooden ceiling of the cellar had been severely damaged by the flames. But such high flames could hardly have reached up from those pieces of wood, since they had burned only superficially. None of them had burned very deeply. Therefore, there had to have been something else that gave such a high, blazing flame when burned ... perhaps the gasoline? Again I wondered whether a liquid had indeed been poured over the wood here. And so, sitting on my improvised work stool, I sorted through all the pieces of wood in the sheep pen, one by one, and after a thorough inspection set them aside. At the top of the pen I found only pieces of wood that appeared to have been gripped by the flame all around, but going deeper into the pile I was lucky enough to find several pieces that had a special "announcement" to make to me. There were some that showed charred, brownish-black surface marks, unmistakably proclaiming that there had been a liquid there that had burned and had thus created the now recognizable black marks in the affected places.

Wherever I found pieces of boards, slats, or beams with these marks I also found the ends of the fluid flow lines directed towards the floor. Moreover, several short pieces of wood with their end grains exposed had deeper burns than wood with other surfaces—a consequence of the fact that in the pieces of wood with their end grains exposed the flammable liquid was much more easily absorbed so that the flames burned more deeply in them. Thus I identified the places where the biggest splash of gasoline had been poured over the loose wood in the sheep pen!

Opposite this pile of wood, in the corner to the right of the entrance to the cellar, some wood had also been burning. Much less gasoline must have been poured on this wood, judging by the smaller burned surface area of the ceiling overhead. Here, therefore, a much smaller amount of gasoline had been used!

When describing the cellar area, I mentioned how some old doors had been put on their sides to create a wood-storage pen. At the front of this—rising to about twenty-five centimeters off the ground—a few wooden slats had been nailed down to make a brace. On one of these slats I also found a small burn mark, which was mainly on the side facing the ground. Above this slat the paint of the door also showed a burned spot, which, however, ran upwards about five centimeters from the slat mentioned above. All this pointed to the fact that something had burnt on this patch, and that the resulting flame had played from below against the batten, in front of it, and then a little above it, against the front of the door. In spite of patient searching, I found no residue of wood, paper, or other matter on the tiles of the floor. Something must have burned there that did not leave any residue at all—undoubtedly also gasoline. However, it had only been a small amount—perhaps a dash accidentally(!) spilled. What happened was becoming clearer and clearer!

Now only one question remained: "Who is the culprit?" Willy W.—the young man, who was still being nursed in the hospital until he recovered from his burns—was "strongly suspected" in my eye. Soon, however—after the Justice Department, having heard my preliminary impressions, had W. W. transferred to the House of Detention upon discharge from the hospital—spontaneous expressions of sympathy were made by family, neighbors, friends, and fellow patrons of the arrested. There were long letters testifying to their sympathy for the simple, kind boy, whom no one, but no one, could suspect of such a mean deed. After all, when the fire broke out, all the housemates (he was living with people!) were deeply asleep. But the old police sergeant had already informed me about the impulsive character of the somewhat eccentric boy, who, on the one hand, knew how to elicit people's sympathy, but who, on the other hand, when under the influence of oddballs with whom he interacted, could sometimes "do strange things."

After the man was transferred to the hospital, the police had confiscated his entire outfit. I wanted to examine it more closely. The blue smock told me that a flame had gone up on the inside along the back of the person wearing it. One of his woolen socks showed light scorch marks, which could have been caused by a low flame that had gone up alongside it. Was that perhaps from the "spilled" gasoline next to the "sheep pen"? Had the gasoline can always been in the cellar in that place where the police found it empty? As I was assured by the housemates, the can was not usually on the floor of the basement. Now the resident's wife told me how, the day before the nighttime fire, she had put the bicycle—belonging to a temporarily absent resident—in the basement "for safety," to prevent any visitors to the house from using it. She had pushed the bicycle over the steps of the flat ladder in the dark, even walking next to that ladder on the narrow strip of basement floor next to the "sheep pen," and on her way had not encountered anything. The implication was that the gasoline can had not been there at that moment! That meant it must have been moved in the basement later, no doubt while preparing the fire! W. W. was the only one who, as midnight approached, had not gone to bed. Claiming that his room was too warm, he had remained in the downstairs room on a divan as the others went to bed.

In my report to the Justice Department, I not only reconstructed the facts, but added that I had the moral conviction that W. W., who had burn marks on his clothes, indicating that he had been standing precisely where the gasoline used to start the fire had ignited, must be the perpetrator of the offense (intentional arson using gasoline). Nevertheless, W. W. maintained his innocence. He had heard noises in the basement, etc., etc., as he had stated in the first instance to the police of the town of M. Even the geniality with which the examining magistrate reminded the accused of the significance of my report did not change his attitude in any way, so that I was requested by the examining magistrate to come to Alkmaar at a time to be determined for an interview with both him and the accused. After receiving that letter I posted my reply, confirming the day of my visit. Just then I received another letter from the magistrate, reading as follows: "You may ignore my previous letter. This morning W. confessed to me that he set the fire, and in exactly the way described in your report. He has gradually realized that he could not stand up to your report with his lies. We are still searching for the reasons for his action, which he does not wish to reveal." Later it came to light that W. W., who was out of work, owed a lot to the couple from whom he got board and lodging, thought he could do them a "good deed" by setting fire to their house, which he thought was well insured. If the insurance money had been paid out, a new house would have had to be built and there would have been work again!

Epilogue by Mattijs Koeberg: Bomb Scene Management

Reading this story brings to mind at least three topics in current crime and forensics: terrorism, bomb scene management, and forensic reconstructions. The context of politically or ideologically driven crimes, as is suspected in this story, is of the time. Currently, international terrorism by fundamentalist organizations and individuals and political extremism are what worries our safety and security organizations the most. As I write this epilogue, the most recent "Dreigingsbeeld Terrorisme Nederland" ("Terrorism threat assessment in the Netherlands") issued by the Nationaal Coördinator Terrorismebestrijding en Veiligheid (NCTV, National Coordinator for Security and Counterterrorism) puts the threat level at three out of five, after having been at four a few years back.

It is interesting to note that forensic investigations of terrorist crimes are no different from "ordinary" crimes, but the dynamics around the investigations are often different. There can be intense pressure to achieve quick results, for example, in order to prevent a possible second attack, or in order to inform the general public that is panicking. This has led to the development of new ways to apply forensic techniques—for example, by rapid response teams using mobile technology to allow for fast indicative biometric, DNA, or explosives investigations.

Although the basics of good crime scene management are the same, most types of crimes/incidents have their own processes and techniques. The investigation of a suspected bomb scene is an example of this. To be ready to do forensic investigations of (multiple) terrorist attacks with explosives, every few years Dutch forensic explosives investigators, together with international colleagues, organize an international bomb scene management training. Here, best practices are exchanged relating to procedures to ensure efficient, complete evidence collection and registration that also assures contamination prevention and chain of custody. Experiments are done with new ways of trace sampling and packaging and working under time pressure. Done correctly, similar levels of evidential value can be achieved in a crime scene investigation of twenty minutes or of two hours. This is useful knowledge for the applications of forensics in unsafe areas such as conflict/war zones.

An important part of the contribution of forensics in the investigation of the scene of an explosion is the reconstruction of what happened. Where was the explosive situated, how were bystanders and cars situated and moving at the time of the explosion, how was the explosive device constructed, and how was it initiated? It is surprising to see the level of detailed reconstruction that can be achieved with a thorough examination of the evidence and logical reasoning. As the extensive and somewhat confusing textual descriptions of the crime scene in this story by Co van Ledden Hulsebosch shows, visualization is an important and powerful way of presenting the evidence and results in reconstructions. Sometimes a drawing of the layout of the scene is sufficient. For more complex/large crime scenes, digital 3D representations are often the norm.

10. Murder in the Celebesstraat

It was still in the early years of my career (July 1903, Mr. Von Baumhauer was still the district attorney) when I was summoned by him over the phone to the property at 24 Celebesstraat in Amsterdam East, where a small shoemaker's workshop was located. Behind it was the home of the shoemaker, who lived there with his wife and his brother. The latter had an unsavory past. He had already served a prison sentence and had reason to be grateful that his older brother had extended a helping hand to him after his release from Leeuwarden, promising to train him in the shoemaking trade, while the younger brother could also count on board and lodging.

After a few customers had visited the workshop for repairs in the morning of that fateful day—as later became clear to us—the neighbors noticed that the house remained closed after noon, and even persistent ringing went unanswered. This seemed so strange that the police were alerted. It appeared as if the neighbors had an anxious premonition. When the police had the lock on the front door opened by a blacksmith, the entering officers beheld a horrifying sight: at the back of the narrow hallway, in front of the threshold of the door to the backroom, lay the lifeless body of the woman of the house, brutally murdered and drenched in blood. The side walls of the hallway were so generously splattered with blood that there was no spot larger than the size of a postcard where there was no blood. They immediately closed the door again and alerted the Justice Department, who—as I began to say—also instructed me to come there.

Thus, I was among the first to witness the crime scene after its discovery. Here, I should note that unfortunately, this was not always a steadfast rule. Indeed, all too often attempts were made to arrive at conclusions without expert help, forgetting that precisely in the initial stages, there is great danger that the "silent witnesses" are condemned to eternal silence, as was the case in the sensational murder of the industrialist L. in Rotterdam, where my assistance was requested ... ten days after the murder, when the victim had long been laid to rest under the green sod, and the cleaning women, followed by the painter and plasterer, had completely removed all "dirt" (as the valuable silent witnesses were called!), and there was hardly anything left for the expert to find as a starting point for any deduction! But to the matter at hand!

I return to Celebesstraat, where I thus had everything, as far as possible, in an untouched state before me. I carefully examined the victim, studied various footprints imprinted in blood on the wooden floor of the workshop and the kitchen, and proceeded quietly on my path. Meanwhile, detectives had learned from one of the neighbors that there had been disagreements between the husband and wife in this house quite often; that the man had gone on a trip to his parents in Groningen

... so it was possible or likely believed that the husband might have murdered his wife—in connection with which suspicion, an inspector of police had already taken the train to Groningen.

I asked a neighbor to provide me with a description of the shoemaker, and she provided me with a few details that gave me little guidance, but alongside those were a couple of more significant pieces of information. She told me, "He's a tall figure with dark brown curly hair," and upon hearing this, I immediately intervened: "Then he's NOT the murderer! The murderer has a completely different description: they are short in stature, they have light blonde, straight hair; furthermore, they are left-handed (there, by that window is their place at the shoemaker's table!), their first name starts with an L, just like their last name, and they live in this house. Their room is upstairs in the back." "But then it's the shoemaker's brother who lives here!" was the neighbor's immediate response. That young man, taken into the house out of pity, had thus taken the life of his sister-in-law!

It was demanded that I immediately explain my deductions, a request I was happy to fulfill. On the victim, who was lying on the hallway floor on her back, I had found a light blonde strand of hair, clamped between a pearl from her pinky ring and one of the frame's little teeth—almost straight, without any curl. There was a root end, which—I could observe it with a magnifying glass—contained extremely small flecks of grease, indicating that after leaving the scalp, this hair root had not scraped against anything, meaning it must have come into contact with the victim's surroundings in her final moments, in other words, it must have come from the murderer, almost certainly. It's remarkable how often a victim grabs their murderer by the hair, so our first attention is always given to a victim's hands, to see if there might be a hair of the murderer clamped within. The perpetrator of this crime therefore had light blonde, straight hair.

The way the wounds were inflicted and the direction they took gave me the intuitive impression that they were caused by a left-handed person. My suspicion turned into certainty when I found a thrown-off shirt under a bedstead in the hallway—of small size—of which the left sleeve was completely stained with fresh blood. The same shirt was marked with the letters L. L.—giving me a lead to the probable name of the perpetrator. The small-sized shirt was in harmony with the small footprints and the small steps that the feet had made when they left bloody marks; all of which indicated a small stature. A comparative examination next to the later stamped footprints of a suspect might yield success.

When I found a single-person upper room with a linen closet, all marked with "L. L.," it became clear to me that the perpetrator must be the inhabitant. Furthermore, when I observed in the shoemaker's workshop that one chair was usually occupied by a small, left-handed man, the deduction that the murderer of this crime and the small, left-handed shoemaker were the same was not a very daring leap. (On his spot, I found a hammer and an awl placed on the table, specifically on the left side, whereas the tools of the other shoemaker were on his right side; the distinct size of the straps, hanging over the back of chair number one, contrasted significantly with those of the other, providing additional support for this deduction.)

While all the discussed traces provided me with accurate information about the identity of the perpetrator, the examination of further silent witnesses, which I won't delve into here, led me to all the specifics of this crime. They revealed the time, motive, and all the details of the horrific act. When the perpetrator—who was identified on posters based on my indications, with a request for his arrest and presentation—realized he couldn't escape, he surrendered himself to the police and gave a "confession" to the examining magistrate that contained numerous inaccuracies. However, I was able to confront him with his lies based on my observations and what the silent witnesses had so clearly indicated, thus compelling him to provide a truthful account of his wrongdoing. The fellow received a life sentence. He brought his life to an end by hanging himself in his cell shortly after his conviction.

Translated by Rick van Rijn.

11. Theft at a Bank Solved by a Police Dog

It was in the days when the Pietershal bureau was very busy with various property crimes, that two detectives from that bureau approached me to ask whether I could take some fingerprints from a receipt for a thousand guilders, which was part of a peculiar case at one of the major banks in the city. About a month earlier, it had been noticed that a receipt for a thousand guilders had disappeared from one of the vaults. The management, which neither could nor wanted to believe that any foul play was involved in this matter, initially assumed that the paper had "just gotten lost" among other documents and would be found shortly. They were disappointed when, after four weeks of patience, the missing paper remained gone, and an official "report" of the case to the police at the Pietershal bureau had to be filed.

As a result of this report, the receipt in question, with its numbers, etc., appeared on a criminal investigations list. One can imagine the astonishment of the bank management when the lost paper was back in its old place in the vault the next day ... but it was also discovered that another, equivalent paper had been taken away in exchange for the returned one. That could indeed be called bold! Thus, it was hoped that fingerprints could identify the person who had held this receipt. I didn't have too much confidence in such an experiment. Firstly, I knew from experience that fingerprints on printed documents are rarely usable, and, secondly, I understood all too well that so many people before and after the thief would have touched that document and that someone who is handling papers all day does not produce sufficient "print ink" in the form of sweat to stamp valuable fingerprints on all of them! Finally, it was the cool season, during which the hands of normal people did not suffer too much from the heat!

And so I pondered another experiment and soon my plan of action was set. I instructed the two detectives to go to the bank in question, and ask the management to draw an imaginary line within which the perpetrator should be sought, and beyond which no one could under any circumstances be suspected. Of all the persons falling within that cordon, the detectives had to confiscate their wallets for a couple of hours, and they had to ensure that each wallet was kept in a new envelope bearing the owner's name. By three o'clock in the afternoon, they should come to the courtyard of the headquarters with these wallets. At that time, we could still carry out an experiment there without being disturbed, as it was not yet a parking lot for police cars.

I arrived half an hour early and met the dog trainer, Water, who had brought his famous tracking dog Albert and another disciple with him. First, I wanted to check if the dogs were well-disposed—yes, that can vary quite a bit from one day to another!—which I would verify with a simple test. I asked the trainer to have his dogs check if there were any papers from my wallet in between and behind the shrubs, which were along the side façade of the building and along the outer fence (there were countless papers; however, only three of them had come from my pocket). Water first gave the dogs a "scent" of my leather wallet, after which the command "search" was given. It didn't take long before the tracking dogs had brought back all the papers that came from me to their master. Then I asked if the dogs could indicate to their master to whom the folded postcard belonged which was laying at the foot of one of the shrubs. I assured him that the owner belonged to a fairly large group of "interested parties" who—more or less as extras—took part in the experiment. After the dogs had picked up the scent of this postcard, they slowly and intensively sniffed along people's legs, and ... suddenly a chief inspector of the traffic department was rightly designated as the owner!

Now that the usefulness and suitability of the dogs had been sufficiently established, the thirty-eight envelopes in which the detectives had brought an equal number of wallets from the bank clerks were handed over to the trainer. He made space and displayed the wallets, each placed on top of their envelope, across the courtyard in such a way that distances of about one and a half meters were left between them, to prevent the scent of one piece from interfering with another. Then the trainer let his puppies take a scent from the particular receipt. There was dead silence, and one could hear regular sniffing movements as the dogs each took "scent" in turn. After walking around for a while, each of the dogs sat down next to a wallet and indicated, by loud barking, that they had found the same scent from the receipt there. It was miraculous—two wallets! Among most bystanders, the first thought was that the dogs must be mistaken, but it could be possible that the scent of two people was on the document and that one of the dogs recognized scent A—and the other scent B.

From one of the windows on the ground floor, one of the deputy directors of the bank watched the search. He asked which names were on the two envelopes under the indicated wallets and assured me that it had to be a mistake. Suspicion had fallen on entirely different persons. He was even somewhat startled when I expressed my request to the detectives to fetch the two gentlemen whose wallets were indicated by the dogs, but I assured him that I had enough confidence in the dogs to act as I did under the given circumstances, and I added a little mischievously that—if it turned out that the dogs had been mistaken, they would not fail to offer their apologies for it, if necessary!

After a good fifteen minutes, the detectives came to the courtyard with two office clerks from the bank. I had about twenty people, properly spaced apart, spread out over the courtyard and arbitrarily placed the office clerks among them. Then the trainer and his helpers set to work again; the dogs' noses were again pressed against the receipt in turns with the command "Smell!," after which the four-legged friends were ordered to search and heard the command "Identify the man!" Dead silence. Anxiously calm, the detectives did their work, sniffing at every trouser leg, moving through the crowd in all sorts of winding lines, until suddenly both, one to the right and the other to the left of the same person, indicated loudly with barking that they found "the" scent. The dog Albert, apparently afraid that his master would still not understand his intentions sufficiently, stood on his hind legs, leaning with his front paws against the bank clerk, who had turned chalk white with fright.

The detectives asked the latter to go inside with them, everyone else returned to their work, including me, and the experiment was finished for today. When I was sitting in my living room an hour later, the phone rang. The deputy director of the bank wanted to be the first to share the achieved success with me. The person in question had soon confessed to the detectives that he was the perpetrator of the theft. The paper that he had taken away, in exchange for the original one, was hidden in one of the bank's toilets, behind a shelf on which the roll of toilet paper is attached with its bracket. After first loosening the top two screws a bit, he had let the document slide behind it and then tightened the screws again! The mystery of how the dogs initially indicated two wallets was also cleared up: the person to whom the second wallet belonged sat at the same double desk as the perpetrator. He had had the particular receipt with him for a couple of days to try to cash it, however, he eventually decided against it and returned it. Thus, a little bit of his body scent had also ended up on the document!

Epilogue by Christianne de Poot: Group-wide Trace Comparison Strategies in Criminal Investigations

The case described in this chapter is fascinating. Although nowadays such cases would be handled by private or corporate investigators who would definitely use other means, it is interesting to reflect on the strategy Co van Ledden Hulsebosch used in this investigation. To my knowledge, this is the first description of a Dutch criminal investigation that targets a defined circle of nonsuspects for a systematic trace comparison. This strategy can be used when the police find a crime-related trace with high discriminatory power at the crime scene, and assume that the perpetrator can be found within a specific group of people, but have no leads to identify a specific suspect. In such cases the police can ask all individuals within that defined circle to provide reference material that can be compared with the crime trace. In this way, the police can exclude all individuals whose reference material does not match the crime trace, and identify possible offenders. Not only the strategy, also the use of a scent comparison test in this strategy, is noteworthy. The "group-wide trace comparison" strategy has clearly gained momentum since the rise of DNA. DNA is an absolute winner when it comes to the investigative information it contains and its power to categorically rule out people as possible donors of a biological trace. However, this does not mean that this strategy was not used before the introduction of DNA, nor that its use increased significantly since then. The strategy faces several challenges that do not solely depend on the nature of the crime trace.

Over the past century, the "group-wide trace comparison" strategy was mainly used when the police assumed that the perpetrator of a serious crime was part of a local community. For instance, in the investigation of a serial arsonist in the Dutch village of Blijham, all men between eighteen and sixty-five from that village were asked to perform a handwriting test for handwriting comparison with a letter in which new fires were announced. This strategy led to the offender. In a murder investigation in Stede Broec, 5,000 men from that community were asked to provide fingerprints and palm prints. When a match was found, after the prints of about 1,700 people were collected and compared, the investigation focused on the identified suspect who confessed to the murder. Until the late 1990s, mainly fingerprints, palm prints, and, in exceptional cases, handwriting were used for comparison when this strategy was applied. The case described in this chapter is the only case I know of where scent comparisons are used in a group-wide trace comparison strategy. Since the late 1990s, only DNA comparisons have been used for this strategy.[8]

As mentioned, DNA offers unprecedented possibilities for group-wide trace comparison strategies. DNA characteristics of biological crime traces can be used to narrow down the circle of people targeted for investigation, and partial DNA matches may reveal kinship information that can be used as investigative lead. In a murder investigation in the Dutch town of Zaandam both characteristics of DNA were used in a this strategy. Thorough DNA analysis of the crime trace revealed that donor was a man with likely roots in the southern part of Anatolia.[9] Based on this information, the circle of individuals targeted for the investigation was limited to 133 men with southern Anatolian roots who lived in a specific part of Zaandam at the time of the crime. Although the offender was part of this selection, he refused to participate. However, the offender came to light because his brother participated. The partial match between his brother's DNA profile and the profile of the crime trace led to a further investigative lead, and to the identification of the offender.

---

8   For these and other examples, see C. J. De Poot and E. W. Kruisbergen, *Circling the Perpetrator: Intelligence-Led DNA Screening as an Investigative Tool* (The Hague: Boom Juridische Uitgevers, 2006).
9   A particular part of the DNA molecule contained a specific combination of alleles (haplotype) that is common in the southern part of Anatolia and not in other areas. At the time of the murder, 3,463 men with these roots lived in Zaandam.

In the Netherlands, there are strict guidelines for the use of the group-wide trace comparisons with nonsuspects since 2001. The strategy may only be used as a last resort for investigations of serious crimes. If there are leads to search for the perpetrator with a "best first search" strategy, these leads must first be explored. This prevents an unnecessary burden on nonsuspects who are asked for reference material. The police must also be sure that traces used for comparison have strong discriminatory power, are crime-related, and come from the offender. In addition, the police must be able to identify a sharply defined circle of people of which the perpetrator is most likely to be part. Next to that, there are legal requirements and practical limitations. For example, the police must be able to properly identify and approach individuals within this circle, and these individuals must be willing to participate in such an investigation. In practice, this combination of factors turns out to be quite exceptional. The example van Ledden Hulsebosch describes, with the nicely defined circle of individuals, who are all willing to participate in his experiment at the same time is a textbook illustration of a group-wide trace comparison strategy that rarely occurs in police practice.

12. He Had the Silent Witness "in Hand"

This happened many years ago—certainly before July 1916. I had not yet been appointed by the municipality of Amsterdam to be the "scientific advisor to the Detective Department," as stated in my first official appointment document. However, from March 1902 onwards, I was called to serious crime scenes, but always by the judiciary. For minor offenses, where the immediate assistance of a scientific investigator was not deemed necessary, they managed without an expert, often resulting in the loss of valuable clues! Several detectives, however, had the habit of seeking my advice when faced with a problem, and I gladly provided it out of a sense of duty to the cause.

So one morning, Detective-Sergeant T. from the Pieter Aertszstraat police station informed me of the following: During the previous night, a break-in had occurred at the residence of X, the horse dealer, a villa located along the Amstel River, beyond the last houses of the (then-existing) "basin." Among other things, a heavy silver inkwell had been stolen. The ink had been poured out in advance. It was a precious piece of art, a reminder of a win in a sports competition. Perhaps by now it had already been melted down for its silver content! Suspicions had arisen against an old acquaintance who had been found walking along the Amstel River that night. T. had promptly visited his home, but found no sign of the valuable inkwell. However, he had noticed stains on the man's right hand that strongly resembled ink stains. When he commented on this, the suspect had replied, "Oh, that's just some axle grease I got on my hand this morning!"

T. asked me if I could determine whether these stains were indeed from axle grease or ink. Undoubtedly, I could do that. However, I was reluctant to offer my expertise, time, and chemicals without compensation. Therefore, I advised T. to approach the public prosecutor, explain how much depended on those stains on the suspect's hand, and inform him that I was willing to assist if I received an official request from the judicial authorities. That way, I could include my expenses in my report. I could no longer afford to provide free assistance. My study trips, new instruments, and books demanded constant and substantial financial sacrifices!

Half an hour later, the phone rang. One of the deputy public prosecutors inquired about the cost of the investigation, which amused me. I dared to ask, "Should it be considered regular work from now on?" The magistrate, understanding that I couldn't accurately measure the required time in advance and knowing well that I had no habit of inflating bills at the expense of *Justitia*, promptly said, "Well, go ahead ... it has to be done anyway, and I trust it won't turn out to be too expensive!" I quickly packed a selection of bottles with chemical solutions into a briefcase, along with some pieces of filter paper, glass rods, and a notebook and then I headed to the aforementioned police station, where the suspect was temporarily being held.

First, I displayed my "chemical inventory" like a showcase on the table, placing a bowl of water next to it, and asked T. to bring in the guinea pig. He entered with a dry "good morning" and at my request sat down on a chair near one of the windows, where I had good light for observing any discolorations that might occur during the treatment with various chemical substances—assuming they were indeed ink stains. There was some risk involved. Paper doesn't have "sensation," however, certain corrosive substances could irritate human skin in an unpleasant way, and I had to be cautious about that. That's why I had a wet cloth at hand, ready to wipe away the foreign substances from the skin immediately after observing the expected reactions!

He sat down on the designated chair and noticing my extraordinary interest in those stains on his hand, he said with a mocking laugh, "Anyone can see these are grease stains; yet, they boldly claim they are ink stains!" I tried to convince the man as kindly as possible that—if they were indeed grease stains—my examination would provide the desired certainty. I asked him to hold out his hand as if he were asking for charity. In a matter of moments, I placed small drops from the various chemical bottles onto the dark stains on the inner surface of his hand. Discolorations appeared everywhere, which I immediately relayed to a temporarily appointed secretary to record. My client followed the operation in silent amazement. Fortunately, his skin provided enough resistance to the action of the chemicals during the brief moments of contact. Once I observed the final discolorations, I hurried to clean the skin with damp filter paper and then with a wet cloth. All of this left the victim in dumbfounded amazement and his mouth had gradually fallen open. He was so engrossed in the experiment being conducted on his skin! He must have found it quite intriguing.

Suddenly, he made a remark, "Wow, the detective work nowadays is really advancing!" He was absolutely right! My examination was over; the acquiescent patient could leave! He looked at me questioningly. Might he know the outcome of my investigation?

I declared my intention to be transparent and revealed that not only had I conclusively determined that the stains on his hand were caused by ink but also could specify the type of ink. I even ventured to express the strong likelihood that it had been Stephens' Blue Black Writing Fluid, the English ink sold in brown stone jars. Detective T. continued the investigation and returned to the victim's house. An hour later, he phoned me, reporting that he had seized an almost empty jar of Stephens' Blue Black ink, the only ink used there and also present in the stolen inkwell. The rascal was caught red-handed and received a conviction!

Epilogue by Eva de Rijke

In this chapter the hands of a theft suspect of a silver inkwell are investigated for ink stains. The suspect claimed the stains on his hands were from axle grease, and Co van Ledden Hulsebosch is called in to determine whether the stains were indeed from grease or ink. The method he applies involves small drops from various chemical bottles, which are not further specified. The results were discolorations that conclusively determined that the stains on the suspects hand were caused by ink, but could also specify the type of ink. Based on this evidence the suspect was convicted.

The discolorations of the ink were most likely caused by a chemical reaction of the methylene blue from the ink with sodium hypochlorite (bleach) that results in the colorless leukomethylene blue. One or more other substances in the ink that reacted with the chemicals in the various bottles were probably indicative for the type of ink that matched with the ink that was present in the stolen silver inkwell.

Nowadays, analytical techniques such as (infrared) spectroscopy and gas chromatography coupled to mass spectrometry (GC-MS) are used to determine the identity of (mixtures of) (volatile) chemicals, such as the pigments in ink. Although GC-MS was invented in the 1950s, it hasn't been applied routinely in forensic investigations since the early 1970s. Its application greatly enhanced the capabilities of forensic scientists to analyze complex samples with high specificity and sensitivity. Since its introduction, GC-MS has become a standard and widely used technique in forensic laboratories around the world for the analysis of drugs, explosives, arson residues, and a variety of other substances relevant to criminal investigations.

13. The Murder of the Cat Farmer

It was a chilly January morning in 1918. In the northernmost part of the province of North Holland, in the village of Breezand, at dawn, the farms were full of activity. The cows had already been milked and the cans of milk were being taken to the road one by one, where the truck driver would soon pick them up to take them to the dairy.

But on one farm all was quiet. The gate remained closed and no milk cans came out. The nearest neighbor, who had already placed his entire milk production on the road, soon became suspicious that something was wrong there, and walked to the front door of the elderly neighbor who lived alone. His knock was not answered. Then he tried the back door, which gave direct access to the barn, where six cows with swollen udders were waiting to be milked. The door was not closed. He walked behind the cows to the connecting door to the house, where dead silence reigned. In the large room, a small kerosene lamp, which the old man was accustomed to placing on the high edge of the fireplace in the evening—in order to spread the light throughout the room—was now in the middle of the table, which surprised the person entering. The glow of the light fell between the thin, white curtains, onto the bedstead. When the visitor turned his gaze there, he recoiled in dismay for a moment. The neighbor lay there dead ... murdered in a horrible manner.

He was lying backwards on the pillow, which was soaked with blood. There was a gaping wound on his forehead and his wrists were tied together stiffly with a greasy rope, which was normally used to tie the hind legs of cows together during milking. His legs were shaking so he needed a few minutes to realize the horror of what had taken place and to run outside, in order to send a servant to the policeman stationed in the village. The latter hurried to the scene of the crime, took a quick look at the situation, locked the house, and gave the strictest instructions not to enter the premises. His telegram to the public prosecutor in Alkmaar was soon sent, and his immediate superior, the brigade commander of the National Police, had of course already received a message to go to Breezand immediately.

Before rushing to Breezand, the public prosecutor in Alkmaar sent a telegram to Amsterdam, to the writer of these sentences, ordering him to come over immediately, for the purpose of the investigation. A train would depart within half an hour. The so-called murder suitcase—containing all the items which might be needed in such an initial on-site investigation—was ready to be taken. It was always packed, ready for any trip *pro justitia* (for the sake of the law).

Everything had remained untouched. No one had entered the room after the officer, who had only briefly gone in to see what had happened, an unavoidable necessity to spare the "silent witnesses." How different from a murder case in the big city! Things are different there! After a policeman called from the street first learns of a murder, he alerts his superiors. The sergeant arrives, followed by an inspector and the chief inspector. But the inspector who had arrived at the station, especially charged with the investigation of judicial matters, also hurries to the scene of the crime. The commissioner is also on his way. He calls in the expert from the police, or—as some commissioners used to do—he leaves the "scientific advisor" at home, for fear that he will clear up the case, which "would be a pity … for if we could do it ourselves for once without him, then he needn't have another success and we would get the kudos ourselves." This attitude is a shame. It results in so much being spoiled, as in the case of a murder in the IJpolder in 1933, where the perpetrator must have left traces but where the commissioner, who was in charge, imagined that he could find and work out those traces himself … which turned out to be a vain hope! If the police commissioner is present, then occasionally the medical service—alerted by one of the nervous neighbors—appears on the scene, as well as the special team of investigators from headquarters, who come to the department offices to help with serious cases. In the meantime, the public prosecutor, the examining magistrate, and his clerk arrive, as well as the expert, who—completely understandable!—in this house full of people, feels ill-equipped to carry out an investigation, which requires total concentration, as well as a quiet environment, free of anything that could distract his thoughts. Everyone thinks he can and may contribute. The victim was already moved a little by one of the first people present, because otherwise hardly anyone could pass in the narrow corridor! This is how things often go in the big city … which is very regrettable! In Breezand, it was much, much better in that respect! Everything remained untouched, until the arrival of the prosecutor and the expert!

My first job was to learn the brief history of the event, which the neighbor—a simple peasant, still reeling from the shock of discovering the murder—explained to me clearly and lucidly. He also told me how the murdered farmer used to run his own little household, cook his own food, and run his small business, always placing his cans of milk at the gate of the driveway in the morning with the regularity of a clock. Also, how that old man always desired light in the room at night and to this end placed the small kerosene lamp, which was not allowed to shine in his eyes, on the edge of the fireplace. Instinctively, entering the death room, he had blown out that little lamp, which was then on the table … but without touching it!

In order to keep everything in the proper form, I was first appointed and sworn in. It must make a peculiar impression on any outsider, when I tell him that I, working for the court since March 1902, nevertheless had to retake the "oath as an expert" for every case I was given to investigate! Here in Breezand, it was done in a jiffy. It was different on the occasions when, for example, I had to make a trip to Winschoten to take the oath for an insignificant investigation which the examining magistrate there wanted to assign to me. A whole day of my precious time was wasted, travel and accommodation expenses, and all to satisfy his whim of wanting to swear me in personally! Fortunately, such instances remained rarities. Usually, an examining magistrate from outside passed on the message to his counterpart in Amsterdam, who then "by letters rogatory"—as the term goes—arranged the appointment and swearing in. So I took the oath and began my investigation.

My first job was to take a good look at the situation in order to get a general impression of the layout of the room and to find out by what route the perpetrator or perpetrators had entered. That would undoubtedly have happened through the small window of the cowshed, next to the door, a little bigger than a toilet window and placed in the wall at about the height of a man.

The old man appeared to have been robbed while lying in bed. He had been bashed in the skull—apparently with a tool lying on the floor about a meter away from the bedstead. It was a wrench, like the one we used to have on our bicycles, with recesses to fit various nut sizes. Only this wrench was much heavier, more substantial, and suitable for larger nuts than the bicycle tool. On the flat middle part of the tool was written, in raised letters, the name "Bamford." This was unknown to me. I inquired around and heard from one of the local farmers, who had come to give us some more information, that Bamford was the name of a large steam engine, suitable for threshing and so much more. Who had such a Bamford machine? Well, to his knowledge there were only three in use in upper North Holland, on the farms of three named farmers. Two of them were easy to reach by bicycle, so I immediately sent the policeman with the spanner to check which of the three farmers was missing the spanner for his Bamford machine. I urged him to leave the greasy piece of string attached to the spanner; this could be another point of recognition.

Meanwhile, I searched the room for traces. The aforementioned kerosene lamp, which was found burning on the table, was in any case one of the objects that had been in the hands of the perpetrator and on which fingerprints might be present. To find them, however, seemed extremely doubtful to me, given the fact that the outside of the lamp was "as greasy as a slug" from the kerosene. If I applied the usual dusting powder—the finest aluminum bronze powder—with a badger hair brush, in order to make the powder adhere to the—perhaps still sticky(!)—lines of the fingerprint, the entire surface of the greasy lamp would undoubtedly retain the powder. Then the badger hair brush would soon be so stained with kerosene that it would make the glass surface greasy in all the places where there was no "adhesive force."

I hardly had the courage to apply the usual dusting process to this and yet I was left with nothing else, and so under the motto "all or nothing!" I began, very carefully, to powder the outside of the lamp on one side and gently brush it off with the brush. I soon noticed that the brush itself started to produce greasy lines. I quickly took a clean brush (that's why it's good to carry several in the suitcase!) and continued the treatment with it. Sure enough, a group of fine lines emerged. Whether I would achieve anything remained a question, and yet I decided to do everything possible, because there was a good chance that this trace came from the perpetrators' fingers. Taking the utmost precautions, the lamp was stored in a small box, and in such a way that the entire surface remained exposed, and the dactyloscopic trace therefore untouched! It joined my luggage and was to be further examined in my laboratory. In order to find out whether it was the inhabitant's fingerprint, I made a so-called dactyloscopic description of the victim according to the rules of the art, i.e., I successively pressed the ten fingertips first on a blackened glass plate and then on a sheet of paper, in the boxes of which one fingerprint at a time was placed. Now the trace found could be compared!

Over a chair rail hung a jacket belonging to the murdered farmer. It could be clearly seen how—when emptying the pockets—the lining fabric had been turned inside out. On the table lay an old, smooth leather pocketbook. Attempts to find fingerprints on it failed. It was not easy to find fingerprints in this dirty environment, because the powder stuck almost everywhere, due to the sticky, greasy coating that literally covered all the objects in the household. One could tell that the contents had not had a thorough cleaning in a very long time! Meanwhile, news regarding the Bamford spanner had arrived. The policeman had found the farmer, who, as the owner of a Bamford mowing and binding machine, had recognized the spanner as his lost property by the greasy piece of string with which the spanner was regularly hung against the wall next to the machine in the barn.

That spanner had to have been taken the previous morning by three men, who had had permission to spend the night in the hay barn. They had been three sinister types. The farmer was asked if he could give a personal description of these tramps. That was a bit much to ask! But still, however little our man could give regarding the identification of the three strangers, he was able to give us approximate ages and approximate heights, and also told us that one of the men had red hair and another a stiff right leg.

Now the criminal investigation department at headquarters in Amsterdam possesses an extensive card system, in which all "clients" have a card on which all identifying marks are noted. Searching through these cabinets of cards is considerably simplified by the presence of colored riders, which can be placed on the top edge of each card on one of the thirty numbered boxes into which the top edge is divided.

So, one particular box gives information about hairstyle. Of the ten types of colored riders (that's what we call the little tin clips that can be put on that one box), each color has its own meaning. The "key" of the card system clarifies this. To give an example, if a red rider on box 9 means that the person described on the card has red hair, then, after opening a drawer containing thousands of cards, one need only hold a ruler over the common boxes showing the number 9 to immediately find the red riders falling in that line. These are the redheads among our clientele. And soon some names were noted down from the card system for further checking.

On another box, mutilations, "defective" limbs, etc., are indicated, and so the statement that one of the three strangers possessed a stiff right leg led us to two cards. The person shown on one of these cards was not walking around freely—he was staying in Leeuwarden at the time at the state's expense—so the other one could qualify. Investigations revealed that he had a solid alibi for the night of the murder. But the investigators managed to find out who his regular friends were, with whom he "went out." And now, coincidentally, it turned out that one of these friends had red hair. The latter and "third in the alliance" were promptly interned and I soon received the dactyloscopic descriptions from the Alkmaar Justice Department, that is, the forms on which the fingerprints of these people were printed. Sometimes this activity is called playing the piano!

The examination of the kerosene lamp was not without obstacles. I had—as I told you—found a group of fine lines of a fingerprint on one side, of which a picture was soon taken, taking into account the rather strong curvature of the surface of the reservoir. Because everything has to be razor-sharp in the photo, of course! Soon I had spotted a certain finger from the identification form of one of the suspects, which could be it, and the investigation continued. But—however much the similarity of form struck me—I kept running into points of difference ... how was that possible? Finally, instead of the photo, I took the photographic negative in front of me and found that the print on the identification form did match! And when I had made an enlarged negative on paper, I could record a sufficient number of points—more than is considered necessary for identification! It was established that this man's finger must have touched the lamp!

The explanation of this strange, very rarely occurring phenomenon is the following. As a rule, when placing a fingerprint, a little matter is left behind, either sweat, or other "stamp ink," which the fine ridges of the fingertip skin deposit on the touched surface. Then, as we call it, the imprint is positive on the object. Where the lines are printed, the fingertip skin touched that object. But, as soon as an object is stained with an extremely thin layer of dust, kerosene or otherwise, it is possible that a dry fingertip, when touching it, will not leave something behind, but, on the contrary, will take something away from the touched object. And now, in the present case, a dry finger, when touching the greasy surface of the kerosene lamp with the so-called papillary lines of the fingertip, took away grease from the glass. Between those touching places, where the glass was thus, strictly speaking, not touched, the thin petroleum skin remained, and took over the aluminum bronze of my badger hair brush, so that, contrary to the usual rule, the lines that appeared in silver-white did not correspond to the papillary lines of the fingertip, but to the open spaces between them! The so-called photographic reversal process thus revealed the proof of identity here!

I immediately telegraphed this first result to the examining magistrate in Alkmaar, who presented my telegram to the man concerned. After reading it, the man immediately made a full confession. He gave a detailed account of the whole journey with his comrade B. to the cat farmer's farm (this was the name of the murdered man in the area, because he, being a cat lover, kept several of these animals in his house) and how they, having arrived at the side of the house, first took off their shoes, and then crawled behind each other through the narrow window of the barn, he, A. in front, and B. behind him. How B. (and here A. started laughing at his story) had walked too close to the edge of the ditch behind the cows and at a certain moment slipped with his right foot and sunk ankle-deep into the unspecified matter, which fact had caused a softly smothered curse to cross his lips. B., then, leaning against the doorframe with one hand, lifted his wet foot and brushed away the mushy matter from his sock with the other!

This was followed by a detailed account of the cowardly, cruel act towards the old man, who was beaten to death in his sleep. His hardness of hearing had prevented him from sensing any danger. After the murder, his wrists had been tied together and a gag stuffed in his mouth, just for fear that the victim might still "recover." When looking for money, only a small amount was found in the man's wallet. After taking it out, the thief—aware of the dactyloscopic possibilities!—vigorously wiped the outside of the smooth leather wallet with a tip of the tablecloth, to "wipe off the fingerprints!"

After this confession, the court immediately ordered detention, provisionally for the first term of thirty days. A. was interrogated several times and gradually everything came to light, down to the smallest details. Even though it was now established through A.'s confession that B. was a coperpetrator, as long as he did not confess and there was no evidence of his actions, no judgment could ever be passed against him.

And so it happened that the examining magistrate asked me, reporting all that A.'s confession had revealed, whether I thought, on the basis of this, I could still do something regarding the provision of evidence. My first wish was to further investigate B.'s shoes, which, after all, had been put on when he left the farm of the murder ... the right shoe over a stocking tainted with cow manure. The question I asked myself was this: Can any of that cow manure still be found in the right shoe? And so one of the policemen in Alkmaar was ordered to confiscate B.'s footwear in his cell, in exchange for which he was given a pair of "state shoes." B. meekly started to loosen the laces of his ankle boots. Then he suddenly turned to the policeman and said: "Be so good as to put down in your official report the statement I am making to you now. I have repaired these ankle boots myself, to the best of my ability. The other day, when I was walking through the cattle market in Purmerend with them, cow manure was seeping in through a hole. I want to see this statement included in the official report!" Bang! This cunning man foresaw my entire intention and was—so to speak—now one move ahead of me on the chessboard! With the shoes I received the relevant official report, in which I read B.'s nifty remark. Is it any wonder, then, that I immediately started pondering a new "move" on the board?

I left the shoes untouched in the package and gladly assumed a priori that dried cow manure was present in the right shoe. For me, the question remained whether it was possible to recognize the cow manure residue as coming from the cat farmer's barn and distinguish it from cow manure from other barns. I wanted to find out, and I did so with the help of our four-legged assistants—the excellent tracking dogs that were still available at the Amsterdam Police Department at the time, especially the dog Albert, who belonged to dog handler Water and repeatedly performed phenomenally well.

And so I instructed the policeman at Breezand to collect twelve well-cleaned jam jars with screw lids, to number them 1 to 12 and to put cow manure from the late cat farmer's barn in one of them (no matter which one!), making sure that the other eleven jam jars contained cow manure from eleven other nearby farms. An official report on the matter, which contained a list indicating which farm each sample of cow manure came from, was handed to me in a sealed envelope together with the twelve jam jars.

At the then police headquarters on the OZ Achterburgwal in Amsterdam, the courtyard had a very different appearance than later. It was surrounded by pretty shrubs. The small pebbles of the pavement were not yet soaked with lubricating oil, etc., of the motor vehicles, which were later stationed in and near that courtyard and made this place unsuitable for experimenting with tracking dogs. But in 1918, things were still going perfectly well, and so, with the aforementioned jam jars, I went to that courtyard, where the various preparations were being made for the so-called "sorting test" of the various samples of cow manure. Dog handler Water was to come with his two tracking dogs. I had seventy-two sheets of paper with me, namely six series, all individually numbered from 1 to 12. The six papers numbered 1 were all sprinkled with a little cow manure from jam jar 1; from jam jar 2, small amounts of material were smeared over the six papers numbered 2, and so on, after which the courtyard was "laid out" in the most random way with the collection of unsavory papers—behind the shrubs, in the far corners, over the open space—in short, the papers were scattered everywhere. In the back, in a room that was later converted into a garage, was the package containing the shoes, and in an adjacent room, the twelve jam jars were on an old table side by side.

The dog handler arrived with his four-legged friends, who took the greatest interest in the shop window in the courtyard, and I immediately expressed my wish to know whether the dogs' noses could detect such differences between the cow manure samples that they could bring me the papers of each kind without making any mistakes. The handler took a piece of paper at random. On it was the number 3. After the command "search," the dogs sniffed among the dozens of papers and neatly fetched, without once making a mistake, the other papers with the same number, to their master. So it went with three other series, which were reunited in equally impeccable fashion.

Then came the big moment. I had the handler expose the left shoe from the package to the air, requesting to have the papers possibly matching it tracked down. I deliberately chose—without telling anyone!—the left shoe, to test that it was free of something that was found in the other one. The dogs sniffed the left shoe, then looked at their master, as if to show with a look of understanding that they had taken in the scent well and then they went around the courtyard, among all the shrubs, sniffing all the papers. Shortly afterwards they came to their master, who could clearly read in their faithful glances, their despair: "You seem to be wrong, old man, because that smell is not here in the courtyard among all these perfumed documents!"

Then the handler let his helpers smell the right shoe from the package. With a determination that was immediately apparent from their firm attitude, without hesitation, and immediately resolute, the animals fetched all the pieces of paper numbered 7, and more or less overconfident about the spontaneous applause of some bystanders—who had meanwhile heard from me, how it had become clear from the official report that the cow manure number 7 came from the barn of the murdered cat farmer—the dog Albert jumped to the table with jam jars and—without compliments—stuck his snout in jam jar 7 and fetched it to his master, who hurried to give his darlings a treat as a reward. Thus, it was clear that the right shoe contained cow manure from the cat farmer's barn! Both men received their well-deserved punishment from the court!

Epilogue by Charles Berger

Cornelis Smit was seventy-three years old when his lifeless body was found on that Saturday morning, January 26, 1918. He had not been the same since his wife, Maartje, died twelve years before, after thirty-one years of marriage. He did not look after himself, but kept some cats. While the villagers gossiped about his presumed wealth, and nicknamed him "cat farmer," his neighbors, Mr. and Mrs. Vestering, were more friendly. Mrs. Vestering would regularly bring him a meal, and Mr. Vestering was the one that found him that morning. While Co van Ledden Hulsebosch describes his arrival in Breezand as very swift, contemporary newspapers tell a different story. He was scheduled to depart by train from Amsterdam Central Station only on the next day, Sunday morning, at 9:20 am. He was accompanied by Jacob Water and his trusted scent dogs. Train personnel, however, refused to let the dogs into the train, and after a heated discussion they had to quickly find a box or cage to bring the dogs in the cargo part of the train. By the time they managed to arrange that, the train had left, causing another half day of delay in their arrival at the crime scene. Luckily the crime scene was left mostly unchanged, and van Ledden Hulsebosch stresses the importance of that.

He also touches upon a number of other topics, such as the inversion of the contrast of the fingerprint, and the use of an extensive card system by the police headquarters in Amsterdam. This system was undoubtedly based on Bertillon's *portrait parlé*.[10] It was a classification system to create searchable databases with physical descriptions of persons, and to efficiently and reliably communicate such descriptions by telegraph.

Finally, van Ledden Hulsebosch goes into the details of the successful use of scent dogs in this case, to implicate the "cunning man" in the crime. Contemporary newspaper accounts also report on this man, claiming that he was being framed by the confessing suspect, and he put forward two witnesses to support that claim. That did not work out very well though, as both witnesses were fellow prisoners and they told the court that the "cunning man" had offered them money to tell the untrue story. He was sentenced to twelve years in jail, with six years for his codefendant.

---

10   The *portrait parlé* (or "speaking portrait") was a card-based anthropometric system developed by French police officer and biometrics researcher Alphonse Bertillon in the late 19th century that included a photographs, body measurements, and physical descriptions of criminals or suspects.

14. Shoe Wax

"There is someone who wishes to speak to you, sir." The errand boy handed me a card with a name like Jansen or Polak, which gave me little information about the person in question. I had him come in and before me stood a small, unremarkable man who—as he declared—earned his living through trade. And not just any trade, but rather in irregular goods, preferably those that carried a risk. Recently, he had purchased a batch of "good" items, of which neither the seller nor himself knew what it was! Only as a "gamble" "I bought it in bulk for forty cents per kilogram, thinking that there was a chance it might be worth a guilder per kilogram!"

I forgot to mention to the reader that the story I'm about to tell took place in the years 1917–1918, when, due to the blockade, many commodities became increasingly expensive, and some items were almost impossible to obtain (or were being held in warehouses, waiting for even more advantageous times). For example, shellac (i.e., female excretion of the Thai and Indian lac insect) and beeswax had significantly increased in price because very little of it was reaching the market. Shoe cream manufacturers had to pay higher prices for the raw materials they needed (beeswax or earth wax). It's no wonder, then, that traders of irregular goods quickly tried to acquire batches of these materials, hoping to sell them at a decent (often indecent) profit.

The same had happened to him now. He had been able to buy a batch of yellow, waxy substance. He didn't know whether it consisted of beeswax or some type of earth wax. Perhaps it was something entirely different … who knows, a rare and valuable substance, which is why he had bought the batch for forty cents per kilogram. If it turned out to be wax suitable for shoe cream, he could sell it beautifully! But now that he was trying to sell his merchandise, everyone asked what kind of substance it was, so he wanted an investigation, a "certificate." He had already conducted tests himself and attempted to melt the unknown material by holding a handful of it on a coal shovel over the fire in the stove, but he observed no signs of melting! Therefore, he asked if I could determine the identity of that unknown substance and provide him with a certificate. He hoped that with the certificate, he could sell the material at a handsome profit, which seemed less likely without it. He paid a portion of the costs in advance, which I found necessary because the client preferred not to disclose his place of residence! He would come by in a few days to see if his report was ready!

The great world war also made the seas unsafe, as various nations found it necessary to lay mines. Many of these dangerous devices drifted freely at sea, with only a small part protruding above the water's surface. Occasionally, one of these treacherous things would wash up on the shore. Along our coasts, the population soon knew it was highly dangerous to touch these mines when they appeared. If even one contact button was pressed, the most terrible explosion would immediately follow. Certain military authorities, fully aware of the construction of these war devices, sent designated individuals to dismantle the primary ignition mechanisms, thus eliminating the immediate danger. They also dismantled the remaining parts, causing the chemical components belonging to the most dangerous explosive substances to accumulate in piles on the beach. Initially, these substances, which were not particularly dangerous on their own (unless they exploded alongside an explosive material, causing everything to detonate), were constantly guarded until they were transported by the government to the artillery ordnance factory at Hembrug.[11]

However, as supervision became less strict; at night, sinister elements would arrive and steal these unfamiliar substances without knowing what to do with them. One of them, who was aware of their nature, handed over a portion of the explosive substance to a young man with anarchist tendencies, who gratefully made use of it in building bombs. Later on, I found that same substance during an investigation of the bombs found at his house, with the aforementioned explosive substance as the main ingredient.

But I did not expect that this trinitrotoluene (TNT) would find its way to peddlers who mistook it for wax and would experiment with it themselves, holding a coal shovel full of that substance over a burning stove, attentively observing if it would melt ... I had not expected that. Yet, that was indeed the case! As soon as I discovered the dangerously explosive material through my chemical examination, I immediately contacted the chief of the central police. Understandably, he was alarmed by the thought that a potentially large quantity of that substance, with unknown proportions, could be accumulated somewhere in the old city and feared that it would not be easy to obtain it all without attracting attention. I reassured him and asked him to leave it to me in confidence. I couldn't reach my client, so I had to wait for his arrival.

The next day when he visited, he inquired about the progress of the analysis, and I informed him that I hadn't finished yet and that I needed a few more pieces because the amount he had provided me with was insufficient. "Oh, you can get plenty of it—I have a whole batch of that stuff, but I don't let anyone know! I'll bring you more in a few days!" As he left, I tried to send a servant after him to see where my client was going, but the servant returned a little later empty-handed with the message that the gentleman had gone to the Central Station and bought a ticket to The Hague ... Yet, the dangerous batch of goods was not located outside Amsterdam, as would soon become clear.

11   A bridge over the North Sea Canal that was built between 1903 and 1907 and connects the Dutch cities Amsterdam and Zaandam.

The next day, the gentleman returned and handed me a handful of brown, waxy pieces, expressing his hope that within a few days, I would be able to tell him exactly what it was. Upon examining the latest sample, I noticed that it consisted of two different substances, both equally dangerous explosive materials. I saw an opportunity in this fact to obtain the entire batch discreetly.

When my client appeared again two days later, I told him that the second sample had not been the same as the first; that two somewhat related substances were present and that I could hardly tell from this handful of material whether the entire batch should be called this or that, or which was the main substance. I said, if I could take a look at the batch one of these days—if I was by chance in your vicinity—it would be easier for me to decide whether it is A mixed with a little B, or vice versa. (I didn't want show too much eagerness to access the material, so I spoke of being "by chance in your vicinity.")

He took the bait! He eagerly agreed—if I could be so kind!

Now that I knew where the goods were, I quickly took action. He wouldn't be surprised if I happened to be in the vicinity of his warehouse by chance. In the meantime, I had requested a few men with a car from the workshops at Hembrug, who would take care of the TNT. They were waiting five minutes away from the building for further instructions when I headed to my client's given address. Two detectives in civilian clothing were discreetly positioned outside the door, ready to carry out my orders promptly.

Upon entering his small office on Nieuwe Heerengracht, he expressed how "pleasant" it was that I could provide him with answers so quickly because the batch was nearly sold again! It had once again changed hands to someone who was equally unaware of the nature of what he carelessly acquired—such peculiar "business" indeed! His warehouse was nearby, so we decided to go there right away. Naturally, I thought that was excellent and followed him to the ground floor of a building, which later became a garage. Inside were rolls of coconut mats and various other items. In the background, four large barrels were visible, standing upright and completely filled—one could say "topped up"—with the brownish-yellow dangerous substance. As we entered the room, my client calmly let a burning cigar dangle on his lip while talking. He even leaned slightly forward towards the nearest barrel, saying, "Here's the stuff."

Now the reader might have wondered why I chose such a cautious and elaborate manner to achieve my goal. Let me explain. Since the establishment of my laboratory in 1883 by my father, my business had enjoyed unlimited trust. It was never our practice to write advertising-like, bombastic endorsement reports about products that couldn't stand up to scrutiny, either because they belonged to the realm of quack medicines or for other reasons that could be looked down upon. The aforementioned trader also came to me because he had confidence in my laboratory. What would that man say if the next day I had sent the police to his doorstep "because he had dangerous substances in his possession," even though he himself was fully unaware? No, that's why I preferred to obtain those goods by using a soft touch and then save him from an accident as a "guardian angel." In doing so, I would achieve my ultimate goal just as surely and effectively, without losing the trust in my business and in myself from my client.

"Here's the stuff." Those were his words. We stood amidst the barrels of highly explosive materials, while my little client, still talking, let the stub of his cigar wobble on his lower lip. With unruffled calmness, I made a gesture towards his mouth, took the cigarette from it, and threw it forcefully into the street. I will never forget the other man's face, which was initially dumbfounded, then briefly smiled, but suddenly showed signs of annoyance. I immediately provided the necessary explanation for this brutish behavior and somewhat theatrically exclaimed, "For God's sake, sir, don't smoke next to this highly dangerous explosive! If an explosion occurs, this entire block of houses, along with everyone inside and nearby, will be obliterated! To eliminate all danger, I had to remove the burning cigar from your mouth!"

The man paled for a moment, then regained his composure and suddenly sprang into action. He hurried upstairs to the names of the people listed there and shouted, "Come down immediately, it's too dangerous upstairs!" Turning to me, he asked, "How can I get rid of this vile, dangerous stuff? Should we throw it into the canal together?" I strongly discouraged him from taking this measure, pointing out the great danger it could pose in the future for a dredging machine once they began dredging the shipping channel. "No, sir," I said, "don't worry about that. I have already taken measures to rid you of this dangerous substance, and competent assistance will arrive in a few moments to remove the four barrels from your premises."

The man, who, had I handled the situation differently, might have been angry about the removal of his merchandise, and who undoubtedly would have trumpeted that "secrets are not safe with me," now had no idea how to express his gratitude for the sensible actions that had averted imminent danger from him, his family, and the entire neighborhood. I beckoned to the waiting detectives outside, giving them instructions to guard the barrels until an automobile with personnel from the artillery ordnance factory arrived for transportation. They received detailed instructions on where they needed to be, and the explosive material was skillfully transported to the artillery workshops, where an examination quickly revealed that the trinitrotoluene (TNT) was of impeccable composition. It was therefore decided to reimburse the last owner for the cost. Thus, he also emerged from the situation "unscathed." All parties involved were satisfied with the outcome—a result that is not always the case.

Epilogue by Arian van Asten

TNT, short for 2,4,6-trinitrotoluene, is a high explosive (meaning that it can detonate, providing a shock wave explosion without the need for a container) that still today frequently occurs in forensic case work. In the period from 2014 to 2018, the forensic explosives experts of the Netherlands Forensic Institute (NFI) reported the presence of TNT in roughly 20% of the intact materials (pre-explosion cases) analyzed![12] Interestingly, in this story Co van Ledden Hulsebosch does not provide any details of the chemical analysis, probably because his memoirs were intended for a broad audience (in its time the book was very popular in the Netherlands and went through five editions).

Nowadays, forensic laboratories use advanced techniques like GC-MS and LC-MS (gas chromatography or liquid chromatography followed by mass spectrometry) to chemically identify TNT. In 2014 my team published a paper where we introduce a GC-MS-based method for the rapid chemical profiling of intact TNT. Based on a sensitive impurity analysis we were able to provide a chemical fingerprint that allows forensic experts to investigate whether batches of TNT could share a common origin, an individualization approach inspired by illicit drug profiling but much less common in forensic explosive analysis.

This story reads like page-turner with the Dutch Sherlock Holmes himself preventing a disaster by swiftly throwing away the burning cigar of the trader. However, it is fair to say that TNT has been so successful as a military explosive because of its stability! It does not easily detonate upon friction and heating. A primary explosive in the form of a blast cap (detonator) is required to initiate the detonation of a TNT main charge. So, if the trader had accidentally dropped his burning cigar in one of the barrels most likely nothing dramatic would have happened. Nonetheless, material in a bad state with extensive TNT degradation could behave in a more reactive and unpredictable manner as the degradation of organic nitro explosives involves the formation of nitric acid or nitric oxides. In any case, TNT and its reaction products create serious health risks. They are quite toxic and potentially carcinogenic chemicals.

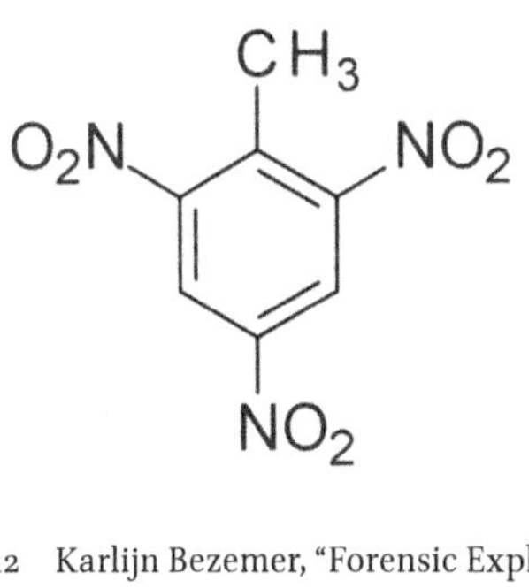

Figure 2. The chemical structure of TNT, 2,4,6-trinitrotoluene, produced by reacting toluene with nitric acid.

12 Karlijn Bezemer, "Forensic Explosives Intelligence," PhD thesis, University of Amsterdam, 2020.

15. Amateur Snapshots as Evidence

Several years ago, the crime magazines presented us with an interesting case of deduction, in which a simple photograph played a prominent role.

In Texas, one day near a girls' boarding school, a peculiar package was deposited, which upon opening revealed an infernal device containing dangerous explosive materials. With timely assistance from a military expert, the device was defused and the dangerous contraption was rendered harmless. A few days later, the police apprehended a suspect, a vagrant deemed capable of committing this despicable attack, but who staunchly denied any guilt. However, this availed him little; he was held in custody, and the authorities felt fully justified since a succession of five boarding schoolgirls came forward one after the other to testify that they had seen the suspect near the boarding school a quarter of an hour before the bomb was discovered. It should be noted that the time the bomb was first sighted was around ten o'clock in the morning; however, the detainee swore that he had not been in the vicinity of the boarding school in the morning, but only later in the afternoon ... which, of course, nobody believed, especially since the five girls all gave consistent statements about encountering the suspect in the morning. Each one claimed to remember the incident even more vividly and definitively than the others! For the individual who adamantly maintained his innocence, the situation became increasingly critical by the day, as such a crime naturally carried a severe penalty! The attorney representing the defendant initially saw little hope of keeping his client out of jail but pondered ways to challenge the reliability of the five girls' testimonies. However, he would only have the opportunity to do so in court during the proceedings.

The day of the trial arrived, and after a prolonged and rigorous interrogation of the defendant, during which he continuously asserted his innocence and strongly claimed that he had only arrived at the scene in the afternoon of the fateful day, the moment approached for the boarding schoolgirls to be questioned. They each reiterated their statements, as previously detailed before the investigating judge.

After this interrogation, the presiding judge asked the defense if they had any questions for the girls. The attorney replied that he wished to question each girl individually. He then pressed them to explain precisely how each of them inferred that it was in the morning and why the defendant couldn't have been there in the afternoon, as he claimed. At this point, doubt arose in a few of the girls' minds; some knew precisely because their friends had also observed it precisely. And the others? They could recall with such precision because there had been a joke about seeing the vagrant while they were standing on the high steps in front of the school entrance, peering over the slanting railing, while a couple of students hurried to take a picture of the group. "And did that picture turn out well?" inquired the lawyer. "Yes, indeed! It's in an album at home; I could go get it and show you!" came the response. The defense requested a few hours' recess in the trial so that they could first examine the said photo.

An hour later, the girl brought the photo. It showed five mischievously smiling girls, standing one next to the other on the different steps, looking sideways over the railing at the photographer. Thus, while this picture was taken, they had seen the man with a package under his arm … which, according to the suspect, contained fabrics—his "merchandise"—a claim that nobody believed. On the right side of the photo, one could see the side wall of the school, against which horizontal planks were nailed, overlapping each other like roof tiles. The defense attorney noticed a shadow on the sixth plank from the bottom, which, based on his knowledge of the school's layout, must have been cast by the gutter point of a side wing of the nearby church building. A glimmer of hope for his client flashed through his mind. Surely, that shadow could testify to the truth about when it fell exactly there. He eloquently presented his view to the judges, explaining how the sun follows a different path each day and, over the course of May (the incident had taken place on May 22), gradually describes a larger, higher arc in the sky until reaching its highest point on the longest day of the year—noon!—and then descending again to the horizon. Undoubtedly, a shadow in this case had to shed light on the matter!

A professor of astronomy was called in to assist. He determined the precise location of the boarding school and the position and height of the relevant gutter point concerning the plane on which the shadow had fallen during the photo shoot. Based on the position of the plank, it was quite easy to pinpoint on the wall itself where the end of the shadow had fallen at that time. The professor reported that, after a thorough examination, he had determined that the photo must have been taken on May 22, at 2:24½ pm! Requiring verification, the court ordered the defendant to be temporarily released and decided to wait until May 22 came around again. If only the sun would shine brightly on that day! And it did. On the grounds next to the boarding school, the professor and several assistants gathered, and—after taking a photo one minute before the critical moment (where the shadow still fell slightly too low)—the snapshot, the "control photo," was taken at the specified time, while another photo was taken a minute later, showing a shift in the shadow by the same distance observed between the two previous shots. Thus, the amateur photograph, elucidated by the professor of astronomy, brought forth the truth and secured the release of the innocent detainee!

Another case in which a photo served as a telling "silent witness" is equally remarkable, although I dare not guarantee its veracity. Let's just say, "se non è vero."¹³ In Vienna, around mid-June, a serious crime was committed, and the police had to search for a long time before they got a lead. This led to an Italian, who had meanwhile disappeared abroad. He was a sportsman who frequented circles of athletes, javelin throwers, and discus throwers. He had been missing for a long time without anyone knowing where he was or that the police were looking for him. The following March, about nine months later, he ventured back into Austria and even showed up in Vienna, where he was soon recognized and arrested.

When questioned about what had happened in June, he adamantly claimed to have been out of Vienna for a full year, having left the city before March of the previous year and not set foot in Austria during the past year. Then it happened. They showed him an amateur photo of him in full, holding a javelin. Based on the javelin and the surroundings, it was determined that this picture must have been taken in the Sports Palace in Vienna within the last year and a half, as there was an addition depicted in it that hadn't been there for longer. They went further and provided evidence that the photo must have been taken around mid-June since considering Vienna's geographical location, only on one of the days near June 21—and only around noon—could a vertically standing spear cast a shadow that is only 45% of the length of the object itself. Thus, it was conclusively established that this man must have been photographed in the mentioned location in the middle of one of the days near the longest day of the year!

Epilogue by Maarten Blom: Chronolocation and Open-Source Intelligence

This chapter stands out for several reasons. Most of the stories in this book show Co van Ledden Hulsebosch at the center of a stunning investigation, a detective in full swing. Why would the author wander away from this successful concept? I do not think he was short of an interesting anecdote. Van Ledden Hulsebosch simply does not appear to me as someone whose inspiration would ever be exhausted. I prefer to look upon this chapter as a reflection of his deep and genuine interest in novel forensic inferences. My conclusion is that van Ledden Hulsebosch felt the urgency to explore and share the concept of chronolocation, even if it meant he could not incorporate his personal experience.

In today's world, we can understand this urgency all too well. Open-source intelligence has become an indispensable tool to investigate publicly available

---

13 Van Ledden Hulsebosch quotes the first part of the famous aphorism by Italian philosopher and astronomer Giordano Bruno (1548–1600): "Se non è vero, è molto ben trovato" ("Even if it is not true, it is a very good fabrication").

evidence. It thrives on the availability of internet resources and tools, and the power of joint investigation through social media. It is embraced by open-source investigative platforms such as Bellingcat, for investigative journalism and official investigation teams alike. In short, it has made it possible for almost anyone to get involved in contributing towards justice and accountability efforts, worldwide.

Just as the scale of the resources have expanded enormously since the time of van Ledden Hulsebosch, so has the impact of chronolocation. Let's turn to a very telling and tragic example. On July 17, 2014, Malaysia Airlines Flight 17 (MH17) was shot down while flying over eastern Ukraine, resulting in the deaths of all 298 passengers and crew on board. On October 19, 2017, the Joint Investigation Team (JIT), the Dutch-led criminal investigation into the downing, published a photograph of Buk 332, the Russian Buk missile launcher that downed MH17. Where and when was it taken? In whose territory was the vehicle at the time of the photograph? On its website, Bellingcat had urged its collaborators to aid in the chronolocation. Many researchers contributed to the analysis and reconstruction, using Google Street View and Yandex images as well as images supplied by local witnesses. On October 20th, the conclusion of this joint effort was published: Buk 332, originating from Russia's 53rd Anti-Aircraft Missile Brigade, arrived in Donetsk from Makiivka around 9am on July 17, 2014, parked at the intersection of Prospekt Ilycha and Shakhtostroiteley, and then eventually turned towards the east-bound Prospekt Ilycha towards the Motel roundabout in Donetsk.[14] It may seem a big leap from a girl's school to this tragic event, but in my opinion, it only underscores the visionary quality of van Ledden Hulsebosch's fascination.

---

14 "New MH17 Photograph Geolocated to Donetsk," *Bellingcat*, October 20, 2017, https://www.bellingcat.com/news/uk-and-europe/2017/10/20/new-mh17-photograph-geolocated-donetsk/.

16. "Visiting Cards"!

Reader—in case you are prudish or, rather than being inclined to find something "shocking" like someone else, know that I want to warn you here not to continue with this sketch, skip it quietly and take the next one—it is much "neater." But there will be many readers who don't find it so bad and also want to be informed about activities from the criminalistic laboratory, which usually remain "behind the scenes" and about which the newspapers—fortunately!—generally remain silent. There, now I have done my duty and given prudish people the opportunity to skip to the next chapter, I can safely continue and want to talk about the "silent witnesses" that burglars occasionally leave behind on their "operating field," and why they are euphemistically called "visiting cards." I have often been asked why burglars often leave such unsavory "dirty" souvenirs for the police. The answer is quickly given. Everyone knows how much the digestive organs are subject to psychological influences and react to them. If something fills us with disgust, it may be that the stomach prepares for a return shipment. If sudden fear seizes us, another part of our digestive tract immediately reacts; many people notice that when they have to visit the dentist or take an exam. Isn't it entirely understandable that burglars also have similar experiences? As soon as he thinks he hears something in his secret work that can disturb him, the "interior" of the burglar immediately shows a greatly increased mobility, with certain consequences attached, right? However, the nervous burglar does not risk moving at that moment, opening extra doors in the house (there might be a police officer behind them!) and thus does not go to the place specifically designated for depositing these calling cards; where he is at that moment, he believes he should leave the surprise there and … (as people say, according to an old superstition of Jewish origin), he attaches special significance to choosing the place to place that visiting card so that the higher temperature of the said "trace" is preserved as long as possible. This is because, as long as the higher temperature is maintained, the police will not succeed in finding evidence of the perpetrator! Isn't it understandable, then, that special hiding places, which provide sufficient guarantees for preserving the temperature of the entrusted contents, are always sought? I found many visiting cards hidden under the soft cushions on a couch, also once in a made bed, in a living room, under a spread-out tiger skin on the floor, and some times covered with stacks of newspapers.

At the editorial office of a small local newspaper—long gone now—everything was in chaos on a certain Monday morning. Burglars had come in the night and the first employees who arrived had immediately alerted the police. They had started their investigation quickly and then the editor-in-chief appeared, who saw with horror the mess his private office was in. As was his habit, he quickly kicked off his rubber boots and put both stockinged feet into a fine fur footrest.... Well, he should have refrained from doing that, because that footrest was being used as a case for "visiting cards," which caused new consternation when the unlucky man later found himself helplessly sitting in his chair with his legs up, ranting and raving about those "vile" guys!

It was my father who first proposed the idea of undertaking a—up till then unknown—study to document the exact changes that our food and beverages undergo during their passage through the entire digestive tract. It was in the last years of the previous century when he undertook this colossal task, sometimes having to restrict his entire diet to just one single item—quite monotonous, I must say!—in order to ensure that whatever he found in his research the next day belonged to the remnants of that particular item. He had to create a modus operandi for this himself and the work was done with the most primitive tools and a microscope, which helped discover the characteristics of each food residue after they had been cleaned through prolonged rinsing and washing.

Based on the results of his studies, microphotographs were made of 360 of the most important microscopic preparations, of which I took care of a large portion, and another part was handled by the photographer Laddé,[15] as my studies at the university did not allow me to spend too much time on making microphotographs. All these photos served as illustrations in the standard work *Makro- und mikroskopische Diagnostik der menschlichen Exkremente* (Macro- and microscopic diagnosis of human excreta) (published by Julius Springer, Berlin, in 1899) that my unforgettable father wrote about these studies and which has not yet found its equal. It is still recognized everywhere as "the" book on this subject in the examination of visiting cards.

During his studies, he had the opportunity to apply the knowledge acquired to cases where the police brought "visiting cards" with the question of what could be said about the depositor. It should be noted here that the examination of these silent witnesses not only revealed the secrets of the menus consumed in the last few days (in some cases even from several days back, when the person leaving the visiting card had a slow digestion!), but could also reveal pathological abnormalities, such as blood cells, eggs of intestinal parasites, or the intact or fragmented remains of the latter "commensals" themselves, during the course of the investigation.

One of the early success stories involved a burglary where the perpetrators gained access to the targeted property through the gutters and an attic hatch of a neighboring vacant house. It was the warehouse of a textile manufacturer. There were crates in the attics containing old "sample cards" with attached fabric swatches. Near the broken attic hatch, the police discovered a visiting card in the gutter. It

---

15   M. H. (Machiel Hendricus) Laddé (1866–1932) was a Dutch photographer and film director.

had been somewhat "watered down" by rain, and the sergeant who found it noticed a reddish color, which spontaneously led him to the conclusion that "the guy must have eaten red cabbage!" This statement was overheard by a curious maid who was peeking through a neighboring attic hatch at all the commotion. Knowing that the newspaper paid a *kwartje* (a quarter of a guilder) for any original news, she quickly ran to the editorial office of one of the major newspapers in the area, where she recounted the preliminary results of the police investigation "in colors and smells." The evening edition then reported how astute the police were in determining at first glance that the suspect had eaten red cabbage the day before.

My father read the news and had a hearty laugh. He knew all too well that the fibrous content of red cabbage, which are excreted undigested through the digestive tract, come out colorless—that is, white—after the usual washing process (at least!) in that the red plant dye is completely digested by the body. In this respect, the remnants of red and white cabbage look the same to the naked eye; only through microscopic examination can the characteristic differences be observed.

Shortly after reading the news in the newspaper, the police brought the surprise—neatly packaged in a jam jar!—to the laboratory. There was indeed something red to see; this revealed itself during the cleaning process as a piece of red flannel, which the great X—for lack of paper material—had used as a "napkin"! The food remnants turned out to be from potatoes and onions—a simple meal!—followed, apparently, by a piece of coconut for dessert.

The next day, the police had suspicions about a certain old customer, who—for various reasons that had come to light—was put under provisional arrest. Of course, the gentleman denied all guilt. Having learned the results of my father's investigation, the detectives thought it would be significant to find out what had been consumed at the suspect's home during the previous days, and they had a chat with the suspect's wife. She had also read in the newspaper about the police investigation and the conclusion: "red cabbage." So when the detectives casually asked what had been on the table over the past few days, the woman triumphantly said, "Oh, you thought we had eaten red cabbage, right? No, you're wrong! We had potatoes with onions and a piece of coconut for dessert. Our neighbor Pieterse can testify to that, because she had lunch with us that day!" What a picture! One can imagine the value of the neighbor's testimony as evidence!

After I succeeded my father in the laboratory in 1902, I conducted police and judicial investigations. Whereas my father, who had no sense of smell, could always perform these types of expertise without any hesitation, his successor occasionally felt some disgust during these investigations—how could it be otherwise? And after thoroughly working out the problem in theory, I constructed an apparatus in which a system of coarser and finer sieves arranged one above the other automatically performed all the less palatable work of preparing, washing, and rinsing the material for examination, connected to the water supply, and sorted the thoroughly cleaned material, ready for examination with a magnifying glass and microscope, onto the bottoms of the various sieves.

When I took a course at the Institut de Police scientifique at the University of Lausanne with Professor Reiss in 1913 and spoke to him about my apparatus, he immediately asked me to have one made for him as well, and he baptized the instrument as the "Coprolysator (or Coprolyseur)," of which the first part, derived from the Greek word "*kopros*," or manure, clearly expresses the purpose. He also invited me to take over his lecture hour the next day to tell his students about the examination of these visiting cards in criminal cases, which I gladly did.

At the beginning of the war in 1914, when there were quite a few German deserters crossing our border, among them were several shady characters. Two of these people committed a burglary in a café, behind which was a bowling alley, wherein there was also a small hanging cabinet, in which behind a glass pane hung a silver laurel wreath and various medals and trophies from bowling competitions. The morning after the break-in, when the café owner had reported the theft and the damaged cabinet—of course, without the medals!—was found on a grass field behind the Central Station, along with a "visiting card," a message came from the police station at Singel that there were two detainees there who had been walking along the Spuistraat in the middle of the night, hiding something under their raincoats, and had lost silver laurel leaves along their path without noticing it! A night watchman who had noticed them had alerted a police officer who had arranged for their arrest.

I received the "visiting card" with an attachment (a part of a letter used as a "napkin") for investigation and reported to the inspector of the judicial service at the Singel police station in the course of the afternoon how peculiar I found this object of investigation. It consisted exclusively of remnants of bread and liver sausage. There were no remnants of vegetables, meat, fruit, or anything else! I expressed my serious suspicion that the person who had left it behind had been on a strict "diet" of bread and liver sausage for several days. The inspector briefly repeated the result given to him and suddenly I heard through the phone hearty laughter erupt in his office. Asking for the cause of that joy, he told me that one of the detainees, a certain Emil K., had just been subjected to a lengthy interrogation an hour earlier. He had denied all guilt, claiming that he had bought the medals found on him from a stranger to use them for "bargaining," etc., etc. But at the end of his statement, to arouse sympathy, he had said: "Have pity. I am miserable. I have only eaten bread and liverwurst for fourteen days!" That matched perfectly. And to top it all off, I could also explain that the "napkin" was part of a letter sent from Elberfeld, starting with "Dear Emil!"

Next is a case that took place in the province of Drente, where, on a certain morning, it was discovered that there had been a break-in at two adjoining dairies.

The modus operandi of these break-ins was the same, so it must have been members of the same gang—there was no doubt about it. What made the case even more remarkable was that in both dairies a "visiting card" had been left behind. They were expertly packaged and sent to my laboratory by the brigade commander of the National Police. In the evening of the same day, I received two jam jars "with contents"—as the accompanying labels indicated—for the purpose of my preliminary investigation.

That the entire life of a detective is a great learning experience was once again evident in this examination. When I compared the various food residues and found significant similarities in the combinations of food and luxury items used (including a raisin bun and peanuts), my initial thought was that the gang members who committed these break-ins must have been staying in the same boarding house, where they would have enjoyed the same menu at the same table, naturally. But when I discovered the presence of eggs from two different exotic intestinal parasites in both visiting cards, I became convinced that both visiting cards—let me continue with the same metaphor—came from the same "printing press"! After I had determined the eggs of the unfamiliar parasites in front of me, I had my findings verified by my former mentor, Professor Sluyter, who, with his renowned willingness, confirmed my results. They were eggs of intestinal parasites mainly found in people who have been in the tropics.

A telegram to Assen was quickly sent to inform the examining magistrate for criminal cases there of this result: both visiting cards were from the same person, who, it could be assumed with a fair degree of certainty, had been in the tropics. Hardly had the brigade commander in Assen read my telegram, when he expressed his suspicion that it could only be P., a former colonial, who was the cause of the problem in the area. That former visitor to the Dutch East Indies was taken from his home. He was silent in all dialects with the police and was remarkably brief in his answers to the questions posed to him. So he stayed as their guest for a few days ... the reader will understand why.

After a few days, the brigade commander sent another jar to my address—the "control sample"—with a request to check if it contained eggs of the same tropical intestinal parasites. That turned out to be the case, and a telegram soon reported the result to my client. The suspect had to appear in the office of the examining magistrate, where my telegram—without further comment—was presented to him alongside the initial wire message. The man silently took note of it all, shook his head meaningfully, made a pitying face, and said the words: "So I have betrayed myself with that...." A full confession followed shortly thereafter, and the case was quickly solved!

Finally, the last act of a drama that unfolded in the old city involves an old woman who was robbed and murdered by her grandson. A friend of the grandson received some ten-guilder banknotes from the stolen money. That friend was picked up the next day and brought to the police station. During the transfer, one of the two detectives noticed that their detainee—while using his handkerchief—put something into his mouth and swallowed it. The unusual efforts he made to swallow it raised the suspicion that something odd was going on. No paper money was found on the friend during the search, and in connection with what had been noticed during the transfer to the police station, it was decided to calmly "wait and see how things unfold." The new inmate had been given a clean bucket in his cell. The next day, it was found to contain what was needed. I investigated it and retrieved three torn ten-guilder banknotes from it that could still be pieced together. After cleaning and drying them, they were sent in between glass plates as "evidence."

As I later learned, the Netherlands Bank immediately provided new banknotes to the family members of the victim in exchange for those fragments, on which all three serial numbers had been reconstructed. Another time, I was tasked with examining a similar bucket to determine whether the depositor had consumed a batch of loose gemstones during a jewelry store robbery the day before. That was a disappointment … there was no gold, silver, or precious stones in it.

Epilogue by Maurice Aalders

As Co van Ledden Hulsebosch detailed in his writings, the innovative study of human feces as forensic evidence was first pioneered by his father (M. L. Q. van Ledden Hulsebosch) at the close of the nineteenth century. His father's meticulous and often monotonous experiments, which involved adhering to diets of a single food item to document the changes in appearance after "their passage through the entire digestive tract," laid the groundwork for the modern forensic application of biological materials. These early investigations culminated in the (for forensic science) ground-breaking publication *Makro- und mikroskopische Diagnostik der menschlichen Exkremente* (Macro- and microscopic diagnosis of human excreta, 1899). Illustrated with detailed microphotographs made by both Co and the photographer Laddé, this work established a foundational methodology for what was then a completely novel forensic technique. This study is still actual and follow-up studies can be found in in recent literature. (see, for example, D. O. Norris and J. H. Bock, "Method for Examination of Fecal Material from a Crime Scene Using Plant Fragments," *Journal of Forensic Identification* 51(4) (2001), 367–377).

Moving into the present, the field (human biological traces) has evolved dramatically, constantly increasing the forensic value of this type of evidence. Today, forensic investigations of human biological material has integrated sophisticated DNA analysis, enabling precise identification of individuals from trace amounts

Figure 3. Leg of a shrimp under 16x magnification. Illustration from M. L. Q. van Ledden Hulsebosch (the father of Co van Ledden Hulsebosch), "Het microscopisch onderzoek van excrementen," Nederlands Tijdschrift voor Geneeskunde *41 (1897), 451–459.*

of the material. Advancements in genomic sequencing now allow forensic experts to extract and analyze DNA from fecal matter left at crime scenes, which can be crucial in linking suspects to criminal activities. In addition to DNA analysis, metabolic profiling has become a key tool. This technique examines the by-products of digestion and can provide insights into a person's lifestyle, diet, and medications, offering another layer of evidence that can support criminal investigations. As we continue to develop and refine forensic technologies, the influence of these early endeavors remains evident, proving that even the most unlikely sources, such as feces, can provide profound insights into forensic and criminal investigations.

17. One Hair Made the Difference

This tale unfolds in the roaring 1920s. Having just concluded a training program for a select group of officers from the National Police focused on improving their skills in the detection and analysis of subtle clues, one of my former pupils swiftly found himself in a position to put his freshly acquired knowledge into practical use.

A message arrived one morning, alerting him to a break-in at the local rectory the previous night. This incident, a rather straightforward one in terms of burglary, unfolded without the use of sophisticated tools such as lock picks, drills, saws, or crowbars. Instead, a rudimentary pocketknife proved sufficient to breach the property. At the back of the premises, a stained glass window had been dismantled with utmost simplicity. The pliable lead strips that held the glass pieces together were meticulously cut away using a small knife, resulting in the window's elements being detached one by one, scattered beneath its frame.

Rural policeman P., leading the investigation, quickly noticed how the weathered and elderly local policeman, deemed to be too old and too near retirement by the mayor to attend my detective training course, observed the actions of his younger colleague with a touch of envy. The old man couldn't resist making quasi-funny, almost sarcastic remarks from time to time. This reminded me of a similar experience I had faced earlier in my career. Back then, as one of the pioneers searching for fingerprints at a crime scene, an old police commissioner—unimpressed with the innovations—stood there, smiling at my work, shaking his head as if he pitied my efforts, and then saying, "What a silly business with all this fuss about finding fingerprints. Just bring me the culprit immediately!" Yes, dear Reader, it took a considerable amount of time before the high value of "scientific detective work" gained universal recognition and appreciation. But "perseverance" was the motto. It was pioneering work!

This policeman was wise enough not to be bothered in the least by the sarcastic comments about his modern sleuthing. He calmly continued his work. In the end, it prompted the old man to think a bit, and he asked the younger one what he was actually looking for, while kneeling beside those pieces of glass under the rectory window. "I'm not looking for something specific," was the brief reply. "I'm searching for any particular object that the perpetrator might have left behind."

Suddenly, the investigator had something between his fingers and thumb and examined it closely with the magnifying glass he had taken from his back pocket. "What is this?" he asked with interest. "A hair," came the response from the other side. Then the old policeman couldn't help but laugh and made a funny comment about a whole wig lying two meters away. "I'm not interested in that—but I am interested in this hair because the perpetrator left this one behind." Naturally, the old man was very curious, wondering how his younger colleague could deduce that the found hair, unlike all the others, must be from the perpetrator. The young policeman was proud to teach the old one a lesson: "Look! This hair was on top of a glass fragment from the window, while a strip of the heavy lead was on top of it. So, it landed on the piece of glass when that was already there and was shortly thereafter secured by the strip of lead that had come on top of it!" The old man stood speechless with admiration. Your observation skills are quite impressive!

Initially, P. didn't know what to do with the found hair. After some contemplation, he recalled that I—at the end of the police course he attended—had expressed my readiness to always provide my former students with small pieces of advice for their investigative work. Consequently, he neatly wrapped the hair, following instructions, in a piece of paper and quickly cycled to Amsterdam. An hour later, he presented me with the question of whether this small clue—a single hair—could reveal anything special; after all, it was from the perpetrator! Naturally, I found the case intriguing and promptly took a seat at my microscope table to scrutinize what this "trace" could unveil. Was it truly a hair? A human hair? Or perhaps a botanical element, a plant hair, or fiber? No! The observation proved accurate—it turned out to be a human hair.

I swiftly provided the following analysis: It is a hair from a wild, fiery-red mustache, belonging to a dirty man who hadn't visited the barber in a long time! Examined at a strong magnification, the hair appeared superficially lightly scaled and revealed a medulla. Utilizing the ocular micrometer, I could measure the thickness of the hair cortex and the width of the medulla in thousandths of a millimeter. This indicated that it must be a hair from a mustache or beard. Numerous scales of a peculiar appearance were visible on the outside of the hair, which I identified as dried nasal mucus. Likely due to a lack of a handkerchief, it had been rubbed between those hairs. This convinced me that it was a mustache hair and not a beard hair, while the presence of these dried masses more than justified the conclusion that we were dealing with a mustache hair from a "dirty" man. The hair did not have the softly curved shape found in a usual mustache. Instead, it had grown in numerous twists, suggesting a mustache that could be called "wild, unruly, tangled," and the color of the hair also indicated that of the mustache. Instead of a sharp-cut end (the natural, original point is only present in baby faces that have never had their mustache trimmed), I found a frayed top section, split far from the tip. Such a thing could not be seen by a barber without taking his scissors to briefly "point" the split hair. And that's how my diagnosis was constructed.

Armed with this newfound knowledge, my former student swiftly cycled back to his post to inquire left and right if anyone had seen "a dirty man with a wild fiery-red mustache" in the village the evening or the night before. After unsuccessfully asking several residents, he finally learned that a stranger, closely fitting the description, had drunk a glass of beer the previous evening in a local café. But who the strange visitor was, the café owner couldn't say. Suddenly, the daughter of the café owner, who had been eavesdropping on the conversation between her father and the policeman, stepped forward and revealed that she had seen that stranger with his wild red mustache talking to the mayor's gardener just before his visit to the café. P. immediately went to the gardener and asked who the red-mustached man was with whom he had been talking on the bridge the previous evening. And—as if he felt some shame because he had been seen in that peculiar company—he said, "Yes, but he wasn't a friend or a good acquaintance of mine! Fortunately not! He was a guy I shared a room with during my military service. I didn't like him back then, and he must have fallen on hard times. His name is so-and-so and he lives in a side street off the canal in Amsterdam, at the corner of a cross street, above a grocery store run by someone named A."

You surely understand how swiftly our state policeman jumped back on his bike to report to the commissioner of the relevant section in Amsterdam and request assistance. He got it and, along with a detective from that bureau, he went to the provided address. They climbed the narrow stairs to the third floor, where the door was closed. They heard soft coughing from inside—someone was home. Well, that "someone" clearly understood that there were policemen at his door when he was commanded to open the door immediately or else force would be used. The door opened ... and they found him in the middle of examining his loot from the previous night! That single hair had revealed it all!

Epilogue by Ate Kloosterman: The Flawed Science of Hair Analysis

In the annals of forensic science, the technique of hair analysis once stood as a pillar of evidence, believed to hold the power of identifying criminals with near certainty. However, as the landscape of forensic technology evolved, the credibility of hair analysis came under intense scrutiny, revealing its inadequacies and the grave consequences it bore on numerous lives and putting innocent individuals behind bars. The story of Gerald Delane Murray serves as an exemplary illustration. Sentenced to death row in Florida for a murder he denied committing, the crucial piece of evidence tying Murray to the crime scene was a single strand of pubic hair, deemed "consistent" with his own by an FBI analyst. Yet, as Murray and a legion of scientists and legal experts asserted, such testimony lacked scientific basis. Unlike DNA, hair lacks the unique markers necessary for individual identification.

The unraveling of hair analysis as a credible forensic tool began in the late 1990s, coinciding with the rise of DNA analysis. In 2015, the FBI reported that FBI testimonies on microscopic hair analysis contained errors in at least 90 percent of cases in ongoing review. The government identified nearly 3,000 cases in which FBI examiners may have submitted reports or testified in trials using microscopic hair analysis. The majority of these cases were trials and the transcript of examiner testimony was reviewed. In the 268 cases where examiners provided testimony used to incriminate a defendant at trial, erroneous statements were made in 257

(96 percent) of the cases. All but two of 28 FBI examiners provided testimonies that contained erroneous statements or authored lab reports with such statements.

Peter Neufeld, cofounder of the Innocence Project, directed efforts to uncover the extent of the damage wrought by flawed hair analysis. The FBI's admission of error in nearly every case reviewed underscored the magnitude of the crisis, shedding light on a systemic failure of justice. Sleuth Co van Ledden Hulsebosch and the criminal justice system, however, can find solace in the fact that the forensic analysis of a single strand of hair led to the crucial breakthrough in this case: the recovery of the stolen loot from the burglary, linking the suspect to the crime.

Fortunately, the availability of DNA analysis has minimized the reliance on morphological hair examination. In a very high proportion of cases involving human hair evidence, DNA can be extracted, even years after the crime has been committed. Although the DNA extraction may consist of only mitochondrial DNA (mtDNA), such analyses are likely to be much more specific than those conducted on the morphological features of hair. Because of the inherent limitations of morphological hair comparisons and the availability of higher-quality and higher-accuracy analyses based on DNA, traditional hair examinations may be presented far less often as evidence in the future. It should be noted that microscopic comparison of physical features will continue to be useful for determining which hairs are sufficiently similar to merit comparisons with DNA analysis and for excluding suspects and assisting in criminal investigations.

As DNA analysis emerges as the gold standard of forensic evidence, offering unprecedented accuracy and reliability, the era of flawed hair analysis fades into history. Yet, amidst this evolution, the lessons learned underscore the imperative of rigorous scrutiny and continual advancement in forensic science to ensure justice for all.

References

Cole, S. A., et al. *Microscopic Hair Comparison Analysis and Convicting the Innocent*. National Registry of Exonerations, December, 2023. https://www.law.umich.edu/special/exoneration/Documents/NREReportMHCA.pdf.

Ebersole, R. "How the Junk Science of Hair Analysis Keeps People Behind Bars." *Mother Jones*, December 2023. https://www.motherjones.com/politics/2023/12/how-the-junk-science-of-hair-analysis-keeps-people-behind-bars/.

FBI. "FBI Testimony on Microscopic Hair Analysis Contained Errors in at Least 90 Percent of Cases in Ongoing Review." Press release, April 20, 2015. https://www.fbi.gov/news/press-releases/fbi-testimony-on-microscopic-hair-analysis-contained-errors-in-at-least-90-percent-of-cases-in-ongoing-review.

Liu, Z., et al. "DNA and Protein Analyses of Hair in Forensic Genetics." *International Journal of Legal Medicine* 137 (2023), 613–633. https://doi.org/10.1007/s00414-023-02955-w.

National Research Council. "Analysis of Hair Evidence." In *Strengthening Forensic Science in the United States: A Path Forward* (pp. 156–161). Washington, DC: National Academies Press, 2009. https://www.ojp.gov/pdffiles1/nij/grants/228091.pdf.

18. Murder or Suicide?

It was a beautiful spring day when the prosecutor in Amsterdam asked me to immediately proceed to the Palace of Justice to accompany him to Uithoorn, one of the towns along the Amstel, where, according to a recently received telegram from the mayor, the body of an elderly man had been found bathed in blood ... possibly the victim of murder! The deceased lay on a grass field on his back, about twenty meters away from the road. A tarpaulin had been placed over him. His wrists showed several incisions, while a deep wound on the left side of his neck, undoubtedly caused by a severed carotid artery, would have resulted in significant blood loss leading to death. Next to his blood-stained right hand lay an open razor, which likely caused the sharp-edged wounds.

I carefully examined the scene, including the state of the clothing, and took some photographs of the body and its immediate surroundings, which needed to be documented before moving the body could take place. Of course, we also searched the immediate vicinity for possible "clues," but nothing unusual was found. Although my on-site investigation didn't take long, I had seen enough to confidently conclude it was a case of suicide. This conclusion brought great relief to the local policeman, as the investigation could have been much more difficult had it been a murder case!

For the purpose of the medical examination—the autopsy—the victim's body was placed in a coffin and transported to Amsterdam to be handed over to the sworn-in medical experts. I contacted them by phone and was informed that the autopsy would take place the next day at three o'clock in the afternoon. The following day, I went to the anatomy room where the medical experts were well underway with their examination. When one of them asked for my opinion, I candidly stated that we were dealing with a case of suicide. However, the medical professionals felt the need to point out that such a conclusion can never be drawn with 100% certainty, since the wounds on the body could still have been inflicted by someone else. Nevertheless, they acknowledged that there was a high probability of suicide.

Various authors emphasize that the conclusion of "suicide" should be approached with certain reservations, as the same injuries could also have been caused by another person. In this particular case, I believed I could argue against this and declared that I could provide evidence that there could be no murder and that it must be a case of suicide. They were eager to hear my reasoning! Here, I must make a remark from the bottom of my heart regarding a fundamentally erroneous practice in my opinion, which is to assign medical experts solely with the task of "external and internal examination of the cadaver of the person." Such an assignment should be much broader unless a criminalist is added to complement the medical examination by deducing information from the clothing. This particular case was once again a clear example of this! To better explain my justifications for suicide, I first took out the clothing of the victim, which had been piled together and apparently overlooked by the medical experts, and pointed out the following points:

- Due to the wrist injuries, both hands were smeared with blood, but there was hardly any blood on the sleeves.
- The blood that flowed from the neck wound ran over the left side of the chest, mainly along the vest; the left pocket (watch pocket) was completely filled with coagulated blood. Lower down, on top of the left trouser pocket, the trousers were soaked with blood up to the left knee.

From these observations, I drew the following conclusions:

- After the wounds occurred, the victim sat up in the grass—otherwise, the blood flow would not have run along the left side of the chest in the direction of the left side and penetrated so deeply into the tissue. Therefore, the victim was fully conscious; after all, an unconscious person would not sit upright in a grass field but would fall over. He was, as they say, *compos mentis*!
- The fact that the bloodstains on the clothing were strictly limited to the areas where gravity carried the blood from the neck wound indicated that the victim remained seated calmly after the neck wound occurred. There were no signs of defensive or other movements. In the case of murder, the victim would undoubtedly defend themselves vigorously, making defensive movements, which clearly did not happen here. This, therefore, was not a case of murder but of suicide!

The medical experts reconsidered their opinion, declared that they agreed with me entirely, and made changes to their notes so that, contrary to the rule stated in the books, they also referred to this as a case of "suicide."

Epilogue by Brigitte Bruijns

For this story it was a bit harder to write an epilogue with ChatGPT, since it gives an "error" that the content may violate the content policy, probably triggered by words like murder and suicide. But luckily it wanted to spit out some interesting sentences about the hypothesis of a forensic investigator once a body is discovered. Nowadays, the discovery of a lifeless body marks the inception of a forensic investigation, setting in motion a complex process to unravel the mysteries surrounding the deceased individual. At this stage, the investigator confronts a myriad of hypotheses, each shadowed by uncertainty and the potential for a multitude of outcomes. First and foremost, the hypothesis of murder looms ominously. The presence of external injuries, the positioning of the body, and signs of struggle can suggest foul play, propelling investigators down the dark path of homicide. Every detail, from the nature of the wounds to the victim's history and associations, is scrutinized to build a case against a potential killer. Alternatively, the specter of natural death emerges as a contender. Here, medical expertise is paramount, as forensic pathologists and doctors scrutinize the body for underlying health conditions, toxicology results, and any signs of disease or organ failure. The goal is to determine if the victim succumbed to natural causes, shielding a potentially innocent party from suspicion.

Beyond these primary hypotheses, a multitude of other possibilities must be considered—accidents, suicides, drug overdoses, and even the rare occurrence of unexplained deaths. Each hypothesis brings its own set of questions and investigative challenges.

19. Petty Thief

The director of the trade school granted an "audience." Three boys, one of whom had tears in his eyes, and the other two closer to crying than laughing, wanted to share their sorrow with him—to report a theft from their overcoats hanging in the school corridor on the coat hooks, which had been robbed of small items that were in the pockets. One lost a beautiful pocketknife he had received on his birthday and of which he was so proud; the second missed a pocket pencil, and the third showed his student tram card, from which the monthly seal, recently affixed to make the card valid for December, had been removed. Yes, it was getting to be a bit too much with these thefts, and the most miserable part was that there was not even the slightest suspicion of who the thief could be. It could happen that a student, who momentarily left the class, committed the thefts, but it could just as well be that a stranger took advantage of the busy commotion in the corridors during the change of lessons to make a grab into the jacket pockets. When the class that had just had drawing lessons had to go to the carpentry room and change classrooms, the corridors were always bustling with activity. There was simply no way to keep an eye on everything.

The director considered it an extremely challenging case to find the thief among those 250 students! When he took a closer look at the tram card in question, he noticed how, in the place where the oblong seal had been affixed, there was now a bumpy surface on the cardboard, over which the thief—who seemed to want to have some fun with it!—mockingly wrote with a pencil the words: "It's off now." That was really too much, thought the director. And thinking further about the difficult problem, a priceless idea suddenly crossed his mind ... yes, that's what he would do to be able to track down the thief!

He cut several sheets of writing paper into small "voting slips"—one for each student—and then visited each class in succession, where each boy was handed a piece of paper, and when the command sounded: "Now, everyone: first write your name clearly on the paper, and below that, write the words 'It's off now.'" Undoubtedly, many wondered in amazement what kind of "joke" this could be. However, the boy whose tram card was robbed of the December seal understood everything, as well as his friends who were in the know! However, most boys did not understand anything, while one (the culprit!) understood the setup so well that he cleverly twisted his handwriting on this piece of paper—so as not to give the game away! Thus, the school principal collected about 250 notes, neatly packed them together with the robbed tram card, and sent them, along with a cover letter, to the chief police commissioner, requesting him to "kindly further investigate this case!"

The addressee handed the package to the chief of the detective bureau, who handed it over to one of his inspectors. This inspector came to my laboratory carrying the invitation from his superiors that I should determine which boy had scribbled the objectionable words on the tram card! It was by no means an easy task! I realized that the thief—in order to remove the seal from the tram card without being disturbed—would have secluded himself in a small room where he found both solitude and water, but no writing desk, the absence of which might have forced him to use one of the walls or the door as a surface for writing. Add to that the fact that the removal of the seal with the help of water had led to the "writing paper" becoming thoroughly soaked, and the reader will understand how many circumstances conspired to deviate the "handwriting" on the tram card. And then to think that the comparison writing of the same boy might be considered "twisted" in other respects—no, it was not easy!

And then the number of comparison slips, about 250 of them! But not to worry! I first thoroughly studied the handwriting on the card, even though it could not be considered normal script, and imprinted its image well in my mind. Then I began going through the slips, most of which could be immediately eliminated and set aside. But there were about eight that interested me more. I couldn't dare to call any of these identical to the writing on the card, but I did consider it very likely that one of those eight slips could have been written by the perpetrator. He must be among them. The handwriting examination, based on the abnormalities I already mentioned, could not provide certainty in this case. And for extensive handwriting analysis, the amount of writing—pencil writing at that!—on the slips was also far from sufficient!

I decided to go to the school at seven in the evening (it was an evening trade school) and immediately asked to speak with the director. It seemed to be a disappointment for him that I couldn't immediately name the thief. He had apparently had a higher opinion of the Amsterdam detective bureau! In his office, I showed him a list of the names of those who had written the eight selected slips. Number one could be eliminated because, as it turned out, he had been absent due to illness on the evening the tram card was robbed. The director thought the second could be temporarily disregarded since that boy lived in the immediate vicinity of the school and presumably had no tram card, hence no interest in a monthly seal! Then number three? The director's face took on a serious expression. Yes, that boy also occasionally gave him an unreliable impression, but … you see … I've had his father at the school once. An incredibly difficult guy, you understand that I prefer not to create any difficulties with him.... Wouldn't we rather start with number four? Well, honestly, I lacked any desire for that.

After the explanation, I was quite eager to meet with that boy and requested that he be taken out of his class and brought to me. The director, noticing that it was becoming "serious," granted my request but, as he later told me, to avoid getting into trouble, he remained in the corridor when the boy entered my office. He whispered in my ear the request not to search the boy, which I answered with an indifferent shrug and a smile. Imagine that: he had already sought the help of the police, and then at a certain moment, he thinks he can give instructions on what should and should not happen!

The young man, about sixteen years old, entered the room. He had something bold, I would almost say cheeky, in his appearance. I gestured for him to take a chair, near the corner of the table. I took a seat just on the other side of this corner point. He had placed his arm in front of him on the table, and soon, I did the same, making discreet "contact" with his arm and—without him having any idea—noting every movement—even every unconscious movement that part of his body would make during the conversation. A conversation about this and that began; about the recent celebration of Saint Nicholas's Day, and whether the saint had treated him well; if he had many siblings and where he lived.

At that moment, I heard an address quite far away, upon which I immediately launched the assumption that he must wear out quite a few soles and heels. No, sir, I have a tram card to reach the school more easily. I showed him my tram card, a service card, and asked if he had one as well. "Oh no, I have a student card," he said, and at the same time, he took out his student card with affixed monthly seals from his pocket. I asked with interest if he had to go to the main tram office to get those seals, to which he explained to me how at the beginning of each month, he bought a seal at the kiosk near him. "And do you have to stick that in the next box?" I asked. No, sir, the lady at the kiosk does that directly; they are gummed, and she sticks the seal in the next box." Throughout this entire conversation, the boy remained calm and composed. Before me on the table lay the tram card with the monthly seals.

I took my magnifying glass out of my pocket and examined the December seal, during which action I did not neglect to maintain contact with the boy's arm through my elbow. Continuing to talk about the adhesive used by the kiosk lady to stick the seals, I focused my full attention on the dried adhesive protruding from the December seal here and there. It seemed milky-white—not Arabic gum—more like white dextrin adhesive found under various trade names. One more remark from me about sticking and the adhesive ... or a slight jolt to the arm and a slight tremor clarified to me how the mood, initially so calm—suddenly reversed. "Kid, listen carefully. This strip was not affixed by the kiosk lady, but by you, and the seal was not bought at the kiosk but peeled off from another card.... You're a thief!" He was immediately caught red-handed.

To make it easier for him, I turned around and ordered him to empty his pockets, laying out all the items he had wrongfully taken on one side of the table and depositing what genuinely belonged to him on the other. Behind me, I heard various items being placed on the table. When, finally, there was silence, and I understood that he was *au bout de son latin* (at his wits' end), I turned around and saw next to me a collection of small knives, pencils, a compass, and various other things—all stolen. And at the other end of the table, there was nothing!

I opened the door to the hallway and asked the director to come in. He still seemed to be filled with fear of this boy's troublesome father. After recovering from the shock of my announcement that I had found the thief and he had already confessed, he declared, to my considerable surprise, that "he" did not wish to file a complaint and did not want to make a "big deal" out of it. Yes, then I immediately made it clear to the director that a policeman who catches a thief has a duty to do and explained that a request not to proceed with prosecution can only be made by the victim—in this case, the fathers of the boys who were robbed. In other words, the director understood that I couldn't be bothered by his fears! This troublemaker needed to be put in his place once and for all, and he needed to be scared out of his wits. That's why I informed him that he was my prisoner and needed to be taken to the nearby main police station.

Then came a flood of tears—perhaps crocodile tears—but there was nothing to be changed about it. Upon arriving at the main police station, I handed him over to the detective sergeant, whom I asked to temporarily place the troublemaker in one of the cells. When he was led inside, I advised him to seriously reflect on what was happening to him. Shortly afterward, the police notified the boy's parents, who could come pick him up around midnight. There was quite a scene! Coincidentally, I was able to observe the boy later on his life journey. The lesson had indeed cured him … and made him a better person. Fortunately, he had returned from the wrong path in time. Most can't do that anymore!

Translated by Rick van Rijn.

20. Simulated Robbery

There are certain families from which multiple members have sequentially become regular "customers"[16] of the police, with the family patriarch and his various sons taking turns in the defendant's dock, some of them more than once. These are people who can safely be called "career criminals." One member of such a family was walking along the Rokin[17] one dusky evening in the company of a postal carrier. Coincidentally, a loitering detective, who was looking for a couple of foreigners, saw the pair approaching. He immediately wondered how a postal carrier, being a state official with a position of trust, could be in such company and—as if he had a foreboding feeling that the saying about close associations with tar and becoming smeared with it could well be applied soon to this postal official—he paid attention to the collar number of that mailman and noted it in his notebook. You never know!

Six weeks later. It is in the early morning at the main post office. The usual hustle of postal officials come to retrieve the locked metal drums from the safe containing valuable items intended for the branch offices in the various districts of the city. Shortly thereafter, the trusted carriers head to their branch offices, where they hand over the drums to the office manager, who appears shortly after. That morning, the manager of the Bloemgracht[18] branch office arrived on his beat, when with horror he discovered how the carrier, who had retrieved the drum, lay immobile on the ground, with his uniform jacket torn open. Fortunately, the patient soon "regained consciousness" and his memory returned shortly after. He managed to explain how as soon as he had entered the office, a strange fellow had followed him, forced him to smell a bottle that was held under his nose, how a struggle ensued, in which two buttons of his uniform jacket had flown off, and how he, lying dazed on the ground for a moment, had been unable to observe anything about his assailant, so he was unable to give a description of the villain. And the drum with valuables was gone!

As soon as the police had knowledge of this crime, a telegram was sent out "for everyone" over all the lines. Barely had the detective, whom I mentioned at the beginning of this account, read the telegram, when he remembered the post officer whom he had seen walking in uniform with a member of the notorious X family. One could never know.... He quickly picked up the phone and called the relevant district bureau, where of course any information that could be useful in the investigation of this strange affair was welcome. The detective simply inquired

---

16 Clearly a joke by Co van Ledden Hulsebosch since in Dutch a "customer of the police" is a euphemism for "criminal."
17 A canal and main street in the city center of Amsterdam between Dam Square and Munt Square.
18 The Bloemgracht (Flower Canal), is a canal in the Jordaan quarter in the city center of Amsterdam.

about the uniform number (collar number) of the postal official who had been unconscious and was not really surprised when he was given the same number he had written in his notebook! He then understood all too well that association with the X family had already taken its toll! And now it was also known which direction to search.

The detectives who had conducted a local investigation at the post office found on the ground, near the spot where the victim had lain, some shards of a small brown glass medicine bottle. But no matter how hard they tried, there was absolutely nothing to be found on the shards—using both their sense of sight and sense of smell. And when those pieces of glass and the cork of the bottle were brought to me, I also had to declare that not the slightest trace of any foreign substance could be found on the glass, just like on the cork. But the detective who brought those glass shards to the laboratory had more physical evidence. He also showed me the uniform jacket of the postal official, from which two buttons were missing, said to have been torn off during the struggle. He also laid these two heavy copper buttons down beside me.

Hardly had I cast a glimpse upon them when I surprised my visitor by claiming that one button had not been on the jacket, but had been deviously laid next to it. To his astonished question of how I could tell, I showed him how that copper button had undergone a repair, where the loop, which had apparently come off, was reattached to the other piece using solder with the aid of candle wax as a flux, and how now, inside the "eye," a quantity of candle wax half-filled the space, and precisely on that side where, under normal conditions—when pulling on the buttons—the thread bundle that connected them to the jacket would have been pulled hardest. In that process, the candle wax would undoubtedly have left its place in the cavity of the eye. This candle wax therefore clearly indicated that this button had not been on the jacket and thus had been laid down as an accessory on the ground afterward—which later also turned out to be correct.

The other button.... Yes, that one could have been on the jacket. But when inspecting the thread bundles that protruded as ruffles from the fabric of the jacket, I also noticed something special: the length of those threads. I will expand on that: When a button is torn off a jacket, or—as can be seen time and again in everyday life—is about to be lost, the cause lies in the worn-through attachment threads that pass through the metal loop; consequently, the thread bundles then fail exactly at the bend that they take, first upward—then downward, back into the fabric of the garment. And the remnants of the worn thread pieces sit together like a frayed tassel. However, I witnessed a different picture: here, the threads emerging from the fabric on one side were cleanly sliced or clipped right "at the ground" and just beside them, the threads stuck out—I would almost say—in full length. Here, the loops were not worn through or torn at their most delicate part—no, the loop parts, which are usually the most worn, had been left intact, while at the base of the thread bundle, the threads had been sharply cut right at the cloth of the jacket. I could even see how this thread bundle had been cut through with two snips: there were four longer and three shorter stumps of thread and—under the microscope, it was beautifully visible how the fibers from which the threads were spun had all been sharply cut by scissors in one line! When the jacket that lay before me on the table was laid straight, I also noticed how the aforementioned thread bundle lay to the right with respect to the short stumps, from which I deduced that a pair of scissors held in the left hand would most likely have cut through the thread bundle. Had the right hand done so, then precisely the threads that now reached up as a free bundle would have been cut at their base. So, it was highly likely that that postal officer was left-handed ... this was something that could easily be checked.

The detective went back to his office, where the postal officer was waiting in his shirt among the agents. To distract him from his boredom, the detective handed him the morning paper, and a little later—as if he had not initially thought of it—asked the other to cut out "that advertisement offering a shepherd dog for sale" for him; at the same time, he placed a pair of scissors next to the newspaper reader on the table. He stayed close by—seemingly engrossed in the reading of a stack of reports—but in reality constantly spying on his guest. The postman seemed to have found the relevant advertisement, and the sound of scissors clipping was heard. The detective was then able to observe cheerfully how the post man was cutting with his left hand—only a left-handed person does that! It should be mentioned that in the post office where the "robbery" had occurred, a small pair of scissors had been found tossed into a distant corner, not belonging there at all. It would have been fruitless to ask the detainee for information about it. He would naturally have shrugged his shoulders and declared that he had "no relation to it." Therefore, the detective wanted to take a different approach.

In the afternoon, he made his way to the arrested man's home, located on the first floor of a building whose street door was conveniently kept open all day. He had no intention of asking the suspect's wife whether the scissors were hers—he well understood that such a question would likely be answered negatively or evasively. So he thought of a ruse. He rang the bell of the first floor after placing the particular pair of scissors behind the front door on the doormat in such a way that—unless the door was fully opened against the wall—one could see the scissors lying there. After ringing the bell, the woman came down the stairs to speak to the "gentleman." He introduced himself as a detective and communicated that he wanted to know a few trivial things about the time her husband had left the house, etc. The woman seemed to need to think carefully about whether to remain silent, to play dumb. She rubbed her hand along her forehead and temples, glanced meaningfully at the floor until her gaze suddenly fell on the scissors. This discovery abruptly interrupted her train of thought, diverting it to other paths. A gasp of astonishment escaped her lips with the words: "Good grief, how on earth did my scissors end up here in the hallway!?" Then the origin of the scissors was sufficiently clear to the detective!

This case clearly demonstrates again how important it is for a detective—even while casually walking along the road in his free time—to remain vigilant, fully taking into account and trying to explain everything he observes around him. It also teaches how carefully one must search for the silent witnesses still untrodden on the territory where the crime was committed, of which there are, all too many, highly sensitive to damage that can so easily diminish or make their value disappear.

Epilogue by Arian van Asten: Every Contact Leaves a Trace

The case of the simulated robbery that Co van Ledden Hulsebosch describes in this chapter has a strong connection to what every forensic scientist knows as Locard's exchange principle: "Every contact leaves a trace." Dr. Edmond Locard (1877–1966) is regarded as one of the founding fathers of forensic science and he introduced forensic investigative methods in France as van Ledden Hulsebosch did in the Netherlands. They can both be regarded as belonging to the group of European scientists that pioneered forensic science and introduced the investigation of physical (trace) evidence as an invaluable source of objective information to accurately reconstruct events relating to an alleged crime. However, internationally, Locard clearly is better known than van Ledden Hulsebosch, even today. He founded the world's first forensic police laboratory in 2010 in the French city of Lyon and also made major developments in the field of dactyloscopy (fingerprint comparison).

The famous phrase "Every contact leaves a trace" was never actually coined by Edmond Locard, but he did introduce the underlying principle that states that when objects or persons are in contact, trace material will transfer from one item to another, or from one person to an item, or from one person to another. This exchange is mutual, which means that a forensic scientist can always find clues of this contact on all objects and persons involved as long as the methods are sensitive enough and the traces persist over time. The observations of Locard were related to violent crimes and the inevitable transfer of silent witnesses when excessive force is exerted. However, more delicate forms of contact can also leave trace material. And nowadays, one can even state the same applies to digital evidence, e.g., when a mobile phone connects to a Wi-Fi network, digital traces of this wireless contact are typically stored on a router and can be used to demonstrate that a person—or at least the phone of a person—was at a certain location at a given time.

Interestingly, at the end of the story, van Ledden Hulsebosch also shows that he was fully aware of the consequences of Locard's exchange principle for crime

Figure 4. The French forensic pioneer Dr. Edmond Locard (1877–1966). Source: Wikipedia, public domain.

scene investigators. What holds for perpetrators also holds for those who enter crime scenes to find and document traces. As soon as these so-called "crime scene investigators," or CSIs, enter the scene, their own actions and contacts will create traces that have nothing to do with the crime. When they secure evidence, there is a risk that the state of the physical evidence is altered such that it affects a correct forensic investigation and interpretation. This is why so many precautions are necessary to prevent contamination at the scene. Accurate documentation including photography, 3D scans, and, if needed, video recording must therefore always precede the physical examination and the collection of relevant evidence items.

21. Who Bears the Cost of the Damage?

It is very remarkable that many people, who, due to some carelessness, cause damage, immediately devise means to blame others and try to make them pay for the damage! Just observe, when in any traffic accident "damage"[19] has been done, as the customary term goes, you will be able to see how both parties try to wash their hands of it, arguing that the blame for everything lies on the other side! Indeed, rare cases occur where the one who caused the accident gallantly admits their mistake and fully accepts responsibility for the damage they caused! As I am going to give the reader some typical examples here, I emphasize that they are not derived from my judicial practice but were dealt with outside of the criminal justice system and the police, in my private laboratory, as the parties left the decision to me.

A large women's clothing store in this city received from one of its customers an evening gown delivered a short time before, with the remark that—shamefully enough!—discolorations occurred on the front of the dress after only one wear. These must be errors in the fabric! When the shopkeeper, who was held liable for the damage, agreed with the angry lady that the chemist's opinion should be delivered first, I received the evening gown for further inspection. After examination, I declared that some stains had been removed with a completely inappropriate stain remover for that delicate costume, so the supplier could not be blamed at all. Although the buyer initially protested vigorously, she later came to tell that, entirely without her knowledge, her sister had worn the gown to a party one evening, got some stains on it, and, assisted by her future groom, had used all possible means—including the wrong ones!—to remove the stains! Thus, the damage could be recovered from the one who was truly at fault.

From a wholesaler of carpet fabrics, I was often tasked with investigations following complaints filed by retailers in the province—on behalf of their "good" customers—which often revolved around discolorations, unexplained stains, sometimes appearing in groups in certain places on a carpet or stair runner, and occasionally even taking on the character of corroded spots with holes in the fabric. And those "good" customers (and therefore also the retailers in the provinces acting on their behalf) always attributed these damages exclusively to errors in weaving or dyeing—so they believed they had every right to demand a replacement for the carpet or stair runner! And time and again—I truly can't remember how many times, but it ran into dozens of cases!—it could be determined that the discolorations and fabric corrosion were caused by nothing other than sulfuric acid—spilled by one

---

19 In the original Dutch text the saying "brokken maken" is used, which literally translate to "making chunks" and means "doing damage."

of the household members while handling radio batteries in a less-than-careful manner. Interestingly, such claims disappeared once modern radio devices made the use of a battery unnecessary!

I remain struck by the brutality—excuse me for using this word—with which those who damaged their belongings through clumsiness still tried to get "free" compensation from the retailer or wholesaler and make him bear the costs! One very amusing case stands out, where I was able to establish that after the damage occurred, an attempt had been made, in a more or less skillful(!) manner, to neutralize the traces of sulfuric acid from the battery and perhaps obscure them for the expected investigation! That too could be determined, and upon further inquiry it came to light that the son of the household—a student of the highest class of the HBS[20]—had expected that after neutralizing the destroyed sulfuric acid components, the eaten-away wires would also reconnect and the destroyed dyes would likewise be regenerated!

Complaints from housewives, whose laundry had been delivered with serious damage by less scrupulous laundries, also frequently came for "treatment" at my laboratory. In these cases the true culprit would often simply claim that it must have been defects in the napkins or bedsheets that had caused the "separation of cohesion" that had occurred. But this excuse rarely held, as the investigation usually made it clear that the damage was a result of mistreatment with corrosive bleaching agents—usually chlorine compounds—which had been applied in an unrestrained manner to shorten the treatment process. I do not intend to cast aspersions on the many good laundries where the laundry is treated with care!

I also had to handle many unreasonable complaints regarding alleged damage caused by self-acting detergents. It's remarkable how easily many housewives, when for any reason—where the self-acting detergent is absolutely innocent!—damage occurs to the laundry, immediately attribute the blame to that detergent! And it's funny how each, in turn, assumes the air of "having a monopoly on the truth" when the manufacturer of the detergent is shown the damaged laundry items with the message: "This is because of treatment with your self-cleaning detergent!" And it could always be demonstrated how far they were from the truth, and how entirely different factors were at play and causing the damage! Perhaps many housewives who noticed damage to their laundry were given information that was too one-sided, especially from the competition, which did not hesitate to cast doubt on the "self-acting detergent" and insinuated all sorts of unpleasant things contrary to the truth! I have read articles myself that proclaimed pseudo-learnedness but actually contained the greatest nonsense.

---

20 The HBS or *hogere burgerschool* (higher civic school) was a type of higher secondary education in the Netherlands that existed between 1863 and 1974. It prepared students to enter a BSc program.

Thus, a manufacturer of self-acting detergent recently sent me a baby apron, sent in by a mother because "during washing according to instructions" stains had appeared and holes seemed to have been eaten into it. And what did the microscopic and chemical examination reveal? That the holes were formed by countless pinpricks and that the stains around those holes were iron stains, consequences of rusty safety pins! I removed those iron stains for the lady—to convince her!—with a little oxalic acid solution and was able to reassure her regarding the use of the aforementioned detergent!

Another lady sent in a bath towel and a pillowcase. Both items showed ugly yellow stains and, once again, the self-acting detergent seemed to be the scapegoat. That lady wrote a note with the shipment stating that "during washing with the specific detergent, the yellow stains appeared on the bath towel and pillowcase!" I reported that I accepted the complaining lady's assertion one hundred percent, that indeed during washing with the prepared solution those stubborn yellow stains had appeared on her towel and pillowcase. But—I wrote to her—nobody will make me believe that "because of" washing with that solution those unpleasant stains could have appeared. Never has a self-acting detergent caused stains to appear—least of all stains like those of an extremely stubborn yellow aniline dye, most likely present in the laundry when, inadvertently, a bright yellow dyed piece of fabric (such as a yellow dishcloth) went into the solution together with the white laundry ... a big mistake on the part of that lady, who, of course, once again wanted to blame the detergent, which, however, was completely blameless!

From the competition's side, there has been no hesitation in spreading rumors that the said detergent contains "sharp-biting granules" that could eat away at the laundry. And that is completely incorrect. Anyone who has ever witnessed the production of the aforementioned cleaning agent themselves could see how the raw materials, ground to the finest dust, are mixed in special blending towers, resulting in a completely homogeneous powder mixture, where no two particles of the added bleach remain together!

One amusing case involved a lady who was persistently convinced that the self-acting detergent had caused holes in her delicate handkerchiefs. Until I scooped up a spoonful of dry laundry powder into a pristine example of one of those handkerchiefs, tied it up into a parcel, and then let the handkerchief soak in boiling water for fifteen minutes. Of course, the concentrated powder dissolved in the water, all the while acting on the fabric at boiling heat. And what was the result? The handkerchief showed no damage whatsoever where the highly concentrated substance had been stored and had had every opportunity to exert its influence on the fabric. The complainant was then convinced and understood that the holes had to be attributed to another cause!

In handling another complaint, it became clear to me that the stains on the laundry were a result of excessively prolonged exposure in an unsuitable piece of crockery (an iron cooking pot poorly coated with zinc!). Nevertheless, the "lady," whose laundry had suffered serious damage from this, was impudent enough to attempt to get "compensation" from the manufacturer of the self-acting detergent!

Several laundry businesses—understandably less pleased with the fact that so many housewives treat their laundry themselves at home—do not hesitate to spread suspicions repeatedly, and in various forms, as if such a solution would be more harmful to the laundry than treatment in their machine laundry! It is often overlooked that—as Mr. Dr. Ir. F. H. Thies[21] indicates—natural bleaching in a bleaching field under intense sun exposure is much more harmful to the fibers of laundry than a correctly applied "chemical bleaching method" achieved with self-acting laundry detergents! Thies and others also rightly oppose the unrestrained use of chlorine compounds for laundry bleaching. It is well known how much damage has been caused by this and how many laundry items have had to be replaced after they have been eaten away.

Scientific experiments conducted by Thies have clearly shown that treatment of the laundry with a self-acting laundry detergent, in addition to effective cleaning, thorough disinfection, and a brightening effect, caused the least damage compared to other laundry methods where chlorine bleach or other methods were used. After washing various test fabrics fifty times with different processes, the tensile strength of the fabrics (the cohesion, the "strength," as the housewife generally calls it) was accurately determined each time with scientific instruments, revealing that the laundry treated with a self-acting detergent produced brilliant results. Similar experiments—yielding similarly favorable results—were carried out by Statens Provningsanstalt[22] in Stockholm. I have seen the reports from that institute and learned how favorably they also reported on self-acting laundry detergents.

Other properties of it—including the germicidal effect—have been thoroughly examined over the years by specialists. For example, Dr. P. Scharlau of the Hygiene Institute of the Westphalian Wilhelm University in Münster established how rapidly, during the prescribed laundry treatment, various groups of pathogens, including typhus, are quickly killed, and this author pointed out in his publication (*Archiv für Hygiene*, vol. 102, no. 1) in the end, how self-acting laundry detergents simultaneously exert a deodorizing effect (thus destroying unpleasant-smelling substances), while the more common disinfectants (carbolic acid, lysol, creolin) are not entirely

---

21 F. H. Thies, *Neuzeitliche Waschprozesse* (Heidelberg: Verlag Melliand's Textilberichte, 1926), p. 2. In the time the book was written, German was the main language used in technical scientific publications. Co van Ledden Hulsebosch also published scientific articles in German.

22 Statens Provningsanstalt (State Testing Institute) was the national Swedish authority for testing and inspection, founded in 1920.

removed after use and continue to make the laundry retain the penetrating odor of these substances in an annoying way. Prof. Dr. W. von Gonzenbach of the University of Zurich also published the results of his survey on the disinfecting action of these laundry detergents (in the *Schweizerische Zeitschrift für Gesundheitspflege*, vol. 7, no. 4). You see how the world of scholars is interested in this group of household aids! But I digressed from my topic. I still want to tell you another amusing case—to illustrate the starting point about "complaining in order to make someone else bear the cost of the damage."

A shopkeeper who had delivered an expensive carpet received a complaint after a few months that the carpet showed discolorations, and—strangely enough—that the discoloration, as well as loosening of the wool fibers, could be observed precisely where the carpet was extra compressed, namely under the table legs. The intensity of the complaint, combined with threats of legal action if the demands for a new carpet were not met, led the shopkeeper to have the central part of the carpet taken out and gave it to me for examination. Yes, there were sharply etched, discolored spots to be seen, right around the flattened places where the table legs had rested. Further chemical research revealed a highly remarkable fact: the results of that research led me to ask the shopkeeper to check if there happened to be a dog in the house of his complaining customer. Yes, there was. They had a large shepherd dog. Then, as a result of my submitted report, the behavior of that quadruped was spied on (especially when it was alone in the room), and the results of my research were fully confirmed. The animal had developed the habit of sniffing the table legs alternately and then—well, "greeting with its backward fascist salute." No wonder that the accumulating elements left behind in the carpet, which remained after drying out, exerted their destructive effect on fibers and dyes! And, of course, nothing remained of the "claim."

Another amusing incident comes to mind, which was investigated by the inspection service, and which I can reveal here, now that I've had a chat about so many "laundry parties at home." A few years ago, a lady from a densely populated district of our city brought a bottle of tap water to the inspection service, which she had just filled from her kitchen tap, but which clearly tasted like bleach! She was truly right. No one understood anything about it, and an inspector immediately went with her to her home, where they took water with a clear taste of bleach from the tap in the kitchen. What was the cause? It was midsummer, and on the third floor, where the lady lived, she did not have a good supply of water all the time. On the fourth floor, with her upstairs neighbors, it was naturally even worse. The lady on the fourth floor had done her laundry very early in the morning and left it in a full tub of water in the sink, to which a dash of bleach had been added. She had tried the tap a couple of times to see if there was any water—but there was none. So, for convenience, she left her tap open, thinking: when the water flow comes later, my laundry will be rinsed clean! Now there was a piece of rubber hose attached to the tap, which hung into the tub water. If the downstairs neighbor on the third floor turned the tap to draw a glass of water (which, due to insufficient pressure, was not yet coming up from the street mains!), she, due to simple siphoning, received the water transferred from the laundry tub of her upstairs neighbor into her glass via that rubber hose! And thus, the phenomenon was explained! As always: examine all things first and draw your conclusions afterward.

Epilogue by Ruben Kranenburg

In this chapter Co van Ledden Hulsebosch describes many entertaining examples of failed attempts of warranty fraud. In most cases, chemical tests and microscopic examinations were performed to reveal the truth. The experiments described in this chapter were performed in van Ledden Hulsebosch's private laboratory at the Nieuwendijk in Amsterdam. Around the same time, the first forensic laboratory in the Netherlands was built for van Ledden Hulsebosch in the head office of the Amsterdam Police at the Elandsgracht. Old pictures of this laboratory clearly show the usefulness of a high variety of chemical tests in these early times of forensic research, as depicted by shelves full of flasks with chemical solutions.

The current illicit-drug analysis laboratory of the Amsterdam Police emerged from this first police laboratory founded by van Ledden Hulsebosch. When I joined this laboratory as a junior chemist in 2009, I surprisingly encountered multiple souvenirs still present from his time at the lab. Also, my predecessor, pharmacist Ruurd Jellema, proudly shared me some stories about our illustrious founding father. For many years, the top of the main closet in the lab was decorated with an old large black metal item that nobody seemed to know the purpose of. That old item was something between a sieve and a closed bucket filled with a siphon. Upon asking, Mr. Jellema told me it was the "coprofractor," which literally translates as "poop sieve." Co van Ledden Hulsebosch's father, Marius van Ledden Hulsebosch, was a pharmacist who created an interesting collection of microscopic stool residue pictures and in 1899 he published the book *Makro- und mikroskopische Diagnostik der menschlichen Exkremente* (Macro- and microscopic diagnosis of human excreta) about this. This collection was useful for forensic investigation because nervous burglars sometimes left a "smelly souvenir" behind. The undigested remnants in such a stool could provide clues about the diet and social class of the perpetrator. Unfortunately, the reference collection had to be created manually by eating a monotonous diet for a week and then carefully rinsing and sieving one's own excrement. According to rumors in the laboratory, father Marius had a poor sense of smell and therefore didn't mind doing this dirty work. However, his son was less inclined to undertake this malodorous task, prompting him to design the "coprofractor."

During my first year at the laboratory, I regularly found old mementos from those early years. These include a copy of the book mentioned above, old bottles of chemicals (e.g., cocaine) purchased in the 1930s and 1940s, manuscripts, old balances, and even original stool residue of the van Ledden Hulsebosch family members stored in formaldehyde.

See Figure 5 (in the insert section) for the "coprofractor" designed by Co van Ledden Hulsebosch and on display at the forensic illicit drug laboratory of the Amsterdam Police.

22. Poison!

This sketch appeared some years ago in a group of provincial newspapers.

If I were to ask you, Reader, to give me an accurate definition of "poison," very few correct answers would sporadically come in. A French professor, who was going to speak about poisons in one of his lectures, began to pose this question to the students: "What is an accurate definition of the concept of 'dog'?" Not one was able to do so. Even though each one considered themselves entirely capable of recognizing a dog as *Canis familiaris* on the street, no one could give such a definition of the concept of a dog that included all types of dogs and excluded all animals that were not dogs! When the difficulty of this task was acknowledged by everyone, that professor declared that it would be just as difficult—almost impossible—to give a completely accurate definition of "poison." And yet, at first glance, everyone knows how to recognize a dog, just as everyone is convinced they know what a poison is. Furthermore: How many poisons are not relative? We know the phenomenon that is called "idiosyncrasy." This is the extraordinary sensitivity of some individuals to certain substances that have a neutral effect on other people but are poisonous to those individuals.

I remember a case from the time when an antipyrine powder was often taken for headaches. A young doctor in the countryside, who had his father visiting, casually gave him an antipyrine powder when complaints of headaches were expressed. The old gentleman reacted quite peculiarly to this, and the son—initially afraid that he had taken the wrong item from his stock—for a moment thought he would lose his father within an hour! The latter had an idiosyncrasy for that particular medicine. This fact has caused the formerly dangerous—for the majority beneficial—headache remedy to recede into the background, and nowadays many young people don't even know the remedy anymore!

A maid could not tolerate any quinine components. The ingestion of just one quinine pill brought her to despair after an hour due to unbearable itching over her entire body, which was covered with a kind of eczema. In another patient, the ingestion of one quinine pill induced symptoms that occur in every other human child as soon as a cup of castor oil is ingested! Hence, it is useful to inform a new doctor in time about any hypersensitivity to certain medications so that the physician can take idiosyncrasy into account when composing the prescription he is going to prescribe.

Thus, a few decades ago, iodophor bandages were still commonly used for wounds. The pungent odor was indeed extremely annoying, but that disadvantage was forgotten when compared to the great benefits in wound treatment. Thus, during my student days, many a student had a small first-aid kit in his bicycle bag—for "first aid in minor accidents"—and in it was also an iodophor gauze. On a joint cycling trip, one of the female students had fallen and injured her ankle. Immediately a gallant knight was ready to dress the wound with a piece of iodophor gauze. Within twenty-four hours, the girl was covered all over her body with a stubborn eczema—as the attending physician called it—the typical iodophor eczema, as a result of that single bandage. She could not tolerate iodophor on her body!

It is well known how sufferers of diabetes are generally not allowed to use sugar. Thus, a young doctor treated one of his aunts for diabetes and prescribed a strict diet for her. Instead of sugar, the patient had to use artificial sweetener in her food and drinks. An old, faithful maid-housekeeper, who had been by her side for many years as her sole housemate, received the necessary instructions from the doctor, which she initially followed diligently, with the patient's rapid recovery as a reward. However, the housekeeper did not particularly favor the recovery. Knowing that she was generously provided for in the old lady's will, she had actually hoped that this would be her lady's final illness. Thus, the diabolical idea ripened in her brain to replace the saccharin tablets and other permitted sweeteners, as before, with generous portions of regular sugar in her patron's food. And immediately, the old lady's condition worsened alarmingly. Her nephew became worried, understanding nothing until he felt suspicions rising and suspected the housekeeper of having replaced the artificial sweeteners with sugar with malicious intentions. Thus, he brought me a dish of applesauce one day, asking me to determine through examination which sweetener was present in it. I had to report that no artificial sweeteners had been added to it, but a considerable amount of sugar was present! He expressed his "suspicions," but the villainess denied it. Only after threatening her with the police or the judiciary did he get the truth out of her—that the sugar I had identified had been intentionally added to her mistress's diet. He had unfortunately bound himself by promise to keep the police out of any potential confession, so that the only punishment consisted of an immediate change to the will, which the hastily summoned notary was able to assist with just in time. That physician surely did not know that he himself was committing a punishable offense by not disclosing the crime he knew to the police or the judiciary! It wasn't until years later that I heard about the circumstances that had unfolded around the investigation of the peculiar applesauce incident!

When we talk about poison, most people only think about poison that enters the body through the mouth. However, it should be noted that harmful, dangerous substances can enter our bodies through various pathways. I need only mention the word "poison gas" to make it clear that through the respiratory tract—yes, even through the skin—poisonous gaseous products can begin their destructive action on our lives. I vividly recall a case where someone, plagued by intestinal worms mainly residing in his rectum, tried to remove them by an enema prepared from a decoction of tobacco and onions. He had prepared this decoction using heavy tobacco that was much too strong and became extremely ill due to a very acute nicotine poisoning via the rectum.

When we hear about poison gas, we involuntarily think of the treacherous carbon monoxide (commonly known as coal gas), which claims victims every year, especially in the cold season. Since our illuminating gas also contains a considerable amount of carbon monoxide, it is also very dangerous. The poisonous effect of coal gas is based on the fact that said gas permanently renders our red blood cells unsuitable for their role, which is to absorb oxygen in the lungs in order to transport that oxygen to all parts of the body. Thus, the blood is poisoned by coal gas, and the victim essentially dies from lack of oxygen, that is, from suffocation, even if they are in an atmosphere where a considerable percentage of oxygen is still present.

I always find coal gas to be a mean, treacherous stealth murderer. Often the victims are caught in their sleep. The gas is almost odorless. (What is perceived, as soon as the stove is not correctly adjusted, is not the coal gas, but the accompanying combustion products, which, however, do not awaken the sleeper!) Thus, most victims of this insidious poison are found dead in bed. It is worth noting that in most cases, the stove was in excellent condition—but not in all.

In March 1925 I was called by the police to a houseboat, located in the Jacob van Lennep canal in Amsterdam. We found an elderly couple inside with five children motionless in bed ... overcome by coal gas. Only the mother still showed signs of life. After treatment with oxygen, she was revived, only to learn that her husband and children had all passed away ... as a result of a defective heating system. I still see the cylindrical stove—a very simple model!—with a kettle on top, before me. The exhaust pipe ran directly horizontally from the stove through the wall to the outside air, and then went up at a right angle. In that vertical section, so much rain had entered that at the bottom of the vertical section, the bend was completely rusted through. As a result, there was no longer an upward flow of heated air with the combustion gases and so the chimney could no longer draw under these circumstances. The egg-sized coals put in the stove just before going to bed remained too cold for too long and strongly promoted the formation of the poisonous gas with the aforementioned fatal result!

But even where there is a well-functioning stove with a properly drawing chimney, accidents can occur, as I have had the opportunity to see several times in my career. It should be considered that the formation of coal gas occurs primarily as soon as a load of new, thus cold, fuel is added onto the fire in the stove. This fuel, while still cold, is capable of producing, from one of the combustion gases rising from the fire at the bottom of the stove, namely carbon dioxide, the poisonous carbon monoxide. If the stove is regulated and burns well, then there is enough "draft"—if the coal gas does not burn with the familiar blue flames on top of the cold coals—to let the poisonous gas escape through the chimney along with the other combustion products. But woe, if, shortly after refilling the stove, the latter is set to "night duty" and the flow of gases to the chimney is reduced or impeded. Then the poisonous products creep into the room through cracks in doors, etc., and ... very little of that poison is needed to spoil the atmosphere and send the sleepers into eternal sleep.

Many have the unfortunate habit of—just before going to bed—refilling the stove and setting it to "night service." This is, as I explained above, disastrous! It exposes you and your family to the greatest dangers. Readers, make it a firm habit to fully refill the stove a few hours before bedtime, so that—as long as the chimney is still drawing normally and the ventilation is proper—the freshly added coals can warm up. The coal gas produced then will not harm us; it will be drawn into the chimney, as far as it is not burned and turned into carbon dioxide. When it's time for rest, set the stove, which now contains only warm fuel, to night service—it will now be safe!

If you live or sleep in a room where smoke from a stove in another—often lower—room is occasionally detected, you must also be cautious. I recall a case where a couple was found dead in bed, even though the stove in their flat was not lit, and yet coal gas was determined as the cause of death. Further investigation revealed that the smoke channel from a large furnace in the basement of the apartment building had cracked at the level of their flat. Wallpaper, stretched tightly over the chimney cracks, could not prevent, under unfavorable drafts—or perhaps a fatal wind direction!—clouds of coal gas from entering the elderly couple's bedroom, with the result mentioned.

Many cases of poisoning are due to fatal accidents—sometimes to human stupidity. When harmful microbes cause an unwanted infection during unhygienic cheese-making, it can happen that in a large cheese, these bacteria start converting the cheese's protein, forming toxic decomposition products that are as dangerous as cadaverine (corpse toxins). If someone unfortunately eats that part of the cheese, they can become seriously ill. We have seen cases where a family became seriously ill after buying a piece of cheese, while the inspection service quickly confiscated the rest of the cut cheese from the shop and found no harmful microbes present. These cheese toxins can sometimes develop very locally.

It's different with meat and sausage products. Not too long ago, an unscrupulous butcher processed meat from a sick horse into steaks and sausages, resulting in entire groups of poor people falling deadly ill. Many still mistakenly believe that by thoroughly cooking "third-rate sausage" beforehand, any danger can be avoided. I already said this assumption is wrong. People think of the often-given advice to boil milk thoroughly before use and draw a parallel with suspect meat products. However, cooking milk kills the harmful bacteria it may contain. In the dangerous meat from emergency-slaughtered animals, the toxins produced by decay or other dangerous bacteria are already present, and these withstand cooking heat completely, just like rat poison does! It's better not to buy such inferior meat and remember that exposing it to cooking heat does not eliminate the dangers associated with using such meat products!

It's often the so-called coliform bacteria that invisibly poison our food. These bacteria are part of our gut flora, play a role in digestion, and are regularly found in feces. If these microorganisms get into food or drink, they can attack the protein substances present and produce toxic breakdown products. In this context, I want to discuss the refrigerator. I'm not referring to modern freezers, which maintain an interior temperature at or below freezing, but to old-fashioned refrigerators filled with blocks of raw ice, maintaining a temperature just above freezing. It goes without saying that even modern fridges—if not set below freezing—keep food and drink just above freezing. This poses a poisoning danger that I hope to clarify.

Everything born has the end goal of returning to dust. Just as all buildings, whether demolished by human hands or natural forces, eventually come down. I once watched the demolition of a large building as a boy. Notably, the contractor always starts with a few quick workers, carefully removing and lowering as many intact roof tiles as possible. This team is always first. Then a few trusted workers come to cut the roof lead from the gutters and honestly deliver it to the boss. When they're done, it's time for further demolition.

It strikes me how Mother Nature also, whenever she starts a demolition, first puts certain "workers" to work, by which I mean the bacteria responsible for decay. These are usually the lactic acid bacteria, whose name clarifies to the reader that they are the silent workers that sour the milk and convert white cabbage into the delicious winter dish called sauerkraut. The fact that we enjoy the formed lactic acid in buttermilk, yogurt, sauerkraut, and other products tells us these lactic acid bacteria—though they start the decay process—are not hostile to us and do not harm our health. But I would warn you: "Keep an eye on them, for their activity, forming lactic acid, is our red signal. Be alert, the decay process has begun, and danger is coming!" As long as these first workers, the lactic acid bacteria, are at work, all other microbes stay away. There is no direct danger to our health as long as the decay is limited to lactic acid formation.

Many housewives, noticing a slight sour taste in leftover cold roast meat, quickly grab the vinegar under the motto: "We'll have hash tomorrow and ... when vinegar is poured over it, no one will notice the trace of lactic acid ... the beginning of spoilage!" However, if you do not let the decay go further, there is no danger to our health. Thus, the first signs of souring in various foods can always be seen as the announcement that the demolition work has begun! It is remarkable how other groups of demolishers patiently wait their turn, which comes as soon as the acid-forming bacteria stop working. They do this when they have developed a certain acidity or when all "raw materials" for their lactic acid are used up. They wait longer if the foods have been given a higher acidity by added vinegar (liver sausage in vinegar, pickled herring).

Then the next groups of bacteria, the dangerous putrefactive bacteria, start their work. They convert the protein substances in food into highly toxic compounds that also develop in cadavers. Then you must be on your guard! And these putrefactive bacteria initially do not reveal their activity because humans do not detect their early toxic products with taste or smell, which makes these bacteria particularly treacherous. What was my reason for linking refrigerators to putrefactive bacteria? Here is the issue: When a nonsterilized food or drink, like a jug of milk, is placed in an old-fashioned refrigerator where the temperature is just above freezing, this cold absolutely prevents the lactic acid bacteria from working. No lactic acid is formed, and the "red warning light" does not appear. However, the putrefactive bacteria, which can live at the prevailing temperature, quietly do their work and produce cadaverine, the dangerous corpse toxins, whose presence is not initially noticeable when using the food or drink.

Years ago, in a large restaurant in Amsterdam, many guests enjoyed coffee ice cream on a summer evening, which—kept overnight in an old-fashioned fridge—was protected from souring but where coliform bacteria had developed significantly. That night, all those who ate the ice cream became very sick and many doctors had a restless night with their numerous patients! The police and judiciary were involved, bacteriological research was conducted, and a mass of coliform bacteria was found. It was wrongly assumed that keeping the delicacy "in the refrigerator" and freezing it daily would prevent spoilage.

In Rotterdam, a large party held a lunch at a big restaurant. Preparations had been made a few days in advance, assuming everything would stay fresh in the refrigerator. But coliform bacteria developed. No one tasted anything unusual, but soon the entire party showed poisoning symptoms. The scenes were terrible as guests, wanting to isolate themselves, found no sufficient opportunity and lined up along the curb to vomit the unwanted food. Toxins had formed during the stay in the old-fashioned fridge.

Notable was the case where an entire family showed severe poisoning symptoms after eating applesauce. When I received a sample of the applesauce for investigation, it was found that a significant amount of zinc had dissolved in it. The frugal housewife had a new bottom put in a pot by a local handyman, who did it neatly but with galvanized iron (zinc-coated iron) instead of tinned iron. The zinc—being a harmful metal—dissolved in the tart applesauce, leading to poisoning, which luckily ended with the patients' recovery!

I also vividly recall the case with a mayor's family in Utrecht. Poisoning symptoms appeared that lasted for days, and a visiting guest from Amsterdam also became a victim. The mayor came to consult me, bringing all the ingredients used in the meal preparation, asking to determine the cause of the unpleasant symptoms. After a lengthy discussion, I set the items aside for a while and expressed a desire to examine the rainwater from the tank used for all local drinking water. Though it had been recently cleaned, chemical analysis showed the water contained zinc. When dredging on my advice, a zinc bucket was found, which a dismissed maid had dropped into the rainwater tank and never bothered to retrieve!

These cases were accidental poisonings. Deliberate poisonings to harm someone or those involving overdoses of medicine intended for treatment are of a different nature. One court case involved a nurse on trial for irresponsibly mixing a medicine (phosphorized cod liver oil) for children in her care, mistakenly adding a hundred times the amount of the highly toxic phosphorus, resulting in fatalities.

In Amsterdam, an old bedridden man was supposed to take a spoonful of castor oil prescribed by the doctor, given by his elderly wife. Without reading the label, she took a bottle of strong carbolic acid, poured a dose, and despite its strong smell, the old man drank it all in one gulp, holding his nose to avoid the castor oil's smell. He died shortly after!

Here I may emphatically point out that such dangerous poisons must **not** be placed in the household cabinet among simple home remedies, and I advise everyone not to open any bottle for use before being well and truly assured that the label indicates the desired item. It is unnecessary to state that bottles, boxes, or bags that do not have a proper label indicating the nature of the substance are taboo! Human lives can be at stake!

History knows many examples of murder using poison. The older generation might remember—perhaps through tales passed down—the story of the Leiden poisoner, who had dozens of victims, mostly small children, who were entrusted to her "care" and—as soon as they began reacting to the administered poison—returned them to their parents to die at home! More recently, readers might be familiar with the Widow Becker in Liège, who stood trial there as a mass murderer. It is peculiar how often this crime is committed by women!

When I pass over cases from my own practice in silence, it is because I want to prevent any readers who were somehow involved in these dramas from setting aside my writing because they prefer not to be reminded of the grief that reigned in their families in those cases. There remains plenty to tell!

Cases of poisoning are sometimes simulated to appear as pitiable victims and to provide a more plausible "cause" for the disappearance of entrusted funds, for example. An official who was responsible for transporting a large sum of money had it taken away by an accomplice. He slightly damaged his outer clothing, broke a bottle—perhaps empty—next to him on the ground, and lay down beside it, waiting for "help" to arrive. In the first moments he feigned extreme confusion. He claimed to have been attacked and resisted vigorously—even his clothing had been torn in the struggle—but the assailant knocked him out by holding the bottle to his face, causing him to fall unconscious, and from that moment on, the "victim" remembered nothing. Such stories can only be believed by those who enjoy Nick Carter novels, but scientists know all too well that such tales are purely fantastical!

Also, travelers who have been "robbed" have claimed that while they slept, some intoxicating liquid was held under their nose, and during the resultant unconsciousness, they were robbed of their entrusted funds. These are old wives' tales. It has long been established that as soon as chloroform or any other intoxicant is held under the nose of a sleeping person, the sleep immediately ends, and the threatened person is instantly wide awake!

Suicide by poison is a special category for the police. Naturally, in such cases, there must always be thorough certainty that it is indeed a suicide, which is usually easily determined. The case I wish to tell you now took place in Vienna. There, the son of a wealthy industrial magnate had somehow encountered a circus performer, the child of an unmarried mother. A romance developed, and one day the young man was bluntly told that no choice remained and a quick marriage with the circus girl was necessary. It is easy to understand how the aristocratic family of the industrialist probably felt about this, but the marriage took place, and after six months, a daughter was born. The spouses both felt that they were not suited for each other, but there was nothing to be done. The marriage bond could not be easily broken "without damage."

One day, the young father, very distraught, reported at the nearby police station that he had found his wife dead in bed upon returning home. A note on the bedside table next to her clarified everything. In it, she begged her husband for forgiveness for her desperate act, urged him to find a better mother for the little girl, and to preserve the good memory of the unfortunate woman. This was taken to be a case of suicide! The note was seized by the police and stored in the relevant files. Sometime later, the mother-in-law seemed to sense something. She expressed to the police justified doubts, claiming to be convinced that her daughter, whose character she knew so well, could not have committed suicide, thus prompting a judicial investigation into the authenticity (or lack thereof) of the note found next to the deceased on the table.

But scholars disagree—even in the capital of Austria. One of them firmly believed that the note was not written by the deceased but by someone else (who that was, was not said!), while his colleague chose to remain neutral—he would neither recognize the note as authentic nor call it false. Thus, the matter was set aside by the public prosecutor. Although this outcome was only half satisfactory to the deceased's mother, she could do nothing to change the course of the case. The father of the young widower, however, who was very displeased with the "meddling" by his son's mother-in-law and understandably angered by the sensational newspaper articles with their bold headlines, found this course of action far from satisfactory. He demanded nothing more or less than the full rehabilitation of his son, whom he trusted completely and believed was wrongfully suspected, deeming it a duty to clear the family name of any stain, no matter what the cost!

Thus, the young man—at his father's insistence—requested exact photographic reproductions of the incriminated note from the judiciary, as well as the comparison samples used in the investigation—handwriting from both spouses—along with some additional handwriting samples from the deceased. He then took these to France, where he consulted a renowned, elderly handwriting expert, sharing the tale of the intrigues he was victim to, finally adding that "money was no object," but the family name had to be cleared of any blemish! He received a report concluding that the deceased had written the note herself. Subsequently, the young man—with his well-filled wallet!—crossed the Channel to England to find an "expert" who could attest to the authenticity of the contested epistle, which he successfully did. With this, he discussed the desirability of also consulting a few more experts on the continent to obtain similar declarations "to clear his name," after which the Englishman promised to arrange for this.

Thus, one of my colleagues in Amsterdam and I received the papers from England with a request to investigate this "simple case, as easy as child's play." To facilitate our task and expedite our report, our English colleague enclosed a copy of his already issued report. However, we did not read it but sealed the envelope containing the copy. We naturally wanted to form our own, unbiased, and completely independent judgment and each set to work. Thus, independently making a thorough study of the incriminated note, each of us soon became fully convinced that it was an artificial product. Numerous corrections, cleverly made to several letter forms, combined with countless signs of artificiality with which most letters were imitated from some example, completely dispelled any thought of authenticity.

Meanwhile, the English expert grew impatient, inquiring by phone when he could expect our report. We advised him to inspect his hands, explaining that he had significantly "cut himself," after which we were unequivocally informed that if we concluded the note was false, he would not use our joint report! The matter seemed highly dubious to us! We returned the papers and received payment for our efforts, but our detailed report did not interest him at all. I then recalled the saying "One man's loss is another man's gain" and availed of the good relations I maintained with the friendly Bundeskanzler Schober in Vienna. As president of the Académie Internationale de Criminalistique, I considered it a particular privilege to count the magistrate among the curators of our institution. He always showed great interest in our work and no less in the report that England did not want! He presented our report to the two Viennese experts, who both fully agreed with it! We had established here that the note must be absolutely false and, furthermore, pointed out a large number of handwriting characteristics that also appeared in the handwriting of the widower as distinctive features.

The case was brought up again, and shortly thereafter, the suspect admitted that he had produced the note in imitation of his wife's handwriting to clarify—in case anyone ever suspected him of poisoning his wife—that she had committed suicide. He claimed to have found his wife dead in bed with a glass smelling of cyanide beside her, became frightened, and then quickly wrote the incriminated note and placed it next to the deceased before involving the police! After our Viennese colleagues unanimously declared that they agreed with our conclusion regarding the falsity of the note and the young man admitted to having produced it, the court in Vienna accepted in its verdict that the deceased had not written the piece of writing, but her husband had. However, it did not deem this proof that he had secretly administered the poison to her! Thus, he remained free, but his reputation was far from unblemished!

Next, I hope to tell the readers about some significant cases where the "criminal poisoning" existed only in the imagination of the "victim"! It is psychologically remarkable how often individuals, fearing they will be poisoned by someone near to them, come to the police with remnants of food or drink to express their suspicions. Naturally, the police, unable to judge whether the complaint is justified, seek certainty as to whether poison is indeed present in that food sample or cup of tea. So, they send it for further investigation to their expert collaborator. Over the years, I have received quite a number of plates with leftovers or cups of coffee, tea, or milk to search for "poison"! It's easy to say, "check for poison," but the layperson must remember that hundreds of poisons of very diverse nature are known, many more poisons are still unknown to us, and detecting poison can be one of the most challenging tasks. The possibility that it may not be detected—for example, if it decomposes or disappears quickly—must always be considered. Hence, as soon as I receive the sample, I feed some of it to a couple of test animals (white mice) to observe their response. Almost always, these animals continue to live fresh and healthy, and we are convinced that the accuser was mistaken! Then, upon further investigation of the circumstances, it almost always becomes apparent that the accuser's own misconduct towards the one suspected led to the complaint. They are in such fear of revenge that they suspect the other of the worst: murder by poison!

Once, a young man of sixteen or seventeen was brought to me. Upon entering, he placed a beautiful apple on my writing desk, looked at me bewilderedly, and earnestly asked if I could examine the apple—a lovely Bellefleur—for any possible poison. I sat dumbfounded for a moment, staring at the boy—"still wet behind the ears"—and asked him what led him to believe that poison might be in this apple. He further explained how another employee at the bank, where he had a minor position, had given him this apple, something that colleague had never done before.

I suddenly posed a perhaps somewhat bold question: "Is my suspicion correct that you played some mean trick on that colleague and now expect revenge?" Blushing, he admitted that my suspicion was entirely accurate. He explained the situation in more detail, and I advised him to openly and chivalrously express his regret to his colleague and added that I would likely value that colleague more than the one sitting before me. The boy quickly packed up his apple and disappeared!

A lady living in the old city turned to the police, as she had serious suspicions that her live-in maid and her lover were repeatedly mixing poison into her lunch to kill her. The police sent me the pot of stew, but—try as I might—I could in no way detect the presence of any poison. Even the test animals, which were fed the stew, continued to live in excellent condition. I reported this in my findings, and a message was sent to the lady about the report's content. The day after receiving this notification, she again approached the police—this time with another leftover meal, because she was sure there was poison in it. She could clearly taste it! Again, I spent several days on an extensive investigation, which again yielded only negative results. This was also reported to her, and—brace yourself, Reader!—for the third time she went to the police station with a pot of food!

At that point, I expressed my serious suspicions that we were dealing with a psychopath and had the police investigate who her family doctor was. As soon as I knew his name, I inquired officially about the lady in question, but received the high-handed response that professional confidentiality(!) forbade him from discussing his patients! As if that had ever been the intention of the makers of the law! But the doctor interpreted his professional confidentiality in that way and remained silent. I foresaw, if this continued, being occupied for the entire year with the investigation of this lady's leftovers, as the police saw no solution and assured me that they could not make a decision themselves, nor dared to refrain from sending me the objects for investigation. There might actually be poison in it one day!

I approached the public prosecutor and complained about my predicament as I increasingly believed that the overwhelming workload of all these toxicological investigations was due to a maniac. But this magistrate shook his gray head and assured me that he could do nothing about it, as the doctor, when summoned, would keep quiet even in front of the public prosecutor based on professional confidentiality! I remained healthy—although indeed there was a threat of the opposite—amid so much purposeless work! Then I had a good idea, which I immediately implemented. I found one of the municipal doctors willing to examine the maniacal lady at the police station—when she was summoned there—to give me his opinion. She received a summons to come to the bureau at a specified day and time. Just as I had expected, her family doctor telephoned me, angrily asking what the reason was for summoning his patient there, to which I calmly replied that whatever it was that he could not reveal due to professional confidentiality would now be reported to me by another doctor. And he responded as if he had been bitten by a poisonous snake! "What? Another doctor attending to my patient?" And I replied matter-of-factly: "Of course, doctor! I too have the right to preserve my health!" And suddenly came the—joyful for me—news that the lady in question was a nervous patient, that I should not take her seriously, and that I could safely return any further food scraps.

I have had several similar cases; I have never calculated how much work such psychopaths have made me perform uselessly! But in the midst of all this, the necessary work continued to bring light to the police and the judiciary. From time to time, questions were posed to me such as: "Is coal gas lighter or heavier than air? Should I, to prevent danger, place a ventilation grille near the ceiling or near the floor, like the grilles in garages that are placed low because of the heavier gasoline vapors?" Chemically pure carbon monoxide has a specific gravity (compared to air!) of 0.97. However, one must not think that because of this, the deadly gases from the stove will rise! When the stove, due to the previously described conditions, lets the gases that should be vented through the chimney into the room, one should not think that chemically pure coal gas will emerge! Carbon dioxide and other combustion gases are mixed in, whose unpleasant odor occasionally alerts someone coming in from fresh air that they smell "coal gas," which is, however, not possible! Coal gas is almost odorless, and what is perceived is the mixture of combustion gases, including tar-like elements found in materials that produce smoke. And that gas mixture, which then escapes, will deviate so little in density (specific gravity) from air that it quietly mixes with it and moves with the air into the corners where the air flows. Anyone who improperly adjusts the stove on the ground floor, whose heat is then drawn via the open living room door and the staircase to the higher bedrooms, should remember that—along with the rising heated air—the toxic stove gas mixture dissolved in it can creep up to do its treacherous work there! And so it became clear to the questioner that installing ventilation grilles—whether near the ceiling or near the floor—cannot prevent the coal gas danger!

A very curious letter came from an interested party who asked me if I did not understand that I was the right person to advocate for his gas heating system! This person seemed to think that I would "just" determine that gas stoves are less dangerous than coal stoves, which can, under certain circumstances, poison our atmosphere with toxins. I refused to! Both stoves undoubtedly have their advantages and disadvantages, but it is too naive to glorify the gas stove in connection with coal gas poisoning! That "interested" reader certainly did not realize that in many municipalities, the light gas consists of one-tenth coal gas (better: carbon monoxide)! I remember from many years ago a municipality where the percentage of carbon monoxide in the supplied light gas was so high that—to counteract the great danger posed by that nearly odorless enemy—they mixed in a strongly smelling, irritating gas, so that any leak, any open tap, would immediately be revealed! Precisely because of that significant content of carbon monoxide, light gas is so dangerous.

Now that the reader has prompted me on this matter, I want to point out another danger that comes up again with every new installation, in every new construction with gas heating, as the same mistake is made everywhere. I am referring to the low placement of the gas tap for the gas fire! Why can't that tap be placed next to the fireplace mantle, well above the floor, to keep it out of the reach of small toddlers who are so eager to turn it? Then a bumping vacuum cleaner or American roller wouldn't be able to change the position of the tap lever! I remember like yesterday a case where a gas poisoning victim was found dead in bed. It was assumed, based on the silent witnesses at the scene, that the gentleman had come home late at night and had roughly taken off his shoes by partially slipping them off his feet and then kicking them away. One of the shoes supposedly hit the gas tap, turning it a quarter turn and releasing a full stream of gas into the small bedroom, turning it into an asphyxiation device!

Another reader showed special interest in what I said about galvanized sheet iron as an undesirable material for kitchenware. I'll let him have the floor for a moment to read part of his letter to me:

> In 1914, I was a conscript soldier and assigned as a cook at one of the forts. Due to a lack of cooking utensils, I asked for a feed stove, which I did not get. Instead, I was given two galvanized iron wash kettles. It so happened that on a Sunday, tutti frutti[23] was cooked. The entire garrison—including the cook—became unwell, but no one knew why. However, another day rhubarb was cooked, and again everyone became unwell, etc., etc. A scapegoat had to be found. The cook was blamed. They claimed he had put pepper in the rhubarb. No one thought that the real culprits were actually the galvanized iron wash kettles!

This case is by no means unique! Last summer, a police brigadier consulted me about his wife. She had cooked a large amount of berry juice and poured the boiling hot liquid through a cloth into a large, well-cleaned wash kettle. The beautiful red color turned a nasty purple—could that be harmful? I had to advise him to pour the entire product down the drain, as it was poisoned by dissolved zinc. It is clear that it was precisely the plant acids that immediately interacted with the zinc: applesauce, rhubarb, berry juice! And what was not visible with applesauce and rhubarb was indeed visible with the berry juice as a "warning signal": as soon as the zinc was acted on and dissolved, discoloration occurred! It is well known

---

23   Tutti frutti (from Italian *tutti i frutti*, "all fruits") is a compote made of dried fruit that is served as a dessert or a side dish to a meat course.

that many red plant dyes "shift" from purple to blue as soon as the plant acid disappears. By acting on the zinc, the acid disappeared, and the purple dye from the fruit immediately changed!

Reading one of my publications on poisons prompted a reader from The Hague to inquire about the extent to which people who work in rooms where smoking occurs daily are exposed to "smoke poisoning" (that's how the reader put it!). While reading that letter, a figure from my childhood suddenly came to mind: an old handyman in a little café where the customers, alternately belonging to the guild of cattle traders and other types of market traders, used to create a smoke so thick you could cut it with a knife with the combustion products of all forms into which the leaves of the tobacco plant can be transformed. I still see that handyman before me, as an example of eternal youth, and I cannot believe that he suffered much from the symptoms of chronic "smoke poisoning."

That doesn't mean that there aren't plenty of people whose respiratory organs are unpleasantly irritated by tobacco smoke, or whose eyelids are painfully affected when the alkaline-reacting products from that smoke act on them. For example, during fierce northeastern winds, the outdoor air on days of intense cold can be painful for the mucous membranes of many a nose without us speaking of "poisoning"! Those smoke products may have a detrimental effect on the respiratory tract of a very few individuals and may be annoying to a larger class—especially nonsmokers!—and yet I wouldn't dare, except "in committee," to speak of smoke poisoning! I know that opinions on this matter will differ, just as in so many other cases scientists disagreed on whether something is "harmful" or "not harmful." For years, there has been debate about whether traces of boric acid (which, although prohibited, were occasionally added to butter to prevent it from going rancid) were indeed harmful to health, in other words, somewhat "poisonous."

The same happened when the question was asked, "Is saccharin harmful to our health or not?" Some gave little thought to this question and simply declared saccharin harmful because whoever uses this non-nutritive chemical substance to sweeten their foods or beverages instead of using sugar, consumes less nutritious substance. But this did not provide a definitive answer to the question posed! Anyone who thinks that a chemist can determine whether boric acid, saccharin, or any other substance is harmful to health by experimenting in a test tube is completely mistaken! The chemist can detect substances generally known as "poisons" and, based on the presence of one or another recognized poisonous substance, can issue a veto. Drinking water in which traces of zinc are found, the chemist declares harmful—potentially poisonous—because the harmful, poisonous effects of most so-called heavy metals are well known and recognized. But he does not establish the toxicity of such harmful metal, no! He knows that toxicity identifies the presence of that poisonous substance here or there, and therefore declares the latter article harmful, or poisonous!

But it is much more complicated and difficult to determine whether an arbitrary substance, which does not yet appear on the "poison list," is harmful or harmless. When this was a hot topic issue with boric acid, a fierce polemic arose. Rightly so, the inspection services, which are responsible for public health, took a negative stance, and seemed to reason thus: if I were to receive butter at my breakfast in which the manufacturer had mixed a tiny trace of boric acid in the interest of shelf life; if I then spread my bread with jam, in which the manufacturer—again for preservation!—had dissolved a small amount of salicylic acid; and if I then—to be consistent—had to tolerate even a single drop of preservative in the milk, because otherwise it would sour so quickly in the scorching hot season, then with such a breakfast I would receive a neat collection of preservatives! I know very well how countless housewives, in the season when their garden yields an abundance of strawberries, currants, and raspberries, make jams themselves. When they lack the opportunity to properly sterilize the closed jars of jam—as is done in large jam factories—they all too often resort to adding (sometimes far too large amounts of) salicylic acid (or benzoic acid) to the jam to prevent it from being attacked by yeast cells or mold! But not everyone knows why these preservatives are detrimental to our health.

Our digestive system is designed to make the consumed foods digestible and to absorb the sugar-like (and other) substances formed therein into our blood, in order to "burn" them in that form during muscle work and so on. A very important function in this digestive process is performed by the collective bacteria, which live inside the intestinal walls and ensure the necessary conversions of the food, and I would be inclined to say: lucky is he who harbors a brilliant bacterial flora in his digestive tract! As soon as foods or consumables are used in which preservatives are incorporated—with no other purpose than to prevent any life of bacteria (and other microorganisms) in them—then it should come as no surprise that those same bacteria-killing substances will just as well launch a destructive action against the bacteria of our intestinal flora. Many rheumatic patients have experienced how their digestion suffered as soon as they followed a salicylic acid treatment for their ailment, and how new concerns arose for restoring the disturbed balance in the relevant department of their interior! But—someone will inevitably ask—how can one then ascertain with certainty whether, for example, boric acid is harmful to health?

I remember a large-scale experiment conducted at one of the major American institutions, where, for that purpose, an advertisement was placed in the newspapers, asking people to come and live at the institution for a few months. This opportunity was only open to those who, after a strict physical examination, were found suitable and were willing to contractually commit themselves to consume exclusively the food and beverages provided "on-site" and to refrain from consuming anything outside. Then the "guinea pigs" were given precisely measured and weighed amounts of food and drink for six weeks. Those with a larger appetite received more, provided the accounting could accurately record the quantities consumed. Efforts were made to maintain the body weight of these individuals (as one person might need to consume more food than another, depending on the kind of work they did!). Anyone who lost weight or gained too much was sent away, leaving a select group of individuals who—while consuming the predetermined amounts of food for each—maintained a constant body weight.

Once this stage was reached, the boarders—without their knowledge!—were gradually and regularly given small amounts of boric acid mixed into their food, with daily monitoring carried out just as rigorously to see how body weight, heart rate, and many other functions behaved under the influence of these small amounts of ingested boric acid. Thus, the answer to the question: "harmful or harmless?" could be determined. One can see that such a puzzle cannot easily be solved! But silent homage is paid to the men of science who—having the means to cover the costs of such experiments—courageously solve the problems that arise in the field of public health!

In February 1933, the Justice Department gave me a quack remedy called Radium Drops for examination. A thief—being held in pretrial detention—had claimed that his tendency to kleptomania was awakened by using these drops!! Unfortunately for him, I could not share that opinion!

Epilogue by Maarten Blom

This is a very lengthy chapter composed of many substories. It is a mixed bag of explanations, anecdotes, and cautionary tales on about every aspect related to the singular word that forms the crux of this chapter: Poison! The topics covered are very wide-ranging: from food decay to the dangers of improperly burning stoves, the importance of accurately labeling medicines, and presenting criminal case examples of poisoning. It is as if Co van Ledden Hulsebosch held a long brainstorming session with himself, elaborating each sticky note into a distinct section, and then seamlessly weaving them together with his sweeping style of writing. Given the mosaic-like nature of this chapter I found writing an epilogue to it quite a challenge. More so than in any other chapter, there seems to be so much in the mind of van Ledden Hulsebosch here that we still can connect with today, in particular, his attention to the interplay between the chemico-physical properties of poison and their effects in the human body and his awareness of the complexity of toxicological casework. Therefore, I would invite the reader to simply enjoy being taken on the journey of this chapter. I am sure you will appreciate its meandering path and be amazed by the power of some of his analogies, for example, to explain the microbial and chemical processes of something as commonplace as food decay.

23. How the Mysterious Thefts in Professor Saltet's Laboratory Were Solved

Since my youth, Professor Saltet and I knew each other through his friendship with my father. He had seen me grow up during my high school years; later, as a university student, I had worked in his laboratory; and when I found my calling, he would often come to me to see my latest gadgets in the field of criminology. And I was always struck by the man's wonderfully cheerful mood, his bonhomie, and his unforgettable laugh when he was truly delighted!

One day, he came to me again, and immediately I noticed from his overly serious face and sad mood that something was going on. In a few words, he told me. There were increasingly audacious thefts occurring in his large laboratory on the Mauritskade. No valuable items could be left in any clothing hanging in the cloakroom. Even a valuable microscope belonging to one of the assistants had disappeared without a trace the previous week. Once again being succinct, the professor concluded his story with a desperate cry: "We are literally being devoured by the thieves."

He had already had a couple of detectives involved from the nearby Muiderpoort police station, but they had failed to solve the mystery, and, in the meantime, the audacious thefts continued, even in broad daylight! He insisted that I help him find the thief, to which I gladly offered my assistance. However, I made it a condition that I would first, without anyone noticing, be able to assess the situation in the laboratory building, which was still new to me. This would only be possible on a Sunday afternoon when the entire building could be assumed to be empty. Professor Saltet would ask his assistant, Miss v. R., to wait for me at a side entrance on the upcoming Sunday afternoon at a designated time. Miss v. R. had a key to that side door, so she could easily show me the rooms where the various thefts had occurred in recent months.

So, as agreed, I was at the designated location at the right moment, and Miss v. R. immediately led me to the first floor, where the professor's office, the library, the librarian's room, and a couple of study rooms were located. In an adjacent room, where all the current issues of various journals were collected, there was a large table where everything was sorted and recorded before being placed in the spacious cabinets. A young employee usually worked in this section, a lively boy of sixteen, agile, courteous, and charming, and as a result, a real "darling child" of the professor, assistants, and laboratory staff. He was always willing to go the extra mile, fetching a bottle of milk for them during lunchtime, buying a box of cigarettes for another, and everyone gladly deducted a small amount from the settlement to give to that nice boy.

However, as Miss v. R. told me, they had just obtained evidence two days earlier that this boy did not adhere too strictly to the principles of honesty. He had been given a piece of paper with the text of a telegram consisting of thirteen words destined for the Dutch East Indies. He had been given more money than necessary for sending the telegram. Upon his return, he calculated the cost of fourteen words and accurately recited the text with fourteen words, making everyone almost believe him. However, he had cleverly inserted a fourteenth word with a slight change of phrasing and did not realize that a carbon copy of the typed note that had been given to him was left behind! They apparently decided not to confront him directly with his fraud and let him believe that they accepted his explanations.

I was delighted to hear this because now there was a greater chance that if he was the perpetrator of the various thefts, he would boldly continue his work, confident that there was no suspicion on him, the nice and "honest"(!) boy. Connected to this room was the office where, at a pedestal desk, the secretary used to work. Money had also disappeared from that desk during the past week, which had been left unattended for a few moments for the purpose of paying the caretaker for sandwiches and coffee. As we walked through the quiet, wide corridor, Miss v. R. led me to the professor's office to show me that as well. Suddenly, my guide turned pale … she had heard footsteps in a side corridor! Impulsively, before I fully understood, she pushed me into an open wardrobe. It would be too absurd if she were found with a man in the otherwise completely deserted building on a Sunday afternoon! The corridor door, which had been slightly ajar, was pushed open, and there appeared the caretaker, who, upon realizing that "someone" was in the building, wanted to confirm the visitor's identity. "Oh, it's you, Miss," and after a brief greeting, he turned around and went back to his private quarters.

I was extremely grateful when Miss v. R. opened the closet door again and released me, as the atmosphere had gradually become somewhat suffocating, and I had great difficulty suppressing an impending sneeze. I had thus had the opportunity to orient myself well and made an arrangement with my guide that I would send her a wallet with marked money—guilders and *rijksdaalders*[24]—which she would deposit on the corner of the secretary's desk. I emphasized to her that she must not open the wallet under any circumstances. She should leave it there for a day, then put it away for another day, and then place it again as bait in the designated spot. She should immediately call me if anything was missing from its contents. "But if I'm not allowed to open the wallet, how can I be sure that something has been

---

24   The guilder (*gulden* in Dutch) was a type of coinage used in the Netherlands from the Middle Ages until 2002. The value of a guilder in 1930 would, corrected for inflation, be about ten euros today. Similarly, the *rijksdaalder* (introduced in 1840 to represent two and a half guilders) would amount to about twenty-five euros today.

taken out?" asked the somewhat nervous assistant, to which I reassuringly replied, "I won't leave the money near the letter scale for nothing." By weighing it—its total weight was known to her!—she could immediately determine the weight loss and ascertain what was missing from the contents based on the fact that a guilder weighs ten grams and a *rijksdaalder* weighs twenty-five grams!

Three or four days passed without incident. Had the thief sensed something and refrained from taking the bait? On Friday, I had to travel outside the city to attend a court hearing, and because I didn't want to risk needing to return immediately that day, I had the still intact purse with money locked away for another day. Then Saturday came. Just as the clock struck twelve, my phone rang. The voice of Miss v. R. sounded like an urgent cry, "Oh, all the money has disappeared.... Can you come immediately?" I promised to come to her right away by taxi and strongly emphasized that all external doors of the building should be locked to prevent anyone from leaving the laboratory. The sudden blocking of all exits was naturally a matter of great significance. Everyone had to accept it—there was nothing that could be changed.

Upstairs, in the vestibule on the first floor, a crowd of assistants, students, and auxiliary staff gathered around Miss v. R., who struggled to provide satisfying answers to everyone's questions. Meanwhile, I had arrived ... and before Miss v. R. could fully comprehend it, I suddenly stood before her in the upper vestibule. "But how on earth did you get in? All the doors are locked?"—"Indeed, Miss, but during my orientation, I noticed that there was still a route that you wouldn't consider now, namely through the large coal shed and past the caretaker's residence!" But I needed to act quickly and, with confidence in success, I entered the previously described journal room of the library, where the "nice" boy seemed to be working alone.

He apparently didn't recognize me and, fully aware of his position as an assistant librarian, stood upright, asking, "How can I help, sir?" To which I bluntly replied, that I wanted to speak with him because I need information regarding the mysterious disappearance of valuable items in this vicinity. "But then, you shouldn't be the one I'm talking to. Why did you turn to me?" I calmly answered: "Because I know that you are a little thief." (I had the carbon copy of the telegram sent to the Dutch East Indies, along with the receipt written by the boy, in my hand.) I identified myself, stating that I wanted to search him, to which he willingly and confidently submitted. No money emerged from any of his pockets. I found that quite peculiar since I had learned that the staff—those receiving a weekly wage—were paid fifteen minutes before twelve on Saturdays. So, he didn't have that pay with him either, and I thought to myself, if he had hidden or somehow embezzled that pay, the stolen money could have been concealed along the same route. However, I showed no signs of surprise, making him feel even more confident that the failure to find the stolen money would exonerate him. But I wasn't finished inspecting his clothing since I hadn't made him take off his shoes yet, so I instructed him to remove his footwear as well. Then, to my surprise, as he took off his boots, a stream of quarters and dimes rolled onto the floor! They hadn't been in the wallet with the marked money! When I asked for an explanation, the boy replied that it was the money he had to keep for a friend, to which I couldn't help but comment that I found it a highly peculiar hiding place for someone else's money!

As he put his shoes back on, kneeling on the floor, I placed a photographic developing tray containing a quantity of fresh plate developer in front of him; with a questioning look on his face, I explained that he needed to wet his fingers in that liquid for a moment. Suddenly, his fingers turned pitch black … which prompted him to conceal them in his fist, thinking that I hadn't seen it. When I asked why his fingers were so black, the "nice" boy had another ready answer. He had been assembling a batch of new lantern slides for the professor in recent days, and the black strips he had to use for framing had left black marks! Silently, I watched as he walked over to the sink in the corner, took the bar of soap, and vigorously washed his hands, revealing that the black discolorations were spreading along the entire length of his fingers. Then I knew enough! "Now get dressed quickly; the charade is over. You have those black fingers because of the substance I sprinkled in powder form on the money in the wallet. You are now in my custody because you stole the money from that wallet. Where did you hide it?" He was trapped—he realized it in an instant—and gave up! Before twelve o'clock, he had handed over all the stolen money, along with his weekly wages, to a friend that had been waiting for him near the front door, as agreed, and it must by now be hidden behind his bed at home! The reader will have understood that I had poured a powder into the wallet. The powder adhered to the thief's skin, while the liquid (photographic developer) turned the contaminated areas pitch black.

Epilogue by Bas Kokshoorn: Every Contact Leaves a Trace

It was Dr. Edmond Locard (director of the Laboratoire de Police Technique de Lyon, and a contemporary of Dr. Co van Ledden Hulsebosch) who in his *L'enquête criminelle et les méthodes scientifiques* (Criminal investigation and scientific methods, 1920) proposed the principle that is now named after him (Locard's exchange principle):

> The clues that I want to show the use of here are of two types: sometimes the perpetrator has left behind traces of their presence at the scene, and sometimes, through an opposite action, they have carried away on their body or clothes the evidence of their stay or their act.

Dr. van Ledden Hulsebosch describes an example here where a powder was "planted" at a scene, which was subsequently carried away from that scene by the offender. More often in forensic casework we focus on the first type of traces; those left by the offender at the scene. With respect to those traces, Dr. Locard stated: "It is impossible for a criminal to act, especially considering the intensity of the crime, without leaving traces of this presence." With the tremendously increased sensitivity and specificity of the analysis methods that are currently employed in the forensic fields, forensic scientists have been able to detect and analyze those minute traces with ever greater efficacy. However, the relevance of the traces, defined as their ability to assist in the reconstruction of the events, has become less clear.

As well as it being impossible for the offender to act without leaving traces, so is it for all of us during our daily lives. Hence the relation between minute traces and the criminal act is uncertain. These developments have prompted ever more research into the dynamics of traces. Under what conditions do they transfer (and are we able to detect them), how may they persist over time under adverse conditions, and what is the prevalence of the traces of interest in the environment? In Amsterdam—particular at the Amsterdam University of Applied Sciences—we study forensic trace dynamics under case relevant conditions. We must realize that there is no such thing as a "silent witness" (a term frequently used to designate forensic traces) and that the traces and their integrity may be affected by actions and environmental conditions prior to, during, and after the incident we are interested in. This includes the forensic investigation itself in which traces may be lost or relocated due to actions performed by the examiners at the crime scene, during packaging, transport, and storage of exhibits, or during the examination in the laboratory. Our research in this area will allow us to have these not so silent witnesses tell us their proper story.

24. A Lame Student Joke, for Which Heavy Penalties Were Paid

As a former student of the University of Amsterdam, I always enjoyed occasionally meeting my professors in later years. This could often happen as I, being a member of the Society for Natural, Medical, and Surgical Sciences, would encounter them alternately in section meetings. Among them, Professor Sissingh, my old teacher, always held a special place in my esteem, and I found him particularly likable. This sentiment had always been the case, and precisely for that reason, I would get annoyed when certain students took pleasure in teasing the humane mentor. They would either start inappropriate applause when one of the physics experiments failed or make untimely interruptions during his lectures.

Even in the years after my student days, this behavior persisted. The professor's kindness was shamelessly abused through various disruptions, as if dealing with a class of mischievous schoolboys wanting to "bully" a disliked teacher. It must have been about a decade after leaving the university when Professor Sissingh visited me seeking help in a peculiar matter. "Two weeks ago," the professor began, "I had, as usual, started early in the morning preparing experiments for my lecture, which, as in your time, takes place from eleven to twelve. It was already past eleven, and not a single student had entered the lecture hall. Assuming they might be delayed in the chemistry class, I patiently waited. At a quarter past eleven, I instructed the assistant to check whether the outside door was locked, preventing anyone from entering. I soon learned that a note was pinned to the outer door, reading: "Professor Sissingh is unable to give a lecture today." I need not describe my feelings when I had all the apparatus packed up and stored again. The next day, I said nothing about it during the lecture, and the matter would have been forgotten by me soon, if it weren't for this morning, where a similar note was again attached to the outer door. As a result, I spent the entire morning working in vain, and no one entered the lecture hall. I have brought these two pieces of paper with me; the handwriting is evidently the same. On behalf of the board of curators (*college van curatoren*), I come to ask you to find out who the author of these notes is."

I hesitated for a moment before promising to accept such a task, with a doubtful chance of success. I emphasized that success would only be possible if the notes were written by one of the students and I could obtain handwriting samples from practically all students as "comparison material." The professor agreed, and I suggested that, on one of the last classes before the holidays, both he and his colleagues should collect all the lecture notes, perhaps under the pretext of examining the note-taking methods. This promise was fulfilled. However, I had no idea what that entailed until one day a porter, escorted by Professor Sissingh's trusted assistant, delivered three large crates to me, filled from top to bottom with lecture notes! It promised to be a lot of work.

My first task was to conduct a complete graphological analysis of the handwriting on the two notes, which I studied for so long that I could imprint the image in my memory. Then the sorting process began. Many of the samples that absolutely could not be considered as being by the culprit were set aside, while a smaller collection of notebooks piled up on the other side, exhibiting handwriting with one or more dominating features of the incriminated notes. After that, with greater interest, I sifted through them again, resulting in three handwriting samples that, in turn, underwent a complete handwriting analysis. It then became glaringly evident which notebook among the three belonged to the guilty party.

When conducting an investigation, the outcome of which could have such significant consequences for the accused, I, like a general practitioner, feel a certain responsibility. I presented my findings to the professor, informing him that I had concluded who the author of the notes was. However, I requested permission to have my results verified by a colleague, which was immediately granted. After a thorough check, my colleague confirmed that he was also convinced of the identified author, and he noted this in the comprehensive report I submitted to the faculty. The board of curators set a date for the meeting at which the implicated student was to appear. The beadle, who, I heard for the first time on this occasion, also has a position equivalent to a bailiff, summoned the "suspect" in that capacity. I was also asked to attend the meeting.

I was given a seat of honor at the green table next to the chairman. It did not take long for the student I had pointed out to enter the room—truly with a certain quasi-indifference and an attitude of "well, who cares?" The two notes were presented to him with the question, "Do you recognize these notes?" to which he immediately responded with a smile, "Yes, I saw those on the outer door of the physics laboratory when there was no lecture." Don't you know them for any other reason?... No?... You must have written them otherwise." "Who claims that?" came sharply from his lips, and I—perhaps a bit boldly—immediately gave my brief answer to that question: "I do." "How do you come to that conclusion? It's not true." I then made the following statement: "Although I am convinced for myself that you are the author of these notes—I am willing to give you the opportunity to convince me of a possible mistake. If my conclusion is incorrect, I will not hesitate to reconsider it and offer you my apologies, although we are far from that point now!"

I had placed writing materials on the table in front of the accused and encouraged him to write a few lines for the gentlemen while dictating. He agreed to do so. As soon as he dipped the pen in ink and assumed a posture to start writing, I explicitly requested him not to write in any other way than he was accustomed to, to avoid misleading. A puzzled look and the question: "What do you mean? I write as I always do!" I had to firmly contradict that. From the many handwriting samples his lecture notes had shown me, I could determine with absolute certainty that he was accustomed to handling the pen in a formal manner, whereas now he let the pen rest between his index and middle fingers, the tip strongly turned to the right. He resisted for a moment, then complied, assuming a posture that betrayed irritation. But at least he now held the pen in his usual way.

During the dictation, several proper nouns with capital letters appeared, and I could immediately determine how he gave these capital letters distinctive forms.... They were fanciful forms! When I made a comment in this direction, he claimed—against better knowledge!—that he always formed these capital letters in this way (and these forms bore no resemblance to those of the two notes). However, I had the lecture notes at hand, made him acknowledge that these notes were written by himself and by no one else, and easily convinced the learned gentlemen that the writer now gave different, bizarre forms to the same capital letters. In short, he was caught red-handed!

He continued to deny his guilt, although the attitude he adopted was highly unsympathetic and dishonest. The chairman frankly stated that this experiment had only underscored the expert's conclusion, and the meeting now had the fullest conviction that no one but he was the author of the two notes. He was allowed to leave the assembly. This student did not wait for the University of Amsterdam's punishment. A week later, he had enrolled as a student at another university to continue his studies there!

Epilogue by Ruben Kranenburg

In this chapter, Co van Ledden Hulsebosch discusses his involvement as an expert in handwriting analysis. This illustrates his versatility: in addition to being a chemist, detective, and pharmacist, he was also experienced in this field. Handwriting comparison has been crucial in forensic investigation for many years. However, with increasing digitization, handwritten material is becoming less common, reducing its relevance in criminal cases. Consequently, the Netherlands Forensic Institute has scaled down expertise in this area in recent years. Another interesting aspect in this chapter is the connection between investigation and science in van Ledden Hulsebosch's work. Throughout his career, he recognized the importance of collaboration with the scientific community. In this chapter, he mentions regularly attending the university as a member of a scientific society. Later in his career, he cherished the connection with the university when he obtained a *privaatdocent* (guest lecturer) position at the University of Amsterdam (UvA). In this regard, he also was a pioneer. An interesting parallel can be seen in the current Co van Ledden Hulsebosch Institute, which is also based at UvA and aims to promote collaboration between forensic science and academia. Nowadays, such collaboration is valued, as evidenced by several extraordinary professor positions and lectureships associated with experts from the Netherlands Forensic Institute (NFI) at universities in the Netherlands. My own appointment as a research associate at UvA, in addition to my position as scientist at the police also is a prime example of this collaboration.

25. The Dishonest Postal Worker

It is usually one of the most difficult problems—once a theft has been committed at the post office—to find out exactly who the culprit is. This is undoubtedly the reason why it often takes a relatively long time before the culprit is found from among the multitude of officials in whose midst the perpetrator is supposed to reside. To this extent, the following case may almost be called unique, especially in view of the speed with which the thief was found.

Here is what happened. At the X bank in Amsterdam, in the late afternoon, part of the staff was busy preparing the postal items, which would soon be brought to the main post office by one of the clerks, and which were deposited in two piles: one for ordinary mail and the other for the items which had money in them, to be sent by registered mail. The clerk, who gathered everything together and took it to the main post, did not—once there—split the stacked letters quite correctly, in the sense that he mistakenly added the bottom letter of the top stack—the pieces to be registered—to the ordinary letters and made it disappear into the slot of an ordinary letterbox.

That letter was addressed to a private individual living in a small municipality in South Holland, which I will call Y. This addressee did not in fact get the letter in question delivered to his home. Instead, he received the familiar "notification" of the arrival of a registered letter and, to collect it, he made his way to the post office after enjoying his breakfast. First of all, he was informed there that the letter bore the inscription "Indicated value 250 guilders." The arrival or this letter in the bag of "ordinary" mail caused a stir and so it was "protected" by adding it to the other registered mail. This attention led to an increase in postage, or a penalty of thirty cents, for the addressee. Although the addressee knew that the letter should have been delivered to his home, and directly into his hands, he appreciated how this lost sheep was taken care of. He paid his penalty postage and the letter was handed over to him.

Hardly had he looked at it closely, when he discovered strange things along the flap edge of the envelope.... He suspected the money had been stolen from the letter and expressed his fears to the lady who had spoken to him when it was being handed over. The latter explained how the postal item—without being registered!—had been put in an ordinary letterbox and how at the arrival office, after discovering this mistake, they had done what they could by adding the letter to the registered mail from then on. "But please open the letter in my presence," said the postal worker, "so we can see whether the value mentioned on the address side is still in the envelope."

This happened, and with dismay the interested party discovered that the 250 guilders was missing; only the "accompanying" letter was present! This caused some commotion.... The local police were called. Not only did the village policeman immediately come to the post office, but the mayor himself—as chief of police—appeared on the scene to take charge of the investigation. He was told what mistake had been made and all kinds of possibilities were discussed. It could well be that an unfaithful employee at the X bank had deliberately deposited the letter with the money already removed and with the letter having a "battered" appearance, into an ordinary letterbox. Otherwise, at the large post office in Amsterdam, amidst the many sorters, one could easily have discovered that there was a bonus containing 250 guilders in the ordinary post.

To be on the safe side, the mayor phoned the X bank in Amsterdam during his investigation to explain what had been found there, and here, too, they considered the possibility that one of the large bank staff could be guilty of the theft. After the fact had been made known at the bank, it had attracted the attention of some superiors, that one lady, who had to enclose the banknotes in the letters, was "acting very nervous," from which some people thought they had to draw a conclusion, all too hastily, less favorable to her! (Afterwards, it turned out that the poor woman was shocked when she heard that the banknotes had disappeared, yet had absolutely nothing to do with it!)

In the meantime, the aforementioned mayor had conducted a detailed interview on the spot with all persons who had had anything to do with the transportation of the mail: the delivery man, who had taken delivery of the mail bags at the train; the person who had accepted the mail, unpacked the bags, and sorted the contents, all of which had taken place the previous evening; and, finally, the lady who had handed the letter to the addressee. Then he closed his statement of interrogation and sent it with the *corpus delicti* to Amsterdam ... where the thief would no doubt have to be sought. The section office, within whose jurisdiction the X bank was located, received the documents from Y, after which they were placed in the hands of one of the detectives for further "handling." He too was slightly inclined to think that the thief was probably to be found at the Amsterdam post office.

The detective came to talk to me. He presented me with the robbed envelope and scornfully remarked: "If I have to look for the thief at the main post office, I will not be finished for a while." Finding little support from me for this assertion, he added, laughing: "It's like when you accidentally fall into an anthill in your swimming trunks and get stung and then try to find out which ant is to blame." In the meantime, I had taken the torn-open envelope in my hand and when my visitor asked me: "What do you advise me to do now?" I replied shortly: "Go for a fifteen-minute walk and leave me alone with this silent witness for a while. I want to try to get him to talk ... and I hope to tell you on your return what information I got!"

He left, and stood in front of me again exactly fifteen minutes later. "That envelope told me everything!" I could tell him. "Quickly prepare a travel ticket to Y. Go there as soon as possible. Inquire who was there, at the post office, yesterday and had the early shift at the beginning of the day.... Arrest that person—that's the culprit!" Without asking for a letter or any explanation, he said, "Yes, sir!," ended the conversation, and left.

By the first opportunity, the detective traveled to Y, where—as required—he began reporting to the chief of police, the mayor, who asked him, more or less astonished, what he had come to do now.... "Arrest the culprit, Mayor!" "Where did you get that idea? You should be looking for him in Amsterdam and not here!" "The one who had the early morning shift at the post office here must have committed the theft, our expert assured me." "What? But how can he know that? Did he perhaps recognize fingerprints?" "Look, Mayor. I have no time to waste and there was therefore no opportunity for me to ask for an explanation. I will get it later. The main issue was made known to me and I was ordered to arrest the guilty person here." "You're not arresting anyone here. Interrogate, for all I care, the person in question, if you like. It's a miss, a girl from a good family."

The detective decided immediately to seize the opportunity offered and was given the postmaster's room for his interrogation. As soon as the miss in question entered the room, the director left. As I heard later, the young lady had from the start given off a certain air, somewhere between astonishment, shock, and self-consciousness, sometimes leaning towards the impertinent. With exemplary composure, the detective confronted the young lady and—based on his full confidence in my statements—he deliberately did not ask her if she could give him any information about the content of the letter in question, but suddenly burst in with the question: "How did you come to commit this theft?," thus showing his firm conviction, his knowledge of her guilt.

At first the lady seemed to want to burst with rage. She then changed her mind, however. The calmness with which the policeman told her that she, and no one else, had robbed the letter overwhelmed her. And his next question, asked when he had discovered an engagement ring on her hand, was, "Did you perhaps do it to help your fiancée?" At that, the sky suddenly clouded over and a fierce sobbing broke out. She reached into the top of her blouse, after which she put the remaining 175 of the looted 250 guilders on the table in front of him! A little later—when the official statement had been prepared and signed—the mayor entered, still amazed at the certainty with which I had made my statement and at the same time curious as to how I could have known all this. His mood did not improve when the detective had to disappoint him, saying that he himself did not know either how the empty envelope had clarified everything for the expert. Then everyone had to know how I had found out, and I had a good time telling all the curious in the first place, how simple it had been for me, and expressing my surprise that no one else had seen those clues.

My "explanation of the riddle" was the following: That envelope had apparently been opened by the flap having been worked loose in order to get the contents out. When the envelope had to be closed again, they used a lick of gum, smeared on the outer edge of the flap, after which the flap was closed and the edge pressed, to make the glue adhere better. While pressing, a small surplus of the thick adhesive squeezed out from under the edge in three places and later dried into a miniature sausage, shiny-brown. Yes, I immediately admitted that these bulges were very, very small, but ... I still had my loupe—even several loupes of different strength—in my pocket and walked with the aided eye along the flap rim, in order to observe everything that could be noticed. In doing so, my gaze met those three pieces of dried sticky matter. "Nothing unusual," I hear you say. No, Reader, of course and very common, I admit, but I also saw one important thing during that walk along the above-mentioned edge: at the office of arrival—i.e., at Y—the letter, as a "registered document," had been given the round stamp on the back, which showed when the letter had been "processed" there. And this imprint showed not only the name of the place with date and year—but also the further indication of time: 6–7 am. (Nowadays the letters am and pm are superfluous, since they are now counted such that the indication 7 pm is 19.)

And now my attention was drawn to that one sticky particle that ran across the number 7 of the stamp! It was obvious that first the stamp had been printed on the letter and that later the sticky substance had flowed over the "7." So the theft had to have taken place in the post office at Y; otherwise the black stamp ink would have been on top of the glue! Whoever heard the solution, nodded his head in agreement and said: "Yes, of course!," fully admitting to me that it really hadn't been that complicated and difficult—which, by the way, is what I've always maintained. Detective work and deduction are simple: infer from what can be observed!

It's too bad that most people do look but don't see!

Epilogue by Charles Berger

Theft from mail is a phenomenon that is probably as old as the concept of mail itself. While the amount of money that is sent by mail will be much less these days, small amounts of money mean that such small thefts are generally not investigated, and will continue.

Co van Ledden Hulsebosch clearly rejoices in his observational powers, his inferential prowess, and in others guessing how he did it. His confidence even brings him to order an arrest, something that surely was not part of his responsibilities. Timing is a notoriously difficult problem in criminalistics, because the actual passage of time is almost never what really matters, but everything that did or could have happened within that time is. Determining the order in which things happened is luckily enough sometimes, as in the case described here. The ability to do so depends on the physical overlap of, in this case, the timed stamp and the glue used to reseal the envelope. The problem is quite similar to determining the order in which overlapping writing was produced, or the printing and signature of a contract. Care should be taken in inferring the order in time from the physical appearance of the materials. In, for example, a laser-printed contract where a signature overlaps part of the print, you would expect to find the thick ink of a ballpoint pen on top of the toner of the print, if the print was there before the signature. But if a thinner ink—such as from a fineliner—was used, the ink might easily permeate right through the toner, and settle in the paper. Someone scratching away the toner and finding the ink underneath might wrongly infer that the ink of the signature was there before the toner from the print.

26. How the First Lamp for Ultraviolet Ray Investigation Came to Our Country

During the tumultuous years of World War I, when our small country swarmed with spies from all warring nations, a dedicated division of our police force was tasked with keeping a watchful eye on these gentlemen (and ladies!), scrutinizing their every move. The chief of this counter-espionage unit occasionally sought my assistance, whether for examining documents for potential invisible ink messages (written with so-called sympathetic ink) or addressing other inquiries.

One day, the leader of the counter-espionage service approached me with a typical stiff linen collar and recounted the following story: Spies from a certain power, armed with entirely fake Dutch passports, attempted to gain access to enemy territory by posing as Dutch citizens. Even if successful, authorities remained highly suspicious of these guests, prohibiting them, for instance, from bringing flacons of hair or tooth water or bottles of "medicines" for fear that they might contain invisible—sympathetic—ink. This ink could be used to convey messages in invisible writing on otherwise innocuous correspondence, which the censor would not object to allowing through. No moisture was to be brought in; even a damp sponge, neatly carried in a rubber sponge bag in a traveler's luggage, would be thoroughly washed out before it could be taken along!

Initially, I found such fears amusing, but later it became abundantly clear that there was ample reason for concern. At that time, I knew more than when the stiff collar was brought to me! To illustrate, I was told how the spy, once in enemy territory, had to manipulate his special collar. He would cut it in half, soak one half in a glass of water overnight, and the next morning, the watery extract, containing everything drawn from the collar, became the "secret" ink. With this solution, he would write on a sheet of writing paper crosswise—along lines running from bottom to top—using a new pen with caution. Once everything dried, no traces of writing were visible. If the pen choice had been less favorable and was somewhat stiff, pen furrows might form, potentially revealing the deception. In such cases, the spy had to take a new glass of water and add as much ammonia as needed to induce a sensation when the liquid was held under his eyes! Using this diluted ammonia, the paper surface had to be gently wiped with a cotton ball before hanging the paper to dry again. This would eliminate all pen furrows, leaving no evidence of the presence of secret writing!

Naturally, I treated the collar handed to me strictly "according to the recipe," producing not only invisible writing but also subjecting it to chemical analysis to uncover the extraordinary substances applied to the collar. I still regret that I failed to unveil the secret. I attempted every conceivable method I knew to make the self-applied secret writing visible, but to no avail. Moreover, the liquid, meticulously examined as it was, behaved like pure water, with only slight traces of starch from the collar suspended in it. I could detect no foreign or peculiar substance whatsoever, leading me to disappoint my client by stating that I could not unravel the mystery.

A few weeks later, this chief walked into my office once again, presenting me with ... a shoelace, which undoubtedly contained the preparation for making secret ink. With this as well, I embarked on the task, but unfortunately, with just as little success. It was terribly frustrating not to achieve a positive result and found myself ... well, Reader, you can fill in the blanks!

Months and years passed, and the end of the war had arrived. Alongside many other things, the service of international trains gradually resumed, and it didn't take long before I fulfilled a long-cherished intention to visit my Parisian colleague Bayle—an excellent physicist and criminologist—convinced that he had much important information to share. I visited him at his large, well-equipped laboratory, where I always marveled at the sophisticated research methods Bayle designed and the equally refined apparatus, he "simply ordered" (the payment was covered by the government! In contrast, since 1902, I have had to finance all my instrument purchases from my modest private purse; neither the state nor the city contributed a single cent!).

On the second day of my visit to Bayle's laboratory, he began to tell me about special investigations he had conducted with stiff collars and shoelaces. I jumped from my chair and declared my extreme curiosity about whether he had succeeded in finding anything in the collar or lace—honestly admitting that I had made unsuccessful attempts to do so. I still recall his friendly smile when I made this confession, and he consoled me:

> Don't be embarrassed, dear colleague I know from reliable sources that the person who prepared this "secret ink"—keeping his recipe strictly confidential!—sent a collar and a shoelace to all the chemical professors of all the universities in his country. They were instructed from higher authorities to look for any foreign material that could serve as secret ink, and ... none of them could discover that secret. if you were unsuccessful as well, consider that you are in "good company," and don't hold your Parisian colleague, who did succeed, too high, for I stumbled upon it purely by chance!

For readers who comprehend the scientific side of the matter, I want to provide a brief explanation here. Bayle possessed a splendid quartz spectrograph worth thousands of guilders. He used it to create line spectra of all "unknown" substances, placing a small pinch of them in the hollowed tip of one of the carbon rods of a projectile lamp. On the detailed photograph of the numerous spectral lines of these emission spectra, he would then group and identify all the lines. He had evaporated the solution obtained from the collar and shoelace and then placed the residue in the hollowed crater of a carbon rod in his carbon arc lamp. In this way, he later discovered the spectral lines of the rare element Vanadium ... and gradually determined that the articles in question had absorbed minimal traces of an organic vanadium compound! I had to confess that I had never encountered the element vanadium. I had never performed identity reactions on it either.

However, the inevitable question arose: "How are the writing lines made with a weak watery extract of that vanadium product made visible?" "I will show you immediately," replied Bayle, "but first, let's enter my darkened laboratory, where I currently conduct various interesting experiments in darkness." He briefly turned on the electric light and showed me an actual spy letter—seemingly very innocent, a heartfelt note from a niece to her dear aunt with delightful chitchat about everything and anything. But after a few moments, I saw—after turning off the light—how the same letter, which lay before me on the table, began to glow remarkably. Right next to it stood a mysterious box, from which a magical, hazy, dark violet-colored light shone on the letter. Across the ordinary ink writing, luminous light blue lines of the secret writing became readable ... phenomenal!

Remnants of the shoelace and collar also emitted a fairy-tale-like hazy blue glow as soon as they were brought into the light emanating from that magical lamp. No wonder I jumped up with delight. What kind of lamp was that? Where did it come from? Soon, Bayle led me to his study, where we sat down at the table for further discussions. Just above Paris lies the industrial town of Suresnes along the Seine. There lived a glassblower who, instead of working with glass, had turned to another material, namely rock crystal or quartz. It wasn't as easy to melt, blow, and bend as glass, and the production of tubes placed much higher demands on the worker's lungs and blowing power than regular glass! The light from these quartz lamps, filled with mercury and mercury vapor, was now shielded, filtered through a prefilter, a piece of dark violet-black-colored glass that blocked all visible rays of the lamp and only allowed the rays of shorter wavelength, falling outside the visible spectrum, to pass through. It was precisely these invisible rays that had the remarkable ability to make various substances luminesce, including the secret ink used by spies!

Shortly afterward, I bid farewell for the day and hurried to Suresnes, where I quickly found the Verreries-Berlemont.[25] The owner himself received me. He was a very affable man, simple and modest in his demeanor, with his right eye covered with a black patch securely tied over it. He took me to his showroom, where various

---

25 A *verreries* is a glassmaking workshop.

glass and quartz articles were displayed. In the middle of the large side wall of the spacious room was a half-open door. It apparently led to an adjacent room where a very powerful, bright blue light radiated. Involuntarily, I walked in that direction, curious about what was there, when Mr. Berlemont suddenly pulled me back by the arm, pointing to the black patch over his right eye, saying: "Attention donc, moi j'ai perdu l'oeil droit, en regardant ma première lampe!"[26]

Those beautiful, bright violet rays from those quartz lamps were not as innocent as they seemed and could cause great harm to the unprotected eye! Mr. Berlemont, noticing my eagerness to take such a lamp back to Holland, initially had to disappoint me. Firstly, the lamps on display (intended for industrial purposes) were already sold, but … if we didn't have direct current in Amsterdam, it was a problem, as these mercury-quartz lamps could only operate on direct current and could not light up on alternating current. We didn't, so I would have to purchase a so-called rectifier to convert the alternating current supplied by the G.E.W.[27] into direct current … and that could be an expensive endeavor!

My delight in everything Bayle had shown me was great, and yet it wasn't the only motivation for wanting such an installation. I understood all too well that this lamp with its shielded ultraviolet rays could provide essential services for many other investigations, and I considered placing an order, even if it meant a considerable expense for me! Then, however, a new shadow passed over. He could not possibly provide me with such a dark violet-black filter to screen the desired shorter wavelength rays. And that was precisely what I wanted! I saw a flat, solid mass of just that kind of ultraviolet glass lying on the table, picked it up, held it against the light, and was about to ask the manufacturer if I could buy that glass plate as a filter when he—understanding my wish—remarked: "That glass filter—a 'home-made' one—comes from Madame Curie, from whom I borrowed it to perform some simple experiments here. I cannot possibly part with that filter."

Then I got an idea. Always receiving support from the Justice Department when it came to my study trips, I had been given a "letter of recommendation" issued by the Ministry of Foreign Affairs, which opened many doors for me on my travels that would otherwise have remained closed. This recommendation also ensured safer and easier passage across borders when I had received—through an exchange of duplicates—counterfeit banknotes or other forged documents from colleagues abroad for study or for my collections. Otherwise, I could easily have been mistaken for a dangerous forger and locked up. I showed him my official papers, and after he had read them, he hurried to the telephone to call Madame Curie in her laboratory.

---

26 Be careful, I lost my right eye while looking at my first lamp!
27 Gemeente-Electriciteitswerken (G.E.W.) was responsible for the generation and distribution of electricity in the municipality of Amsterdam.

I overheard him speaking for some time, making the remark, "But this gentleman, a legal chemist, is accredited by his government!" Shortly after, he informed me with a delighted expression that Madame Curie was willing to lend me that light filter for three months. She would soon provide me with an address in America from where I could obtain beautiful, flat glass plates of the correct composition. The deal was soon sealed. Within three weeks, not only would a mercury vapor lamp with an automatic switch be sent to me, but also, in a second large crate, a mercury-vapor rectifier to convert alternating current into direct current. (Undoubtedly, many will recall from earlier decades the blue light glow that emanated from some cinema theaters' projection booths through the windows in the evening, originating from such rectifiers. Direct current was needed for powerful carbon arc lamps, and it was obtained with similar devices from the alternating current supplied by the electrical plant!)

Over the next few weeks, I found myself in the mood of a child eagerly anticipating the approach of Christmas, counting the days within which the shipment from Suresnes could be expected! An expediter, tasked with clearing the goods, took over the papers that had been sent to me, and a few days later, two large crates were delivered to my home. It is impossible for me to describe all the impressions that overwhelmed me when I stood next to the closed crates and saw balls of mercury rolling out of one of them on the floor! Was the quartz lamp? It soon turned out that this assumption was correct. I quickly concluded that insufficient care had been taken with the packaging and telegraphed the supplier about the receipt of the broken lamp, requesting an immediate replacement—but this time wrapped up correctly.

My anxiety had another cause. I had committed to the Amsterdam Police Inspectors' Association to give a lecture with demonstrations using the new lamp. The date was fixed, and I needed the installation soon! Berlemont promptly dispatched a new lamp—this time even better wrapped in cotton and wood wool and packed in an incredibly large crate to accommodate more flexible packaging material around the fragile object. But even this second lamp arrived broken in my laboratory! The disappointment grew even more significant when I read that the insurance company had refused to cover the risk again, and the lamp was thus dispatched "at my own risk and responsibility!" So, taking the utmost care, I telegraphed Berlemont that he should send someone with a lamp to Brussels, so that the courier could personally hand the lamp over to me at the designated place and time! And so it happened that I traveled to Brussels and waited for the arrival of the Parisian courier at my hotel near the Gare du Nord to take possession of the precious, fragile instrument from his hands. As carefully precise as he—and later, myself—carried the package, never will a young mother have carried her baby!

I came home safely with it. A friend who was an electrical technician assisted me with the connections, and soon I could enjoy my studies with the mysterious, invisible ultraviolet rays that opened up a new world for me, making me the first Dutchman to work in this field of this new creation of technology! Undoubtedly, the reader will ask what I did with that mysterious lamp. Therefore, I want to tell something about it, especially since my research and discoveries provided material for the first publications that appeared in the professional literature on this interesting subject, and sparked many new studies undertaken everywhere in this fascinating field.

The mercury quartz lamp emits a sea of rays with very diverse wavelengths. Quite remarkably, the shorter wavelength rays cannot pass through glass. They are stopped by a window glass pane, as if one were placing a wooden plank in their path! Quartz allows them to pass through easily. Hence, for a couple of special devices, lenses and prisms made of quartz are required. There are numerous materials that, in the dark, as soon as the invisible shorter wavelength rays—especially those of 366 millionths of a millimeter wavelength—fall on them, begin to "shine." The latter rays—falling outside the visible spectrum and belonging to ultraviolet rays (hereafter simply referred to as UV rays)—do not emit visible light themselves. However, they reveal their presence by causing many substances to emit light—often colored!

I discovered that white writing paper from different notepads exhibited different colors when exposed to the mysterious UV rays in the darkroom. Thus, it was quite easy to determine from which notepad a particular sheet of paper could have been taken and where it could not have been taken! Remarkably, many substances that Mother Nature creates exhibit beautiful luminescence: ivory (including our own teeth!), tortoiseshell, silver-white hairs, nails, and even diamonds. Even more remarkable is that everything that humans create as artificial material (celluloid, galalith, imitation diamonds, etc.) does not emit light under UV rays.

It occasionally happened that lacquer particles played a role in postal thefts.[28] The examining magistrate expressed a desire for me to investigate whether such a lacquer particle found in the pocket dust of an unfaithful postal worker could originate from the sealing wax of a specific postal item or from a specific stick of sealing wax. This was always dangerous territory. The chemical composition of the five wax seals on a letter often varies, and sometimes quite strongly, from the composition that the sealing wax stick itself possesses. This may sound unbelievable to many, and yet it is true. I will give you an explanation. A stick of sealing wax consists of a certain percentage—let us assume for convenience's sake half—of meltable organic substance (shellac) and the other half of mineral filler. When sealing an item, the sealing wax stick should become somewhat soft and plastic at through heating; however, many people prefer—probably out of convenience, as it is faster!—to hold the sealing wax stick in the flame of a candle or spirit

---

28 See Chapter 48: "*Souches*," or Physical Fits.

burner in such a way that the resinous substance starts to burn on its own. One even sees how occasionally the sealing wax mass is burning firmly on the items to be sealed, while the sealing wax stick stirs it! That is, in a word, foolishness. The essential part of the sealing wax—the resinous substance, the shellac, as the most valuable component—is allowed to burn! The consequence is that the percentage of noncombustible filler accordingly increases, making the seals extra brittle, less firmly adhering to the paper, and thus poorly fulfilling their purpose! Often, it is observed that when applying the first seal to a letter, the sealing wax is neatly "melted"; with the second seal, the sealing wax mass briefly catches fire; if impatience plays a role, the sealing wax pipe is set on fire for the subsequent seals, and the liquid mass drips onto the envelope in a modified chemical composition, as part of the combustible substance has disappeared, and the noncombustible substance has increased proportionally. That is how it happens that the seals on many letters have different chemical compositions and do not match those of the sealing wax stick ... even though they were applied with it on the letter!

I discovered that different brands and types of sealing wax exhibit an incredible richness of "luminescent colors." I found in it the means to recognizing the smallest differences in shade, so that the luminescent colors of a sealing wax seal proved to be independent of the treatment the seal underwent during placement! Various pipes of red sealing wax exhibit the greatest variety of colors when viewed in UV light, where they begin to "shine."

I just used the word "luminesce"—as a synonym for "shining" in a specific color. This phenomenon immediately ceases as soon as the illuminating object is no longer under the UV rays. However, there are also a number of substances that, after the UV rays have made them luminous, continue to glow for some time away from the influence of the rays. You are already familiar with this if you own an alarm clock or a wristwatch with so-called luminous hands and numerals. The phenomenon we observe there is called phosphorescence. To this class of substances—mostly all artificially prepared!—belong luminous paints, as well as a number of substances manufactured by a Parisian company to create luminous flowers, pearl necklaces, postcards, etc. However, it is unfortunate that phosphorescence only lasts a relatively short time after the removal of UV rays (unless radioactive substances are applied, and those are extremely expensive!). All these phenomena are most observable in rays of the aforementioned wavelength of 366 millionths of a millimeter. They appear quite purely when the UV glass light filter—which I initially borrowed from Madame Curie; later, I ordered several from the US myself—is engaged. Almost no visible rays emerge then, only a few of the darkest violet from our sun's spectrum.

In those days (in 1924), after my first experiments with the UV lamp, I received a letter from the archaeological service of the University of Groningen. Professor Van Giffen asked me to determine whether certain "bones," found under a dolmen in Drenthe and believed to be remnants of primates, were from buried or burned beings. My new lamp provided the solution to this problem. If the bones were first superficially cleaned to remove adhering dirt, the bone material luminesced blue in UV light. Comparative experiments with bones of buried humans next to those of burned bodies had taught me, however, that bone remnants cease to "shine" in UV light due to the burning process.

Gradually, I discovered how grease stains on paper and light-colored fabric take on very diverse colors as soon as they are viewed in UV light. Thus, it became possible to determine, during the examination of a forged promissory note, whether the stains on it were caused by motor oil or linseed oil, influencing the choice between a bicycle messenger and an apprentice from a painting workshop! And so, I became the first researcher to view oil paintings by old masters in UV rays to discover signatures that were entirely invisible under normal light. This possibility became particularly evident if the painter had applied his name to the painting with one of the paint types that luminesce conspicuously, such as zinc white and other zinc-containing paints, or with nonluminescent paint on a luminous background.

Nevertheless, the UV rays play the most important role in the examination of documents when it comes to erased writing. For this, rays of even smaller wavelength than those encountered in luminescence and phosphorescence experiments are required. The most important spectral band following that of 366 millimu (meaning millionths of a millimeter) is the one with rays of wavelength 313 millimu. This one is much less intense; it can even be called extremely weak. The surfaces suitable for luminescence, where we let these fall, only "shine" extremely weakly, not even perceptible to our eyes! Yet, they are of great significance for the examination of documents. While in the 366 rays (let's conveniently call them that) all types of white paper luminesce (as mentioned, in all sorts of colors—blue, purple, gray, etc.), the 313 rays induce only a very weak luminescence in virgin clean paper—and not on places where invisible components of writing ink have penetrated the paper, albeit invisible to our eyes. This happens when we pick up the pen and write. The dark part of the ink settles on top of the paper surface, which we see. But, in addition, colorless components of that ink penetrate the paper at that location, and those our eyes do not see. If a bungler erases the black writing, he stops when his eye no longer perceives anything, and he does not take into account that the invisible substances from the ink remain in the paper.

How do these behave with respect to the 313 rays? I already mentioned that these rays can induce an extremely weak luminescence on virgin clean paper. However, where the aforementioned—invisible—substances have penetrated the paper, the paper does not luminesce. Thus, the places with those invisible substances, deposited according to the letter forms, stand out against the weakly glowing background of the paper and provide an image of what was erased on the photo. We absolutely cannot see the weak luminescence of the paper in these 313 rays. It is much too weak. But—if we just let the photographic plate "look at it" for long enough (i.e., expose it for a very long time—eighteen, twenty, sometimes twenty-four hours in a row!)—thanks to the so-called "additive" action of light impulses on that plate—we get an image of the erased writing.

It goes without saying that such shots must be taken in complete darkness, where only the filtered 313 rays, and no other UV, much less the "visible" rays of the quartz lamp, can directly or indirectly reach the paper under investigation. It is quite a task to meet all these requirements and then, while staying outside the darkroom, ensure that inside that room, the 313 rays can do their duty, that absolute darkness prevails there, and that the lens of the camera is opened from the outside and closed again after so many hours. The results of such work are indeed surprising. To see, alongside a forged check that shows absolutely nothing suspicious on the outside, a photo that depicts an image of that check, where, adjacent to the current writing, the erased primary writing is also readable, is truly striking! The expensive device used for these tasks contains lenses and prisms that are entirely cut from rock crystal. The apparatus is a copy of the one built by Carl Zeiss according to the instructions of Professor Kögel in Karlsruhe, and it is the only one of its kind in this country. Understandably, it is not used daily and thus is a particularly luxurious instrument since it barely yields the interest on the money I once invested in it.

Epilogue by Maurice Aalders

Co van Ledden Hulsebosch's early and pioneering work in developing, experimenting with, and implementing innovative technologies to examine and visualize evidence has had lasting impacts. His pioneering work involved the development, experimentation, and implementation of various very innovative technologies designed to examine and visualize evidence. The highlighted technique in this chapter is a good example, visualizing traces using their distinct optical characteristics, in the case of ink, the intrinsic fluorescence properties of the ink, and many other organic components. By utilizing short-wavelength light, UV (ultraviolet) with, for mercury lamps, typical wavelengths of 313 and 366 nanometer (or "millimu" as van Ledden Hulsebosch uses), as an excitation source, fluorescence is generated, a principle that is still routinely used in contemporary forensic practices. In fact, current photography setups are very similar the one described in this chapter. The cameras are, of course, far more sensitive, requiring shorter exposure times, the filter settings can be switched and therefore optimized more easily, and the once hazardous mercury lamp has been replaced by lasers, filtered broadband sources, or rechargeable flashlights equipped with power LEDs and a wavelength-selective filter. Over the years, extensive research has been conducted on this technique, advancing the use of increasingly powerful light sources across a broader wavelength spectrum. Modern sensitive and fast cameras, augmented with AI-based enhancement techniques and spectral analysis, are now under investigation for their potential the enhanced the precision and efficacy of forensic investigations. With a single recording, localization and analysis of traces at the crime scene can now be achieved. Looking at modern crime scene investigations, it is clear that van Ledden Hulsebosch stands as a clear pioneer in laying the groundwork for the currently used techniques and future advancements.

27. The Treacherous Glass Splinter

When notorious types have "served" their sentence and regain their freedom—often only for a very short time, as they are quickly picked up again for a new offense!—the administration of the respective prison informs the police of some large cities of the imminent departure of the guests. And so it happened that one day a message arrived stating that the B. brothers—very "heavy" boys[29]—would be released on a specified date (into society!). It was foreseeable that these customers would soon try to strike again, and therefore the central investigation unit of the capital[30] was given a special assignment to keep an eye on them.

As night began to fall, two detectives cycling through the city center spotted an old small car with the two brothers sitting in the front seat! Undoubtedly, they also attracted the attention of the cruising "old acquaintances" who hurriedly drove past, turning into a side street to get out of the reach and sight of the "cops." But then suddenly their sharp eyes in the darkness spotted a few other detectives who also recognized the car with its occupants. No, it wasn't easy to stay out of the reach of the law! They took another detour, outside the city center—just to cause confusion—and then returned to the old neighborhoods of the city center. At one point, the car stopped in front of a jewelry store on Kalverstraat.[31] Quick action seemed necessary. For a moment there was not a soul to be seen nearby ... not even detectives! With a hammer or another hard object, a window in the store's entrance was smashed, the plan being to reach for the desirable items through the resulting opening, when suddenly a couple of cycling policemen appeared at the end of the straight section of the street. At a signal from the man at the wheel, the other one jumped into the car without having a chance to make a good grab, and "full throttle" was given as the car sped away ... as later it turned out, towards a garage in the northwest of the city.

The police found the broken window. They soon realized that it had only been smashed and went in search of the car and its occupants. The next morning, they had the brothers in custody and the car seized. One of the detectives further examined the front seat, which included a mattress-shaped cushion, using a magnifying glass to good effect. And so, the presence of a miniature glass splinter was discovered. To give you, Reader, an idea of its dimensions, I ask you to imagine that you could slice a soaked match head with a razor blade into a few pieces. The middle slice would give you, in terms of shape and size, an idea of the dimensions of that small glass shard.

---

29   Notorious felons.
30   Amsterdam.
31   The Kalverstraat is a bustling and iconic shopping street located in the heart of Amsterdam.

That small fragment was delivered to the laboratory, while I—for the purpose of comparative analysis—obtained a piece of glass from the shattered window. Now one must consider that in the preparation of glass, various materials (not all of the purest kind!) are weighed with a rough scale or measured into "bags" to be melted together; just as two pots of *snert*[32] will not have absolutely the same chemical composition (there the cook tends to add salt and other ingredients "by eye"!), likewise two "melts," which must be processed into window glass, mirror panes, or car lantern glass, will not have products of the same composition. There are always small differences that can be observed with the now so perfectly crafted instruments and methods, developed to the highest perfection. And so, it turns out how two melts, "prepared according to the same recipe" (just like those two pots of *snert*!) reveal differences in their physical properties. For example, however small and insignificant the glass splinter may be—its specific gravity is determined. The same is done with a shard of glass from the particular window. Furthermore, the so-called refractive index—related to the degree of light refraction—is determined for both samples, while, finally, the color of the two shards is compared in light rays of very short wavelengths—so-called ultraviolet light. If the shards match completely in all three of these points, then there is a probability approaching certainty that both come from the same window. We have absolute certainty that they must come from the same melt, and thus, in other words, belong to windows that were cast from the same crucible.

The judge who had to render judgment in this case knew how to appreciate these "indications"!

Epilogue by Lisette Kootker and Gareth R. Davies

In the realm of forensic investigation, the analysis of glass fragments has undergone significant advancements through the use of cutting-edge methodologies. Forensic glass analysis involves examining two or more fragments to determine their common origin. Presently, forensic researchers employ a comprehensive approach that blends traditional techniques with state-of-the-art methodologies to accurately match glass splinters to crime scenes. In ideal scenarios, a recovered glass splinter, if it exhibits a so-called fracture physical fit, can be used to reconstruct the original shape of the broken glass object. Such fits represent the highest level of association, unequivocally linking the glass fragment to a crime scene. However, physical fits are susceptible to errors, and most small or highly fragmented fragments are unsuitable for this technique.

---

32 *Snert*, also known as *erwtensoep*, is a thick and savory split pea soup that is a hearty, traditional Dutch dish.

Over recent decades, forensic researchers have turned to (advanced) microscopy techniques to meticulously examine the microscopic characteristics of glass fragments and their potential sources. Today, high-powered microscopes with sophisticated imaging capabilities allow for the visualization and examination of minute features such as physical properties (color, fluorescence, density, etc.), optical properties (refractive index), surface topography, internal structure, and even elemental composition. These microscopic analyses offer invaluable insights into the origin and manufacturing process of glass fragments, facilitating their comparison to potential sources.

Additionally, spectroscopic methods play a pivotal role in the forensic analysis of glass evidence. Nondestructive techniques such as Raman spectroscopy and infrared spectroscopy enable researchers to identify the chemical composition of glass fragments based on their unique spectral signatures. Furthermore, perhaps one of the most revolutionary advancements in this field, is the application of (semi-)destructive methods to determine the trace element and/or radiogenic isotope compositions. New technology such as inductively coupled plasma mass spectrometry (ICP-MS) allows the determination of almost all elements in the periodic table, which ideally can be combined with strontium (Sr), lead (Pb), and neodymium (Nd) isotope ratios that can be obtained by means of thermal ionization mass spectrometry (TIMS) or multicollector inductively coupled plasma mass spectrometry (MC-ICP-MS). By measuring the trace element and isotopic composition within glass fragments and their potential sources, forensic experts can discern subtle variations that serve as unique signatures of a specific source. This method offers unparalleled precision, potentially enabling investigators to differentiate between glass samples with remarkable specificity. However, to date, limited knowledge about the chemical and isotopic variation within different batches of industrial glass (i.e., trace element and isotopic heterogeneity) restricts the differentiation power of the method. Nevertheless, generating more elemental and isotopic data, and by establishing reference databases and datasets, may consolidate the position of geochemical analysis within forensic glass research in the coming years.

Together, these state-of-the-art methodologies enable forensic researchers to further decipher the complexity of glass evidence with unprecedented precision and reliability. By leveraging the latest advancements in analytical technology, forensic science continues to push the boundaries of glass investigation capabilities, ensuring that even the smallest glass fragments can yield crucial insights into solving crimes.

28. The Corpse in the Suitcase

It was on the beautiful tenth day of August in 1939 when a small truck, empty of the baskets that had be used to transport poultry to the Deventer market, was returning to Amsterdam, following the highway from Apeldoorn to Amersfoort. The three men inside the truck were thirsty, and knowing that there were plenty of blackberries growing on the other side of the grass field beside the road, in the hedge along a dry ditch running parallel to the railway line, they pulled over and walked to the mentioned hedge to quench their thirst.

While they enjoyed the juicy blackberries, one of them spotted a large suitcase behind the hedge, in the dry ditch, with one of its bottom corners embedded in the soft ground and the other end sticking out. Squeezing through the barbed wire fence, he approached the suitcase and soon realized it was a "weighty" one. With combined effort, they lifted the suitcase over the barbed wire fence and placed it on the grass field. One of the men quickly went back to the truck to fetch a screwdriver, with which he managed to open the suitcase without too much difficulty. In the moments that it took to open it, their minds were filled with the most fantastic expectations, imagining that it could be a stolen suitcase filled with treasures that the thieves had temporarily left here out of fear that their pursuers would find it in their possession! However, their surprise and horror were immense when they opened the lid and found a decomposing torso of an adult human body.

The overwhelming stench made them recoil, and they hastily closed the lid again. One of them hurried to notify the local policeman, who lived nearby, and because the policeman immediately alerted the mayor as well, the authorities arrived promptly to the scene to investigate the gruesome discovery. Since the location of the suitcase fell within the jurisdiction of the Utrecht District Court, the public prosecutor office from Utrecht was immediately informed, and, as a result, a public prosecutor soon arrived in Terschuur to take note of the finding.

The suitcase with its contents was transported to the hospital in Utrecht for further examination. In addition to the human torso, there were pieces of coconut fiber matting, a couple of blankets, a towel, and fragments of fabric, presumably from undergarments, found inside the suitcase. The news of this macabre discovery spread throughout the country in a short period through telegraph and radio, while the police in major cities received various details, including the information that a laundry number, 273, written with black ink, was found on one of the pieces of underwear.

It so happened that about a month earlier, a steward residing in Pijnackerstraat in Amsterdam, who worked on one of the ships of the Netherlands Steamship Company, claimed that his wife had suddenly "gone missing." He seemed to accept the situation, believing that she had left for Rotterdam with a "friend." The detective who had taken the report and fruitlessly searched for the missing woman began to dig deeper. It became apparent that the wife, who was often separated from her husband for extended periods during his trips to the Dutch East Indies, was financially "restricted" by him to such an extent that she sought additional income as a cleaning lady. In the family's home where she had worked until the day before her "disappearance," there still hung an apron that belonged to her, and on that apron was the same marking, 273, clearly written by the same hand, with indelible black ink. Therefore, it was no wonder that just twenty-four hours after the suitcase was found, and a postmortem examination had been conducted on the torso in Utrecht, revealing that it belonged to a woman, the attention of the police in Amsterdam was drawn to the residence of the steward, or rather his wife, who was now "on the run"(?).

In the meantime, it was discovered that shortly after the woman's disappearance, the steward had sold all the household belongings, vacated the property, and was in the midst of yet another journey to the Dutch East Indies. The house was still unoccupied. On the evening of the eleventh of August, I received a phone call from the public prosecutor in Amsterdam, summoning me to his office at the police station on Pieter Aertszstraat as soon as possible. It was ten o'clock at night when I arrived and found him in the company of higher- and lower-ranking police officers, engrossed in discussions about the likelihood that the marking could indeed establish a connection between the crime and the mentioned address.

Detective U., who had previously searched for the missing wife without success, shared some important information gathered from the immediate neighbors. It became increasingly evident that we were on the right track. A message came through that a police car from Utrecht had arrived at the garage belonging to the police station, bringing us the suitcase with everything found inside it, apart from the torso. The body part remained in the hospital's morgue in Utrecht. Under artificial light, I conducted my initial examination of the suitcase. Nobody got in my way since all onlookers, no matter how curious they were, were kept at a safe distance due to the indescribably penetrating stench emanating from the object of examination. However, the dark garage was not an ideal environment for a scientific investigation, so I proposed that the suitcase and its contents be delivered to my laboratory the following day.

Discussions continued in the upstairs room of the police station, and when Detective U. informed us that he had managed to obtain the key to the vacant house, despite the late hour, we decided to proceed there. For the layperson, there wasn't much to discover. After the resident had removed all the usable items and left behind only rubbish and dust, a jobless neighbor had volunteered to sweep and clean up so that the vacant house would look more presentable to potential tenants. In the kitchen, the municipal garbage bin belonging to the house was filled to the brim with all the waste that the cleaner had disposed of. I soon spread its contents over the granite kitchen floor. Some sensitive noses detected a "rotten smell," prompting me to set aside some pieces of floor covering and paper that were clinging to a soft, decomposing mass for further examination in my laboratory. However, in the empty house, which had no electricity connection, and where we had to make do with flashlight beams in the middle of the night, it was a challenging "search." Nevertheless, I discovered traces on the kitchen counter and on the tiles leading from it, which strongly suggested they had been left behind by blood. I would obtain certainty about that after chemically analyzing these traces.

The subsequent discussions at the mentioned police station led to the public prosecutor composing a telegram, requesting the arrest and detention of the steward. Inquiries with the night porter of the Netherlands Steamship Company revealed the exact location of his ship, and thus, the telegram was sent to the public prosecutor in Bandoeng. After the discussions, I took the telegram with me to drop it off at the telegraph office on my way home! A news article in the newspapers caused sensation everywhere, including abroad. Scotland Yard telephoned the next day from London to congratulate the police but also to inquire how they had managed to shed light on this horrifying story in such a short time. "One day we read about the discovery of a suitcase with a human torso, and the next day the authorities are telegraphing to the other side of the world to have the presumed perpetrator arrested … it's remarkable!" Yes, it was remarkable. Everything fell into place!

The detectives at the aforementioned police station now worked day and night, aided by an alert investigator from the mobile brigade of the central investigative unit at the headquarters. The latter managed to compile a kind of diary of all the events, as if it had been maintained daily in the Pijnackerstraat residence. When the unfortunate woman, who loved her husband dearly, was expecting him home from his journey to the Dutch East Indies, she had made an effort to prepare a menu with his favorite dishes for their first evening together. The butcher could provide interesting details about the woman's last visit to his shop. This fact alone was such that it cast doubt on the possibility that the woman intended to run away with someone else or commit suicide within twenty-four hours!

But the investigation by the detectives uncovered much more! Through the reconstruction of the events, they were able to determine the hour at which the woman must have died. The suspect had then dragged the body to the bedroom at the back of the hallway and placed it on the bed, after which he locked the bedroom. He had then gone to a café and later invited three neighbors to join him for drinks in the evening. He claimed that his wife had run away. One of the friends, who went to visit the house, made the remark that the bedroom was locked and received the reply that it was the work of his wife; she had taken the key! The later dragging of the body from the bedroom to the kitchen resulted in the "dissection" of the body on the kitchen counter, releasing a considerable amount of blood, which was partially disposed of through the sink and partially into the toilet. In the harbor district, the steward went to buy a couple of suitcases, a trunk, and two smaller cases, which he transported home himself in a rented car (without a driver). A neighbor—a cigar store owner—had the steward visit him the next day, asking for assistance in carrying a case of books downstairs. A rented car was parked outside (the steward would drive it himself), and the neighbor helped carry the "heavy" case downstairs. He later positively recognized the suitcase found in Terschuur as the one he had helped transport, and the supplier also positively identified it as the one he had delivered to the steward. Numerous incriminating facts came to light, and link after link was forged to form a tight chain in which nothing was missing.

One evening, my assistant, Viëtor, and I went to the house on Pijnackerstraat for further investigation. I applied the new method to bloodstains—no matter how small—that Specht had just published ... in complete darkness. Using a vaporizer, I sprayed a fine mist of the liquid I had brought onto all surfaces where the presence of slight traces of blood was presumed. And wherever there was blood, a beautiful phosphorescence occurred, emitting a mysterious blue glow that provided certainty that there were traces of blood. Thus, I was able to detect blood on the floor covering in the toilet, even though it had been cleaned, as well as on the doorknob, the flush lever, and many other places. At the base of the door frame of the bedroom door, there was a wipe of blood with a strand of hair; apparently, the dead body had scraped along it when being dragged to the kitchen. Numerous garments of the murdered woman were found in the luggage depot of a railway station, where the steward had placed them in a suitcase for safekeeping. They were positively identified by a sister of the victim, who had purchased several items together with the victim.

Accompanied by a police officer on leave from the Dutch East Indies,[33] the steward returned to the Netherlands as the arrested suspect. Although he initially denied knowing anything, he couldn't refute the overwhelming amount of evidence and admitted to having cut up his wife's body. However, he claimed that her death had been caused by innocent fighting and horseplay, during which she had fallen and hit her head on a protruding corner of the fireplace. The other parts of the body were never found, so his claims about the cause of death could not be verified through examination of the head. I conducted an investigation in the hut where the steward had lived during his last voyage to the Dutch East Indies once the ship *Johan de Witt* arrived, but nothing incriminating was found. The steward, who had formed a relationship with a young girl in the Dutch East Indies, had assured her

---

33 Modern Indonesia.

that they would marry because he would find a way to get rid of his current wife. This testimony had worked against him! The judge took this into account when determining his verdict.

Epilogue by Josita Limborgh

Together with the forensic investigation team of the police, I was present at a crime scene in 1996, where we strongly suspected that parts of the scene had been cleaned to remove any traces of blood. A year earlier, a project had been initiated in collaboration with the police to study chemical agents suitable for visualizing and enhancing shoeprints made with blood. During the literature review for this project, I came across several articles about luminol, a reagent used to visualize latent (invisible) bloodstains. We decided that this was a great opportunity to investigate whether luminol could indeed reveal removed bloodstains at this crime scene. And yes, the results were very good. In my humble opinion, I thought we had a scoop and that this was the first or at least one of the first cases in the Netherlands where luminol had been used. Only when reading this book I was very surprised to discover that this was not the case at all; Co van Ledden Hulsebosch was already using this substance in 1939!

Apparently, luminol fell out of use at some point and was left uncovered for decennia to come. Van Ledden Hulsebosch indicates that he was inspired by an article by Specht. This concerns the article "Die Chemiluminescenz des Hämins; ein Hilfsmittel zur Auffindung und Erkennung forensisch wichtiger Blutspuren" ("The chemiluminescence of Hemin: An aid for detecting and identifying forensically important bloodstains") by Dr. W. Specht, published in 1937 in the journal *Angewandte Chemie* (Applied chemistry), where the use of luminol for visualizing bloodstains is first mentioned. This article describes how the solution is prepared and applied. Van Ledden Hulsebosch was, apparently, well-informed about the recent scientific literature and saw its added value for his investigation at the crime scene. It's remarkable to realize that both van Ledden Hulsebosch and myself must have felt the same euphoric sensation when we stood in the dark at a crime scene and suddenly saw for the first time the various invisible bloodstains emit blue light.

Luminol is a chemical substance that, in solution, very slowly reacts with hydrogen peroxide. Hemoglobin in red blood cells acts as a catalyst, accelerating this reaction. In the presence of bloodstains, luminol manifests a bluish luminescence which can be seen in a darkened environment. Due to the high sensitivity of this chemical reaction, the luminol reagent is highly suitable for detecting extremely small amounts of blood. As a result, even traces of previously cleaned-up bloodstains can be detected using luminol. However, luminol not only reacts with blood but can

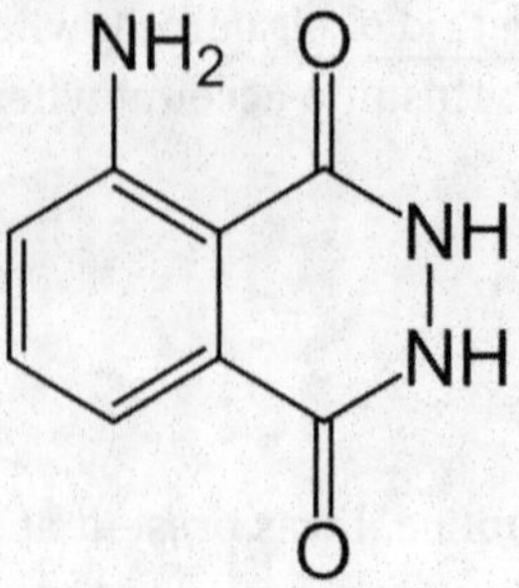

Figure 8. Chemical structure of luminol.

also give a positive reaction with substances such as jute, sisal, oxidizing metals (like rust stains), paint, wallpaper paste, some chlorine-containing cleaning agents, and certain types of vegetables and fruits. Therefore, when luminescent stains are found, they must always be additionally tested for the presence of blood using a more blood-specific test. Only the traces that show a positive reaction in this test are sampled for potential DNA analysis at a later stage.

See Figures 6 and 7 (in the insert section) for a color illustration of a cleaned "scene" and the chemiluminescence occurring after luminol application. (The photos are not from a real crime scene.)

29. The Severed Head of a Woman

On May 28, 1941, near the lock of the Merwede Canal near Amsterdam, a sailor was sailing in a small boat. A rain shower approached, and the sailor decided to take shelter under a nearby bridge. In order not to drift away, he stuck his pole hook in the shallow water next to the sailboat. When he lifted the pole again, he felt that something was hanging on it. To his astonishment, he saw a tightly knotted cloth with contents dangling from the hook, wrapped around by a bandage like a "cruciate ligament," and upon opening this package, he discovered the decomposing head of a woman. He immediately reported his gruesome find to the police, and soon an official announcement was published in the newspapers.

The Linnaeusstraat bureau, within whose jurisdiction the finding of the gruesome package fell, understandably took a special interest in it, and the detectives immediately started their work to find clarity. The autopsy, performed by the medical experts the following day, suggested that approximately two weeks had likely passed since the woman's death.

When the aforementioned detectives consulted a list of women reported as "missing" since January 1, they naturally focused on the reports from the last two to three weeks. Among them was one from a resident of Balistraat, whose wife—according to the report—had moved to Rotterdam without leaving a note! In Balistraat, they found the resident's seventeen-year-old son, who openly expressed his doubt about whether his mother had actually moved to Rotterdam. Since her departure from home, he had already been to the mentioned family in Rotterdam, where he learned that his mother had not been seen there in recent weeks! He distrusted his father—as things were far from harmonious(!)—and his father had special relations with a woman in Hillegersberg, of which "mother" knew everything. During the days of his mother's disappearance, the son had found bloodstains on a door panel and had brought it to his father's attention. He had wiped them away with a shrug. But the son had continuously wondered where his mother could be with an anxious foreboding…. The husband was visited and, suspected of murder and hiding a corpse, was temporarily detained.

After the medical experts conducted their examination of the severed head, I received it in order to make a death mask, which might contribute to the identification of the head. For this purpose, I had taken it to my laboratory. From the moment the head emerged from the water, the decomposition processes—with strong gas formation—increased rapidly, causing the thicker, fleshy parts to become considerably larger, thereby diminishing the chances of recognition with each passing day. External treatment with formalin had no effect. But one thing struck me as particularly peculiar: the profile line, the line running along the forehead and nose, which hardly changes under such circumstances (as there is little tissue underneath, as the skin almost adheres to the bone), showed something very distinctive: a deep-set nasal root, a concave bridge of the nose, a rounded nasal tip, and a slanting downturn of the nasal base, resulting in an observable "pug nose," which I had also noticed in the son during my first visit to the house on Balistraat.

While I was working on the head, my investigation also extended to everything else that had been part of the package, namely: the square cloth—a tea towel with gray checkered pattern; a flannel bandage over four meters long; and two longitudinally split pieces of bricks. Why were these items of particular interest to us? Because in the aforementioned house, eleven similar tea towels were found, as well as several similar flannel bandages and bricks of the same kind as the ones found. There was no difference between the tea towel from the package and the one from the house; the bandage that had been wrapped around the package was also 4½ cm wide, just like the ones found in the house (there were several since the son bandaged his ankles when he played football), and the pieces of brick that had clearly been a whole showed scratch marks made by a knife or chisel. The bricks found in the suspect's attic workshop were similar and used for the same purpose!

When the arrested suspect continued to proclaim his innocence and insisted that the head shown to him in the laboratory was not that of his wife, the detectives did not remain idle and also conducted their investigation at the woman's house in Hillegersberg, where the suspect had apparently hurried to shortly after his wife's disappearance. There, they found the sewing machine that had been taken from the house in Balistraat. The man had simply explained to his astonished son, upon seeing mother's sewing machine being packed, that he would have it nickel-plated so that it would be a surprise for her when she returned! Likewise, beautiful shoes, a tablecloth, nice coffee cups, and other "gifts" were found there, which had been dragged away from the house in Amsterdam. There was even a beautiful coat belonging to the missing woman! Everyone was deeply convinced of the man's guilt, including his own child, but he continued to deny everything.

We revisited the aforementioned house, but found no traces of blood anywhere that would indicate that a dissected corpse had been there in that cramped space, and we suspected that the victim must have been dismembered elsewhere, which turned out to be a wrong assumption in hindsight. A few days later, one of the detectives told me that the son of the household had informed him how he had gotten specks of tar on one of his flannel bandages when he walked on a freshly tarred road, and how he now missed that bandage. I then examined the bandage found in the mentioned package in that regard and found the mentioned specks of tar! I informed the examining magistrate of this discovery and he questioned the suspect again an hour later. He was confronted with this new evidence, which made him realize the hopelessness of his situation, and he burst into tears and fully confessed.

During an argument, she had slapped him in the face, after which he grabbed her by the throat and then wrapped a piece of cord around it, fearing that she would regain consciousness and start screaming again. After taking a breather, he had carried the body to the attic, undressed it, and above a large wash basin—to avoid a bloodbath in the attic room!—he severed the head from the torso, which was then wrapped with the aforementioned items. A handkerchief had been stuffed in the mouth, of which several similar ones were also found in the house. Having difficulty dismembering the limbs, he had separated them from the torso with a saw! The empty torso was wrapped separately and thrown into the water under a bridge using a rented boat, weighted down with stones. The limbs were disposed of in a similar manner at another location.

We took him by car to accurately indicate the places, and the police carefully dredged the indicated spots. The torso was found, but the limbs had come loose from the wrapping and had floated away, so we could not retrieve them. The medical experts determined that this was the corresponding torso belonging to the same woman whose head had been examined a few days earlier. Certain organs, which were approximately halved during the dissection, were found to have the same cross-section both in the head part of the neck and in the neck part still attached to the torso, confirming their connection. Needless to say, we no longer needed to proceed with the initial plan to publish photos of a plaster death mask of the head in the newspapers for identification. It was no longer necessary! Inside the wash basin, I was able to find dried traces of blood along the seam lines.

Epilogue by Jan de Koeijer

What stands out to me in his stories is the excellent synergy between tactical investigations and forensic science. With limited forensic capabilities but a lot of resourcefulness, Co van Ledden Hulsebosch is consistently able to bring the investigators one step closer to solving the crime. Since then, forensic science has played an increasingly significant role in solving crimes, but at the same time, the perpetrators' forensic awareness has also grown and alternative scenarios for the presence of incriminating traces are often given. If we zoom in on this case from today's perspective, we don't actually have a lot of additional investigative possibilities. Of course, DNA could play a role in determining the common origin of the body parts, and there is also a slight chance of finding the perpetrator's DNA on the materials (tea towel, handkerchief, flannel bandage, and brick halves) used to package the head.

However, if DNA is found on these materials, the immediate question arises: What does this mean? Yes, it establishes a connection with materials from the suspect's residence, but does that mean the suspect is also the perpetrator? Couldn't his DNA have ended up there innocently? Such questions, which are quite common now, would warrant an evaluation at the so called activity level. Van Ledden Hulsebosch is aware that the combination of similarities between materials found near the severed head and materials originating from the residence together form stronger evidence regarding their origin (source level). However, it is uncertain whether this reinforcing effect also manifests at the activity level. After all, at this level conditional independence of the evidence is more often an issue (if you find one item from the residence, it becomes more likely that other items from the residence were also used in packaging the head). Thus, combining evidence can suddenly become a complex matter where specialized knowledge comes into play.

For this purpose, the Netherlands Forensic Institute (NFI) established the Interdisciplinair Forensisch Onderzoek (IDFO, Interdisciplinary Forensic Research team). Using graphical models (evidence schemes), evidence from different traces is combined at the activity level in the context of the scenarios presented by both the public prosecution service and the defense. In an interdisciplinary report, the overall strength of the evidence resulting from all forensic investigations is then reported. The diagram in Figure 9 shows an example of an evidence scheme containing the relationships between the suspect and the actions in the crime scenario, as identified by van Ledden Hulsebosch.

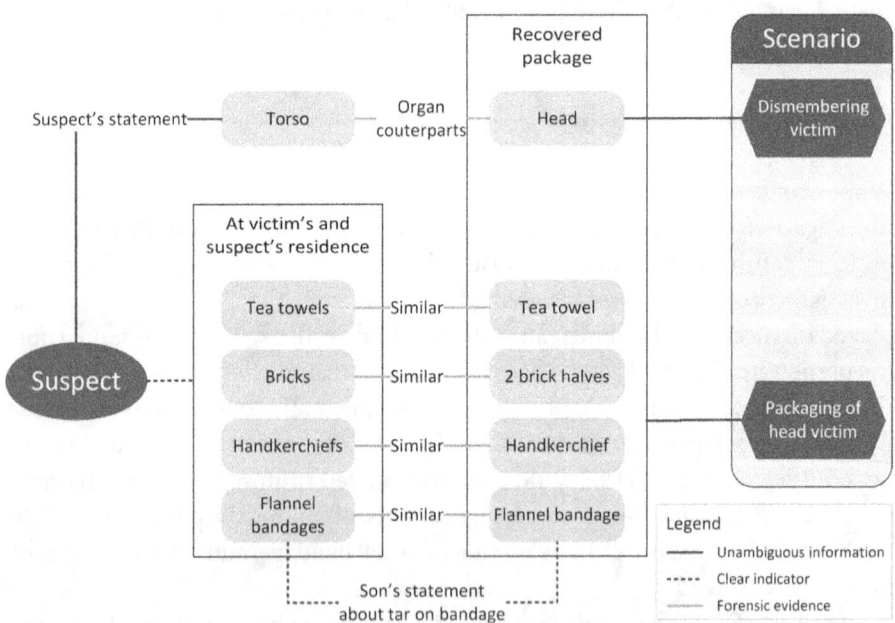

Figure 9. IDFO evidence scheme for the case discussed in this chapter.

30. Dust Provided the Evidence

It was the usual crowd on a Saturday evening in a small café in a working-class neighborhood on the border of Amsterdam. Among the regular customers, the innkeeper observed one strange face. Had this face inspired more confidence in him, the innkeeper would undoubtedly have been delighted at the thought of a new regular. However, this was different. He watched the stranger with suspicion, but he did not annoy the others and, on the contrary, seemed to be there just to have a good time! Around eleven o'clock—the prescribed closing time—the customers disappeared, and after the last guest had left, the owner of the establishment began, according to his rock-solid custom, to gather the chairs on the tables so that the floor could be neatly swept, after which all the furniture was dusted and put in its place. Then he went to bed.

The next morning a strange surprise awaited him. There had been a break-in and a not inconsiderable amount of liquor—already becoming scarce!—appeared to have been stolen. He rushed to the police, who sent an investigator to take stock of everything. He found a piece of shoelace, at one end of which there was a metal tip, while the other end had a frayed appearance. It was about ten centimeters long. Obviously, the cleaning of the café at the end of the night before gave full assurance that this piece of shoelace must have been left behind by the nocturnal visitor. It had not come from the shoes of the owner, nor from anyone living in the house, so it had special significance.

The detective soon figured out who had been the strange visitor from the previous evening … an old acquaintance of the police, who was unable to provide a proper alibi for the night. Of course, he tried to talk them into believing that he had been in this part of town only in the evening, but it was soon established that he had been there during the hours in question—between midnight and four in the morning! He had knocked on the door of a family member living in that area and asked if he could stay there until dawn, but he was refused because they could feel that something odd was going on! The best part was that the man's left shoe had a full-length shoelace, while the right shoe was held in place by a shoelace that was apparently missing a piece.

It took little effort to determine how the piece of shoelace found, in terms of its length, could very well be the missing piece, so that, when added to the piece from the right shoe, matched the length of the intact shoelace from the other shoe. But that evidence could hardly be considered sufficient. Then they tried to construct a *souche*. As one knows, a *souche* is a "separation of cohesion, which can prove the solidarity of two pieces." A shard from the edge of a plate, a broken-off knife tip or key blade, a piece of paper torn in half—they all show dividing edges of such a characteristic form, that they can only fit to that part, with which it had previously formed one whole. But the disintegrated nature of the broken shoelace did not lend itself at all to the recognition of any *souche*.

Then something else came to me. I thought about how the laces of our shoes exist just a short distance from the surface of the road, regularly in contact with the swirling dust, and how parts of the dust could be hidden between the threads of these laces. Undoubtedly, both shoelaces of a walker would be "dusted" in the same way, so I immediately decided to collect the dust for further microscopic research. Thus, I separated a very small heap of dust from the three pieces:

- The piece of shoelace that had been found in the café
- The fragment of shoelace found in the right shoe
- The full-length shoe lace from the left shoe

Curiously, each of these dust piles contained dust particles of varying color and origin, but … the combination was in all three of these dust piles one and the same, so that, without any hesitation, I could conclude that the found piece of shoelace must have come from the right shoe.

Our friend tried to deny everything and anything, but the prosecutor, in his indictment, asserted how the nonliving (silent) witness spoke in a much clearer language and told more truth than any living witness in this case and demanded a sentence of six months' imprisonment. The police judge immediately ruled and sentenced in accordance with the claim. The condemned did not appeal!

Epilogue by Mattijs Koeberg: Background Levels and Frequencies

A recurring theme in the epilogues to the chapters in this book seems to be lack of serious consideration of an alternative (non-crime-related) scenario. What is the chance of a similarity between (the traces on) two items being a random match? In this story, the evidence focuses on dust particles in laces, but the same questions hold for almost all forensic traces. For many forensic specialties it is thus very relevant to know and understand the background levels and frequencies of the relevant trace materials. Traces of drugs, fibers, evidence of human contact, car paints, types of soil or diatoms, etc. Only if there is some information on the frequency of occurrence in the "background" can proper statistical assessments of the evidential value of (similarities in) recovered traces be made. For other areas or types of traces this is less relevant, but it is still important to have shown that this is the case.

For example, for different type of high explosives, such as TNT and Semtex, it has been shown in certain areas in the world, for certain types of surfaces, that they are not typically found in the background. This means that detecting even low levels of TNT traces is significant. By the way, for other types of explosives, such as pyrotechnical materials, it has been shown that they do occur in the background, making it necessary to at least take relevant reference/background samples to determine if detected levels of traces are significantly higher than in the background. Several forensic labs have studied and published studies of background levels of pyrotechnic traces to support evidential considerations.

In this story of a burglary, the dust that is collected from three pieces of lace seems to be a complex mixture of different types of dust. This could be unique to a certain history of these laces, or it could be that everyone living in the same area at some point will collect. It would have been useful if Co van Ledden Hulsebosch have looked at dust from his own laces, too. At the Netherlands Forensic Institute (NFI), it would not be considered unusual if a forensic examiner sent out an email to all her colleagues asking them to donate their shoelaces for science.

31. Assisting Criminal Justice in Belgium

This happened somewhere in Belgium between 1914 and 1918. Justice authorities had seized several documents during a house search, including one that had arrived by mail from across the border. In one of these significant portions of text had been rendered completely unreadable by a censor. The people in the laboratory of police official Ernest Goddefroy knew various tricks used to decipher portions of text that an ordinary person would consider illegible. They employed exploratory photography, sometimes using special light filters and other times using infrared rays. In this case, even the great detective of Brussels faced an "unsolvable" problem; the letter's text had been written with a purple aniline pencil, and the censor had used graphite pencil to scratch deep black lines over large portions of the text, rendering it unreadable. Goddefroy had tried everything in the laboratory, located on one of the upper floors of the Palace of Justice in Brussels, but none of the known methods helped unveil the hidden text. And this was particularly frustrating because judicial authorities were eager to learn the content of this specific document. Facing Goddefroy, the public prosecutor (*procureur du roi*) didn't hide his opinion and regret, yet he couldn't blame Goddefroy, a self-taught expert in chemistry and physics, for not finding a solution.

At his wit's end, Goddefroy requested permission to take the mysterious letter to Amsterdam the next day to have it examined by me, and his request was gladly granted. Goddefroy took the first available train to Amsterdam, so he was standing before me with the enigmatic letter the next morning. After recounting his futile attempts in various directions, he took my suggestion and visited the Rijksmuseum, as I preferred to conduct my investigations "all by myself" to avoid distraction, while I devoted my full concentration to the problem. I suggested that he come back in the afternoon before catching the evening train to Brussels, to see if I might have reached a solution by then. I worked tirelessly throughout the entire afternoon—first sitting still for half an hour, thinking, and then suddenly having an idea. Immediately, I retrieved the necessary tools from the cabinets and set up the apparatus to start experimenting.

When Goddefroy returned to the station in the afternoon, burning with curiosity about whether I had found a solution, he was taken aback when I handed him an unchanged copy of the entrusted document and a photograph of the complete letter as it had initially been—all portions readable, the ones that had been rendered illegible by censorship with the deep black pencil were now visible. He couldn't believe his eyes, suspecting for a moment that I was playing a trick on him and had "created" something, but he soon realized that I had genuinely provided him with the solution. "And how did you accomplish that, Mr. v. L. H.?"

I, of course, had foreseen that question, and I had considered that, before publishing the entirely new method I had discovered, it would be better not to discuss it with anyone. Previous unfortunate experiences led me to this decision. In the past, I had openly shared a discovery, only to see it published as a novelty in the media by someone who had heard about it indirectly. So, I wisely stayed silent to avoid being accused of plagiarism. Since then, I made sure to keep new findings to myself until I published them in a journal as the results of my work. But, "revenons à nos moutons" ("back to our story")! Goddefroy returned to Brussels half-satisfied. On one hand, he was delighted that the trip had been successful, and he had a photograph of the entire content of the elusive letter in his hands. On the other hand, he regretted that I hadn't immediately revealed my new method of working. And the method was not really so complex!

I couldn't achieve anything through photographing the document using a variety of light filters. I had to find another approach. After some consideration, I decided to try the following experiment: I placed the letter on a hectograph, where both the writing and the cancellations came into contact with the sticky surface of the gelatin adhesive layer. I left the letter on the hectograph for about fifteen minutes. I had reasoned that the aniline pencil-produced writing could locally stain the hectograph's surface and penetrate it, while graphite, being a completely neutral substance, wouldn't transfer anything to the sticky adhesive surface. Indeed, a mirror image of the aniline writing appeared gradually on the hectograph. I then covered the hectograph with a piece of smooth white paper, which had been made "more sensitive" by holding it above a pan of boiling water. I left that paper in contact with the hectograph under light pressure for an hour to transfer the pale purple writing from the adhesive layer. To create a high-contrast reproduction from the very pale purple image, I took the photo under sodium light—the familiar yellow light that was used to illuminate many major roads in our country in the evening before the mandatory blackout period. In that powerful yellow light, the purple lines of the hectographed letter appeared gray-black (in yellow light, violet cannot be distinguished), and, thus, I obtained a striking photo that showed the aniline writing of the censored letter, but not the pencil markings that had been crossed out! It really wasn't that complicated at all!

Epilogue by Brigitte Bruijns

In the following story a hectograph is used to reveal the answer in a case of a document made unreadable. The term "hectograph" comes from the Greek words *hekaton* (a hundred) and *graphein* (to write). In the past, a hectograph was used to duplicate multiple copies of documents or images. It involves transferring ink from a master copy to a gelatin or gel-like surface, which can then be pressed onto paper to reproduce the original image or text. Hectographs were popular before the advent of modern photocopiers and printers. If one writes on a piece of paper with suitable ink, then, when pressing this piece of paper with the written side onto the gelatin plate, a large portion of the viscous ink will be held by the sticky mass. Subsequently, placing an unwritten piece of paper on the gelatin plate, pressing it without shifting, will yield a sharp impression of the written text or image.

Gel printing, also known as gel plate printing or monoprinting, shares some similarities with hectography (and stencil printing) in terms of ink transfer principles. Gel printing involves using a gelatin-like surface, typically made from gel plates, as a medium for creating unique prints. In gel printing, the gel plate acts as a temporary surface that holds the ink or paint, similar to the gelatin surface in hectography. The ink or paint transfers from the gel plate to the paper or other surfaces, resulting in a one-of-a-kind print. It's a versatile and creative technique used in crafting and art, offering the ability to experiment with textures, layers, and colors. I never realized when I was using my gel plate, that I made use of a (forensic) technique that was also used by Co van Ledden Hulsebosch!

32. The Anonymous Letter

Many anonymous letters are written, driven by various motives. Sometimes, these missives are penned with the most amiable intentions, such as during the celebration of Sinterklaas. More often, however, they are crafted with the malicious intent to hurt, offend, or extort. In such cases, one question consistently arises: "Was this epistle authored by the same hand that produced the accompanying comparison documents?" Those who dispatch such anonymous missives are motivated by a wide array of thoughts and intentions. In most cases where my assistance was sought, the accused party was of the fairer sex! It is widely agreed that more women than men engage in this cowardly act. One case stands out as particularly illustrative.

The father of a student at a *hogere burgerschool* (HBS) in Amsterdam discovered, one evening while emptying his mailbox, a letter addressed to his fourteen-year-old daughter. The address was clearly written in a distorted hand, raising suspicions. He decided to open the envelope and was left stunned by its contents: a letter overflowing with the vilest, crudest expressions interspersed with sketches (supposedly drawings) of the most obscene nature. Indeed, even the most ardent aficionado of obscenity would blush upon reading this letter. Several expressions and names mentioned in the letter indicated a connection to the school class. Consequently, the headmaster of the respective HBS, upon being informed, took immediate action. In consultation with a teacher known for his psychological insight into students, a few boys in the throes of puberty, who were expected to be among the potential authors of the letter, were selected. Their notebooks, featuring the necessary handwriting, were placed alongside the anonymous letter in my hands for analysis to determine the author. I unequivocally declared that none of these boys could have been the author of the anonymous work. Subsequently, the notebooks of all the other boys in the class were examined, and again, none could be identified as the author.

Consequently, I proceeded to request the notebooks of the girls in that class as well. Then, ultimately, even with these notebooks, no clue was found. At this point, I inquired whether they would be willing to send me the homework notebook of the young girl who had received the offensive letter. They complied with this request, albeit with surprise. The resolution to the puzzle soon became clear: the girl had written the erotic letter herself and sent it to her own address! According to the testimony of many, she was such a well-behaved and reserved child that literally no one could have imagined such a thing from her. This case is not unique; in my many years of practice, I have encountered several similar cases where young girls, in their emerging puberty, outwardly presented themselves as perfectly modest, adhering to the impeccable upbringing they had received. However, internally, they simmered with almost uncontrollable desires. To soothe these desires, they confided various messages and expressions to paper, things they would never utter aloud, but reading them back—providing a unique sensation(!)—held a certain allure. The intriguing notion of receiving a letter containing forbidden content from "someone" also enticed them. Consequently, such a child would decide to include a collection of erotic phrases—often devoid of any logical connection—in a letter sent to her own address, because ... receiving such a letter was indeed something quite extraordinary!

Epilogue by Brigitte Bruijns

Crime rates and the gender of offenders can vary widely depending on the type of crime and location. Generally speaking, crime statistics have shown that men are more frequently involved in criminal activities compared to women. This holds true for various types of crimes, including violent crimes such as homicide and assault, property crimes like burglary and theft, and drug-related offenses. Men tend to be overrepresented in the criminal justice system across many countries. However, in certain white-collar crimes, such as embezzlement and fraud, men tend to be the predominant offenders, but women are also involved in these crimes. Also property crimes like shoplifting, petty theft, and shoplifting often involve a higher proportion of female offenders. While engaging in prostitution itself is not always seen as a crime in many jurisdictions, women are sometimes arrested for prostitution-related offenses. It is important to note that while women may be involved in these types of crimes, they are still less likely to be arrested for or convicted of criminal offenses compared to men.

33. Fine Sleuthing by Dogs!

Prologue by Adee Schoon

I first read the memoirs of Co van Ledden Hulsebosch in 1996, when they were gifted me by Professor Groeneveld, director of the National Forensic Laboratories and professor at Leiden University. At the time Professor Groeneveld was supervising the completion of my PhD thesis on "the performance of dogs in identifying people by scent," and he had added a note to the book saying he considered the work with the dogs in the book "scientifically weak." This opinion I do not fully share—given the knowledge available a century ago, and combining the three stories where dog Albert plays an important role in this book with the more extensive memoirs of policeman Water, Albert's trainer and handler, I think they did a pretty amazing job. Both van Ledden Hulsebosch and Water were keenly aware of the necessity of introducing odor controls and testing what Albert was actually capable of, before attempting to solve the forensic problem at hand. The work with van Ledden Hulsebosch and Water made Albert quite famous—there still is a statue to his memory in the Oosterpark in Amsterdam. But more importantly, what Albert did was the result of good training.

In an epilogue to his memoirs, van Ledden Hulsebosch declared it was necessary to breed good dogs and train them well to reach Albert's high performance, if dogs were to be forensically useful. This feeling was shared by the Ministry of Justice and led to the founding of the Rijksspeurhondenschool (the National Sniffer Dog School, the Dutch school for training police sniffer dogs) in 1919. This school still exists as the Canine Unit of the Netherlands National Police Agency, and I believe that it has to a large extent realized van Ledden Hulsebosch's ideas. Dogs are not bred at the center but there is a careful selection process, and they are trained up to a high standard by trainers that share Water's passion and critical thinking.

Van Ledden Hulsebosch had a second condition that needed to be met for dogs to be forensically useful: to not trample the crime scene and contaminate it (with human scent) prior to calling in the dogs. Sadly enough, that condition is sometimes still not met. Even though crime scene management has improved a lot during the last decades, first responders are still sometimes unaware of canine capabilities and how to optimally preserve a crime scene for a dogs sensitive nose, making it difficult for dogs to always excel.

The story below, "Fine Sleuthing by Dogs," is one of several cases in the memoirs of van Ledden Hulsebosch involving a lineup. In such lineups, Albert would match the scent of the perpetrator on a murder weapon to the scent of a person suspected of that crime, and so identify the murderer and solve the crime. There are two lineups in this story: one matching the scent of the perpetrator on a crowbar to a lineup of caps, one of which belonged to the suspect, and a second one matching the scent on the crowbar to a lineup of people, including the suspect. In the second lineup, the dogs could have been responding to memory of the scent on the cap from the first lineup, or perhaps responding to the nervousness of the suspect standing in the lineup, so this second one is "scientifically weak" as Professor Groeneveld would have put it. But the first lineup certainly meets most essential criteria. Scent lineups are still in use is some countries but were discontinued in the Netherlands in 2011 after a group of handlers knowingly ignored correct procedures, which led to approximately 2,000 cases having to be reviewed by the courts. This coincided with significant technological advances in DNA analysis, which has since become a standard.

Nowadays dogs contribute in other ways: for example, by locating minute blood or semen traces that are difficult to find by other methods. Traces that can yield useful DNA profiles to help solve cases. Nonetheless, the exploits of Albert and his handler Water are interesting to read, as are van Ledden Hulsebosch's strategic use of them in the cases he was asked to consult in. Rereading this chapter, I vividly recalled reading it for the first time. I was shocked again by the same detail as I was the first time: the completely natural acceptance that van Ledden Hulsebosch traveled first class by train, and that Water and his dog Albert were in third-class carriages. Times have changed!

See Figure 10 (in the insert section) for a photo of the tombstone for Albert the police dog placed in the Oosterpark in Amsterdam in 1924.

. . .

During the previous war (1914–1918), a service revolver belonging to the local policeman was stolen at the Town Hall of a small village. Various unsavory people—mostly people living in caravans—had visited that morning to collect food coupons, and one couldn't help but suspect someone from that group had stolen the revolver. A few days later, at breakfast, I received a telegram from the prosecutor in Tiel (back then, Tiel still had a district court, which was later abolished, along with the courts in Winschoten and Zierikzee), reporting that the mayor of the village of Beesd had been shot dead by an unknown perpetrator during the night.

I was requested to come to Geldermalsen by a specified train, where I would be met at the station. Given the gravity of the crime, I decided to mobilize all available resources immediately. This included calling and bringing along the dog trainer Water with his two invaluable assistants, who had demonstrated their remarkable skills on many occasions. Accordingly, I phoned Water directly to meet me at the station at the agreed time, accompanied by his pair of four-legged detectives, to join me on the journey to Geldermalsen and Beesd. Upon arriving at the station in Geldermalsen, the judicial authorities greeted me on the platform, informing me that there was just one seat available in the car for me. I pointed out that I had brought company, namely the trainer and his two dogs, which seemed to provoke undeniable irritation. They had only called for my assistance, etc., etc. Somewhat upset by such reprimanding, I noted that—when called as an expert for the investigation of any case—I must reserve the right to choose my tools, whether inanimate or living, in the form of tracking dogs. And what dogs they were! None in the world could match their abilities, especially in conducting lineups.

Yes, ... but then a second car would be needed! Well, if it must be ... and they saw the justifiable and necessary nature of the precautions I had taken. (Later, it would turn out that the dogs' assistance was crucial to the swift success of the affair!) Upon arrival in Beesd, the elderly village policeman Van Trigt stood like Cerberus at the door. I was on familiar ground! My uncle, who had been the mayor of Beesd for thirty-nine years, had lived in this large building with his family for many years, and I had spent many a pleasant holiday week here as a boy. Later, I had visited the family several times, and a friendly relationship had remained with Van Trigt from those old days.

It truly pleased the old fellow to be able to concisely confirm that no one had been on the premises after the attack had been discovered, so all traces had been preserved intact. (This is in stark contrast to the situation in some large cities, where, upon the discovery of a serious crime, detectives, senior police officers, medical services, forensic teams, the central detective bureau, and often the public prosecutor's office might completely fill up a small house when expert examination had yet to begin! Everyone present quietly hoped that fortune would allow them to find something that could untangle the web; but ... what became of most "silent witnesses," I need not say. Fortunate, then, when such a simple village policeman takes his duty as seriously as old Van Trigt, and hands over the crime scene to the judiciary—and then to the expert—in the same state as the perpetrator left it!)

At first sight, it became clear to us that the perpetrators (there must have been at least two) had dragged a long ladder—from a farm ten minutes away—and placed it against the back wall of the house at the center window of the first floor, which opened onto a corridor running from front to back. To clarify further, let me explain the following: When my uncle resigned from his office, he was succeeded by a bachelor mayor who did not need the large building where my relatives had lived for so many years. He occupied the rooms on the ground floor and a single room on the first floor, which was furnished as his bedroom. The remaining rooms on the upper floor were used for the secretariat. To access these rooms, a staircase had been built against the outside of the house with a landing, from where a new door opened to the first floor. Right next to the corridor, at the back of the house, lay the mayor's bedroom, such that the bedroom door was immediately adjacent to the aforementioned window through which the nocturnal visitor had entered.

Awakened by the noise of the sliding window, the mayor had opened his bedroom door and at that moment received a shot in the chest, resulting in immediate death. Upon arrival, my first thought was that if the ladder was brought by the perpetrators, their hands could have left scent on it for the dogs. Therefore, I asked the trainer Water to first let the dogs sniff the ladder and see how they would react. The four-legged detectives sniffed both sides of the ladder, put their noses to the ground, and followed a trail into the deep garden at the back of the house. Curiously enough, the trail did not cross the gravel path but went over the lawn and through an empty flowerbed, where a footprint in the garden soil caught our attention when the dogs barked loudly. I noted it was a clumsily modeled right shoe with a fixed round rubber disc under its heel. (When the public prosecutor asked how I came to declare that the rubber disc was fixed, I replied, "Because it's worn unevenly; as long as it can rotate, it doesn't wear unevenly.")

Meanwhile, the dogs, enthusiastic about their task, dragged their master on long leads to the back part of the garden, where a fairly wide mud ditch separated the garden from a cherry orchard with tall grass. Reaching the ditch, the dogs did not hesitate and ran across a rotten, creaking plank that had served as a bridge in its better days, but which no human being would now trust. The plank creaked and groaned even as the dogs ran over it. Now their master had to get to the other side. His enthusiasm for tracking was great, and, accordingly, his courage rose. A good run-up ... a strong push-off ... and he made the jump successfully! In the cherry orchard, the dogs quickly relocated their trail, sniffing nervously, their noses moving back and forth continuously as they advanced ... dragging their guide along at an increasingly faster pace, for—their behavior revealed it—they were clearly on the trail and were now figuring out where it would lead.

Suddenly, both dogs stopped and announced by loud barking that they had stumbled on something. The trainer quickly approached, bent down, and picked up a moderately sized crowbar from the tall grass. It could not have been there long, given the wetness of the tall grass and the lack of rust on the crowbar; indeed, it seemed as though it had been thrown down there just moments ago, given the state of the crowbar. It would undoubtedly have emerged red and heavily rusted from that wet grass otherwise, leading us to believe that this tool had been left behind by the perpetrators during their escape.

To preserve the personal scent of the perpetrator as much as possible and especially to avoid introducing foreign scents, I left it to the trainer to pack the crowbar, using the inner sheets of a notepad that no one had recently touched. And the trainer could safely wrap it, because during the lineups performed later, his own body scent could do no harm; the dogs were accustomed to it throughout their training. The dogs automatically exclude that scent when they follow someone else's trail and take scent from an object left or lost by that person, to then—on the firm command "Find the man!"—search for the person who has matched that body scent.

Before the crowbar was completely packed by the trainer (it never crossed my mind to allow anyone present to handle it!), it was briefly compared with a tool mark under the sliding window upstairs and in the window sill, where a preliminary examination already showed a high degree of similarity. No doubt, that crowbar had been used to push up this window the previous night. The harvest of fingerprints was not rich. On the window sill, the coarse outlines of a left hand were visible, which, however, were not sharply printed, thus useless for identification, except for a few lines from the tip of the middle finger, with a peculiar central figure in them—insufficient material by themselves to reach absolute certainty of identity, excluding all other Earthlings. Yet, I took an image of it to my laboratory. I had already made a plaster cast from the shoe print in the flowerbed, and placed it with the luggage.

A few hours later, my friend Hulst—the well-known Leiden pathologist—arrived. He had performed the autopsy on the victim and removed the deadly projectile, which he handed to me for possible comparison. Before the arrival of the forensic pathologist, I had declared that the shooting must have been done with government-provided ammunition from a large-caliber service revolver. I had found a small round disc of paraffin paper next to the victim on the carpet, as was typically found between the powder charge and bullet in the specified caliber of government ammunition to block moisture seeking its way to the powder charge. When the bullet was later recovered from the chest cavity, everyone was convinced of the accuracy of my statement, based on the paraffin paper disc and its dimensions.

Due to the train schedule, one of the cars would take the trainer and me with the dogs back to Geldermalsen, and so I said goodbye to the public prosecutor and the examining magistrate. Our train had just left Geldermalsen when the Utrecht police called the Beesd town hall looking for the public prosecutor. The public prosecutor was told that the Utrecht police had taken the route to Geldermalsen via Houten and Schalkwijk by car, and had stopped a caravan on the road with some suspicious characters. They had been among the caravan dwellers I referred to at the beginning of this story who had collected food coupons on the day the service revolver had been stolen.

The Utrecht police had taken the group to the headquarters in Utrecht, and further action was now up to the Tiel public prosecutor. Yes, it was unfortunate that the expert had just left, but he could not yet have passed Utrecht by train; if some detectives quickly went to the Central Station in Utrecht to wait for the train, they could ask the expert to disembark and assist with the tests he might still want to conduct on the detained suspect. And so one of these detectives soon found me in my compartment, insisting that I accompany him to headquarters. It goes without saying that I had my "entourage" picked up from the third-class wagon, where trainer Water traveled with his dogs.

The spacious courtyard behind the (old) headquarters served as the field for my now to be conducted tests. A couple of masons looked up from their work from the scaffolding against an adjacent building they were working on. Since I wanted to take a purely objective test first, I asked one of the detectives to fetch the cap of the caravan dweller and lay it at the base of the surrounding wall. A few detectives also had caps, and at my request, the masons (amused by the situation) threw down their headgear from the scaffolding as well. Soon, a dozen caps lay at intervals of over a meter in rows. Then the trainer was called with the dogs from the waiting room. The dogs were given the opportunity to sniff the crowbar, after which their master sent them towards the caps to search. Both dogs decisively barked at one of the caps. It was that of the arrested caravan dweller. Then—in the absence of the trainer and the four-legged detectives—alterations were made in the order (whereby the valuable cap of the gypsy was moved using special tools to avoid adding new human smells to it!), and the test was repeated, with the dogs again identifying the same headgear as matching the scent they had also smelled on the crowbar.

Then I set up the following test: I had twenty-five people spread out in the field. To never hear the reproach from any defender that the police dog, which had to identify one "chap" among city gentlemen, always barks at the latter, I invited the curious and eager masons to set a ladder over the wall and assist me by joining the lineup. They naturally found this extremely interesting and were with us in a jiffy. The place was crowded with people. The detainee was then brought and placed somewhere in the middle of the crowd. In the waiting room, I once again had the trainer present the scent of the crowbar to the dogs' noses, and immediately after coming outside, the dogs received the command: "Find the man!" There began the sniffing, during which the dogs wandered among all the people, who remained completely still, sniffing attentively at each leg or if the scent of the crowbar was detected on them. Then suddenly, triumphant barking—a duet—and there stood the gypsy, dumbfounded, with his hands crossed in front of his chest, and on each forearm, two dog paws. The four-legged friends stood neatly beside him and barked somewhat fiercely in his face. The fellow was far from reassured and kept asking if they were going to bite! Laconically calm, the trainer said that the dog does not bite as long as the truth is spoken, but woe betide if gross lies were told!

I quickly approached the caravan dweller, let everyone else—thanking them for their assistance—leave the courtyard, and said that I had a few questions. First, he had to show me the sole of his right shoe for inspection, because—as I told him—you'll see now how there's a worn, fixed rubber disc under your right heel. And indeed so it was! Then I had him present the tip of his left middle finger, which I examined attentively with my magnifying glass. Then I added: "Well now, friend, you can confess safely!" And suddenly the full confession came from his lips.

He had stolen the service revolver in Tricht at the secretariat and had shot the mayor of Beesd with it at night. A precise account followed, where they had taken the ladder, how they had crossed the ditch at the back of the garden, and left the crowbar in the cherry orchard. They had thrown the service revolver into the water of the Linge while crossing the Linge bridge. I had the specified place searched with powerful magnets, and the service revolver was also found. Thus, on the same day the crime was committed—thanks to the help of our brave police dogs—everything was fully clarified, and the perpetrator was locked up after making a full confession. It couldn't have been more perfect. The gentlemen of the Tiel Court will probably never again object when an expert they summon arrives "with an entourage" consisting of four-legged helpers and their leader!

34. The Murder of Tania Schovers

In the late autumn of 1906, a forester from a large estate in the Achterhoek region (in the eastern part of the Netherlands, near the German border) was walking through the somewhat remote parts of the extensive forest along a narrow forest path. On his left, there was dense coniferous forest, and on his right, an area overgrown with tall oak coppice separated from the path by a wide, damp ditch. Many of these foresters have "eagle eyes" and this one was no exception. At a certain point, he noticed that some of the thinner tops of the oak coppice shoots along that ditch had fresh breaks and were bent over. This was enough indication for him: someone must have passed through here, breaking the branches, for some purpose or another.

Curious to find out more, he leaped over the ditch and made his way through the same spot where the unknown person had snapped the twigs. A few meters inside the coppice, he arrived at an open space, perhaps five or six square meters in size. There, with a start, he beheld the remains of a human being in an advanced state of decomposition. The head, consumed down to the bone by field creatures (so a Frenchman collectively called the beetles, worms, ants, etc., characterizing them as "the workers of death"), had rolled like a bowling ball to the slightly sloping part about a meter away from the torso. The rest of the skeleton was scattered, and only a few ragged fragments of clothing remained. A tightly knotted cloth that had clearly been the belongings of this person contained a few pieces of clothing and a letter from which the person's identity could be inferred: it was the remains of a certain Tonia Schovers, a laborer who, during the "hay season," moved from one farm to another for work, a pariah with no blood relatives. Hence, no one had noted her disappearance; she was essentially missed by no one!

Upon inquiry, the police learned that she had been last seen during Pentecost that year and not seen again afterward. At first, nobody immediately thought of a committed crime upon finding the remains, except for the prosecutor, who considered how the perpetrator of any crime against life often succumbs to the mysterious urge to see something more of their victim *a posteriori* ... even if it's the burial ceremony. (It's wise, therefore, that in America, it was early on introduced as a good practice to film the entire crowd of spectators who show "interest" around the door of the deceased's house and later attend the burial of victims of murder by unknown perpetrators without their knowledge, in order to later play the film for the circle of investigative officials ... hoping that one of them might recognize an old acquaintance among the crowd filmed, whose presence could be the result of the aforementioned mysterious urge.)

A thorough investigation was carried out, revealing that Tonia Schovers had been in the company of a certain Johannes R. during Pentecost. Johannes R. was a dangerous character with peculiar inclinations. He liked girls, but women and girls had warned each other about how dangerous Johannes was. Initially charming during courtship, his affection would often inexplicably turn into a murderous rage, making him as dangerous as a wild animal! It was known that this wild man had been in the area around Pentecost. Afterward, he had disappeared across the eastern border of the country to work in Germany ... where, no one knew. He was a chair mender and worked wherever he could find employment. Further investigation also revealed that he had been briefly in the vicinity the day before the forester found the remains of Tonia S.

Naturally, attempts were made to connect the two incidents. However, the man had vanished, and it seemed impossible to discover his current whereabouts. The clothing remnants were gathered as best as possible and, once dried, deposited in a package at the clerk's office of the Almelo Court. The remains of the body were collected into a box and laid to rest in the soil of the cemetery in Diepenheim. After the presumed murder, two full years had passed, and in the spring of 1908, Johannes R. dared to set foot on Dutch soil again. He likely believed that no one would remember Tonia or him anymore. However, the local police remembered everything all too well and arrested him. Now, the task was to try and construct some evidence of his guilt. But that proved to be far from easy!

One day, the examining magistrate for criminal cases from the Almelo Court visited me when he had to be in Amsterdam for a family visit. He asked if I could contribute anything to the reconstruction of the criminal act that had been committed two years ago. He pointed out that the murder had occurred two years prior, the victim's remains were found and buried half a year later, and a year and a half later, the suspected perpetrator was arrested and was currently incarcerated in Almelo.

I truly didn't know what to answer. Where could I possibly find "silent witnesses" now who could have something to say? In any case, I promised that I would do my best to find something. To start, I wanted to visit the scene of the crime, even though it had become overgrown with new coppice in the past two years. Secondly, I wanted to subject the box containing the remains of the clothing to further examination. So, they began sending me the clothing remnants, and we scheduled a day for me to visit the site where Tonia's remains were found. From what I heard, Johannes R. denied all guilt. He couldn't deny knowing Tonia and being in her company on one of the Pentecost days two years prior, but that was the extent of his admission. For the rest, he literally denied everything, even knowing the location of the particular estate, let alone the secluded lane where Tonia's remains were found in the undergrowth. His persistent denial and statements about being unfamiliar with the location where Tonia's remains were found proved to be his downfall.

In my laboratory, I had begun examining the remnants of Tonia's clothing, which must have originally been in a very poor state, judging by the descriptions of her modest appearance and poverty. However, the gnawing field creatures that often feed on the blood of a victim's clothing also chew the fabric everywhere, making the remains barely recognizable and unable to determine what type of garment they belonged to. There I needed the assistance of women, although that assistance was provided with some reluctance due to the "creepiness" of the situation. To proceed with the reconstruction, I used a small bundle of wood shavings, slightly tapered in the middle to serve as a "mannequin" for the torso. The clothing fragments that were recognized by the women's eyes through buttons, hems, or other features were then placed around it. Once all the rags (not yet suitable for cleaning!) were arranged in this way, a further investigation could commence into the many "separations of cohesion," as we call them. Firstly, there were countless tears identifiable by their direction (running exactly along the warp and weft) and the frayed individual threads of the fabric. Secondly, many edges of such separations were found, seemingly nibbled away by field creatures, with several spots marked by bites that sharply cut the threads.

But after some searching, I discovered a short cut with sharp-edged adjacent threads in the upper half of the "torso"(!) of my mannequin, within the clothing remnants. What was most remarkable was the observation that this cut, equally wide and in the same direction, could be found in all overlapping rags in the same corresponding place. There was no doubt: a knife must have penetrated through all layers! Could there be any trace of this on the remains of the body? Then, I consulted with the examining magistrate and advised him to visit the scene of the crime with the suspect and, on the same day after obtaining a court order, exhume the remains of Tonia for further examination and transport them to Amsterdam. The plan was fully approved, and a day was set when I would arrive early at the Goor station, where they would await me. On the platform, I found the examining magistrate, the prosecutor, a clerk, two military police officers, two national policemen, two municipal policemen, and Johannes R., heavily handcuffed, standing in the middle of the circle of his guards. First, I heard that the suspect continued to vehemently deny everything, claiming that he didn't know where the place outside was where Tonia's remains were found. He even claimed not to know how to get to that park. Then, I had an idea.

During the preceding winter, I had attended an evening at the Concertgebouw in Amsterdam, where the then-famous telepath Rubini[34] performed astonishing feats of telepathy. The entire hall was amazed at the certainty with which he executed commands, about whose form and nature only a few confidants in the hall knew (carefully selected to avoid having a spy among them! Two doctors and the author of this text constituted that committee). After that evening, I enjoyed attempting

---

34 Eugene de Rubini, the Czech "telepath" who sold out theaters in Amsterdam from 1919 onwards.

to replicate his actions, and indeed, I succeeded to some extent in performing similar tricks. So, when suspect R. continued to insist that he didn't know where the estate was, nor which direction he should take to get there, and claimed to have never been there, I decided to test the accuracy of these statements. At my request, the psychiatrist Dr. Le Rütte from Deventer was present as an expert. I briefly consulted with him, after which I took the prosecutor aside. "I can assure you," I said, "that I have never been in this area before. I am on completely unfamiliar ground here. However, I'm willing to try leading you to the spot where Tonia's remains were found, walking ahead of you, provided that Johannes R.—without his handcuffs—walks beside me, and I will hold onto his wrist!" If things happened as I expected, it would conclusively demonstrate that the suspect unconsciously directed me to that location!

That plan was agreed upon. The suspect—freed from his handcuffs—was sternly warned that he need not attempt to escape while walking between the two experts, as they would walk ahead of him. This was because two sharpshooters with loaded rifles followed closely behind him. The journey began. As soon as we left the station, I immediately sensed the direction in which the walk should start. Whenever the road forked or had a side path, Johannes R.'s pulse told me with certainty how I should and should not proceed to get closer to the desired spot. Dr. Le Rütte and I both counted the pulses. I conveyed their number in Latin each time, after which he quickly made a note. Ten meters behind us were the policemen and members of the court, and, as I later heard, they were amazed at how confidently we followed the shortest route to the specific lane! Finally, we arrived at "the" lane; I could clearly perceive it from the arrestee's pulse and his breathing. Upon reaching the middle of the lane, I suddenly had to stop and remark, "We are now going too far; we have just passed the exact spot." After that, I pointed out to the examining magistrate the place where it must have happened; it was spot on! I still hear the words of the prosecutor: "If it weren't a tragedy, I would applaud your achievements!" Yet, I found this experiment not so difficult myself. This experiment, crowned with success, gave everyone the moral conviction that no one other than the suspect had guided me to this location, which he must have known. (It goes without saying that Dr. L. R. was also unfamiliar with the terrain on-site).

During the subsequent renewed questioning of R., he lied so blatantly in all his answers that, upon learning that I had found a knife stab through the clothing, he adamantly declared not to own a knife and never to have used one! And that while his profession was that of a chair caner! In the oak coppice, as expected, there was nothing more for me to discover. The spot, now densely overgrown, was hardly distinguishable from its surroundings. However, a mark made by the forester on a tree on the other side of the footpath firmly established the exact location! Now, the excavation was in order at the simple cemetery, where the gravedigger had already exposed the top of the relevant coffin. After verifying, based on the cemetery register, that the remains found in the park on that particular day were indeed stored in this box, the disarranged skeletal parts, still bearing small pieces of clothing fabric, were transferred to a so-called starch box, which could easily hold the entire collection of bones. Due to my train's departure time, I bid farewell there, and a carriage that had arrived took me to the station with my luggage.

An unusual surprise awaited me there. The stationmaster, apparently well aware of legal regulations, approached me and happily informed me that he just happened to have an empty freight car on the platform. When I asked him what he meant (I understood where he was going!), he told me, "Corpses can only be transported in a separate car, and didn't you just unearth a body in the cemetery over there?" I indicated to him that there must be a misunderstanding on that matter and asked in return, "If a medical student from Leiden wants to continue studying in Amsterdam, should his "Grim Reaper" be transported in a separate freight car?" His response was, "No, of course not, because that's a skeleton, not a body anymore!" "Do you know, Mr. Stationmaster, where a body stops being called a body and can be called a 'skeleton'?" "That's the thing, I don't know!" "Well then, chief, I know; I'm an expert and I take full responsibility; in this box is a dried-out skeleton that has turned to dust, and it can no longer be called a 'body.'" "Well, then, it is for me—and, in accordance with my request—the starch box with the bones was weighed and registered as passenger cargo, after which I received my receipt.

For the examination of the skeletal parts, the examining magistrate appointed Dr. Schoo from Amsterdam as an expert, at my request, whose friendly collaboration *pro justitia* (for the sake of the law) was always an indescribable pleasure to me. We often worked together in criminal cases for the Amsterdam Court. Unfortunately, he was taken from his family, his many friends, and his beloved work through a lingering illness in the prime of his life. Together, we carefully inspected the contents of the starch box, where a scratch on the sternum was discovered, evidently caused by the deflection of some sharp object—presumably the knife during one of the administered thrusts. Now, the series of slits in the clothing where the knife had passed through were more to the side of the midline, and it was evident that—after a stab that had hit the sternum—a second one, situated more to the side, would have been inflicted. My friend Schoo cleaned the bones meticulously and reconstructed the skeleton to its full extent using copper wires. However, several joints were missing from the fingers and feet. It is likely that larger field animals had dragged them away, as I was assured that during the collection of the remains, every effort had been made to meticulously search everything, so as not to overlook any part.

And now, Reader, are you curious about the final outcome? Based on the data collected from this side, the examining magistrate succeeded in extracting enough from Johannes R. that the prosecutor could charge him with "severe assault resulting in death." The court sentenced him to a prison term of fifteen years, a verdict to which he acquiesced.

Epilogue by Jaap Knotter

Based solely on the gathered evidence, a conviction in this case would not have been successful. The way in which the suspect could be linked to the crime scene can be considered creative, but it doesn't necessarily indicate his involvement in the committed crime. The same applies to the link with the presumed murder weapon. The breakthrough seems to have been the suspect's confession to the interrogating magistrate, despite his previous denials. If he had chosen to remain silent, it would have been difficult to secure a conviction.

35. Bombs

During World War I, it happened that a shop in the Kalverstraat, behind whose plate glass a large collection of Brownings and other automatic firearms was displayed, had its plate glass smashed during the night, and before a policeman had appeared on the scene, the "people" had already left, taking all these weapons with them.

The central criminal investigation department put out all its feelers. One of them pointed in the direction of an anarchist, living on the Haarlemmerweg, and within a short time the court had issued a search warrant for his house, upon which the public prosecutor, the commissioner of the court, the clerk of the court, and several inspectors of the central criminal investigation department went to the house. The occupant was not at home—but his spouse was, who was unhappy that during the absence of her husband, whose comings and goings were well known to her, everything in the house would be searched.

In the front room stood—diagonally covering the corner of the room—a couch, behind whose railing one of the peeping eyes discovered a collection of objects, which undoubtedly had to be bombs: pieces of iron pipe five to six centimeters in diameter, twelve to fifteen centimeters long; at the bottom—by autogenous welding—fitted with an iron base, while at the top a grey head like half a billiard ball, made of concrete, formed the seal. Hardly had this collection of dangerous objects been discovered, when the woman warned everyone to be extremely careful with them, because "taken in your hand, they could explode."

The public prosecutor immediately ordered to telephone the expert v. L. H. to come and give his assistance.... Let me tell you straight away that, although I may have known a little more about the chemistry of explosives, my knowledge of bombs was far from adequate. I could have mentally equipped myself in every area in which I would have to assist as a criminalist, except that of "bombs." You will ask why: in the literature one finds nothing on this subject—perhaps fortunately!—since a book on the composition of bombs would perhaps be bought more in the big underworld than in the small circle of criminalists. And—if I tried to enrich my knowledge at those institutions, which were involved in the manufacture of bombs (here I am thinking first of all of the artillery ordnance factory at Hembrug!)—I came home with a sore head, because there strict secrecy was imposed and even with regard to a police expert no exception could be made!

So it was that I always felt "poor" in knowledge, as soon as the Justice Department brought me in as an expert on a bomb situation(!) However, by a very strange coincidence, I had come into possession of a brochure entitled *The Practical Anarchist*. It was a little work translated from the French, but how had it been translated! By no means by a chemist, but undoubtedly by a layman, who had to look up all the scientific terms he was unfamiliar with in a dictionary and—when he didn't find them there—choose at random translated terms that "looked a bit like it." I remember that *benzène* (benzene) was translated as "petrol"; when he read "acetone" in one of the recipes and couldn't find that word in his dictionary, the Dutch translation simply said "acetic acid"! So there were numerous mystifications in that booklet, which of course had to lead sometimes to the desired end product not being achieved because it couldn't have any explosive tendencies, but then again to enormous dangers for anyone who, when following the recipes, wrongly took a "quid pro quo"! However, what I could understand in that booklet—which, of course, was by no means intended for the eyes of a criminalist!—was the technique according to which some kinds of bombs had to be made, and I had studied it well!

So when I saw, among the finished bombs sealed with concrete, one half-made product that—for one reason or another—had been put away halfway, unfinished, I immediately understood what type of bombs I was dealing with and according to what instructions these dangerous things had been made. It also became clear to me immediately why the lady of the house anxiously said: "If one falls over, it could explode ... even if you turn it upside down in your hand!" Now I knew enough! My mind was made up. I calmly grabbed the two largest specimens—upright, of course—and asked, which of the detectives was willing to follow my example, to take them together to the neighboring police station (Post Haarlemmerplein).

I had assured them that—as long as these objects were kept upright—nothing could happen; my word and the example I set led to each of them picking up two of those bombs and following me. I will never forget how suddenly a friendly voice came up behind me and—before I wanted to walk down the somewhat steep stairs—said: "Mr. Hulsebosch, it would not be at all appropriate for me to criticize your actions, but I would like to suggest to you: give me those big ones and take some smaller ones; I don't have a wife and children at home—you do! Thus spoke the—then still young—Inspector of Police Broekhoff, who later became one of my best friends and left the service as acting chief commissioner in 1941!

I can still see the frightened look of the sergeant-in-charge at our entrance with the bombs! It took persuasion on my part to reassure him and convince him that these objects—quietly placed in a few cupboards, which I would lock and seal—could do no harm. So gradually all the bombs came to the post house temporarily; the next day I would take them to the artillery ordnance factory at Hembrug, but first some arrangements had to be made. In such matters, I always enjoyed the cooperation of Ir. Berkhout—a chemist at the factory—who was appointed by the court as a fellow expert. He would wait for me to arrive with the bombs the next day. The chief commissioner placed one of the police boats at my disposal; it would dock exactly behind the old Haarlemmerpoort (which housed the said post house). Artillery Captain B. would send me six artillery soldiers to assist in transferring them onboard. On the deck behind the pilot's chair, a long line was wound in such a way that the bombs could be placed safely within this fence, so that—should a collision occur unexpectedly, or the boat get an unseen knock while mooring—none of the dangerous objects could fall over. The space between the objects was filled with paper wadding. My friend Berkhout was already waiting for us at Hembrug. The soldiers again very carefully and cautiously carried the lot inside, where it was put away in a separate shed.

The next day our investigation began. The semi-finished product gave us—as I already mentioned—an insight into the construction method and the load. From this we could immediately deduce that they would not be "gentle" if exploded. We had enough material, so we wanted to make sure of its functioning—its effect! We used the so-called explosive pit, a deeply dug grave. This is what it looked like: instead of planks against the sides, heavy thick beams—old railway sleepers and the like—had been placed here, while the pit was about two and a half meters deep. Next to the pit was a lifting device—a crane—which was used to pick up huge heavy iron plates—as big as large tombstones—and place them over the pit, once objects had been put down there for explosion. We made a small table on three legs, placed at the bottom of the pit, on which one of our bombs would be placed. Attached to one of the legs was a wire, which ran to the top and reached up to about fifty meters from the pit. Pulling the wire would cause the table to tilt and the bomb to move into its dangerous position.

I descended a ladder into the pit, set the unstable table down, and placed one of the bombs on top of it. The wire was attached to one table leg. Then, very carefully—so as not to pull the wire or get my foot caught in it—I left the pit via the ladder, pulled up the ladder and had the heavy iron plates placed over the pit—and then distanced myself like hell. I then pulled the wire. Patiently we waited, minute by minute … until after twenty minutes there was a huge explosion. Clouds of dust rose up alongside the iron tombstones. Then we rushed to the pit to have the iron plates removed. After some mist lifted, we looked down—but we saw nothing but the empty pit! No bomb remains, no table … everything had apparently disappeared! Closer inspection showed us the following: the bomb had included a lot of old wire nails and bent square nails, such as one sometimes finds at the blacksmith's. All these had been destroyed by the force of the explosion. They had been driven into the timbers of the sleepers—most of them headfirst, pressed deep inside, so that none of these pointy, sharp iron objects protruded beyond the surface of the beams!

We had workers shovel the sand at the bottom of the pit into buckets and dump it next to the pit, passing everything through a sieve. This is how we collected the small debris, the shards of the bomb's casing and the small splinters of wood from our "table." All these fragments had been pushed into the ground more than a meter deep by the force of the explosion! Our task was also to defuse the rest of the bombs.

Meanwhile, we were eager to try to establish with the desired certainty that the completed bombs had indeed been manufactured according to the same which the incomplete specimen had been manufactured. For this, it was necessary to remove the concrete cap (which was held firmly together by the iron nails and chain pieces cast into the concrete!) from the cylindrical part; we could not dare to do that by hand. So Ir. Berghout suggested the idea of putting a weak explosive charge as a noose around one of the bombs, after it had been buried largely vertically in the ground—the head only above the surface of the blast pit floor. This was done. Four bombs, equipped in this way, disappointed us, as the bomb's charge detonated along with our auxiliary charge, but with the fifth, the weakness of the explosion we observed gave us hope that only the concrete head had have been detonated. And so it turned out to be! It was now absolutely clear how the bombs were built and what chemicals they contained, but also how intensely dangerous they were! It goes without saying that, here again, I anxiously conceal the construction and the load!

The court gave the maker a prison sentence. However, this did not bother him as much as—after his dismissal—the fact that not one house owner in Amsterdam wanted to rent him a house! And I can be brief about the attitude of the neighbors upstairs and downstairs of the large building when they noticed what the police had found at H.'s place. The woman left quietly, because the anger of the people living upstairs and downstairs was indescribable! A few weeks after the aforementioned investigation had been completed, the police received a hint from an informant that a batch of the same bombs was also hidden in a warehouse on Bickerseiland. It was a kind of shed with an earthen floor. In one of the corners of the room where water poured from a watering can over the floor sank faster into the ground (indicating where the ground was looser!), we went digging, and soon twelve grayish round heads of bombs similar to those found over there were sticking out of the sand. These bombs, too, were defused at the Hembrug. It could never be proven who had made them or hidden them there.

During World War I, I was involved in another investigation dealing with bombs. One morning—still in bed—I received a telegram by phone, sent by the judge commissioner for criminal cases in Maastricht, which read approximately: "Expect you at the next opportunity here for investigation regarding an international bomb affair." I hurried to catch the first train to Maastricht. At the Palace of Justice in Maastricht, I learned what had happened the previous day on and around the small steamboat that still ran a regular service between Maastricht and Liège in those days.

Someone—unknown to any of the boat crew—had brought four large iron barrels on board—said to contain carbide—destined for "someone" in Liège. When the boat mate—to make some space for further deck cargo—wanted to move the barrels a little closer together, he heard a metallic clink, caused by the contents knocking against each other. This could not be carbide, so he immediately warned the captain of the boat. The captain investigated and recognized that the boy was right. He decided to open one of the barrels. Then he was shocked to see yellow copper bombs—1,098 of them!—which had been brought on board as "carbide." He hurried to move them onto the bank and alerted the police. At the same time, the stranger who had brought the lot on board hurried to get away. The combined barrels were housed in a basement of the Palace of Justice. In one of the barrels was a long explosive fuse, which—as I heard later—was meant to be laid zigzagging in a basement of a barracks in Liège, after which the 1,098 loose copper bombs were to be laid down across it. If the aforementioned explosive fuse exploded, the other items would explode at the same time.

My assignment was to investigate the nature of the bombs and, before that, to check for possible fingerprints on the smooth copper sheaths. So that's where I started. Oh, what a tedious job, and how monotonous! And the most tedious part was that not a single usable fingerprint that lent itself to identification could be found on any of these objects! The bombs, which apparently needed a so-called initial explosion to detonate themselves, had to be brought to the Hembrug. Of course, I could only examine them there and not in my own laboratory! But now came the great difficulty: How to get a limited number of these things to Amsterdam and to the Hembrug? There was a conferral, but nobody knew how to get them to their destination. Then I decided to commit an offence; in each inner and outer pocket of my jacket and overcoat, I put a bomb, fully convinced that—without an initial explosion—they could never be detonated. The examining magistrate thought it was "creepy," but didn't know any other way out! And that's what happened.

The next day I took the evening train to Amsterdam "packed and unpacked," and the following day to the Hembrug. It turned out that all the canisters contained picric acid. A test taken with one of these objects in the aforementioned explosive pit showed the fabulously strong effect of the explosion. No matter how hard we searched, no proof of guilt could be found against any of the people initially arrested. So the perpetrators of this setup were never found.

And—while I am writing down these memories from my practice—we are again in a state of war and elements appear now and then to disturb the order, frighten us, and pose as heroes in the eyes of their "friends." I'd like to tell you about a few "bomb scares" from this period, too. Certain nervous tension among the public, all kinds of reports about bomb attacks abroad, led to people—more easily than before—feeling anxious, "seeing dangers" where in fact there were none. And then there were always pranksters who took pleasure in frightening their nervous fellow men.

I still clearly remember how on one evening—at dusk—an alarm came over my duty phone reporting something like the following: "Police station number such and such notices, that a police officer, having been warned that a bomb with a smoldering fuse had been placed in the portico of bank building A, entered this portico at risk to his own safety and was able to extinguish the burning part of the fuse. The bomb has been seized; expert examination is demanded; for this purpose, the bomb will be transferred to the police laboratory—v. L. H. to be transferred."

To be honest, I could well imagine the dismay of my family and my staff at such an order; after all, the question remains whether it can be considered responsible to bring a bomb—the nature of which has not yet been established—into a house in which my family lives and which also houses my laboratories, where—at that time—my assistants were working! But, be that as it may, I was brought home. And then I soon had good fun! Firstly, the bomb consisted of a copper shell—a tube into which my thumb could barely be inserted. At both ends it was sealed with something strongly reminiscent of bread dough. The filling consisted of a mixture of dry sand with some cement, and the fuse was nothing more or less than an end of shoelace, one end of which was pushed into the sealing compound, while the free end was found smoldering (causing all sorts of memories to pop into my brain of mischief at school, such as secretly bringing in a smoldering piece of shoelace, which was then called a "stinker"). In any case, I was soon able to reassure the authorities, after which the calming message was immediately passed on to the higher "echelons," who had already been dutifully informed about the "bomb attack"!

An even greater panic took hold of the crowd during the war days in May 1940. When everyone rushed to the shelters during an air raid, people repeatedly dropped things, sometimes a bar of chocolate, sometimes a packet of cigarettes, or something else. It didn't take long before the supposition put forward by one fool, that hostile elements had poisoned these chocolate bars, these cigars and cigarettes, and had deliberately deposited them on the public roads, was embraced by many and shared from mouth to mouth. Convinced of the "truth" of these reports, they passed them on as absolutely reliable and correct.

Of course, I immediately began to carefully examine the cigarettes sent to me for examination by various section offices until I became convinced that the fears were all nonsense. All the police authorities who had thrown such an investigation at me were very curious about the results, and my telephone was constantly occupied by them to inquire how far I had progressed with their investigation. One of them, who was convinced "that the cigarettes must have been poisoned" and expressed his doubts whether I had overlooked some poison, only regained his composure when I assured him that, having found nothing, I had quietly lit one of the cigarettes. "Oh, Mr. Commissioner"—I said to him over the phone—"I am so convinced of the harmless nature of these cigarettes that, while I am talking to you on the phone, I am having a nice smoke!" When he inquired a few hours later whether I had done well and heard that I had smoked another one, he fortunately calmed down. People were also terribly afraid of the chocolate bars, although neither the packaging nor the mechanically applied shiny surface of the bars showed the slightest abnormal aspect.

Then—one evening—the director of one of the big hospitals called me. Not far from the hospital, someone had found a peculiarly shaped bottle of mysterious red liquid. It had to have a deeper meaning. It had been brought to his office by the analysts of the clinical laboratory, but, in his opinion, such a strange object belonged in my home under the present circumstances! So, half an hour later, a confidant of the aforementioned hospital director brought me the mysterious bottle, which he handed to me with a serious look. Hardly had I held it in my hands when I burst out laughing—to the amazement of the messenger, who was still looking serious and worried. Do you know, Reader, what he handed me? A piece of children's toy from a miniature magic box, as I had seen several times before.

Many of you will be familiar with fake glasses, double-walled, with red colored water inserted between the walls. If such a glass is on the table in front of you, you might think that you have been brought a glass of liqueur. When you lift the glass, the liquid moves into the space between the walls ... but no matter how you swirl it and put it to your lips, nothing enters your mouth! Well, a greatly reduced edition of these fake-like glasses—only a few centimeters in size—was handed to me! The "stem" of the glass was hollow. Through it the red liquid was placed in the space between the two walls, after which an extremely small piece of cork had to provide the seal. Now when people held the glass upside down, the cork "pushed deep into the neck of the flask" could not be removed without endangering the flask itself, and the actual hollow part of the flask was considered to be a deep "punt" in the flask. Never have I had such fun with such a fake glass as on this occasion!

In 1941 and early 1942, there were a few occasions when certain terrorists exercised their power by detonating homemade "bombs," whose explosions caused more terror and material damage than personal accidents, which is very fortunate! After I was first called to investigate a building on the southern border of Amsterdam, where a bomb placed under the façade caused damage to the house and a garage, as well as many broken windowpanes on the other side of the street, I could only deduce which components had been used in the infernal device from the components of the residue deposited on the stones of the façade. Sometime later, a bomb exploded in Amsterdam West, again causing minor material damage and no personal injuries, but, in the quiet of the night, a lot of shock. There, too, I determined which chemicals had been used to make the bomb.

In the course of one night in January 1942, at around one o'clock in the morning, a bomb exploded in one of the windows of the basement of a large mansion on the Weteringschans, which at the time housed the Studentenfront (Student Front) organization, with enough explosive force to smash windows here and there in the upper floors of the houses across the street. A little later I was awoken from my sleep. The police asked me to come to the scene immediately to investigate. I made serious objections to this. As an expert, I had to search for clues. I could never do that in Egyptian darkness, such as prevailed this night. Even the police couldn't illuminate the spot, so how on earth could I work in the darkness…? So I agreed with the inspector on duty of the police section concerned that I would be there—as soon as daybreak—to start my investigation.

And so, it happened. Just after nine o'clock, as soon as I could drive my car without artificial light, I set off, taking the suitcase with my necessities with me. The trellis in the window frame of the basement was shattered. The two-piece window behind it was completely destroyed. From the seams between the neighboring cement tiles of the pavement I was able to collect granulated chemical residues, which were taken to my laboratory for further identification. As I learned, the police had already found some of the bomb shell's remains on the road during the night and deposited them at the Stadhouderskade office. I went there briefly to receive them from the inspector for further chemical analysis, and drove back to the building where the explosion had occurred.

Then followed the curious discovery that in the second window frame, between the hedge and the window, there was also something strange. It seemed to be a cylindrical package wrapped in dirty rags, which were tied up with straps. On one of the rags—at the top—I saw black spots, which at first, I thought were charred spots, which made me assume that—after lighting a fuse—the fire had been extinguished and therefore this bomb would not have exploded. I re-entered the house through the front door and descended to the basement, where—through the cellar, which contained the central heating boiler—I reached the back of the window in question. I carefully removed the bomb and walked up the stairs to the first floor. There I found, among others, an officer from the German Police, who was as curious about this find as everyone else present. On a ping-pong table in the middle of a back room, I put the package down and unbuttoned the straps holding the pieces of fabric—apparently old, dirty cleaning cloths—together, and soon the infernal tool lay exposed before our eyes. It was a piece of iron pipe, over five centimeters wide and about twenty-four centimeters long. It was threaded at one end and closed with a screwed-on cap and closed at the other end by a disc of sheet iron, which was connected to the cylindrical part as a bottom by autogenous welding. "This far and no further" said my intuition, and I immediately thought again of my married former collaborator, Viëtor.[35]

---

35 [This note appears in the original Dutch text of this book.] Berend W. Viëtor worked at my laboratory for ten years, first as an apprentice, later as an assistant. I trained him entirely for criminalistic work. Mobilization called him away from me. Shortly after the war, when he left the military service, he received his destination: he was assigned to The Hague criminal investigation unit as a police expert, where he was soon held in high esteem by all his superiors. On July 23, 1941, he took an interest in a canister with

The representative of the German Police—realizing that I did not wish to continue with the anatomy lesson—also thought it would be better to leave the further dissection to a *"Feuerwerker."*[36] In anticipation of his expected arrival, I placed the suspect object on the mantelpiece, against the chimney wall, where it lay calmly, and supported it at the front with the rags that had been wrapped around it. Then I returned by car to my laboratory, to examine the deposit on the fence, the chemicals found and the remains of the infernal contraption, further chemically. On arrival, I left the car, saying to myself, "I won't put the car away yet. I have a notion that something else will come up there!" I went to my private laboratory to delve into the research. Ten or twelve minutes must have passed when the phone rang. The inspector at the office on Stadhouderskade informed me that the second bomb had just exploded with a loud bang, causing serious damage to the suite on the first floor!

My car was still waiting in front of the door. I rushed to the Weteringschans. The two policemen looked at me with grateful faces who, as guards in front of the house, made sure that curious passers-by kept going. Grateful, indeed! Had the dangerous thing been left where it was deposited, the two policemen would undoubtedly have been hurt! For now, everything was limited to material damage. Nobody had been injured by the explosion, except for the caretaker, who—standing at the outer door—had been hit by a shard of one of the large mirror panes falling down on his forehead—a cut that was quickly stitched at the guesthouse and further bandaged. I had crawled through the eye of a needle! Had I gotten up half an hour later and had I started my work that much later—then this infernal machine would have brought the Amsterdam police chief the same fate as the infernal machine in The Hague brought to Viëtor!

People congratulated me on this happy ending. The back room was quite devastated. The mantelpiece was completely shattered; in the standing flue a hole had been made in the brickwork; in the front and back room the panes of the windows were shattered; one shard of the iron pipe had made a big crack in the wall of the front room. I was told that, entering the room immediately after the explosion, a dense smell of gunpowder had been detected. The chemical analysis showed similar explosive charges. I did not hesitate to state emphatically that I

---

a screw cap whose meaning no one knew. He unscrewed the cap with the terrible result that a horrific explosion shattered his body; the building was also severely damaged and two other persons were seriously injured. At the cremation ceremony it became clear once again in how many hearts he had managed to win a good place. Not only did his young wife and sweet little daughter grieve, but also his many friends, including his old teacher, were weighed down by the loss of this good man. Later, I learned that the strange object had been found on the beach at Scheveningen; nobody understood what it was and, suspecting no wrong, it had been stored on the top floor of one of the buildings belonging to the police headquarters! There it had been lying incognito for seven months!

36 That is, an expert in explosives.

could not explain anything about the technical construction of the infernal device. As I explained above, as a police scientist I never had the opportunity to inform myself on this subject "comme il faut"! Despite this, it is "the police expert" who investigates such matters!

Epilogue by Mattijs Koeberg: Safety: Collaboration of Different Forms of Expertise

Co van Ledden Hulsebosch addresses three main issues in this chapter that are just as valid today: safety, expertise, and collaboration. Especially around crime scenes and investigations that are dealing with hazardous materials, these three are crucial and interconnected. Many kinds of expertise are required to safely handle the investigation, and all parties have to understand each other's expertise in order to work together optimally. Van Ledden Hulsebosch knows his limitations in the knowledge of explosive device construction and excels in chemical knowledge and logical reasoning.

This is not only true for explosives investigations, but also for the investigation of, for example, drugs labs or chemical, biological, radiological, and nuclear (CBRN) materials and instable crime scenes (such as collapsed buildings and airplane crashes). One example of how this is dealt with nowadays is the forensic training that Explosive Ordnance Disposal (EOD) personal receives from forensic experts of the Netherlands Forensic Institute (NFI). In this training the military experts from the EOD get a better understanding of the (procedures of) relevant forensic disciplines, such as DNA, fingerprint, electronic devices, micro traces and explosives. The other way around, getting to know the EOD procedures and techniques is part of the training of NFI forensic explosives experts. These training are not meant to be able to do each other's jobs, but to be better able to collaborate, knowing what the other's party's role is in the collaboration. The same is true for explosives safety officers and forensic experts of the National Police. A joined knowledge database, the Dutch Bomb Data System, further supports this collaboration.

This exchange of knowledge also helps in determining where the border is between "safety first" and finding the perpetrator and finding out what happened. "Safety first" does not have to mean that no forensics is possible in dangerous situations. Investing in knowledge exchange ensures that in the Netherlands, in most cases involving hazardous materials, we have the knowledge and collaborations in place to do very extensive forensic investigations, while keeping everyone involved safe!

36. Cigarettes with Water Damage

This time it wasn't a matter for justice or the police, but for an insurance company in Amsterdam, which called me one day in late autumn of 1918—several weeks after Armistice Day—and asked if I would be willing to conduct an investigation for a group of insurers, mainly in Dusseldorf. About fifty large crates, containing big cardboard boxes, which, in turn, held small cigarette packets, had arrived in Dusseldorf with significant water damage from the Rotterdam ship that transported the valuable cargo. After ensuring I would obtain a visa to enter that area, occupied by the Belgians, I accepted the assignment. I received the necessary information about consignors, freight forwarders, consignees. I also reviewed the report of an expert from Dusseldorf who had "inspected" the shipment, extensively describing the water damage, deeming the consignment practically worthless.

It was twilight when I arrived in Dusseldorf, so I postponed commencing my work until the next morning. I attempted to meet the expert to propose his presence during my examination, a gesture of generosity in case we disagreed on any aspect. I vividly recall, in order to pass the Rhine bridge, I had to had to pass through the customs warehouse, which had to pass over half the length of the bridge, over the full width—from one handrail to the other—was built upon it. Belgian military personnel meticulously checked the papers of everyone crossing the bridge! The precious cigarette shipment was stored in a spacious warehouse with a glass roof, providing excellent light for the investigation.

As we entered, I observed several crates already opened, revealing soaking wet cardboard boxes and others partially saturated with water. My enthusiastic "colleague" emphatically drew my attention to all of this, insisting that due to this water damage, everything was rendered unusable and practically worthless. It was not difficult for me to understand that he represented the owners/senders. When he suspected my lack of enthusiasm for the established fact of water damage, he attempted once again to convince me that literally nothing usable remained in the crates. Everything had been damaged by water.

However, the captain of the shipping company that brought these crates from Rotterdam to Dusseldorf had filed a statement, clearly establishing that no rain had fallen during the journey, and the cargo could not have suffered water damage in any other way. So the damage must have occurred after the shipping company handed over this shipment to a forwarder, responsible for transporting everything to the warehouse. Since the insurance covered the entire journey of the cigarettes, including that final part between the dock and the warehouse, it was now a matter of determining where and how this damage occurred!

As I was led from right to left through the warehouse, inspecting one opened crate after another, particularly focusing on the stack of wet boxes brought out from those crates, I requested the warehouse staff to close all the crates examined by my colleague and place them in a separate area. Then, I asked for assistance in dragging forward a couple of crates I chose from the inventory. Everyone looked somewhat puzzled. What could he be thinking? What does this Dutchman want? Does he believe that the other crates contain dry boxes? We just took them out randomly! I noticed clearly that, at that moment, they found me a puzzle, which left me unfazed. Two crates were placed in the middle of the floor, and the warehouse workers immediately grabbed their tools to open the crates for me. However, I politely approached them, requesting a moment's delay to carefully inspect the external surfaces of the crates. Sitting on a lower crate, I examined the edge of the lid with a magnifying glass. Soon, my "colleague" curiously asked what I was staring at. "Oh," I remarked, "I am just making sure there isn't a single rusted nail head." All the nails hammered through the edge of the crate lid shined like a mirror, declaring one after another that they had not experienced a shower! I sensed a certain shock in my "colleague." This observation of mine regarding the nail heads did not fit into his reconstruction of the damage and somewhat jeopardized his report. He admitted he had completely overlooked it but found my view "indeed" interesting.

Next, I touched the exterior of the crate planks at numerous points with my aniline pencil to draw a short line. Nowhere did the familiar lovely purple color appear, observable as soon as a wet plank is marked with such a pencil. The wood was dry! Internally, yes, on the inside of the crate, there were enough traces of moisture. When I lifted the lid, eager helpers wanted to start immediately and begin lifting the cardboard boxes out of the crate. I expressed my gratitude for all their helpfulness, but preferred to take another moment to observe before personally removing box after box from the crate. One of the boxes from the top layer was completely wet. However, the section of the lid that had rested directly on top of it and a piece of paper that had been between the box and the lid were dry! This cardboard box exhibited a wet spot on its side, where it had been pressed against another box. So, had water "penetrated" through that gap between the two boxes? But why did the neighboring box not show a similar wet spot in mirror image on its side? No, indeed, that neighboring box was completely dry but revealed a thoroughly soaked bottom on the side that stood on top of a dry box. I quickly became convinced that the water, which had spoiled all these cigarette boxes, had not drenched them after they were packed in these crates, but before. My "colleague," who had only declared in his report that the shipment had proven entirely worthless due to water damage, requested his report back to add something to it(!).

Naturally, my clients were extremely satisfied with my report, and the Rotterdam firm that had submitted the claim about the "cigarettes spoiled during the journey to Dusseldorf" received a stern letter. In response, they received a note that they themselves had known nothing about it, but upon inquiry, it was discovered that the cigarettes, which had been stored in a cellar in Rotterdam, had suffered serious damage after a "high water" event from the Maas. They had sought a way to have someone else compensate for this damage and sent a dummy buyer to Dusseldorf to whom the shipment, neatly packaged, was sent.

In hindsight, they probably thought: how foolish not to use rusted nails and ensure that at least the crates were properly dampened. But then they would have neglected something else. The truth eventually comes to the surface, sooner or later, like water!

Epilogue by Brigitte Bruijns

Phil Collins's song "Both Sides of the Story" resonates with the complexities inherent in forensic research, where every piece of evidence tells a story from multiple perspectives. Just as the song explores the different viewpoints in conflicts, forensic investigations demand a comprehensive examination of evidence to uncover the truth. In forensic science, each detail, whether minute or significant, contributes to unraveling the narratives embedded within crime scenes, accidents, or historical events.

37. Ill-fated Bloodstains

On the evening of February 10, 1942, I received a phone call informing me that a gentleman living alone in a ground-floor apartment on the Van Hillegaertstraat in Amsterdam had been found murdered in the front room. It was late in the evening, and due to the blackout measures, on the one hand, and the thick layer of snow, which made some streets impassable, on the other hand, the public prosecutor deemed it preferable to postpone the start of the investigation until the next morning. Therefore, I was instructed to go to the indicated address the following day. Since I was driving my own car—as I was taking along all the suitcases with instruments that I might need—I decided to pick up the prosecutor and the examining magistrate on the way.

Upon arrival, we found members of the relevant police division and Inspector Posthuma from the central detective service (headquarters) already present. As will become clear later, Inspector Posthuma played a major role in the laurels that accompanied the resolution of this murder case. The small apartment quickly became crowded with people, actually far too many to allow for a calm search for evidence of the crime and its perpetrator. In the narrow hallway, the people present were packed like sardines after a neighbor and a good friend of the deceased were let in, hoping that they could provide valuable information.

The said good friend informed us that he had made an arrangement with Freddy, as he called the deceased, to pick him up on Sunday afternoon but that he had not answered the door. Later that afternoon, he had tried again but with equally little success. On Monday, he had attempted once more and eventually gave up, assuming that his friend had left the city for a few days. My friend Hulst from Leiden, the forensic pathologist, was also present. We examined the position of the body and the bloodstains on it and on the surrounding objects. Soon, we got the impression that the victim had been struck on the head with some heavy object, first while standing and then again, while lying on his back in front of the fireplace on the small carpet. Fragments of a teapot, a cup and saucer, and a blue decorative plate were scattered in the immediate vicinity of the corpse. Otherwise, the small room, which made a "crowded" impression with its many pieces of furniture, showed little evidence of the committed crime. Everything appeared to be in its proper place. There were no signs of a break-in. No money was found in the wallet located in the inner pocket of the jacket, but a sum of a hundred guilders was discovered in a pocket of the vest. Whether any money had nevertheless disappeared from the mentioned wallet, and whether greed might have been a motive for this gruesome crime, remained a mystery for the time being.

The autopsy conducted in the afternoon revealed that the skull had been fractured by several blows with a heavy object, while the lower right jaw had been shattered. Rib fractures and stab wounds, including one that pierced the stomach wall, were also observed. Therefore, it was presumed that we were dealing with the work of more than one perpetrator. The upstairs neighbor drew the attention of the police to the fact that a new bicycle, which the deceased had not owned for very long, had disappeared from the narrow corridor. It was reasonable to assume that a perpetrator had made his escape with that bike. However, what brand, what number, what other identifying features could be provided as a description of that bike, necessary for a rapid investigation? All they knew was that the man had recently purchased a beautiful new bicycle, and that was it!

While the police did not have any immediate leads to follow, Inspector Posthuma followed his own path and calmly sniffed around the house while the experts were at the autopsy table and the judicial authorities had resumed their activities elsewhere, without knowing exactly what he was looking for! In the deceased's writing desk, there were folders with papers related to his administration. He had also lent money to various individuals. Could one of them have committed the act and searched for their promissory note? No, the order prevailing in the archive spoke against it.

Continuing his search, Chief Inspector Posthuma stumbled upon a folder in which the deceased had stored various papers related to insurance policies. There was a fire insurance policy, a burglary insurance policy, and ... to his surprise, a recent insurance policy specifically for the newly purchased bicycle! Suddenly, he had all the details he needed: the brand, color, frame height, frame number, saddle type—everything! Posthuma quickly composed a notice that should appear in the newspapers that same evening, requesting the whereabouts of that particular bicycle. The next morning, he received a phone call from someone who had been present in a small café when a bicycle matching the given description was sold. The caller didn't know the seller's identity (although he was sure he would readily recognize the man), but he could immediately provide the name of the buyer who had paid a hundred guilders for it. You will understand the urgency with which Posthuma hurried to the address of the new owner, where, upon entering the premises, he found the bicycle standing in front of him. The question of how the man obtained the bicycle was promptly answered. "Please don't think that I stole this bike! I bought it fair and square and even asked the seller for a receipt, which I can show you now!" And just like that, Mr. Posthuma found himself holding a document that could be called "the beginning of it all." The most remarkable aspect was that the receipt was written and signed by ... the same good friend of the deceased who had willingly provided us with information and had often been turned away at Freddy's front door!

That friend, whom we'll call Chris, immediately received a message to come to the police station to provide further information, to which he readily complied. With remarkable calmness and self-control, he answered all the questions ... in a way that suited his narrative. However, at a certain moment during the interrogation, when the chief inspector silently placed the aforementioned receipt on the table, Chris's expression momentarily changed before he quickly recovered and offered what seemed to be a plausible explanation. It went something like this: "On Saturday, Freddy allowed me to borrow his bike to run some errands in a distant place. I was supposed to return the bicycle to him on Sunday, when I planned to pick it up shortly after noon. I rang the doorbell several times, but no one answered. Even after driving around for an hour, I still found the door closed. On Monday, I resumed my attempts, but with no success. Driven by financial difficulties due to gambling debts, I foolishly sold the bike for a hundred guilders."

Naturally, from that moment onward, Chris was kept in custody, even though there was still no concrete evidence linking him to the murder of his friend, Freddy. A couple of detectives were sent to Chris's residence, where nothing particularly suspicious caught their attention. In the wardrobe, there hung a neatly pressed Sunday suit, flawlessly draped over a hanger, with no signs of anything untoward. Nevertheless, they decided to take it along as a precautionary measure for examination by the expert. The same fate befell a heavy hammer—a mallet—that was found in Chris's toolbox, under the motto: "You can never be too careful." The fact that these investigators could hardly observe anything on the mentioned clothing or the hammer made them skeptical. Nevertheless, I took those silent witnesses to my laboratory, where I subjected them to a very rigorous "interrogation."

During this process, something very important came to light: there were extremely fine blood specks on the lapels of the jacket, so small that they couldn't be seen with the naked eye. However, under the microscope, their presence became clear. Additionally, I found it interesting to measure the size of these specks, which amounted to 0.075 millimeters! It's no wonder that these "bloodstains" had eluded the detectives' attention. Further examination revealed similarly fine blood specks on the lower ends of both trouser legs at the front.

To explain the significance of these extremely fine bloodstains to the reader, I must first provide some general information about bloodstains. As blood flows from a wound, it may result in a stream of blood. Drops of blood may also form when blood drips. However, when a blood-rich tissue is severely injured by a hard blow from a heavy object, extremely fine particles of blood—likely originating from the so-called terminal blood vessels of the skin—are propelled away. These specks are finer than what we observe in any other type of injury. Such fine spatter therefore only occurs where blood-rich tissue is struck by a very powerful blow. We refer to them as "murder specks" here in the laboratory. If someone has them on their clothing, they don't need to regale us with stories about a nosebleed or witnessing a clandestine slaughter somewhere. Such minuscule bloodstains never occur in those situations. The presence of these specks on both lapels and at the bottom of both trouser legs suggested that they resulted from the splattering of blood from head wounds while the victim was still standing, as well as from the administration of one or more heavy blows to the head when the man was already on the ground. Yes, it was indeed blood. With the help of a dissecting microscope, I isolated a few individual wool fibers from the fabric of the jacket, to which tiny crumbs of dark red matter adhered. This allowed for the identification of fresh blood.

Once all of this was established, I hurried to inform Mr. Posthuma of the findings. He happened to be engaged in another interview with his client at that very moment. As I later learned, my findings had been particularly welcomed by him at that precise moment because he was running out of conversation topics. However, armed with the knowledge of my results, he could now launch a new attack "with a powerful lever," as he put it. Chris was then informed that the phone call, for which Mr. P. had just been briefly called away, concerned evidence that conclusively indicated that Chris must have been "right there at the scene" when Freddy was murdered. New desperate moves ... a new story ... a last-ditch effort to explain away the presence of those bloodstains on the clothing of a "completely innocent" person.

He would not have made that Sunday afternoon call in vain but would have been let into Freddy's place, where he found two unfamiliar guys introduced to him as Jan and Piet, who were negotiating with Freddy. Suddenly, one of these men pulled out a mallet and attacked Freddy with it, while the other allegedly threw himself at Chris to prevent him from aiding his friend. And then, at some point, those guys walked out of the house! While the chief inspector listened to these stories, I occupied myself with examining the aforementioned mallet, which had been submitted to me for investigation along with the Sunday suit. The handle was somewhat battered near the head, and the wood, though somewhat fibrous in that area, had a reddish color. I found traces of fresh blood (albeit diluted with water) between the wood fibers, and the microscopic analysis of the hammer's striking surface revealed tiny indentations that also contained remnants of blood. I quickly reported these findings to Mr. Posthuma.

When the chief inspector heard from his arrestee's fantastic tale about a mallet being used to strike down Freddy, he dryly remarked that the mallet had already been found ... and that it turned out to be the one from Chris's toolbox. At that point, the case was quickly resolved. The suspect soon realized that further evasion and lying would be futile. He made a full confession, revealing some highly remarkable character traits. He had struck down his friend, motivated by a few pieces of silver, using a mallet specifically brought from home for that purpose, and he had stolen Freddy's bicycle and sold it. Yet, he willingly entered the house with great "readiness" to provide the police with some "information," showing absolutely no emotion. And a few days later, Chris—still free at that time—accompanied his mother to the cemetery to pay his last respects to Freddy.

Epilogue by Bas Kokshoorn: Forensic DNA Analysis as an Investigative Tool

The bloodstains on the clothing of the suspect as well as on the mallet in his toolbox were considered damning evidence against him. While the mechanism by which they ended up on the location where they were found is discussed at some length (in light of the crime scenario only), it remains unclear whether these stains are human or animal blood. And if we assume that the stains are from human blood, whether this is blood from the victim. Today it would therefore be unthinkable that—in a case like this—the stains would not be subjected to DNA analysis.

With the advent of forensic DNA analysis in the late 1980s, it became possible (beyond the low diagnostic value of blood group typing, for which a large quantity of blood was needed) to determine who the source of such stains may be. The nature of the biological stain may also be determined, for instance through mRNA analysis. This technique, which was advanced significantly at the Netherlands Forensic Institute, allows for the determination of common human body fluids and cell types, and even organ tissue types. The technique has been successfully applied to a large number of forensic cases, for instance, to identify blood, but also brain or muscle tissue on tools used in violent assaults. Forensic DNA analysis has become one of the most powerful tools to identify potential perpetrators of crimes. Minute quantities of invisible biological deposits (for instance latent traces deposited through touching an object) may result in DNA profiles that can be uploaded to the Netherlands DNA database for criminal cases (founded by law in 1994 and operational since 1997). Roughly half of all traces from unknown sources are at one point in time linked to a reference DNA profile of an individual. This may happen immediately if the database already contains a corresponding reference DNA profile, or occasionally decades later when such a reference DNA profile is uploaded through another case. Since 2008 DNA profiles from the national DNA database are compared daily to those in databases from other European countries. This results in investigative leads for the police in cross-border crimes.

Forensic DNA analysis currently provides us with further investigative tools. Through familial searching in the national DNA database, traces left by unknown persons may be searched to find possible family members like brothers/sisters or parents/children. Names of such potentially related individuals may help police to identify the donor of the DNA. Subsequent direct comparison of a reference DNA profile of a person-of-interest to that of the trace will show whether this person may have donated the DNA. More recently the application of investigative genetic genealogy in the United States as well as several European countries allowed for the identification of remains of unknown individuals as well as potential suspects in criminal cases—thereby increasing the power of forensic DNA analysis as an investigative tool even further.

38. Arsonists

Once before the Court of Justice in Amsterdam, a criminal case was tried concerning an intentional act of arson. The person who had the dubious honor of being in the defendant's seat passionately asserted that he was completely innocent. However, the smart court president, who had many case files in mind, casually remarked, "When no plausible cause for the fire is found, I always consider it a case of intentional arson!" Those who heard this were taken aback for a moment; initially, they found it somewhat unheard of to entertain such an evil thought. Still, the better informed—including myself—felt that there was some truth to that reasoning.

As I write this, we are again living in wartime and—to a greater extent than in the years 1914–1918—we are witnessing how consumer goods are depleted, sold out, and no longer available! And—just as during the years of the previous war—statistics show that the number of fires has also decreased significantly! Truly, Reader, the court president had every reason to be suspicious. I myself have also defended in small circles the proposition that "the majority of fires of unknown origin are intentionally set! The insurance companies bear some responsibility for this!"

Several cases in which I had taken part in the investigation taught us something like this: In the lowest social class, two people will get married ... much sooner than originally planned, but ... it was necessary! And hardly was the wedding announced (sometimes the news got out even earlier, and some insurance agent knew about it) when several representatives of fire insurance companies show up to sell them insurance policies. Oh dear! Then they discover how meager their household inventory is. It couldn't be any simpler or poorer; the possessions in their future home is worth barely two hundred guilders. If the man doesn't take out a policy for at least a thousand guilders, he won't get any commission, so he convinces the future couple that, of course, they will buy some more things and that soon, when the stork visits them, a cradle and many other necessities will increase their possessions. "Come on, let's make it a nice round sum of a thousand guilders!" The poor fellow is momentarily dazzled. Is it any wonder that—in the midst of his poverty—the idea grows stronger in him that if his possessions should ever fall victim to a fire that those kind gentlemen from the insurance company will hand him a thousand guilders? By far, the most cases of intentional arson are motivated by someone seeking to get out of financial trouble by "getting themselves out of the fire."[37] But clumsiness in one part of the process or too talkative neighbors could lead the police to become suspicious and investigate the case. Following an order

---

[37] In Dutch, this saying means "getting yourself out of trouble," so Co van Ledden Hulsebosch is making a pun here.

from the court, a thorough expert examination was often carried out, and all too often "silent witnesses" were found that shed light on the obscure case and proved the crime of premeditated arson. In most cases where the "red rooster was put on the roof,"[38] the occupant acted in his own interest; sometimes, while constructing a perfect alibi for himself, he had an accomplice set the fire.

Such fires were, so to speak, isolated and had no connection with other fires. However, at the beginning of this century, a group formed with the goal of systematically making money from arson. The mastermind behind this was an "expert," which early on referred to the person who acted as an intermediary between the one whose house had caught fire and his insurance company. This intermediary tried to extract as much as possible for his client, and his salary increased proportionally to what the insurance would pay out! Several officers at the Amsterdam fire department had noticed this agent and saw him arrive at numerous fires shortly after the alarm was raised ... which quickly raised suspicion. It was noticed that all those fires where this person was seen on the scene were "suspicious fires"! In various directions, the police investigated the actions of this suspect.

Meanwhile, in a city in Brabant,[39] another suspicious fire broke out; the day before the "festive" opening of a new establishment, the whole place burned down. It was a shop on a street corner and the windows were still smeared with chalk to prevent the interior from being seen from the outside. In the shop area, a shipment of bicycle crates, tires, rims, saddles, lanterns, and many other items was still to be unpacked. A few crates containing cans of solvent and carbide were already unpacked. And now, due to an unknown cause, a fire broke out. The shopkeeper considered himself fortunate that he had insured his establishment in time; everything was covered! During the difficult task of the fire department, it was noticed how carbide and solvent cans were alternately placed on the display shelves, and the lids were left loose on top. The cans with solvent naturally burned like torches, and no matter how energetically the fire department sprayed water over them, the fire spread furiously. This was a natural consequence of spraying the extinguishing water into the open carbide cans, which produced large amounts of highly flammable acetylene gas. That made the matter highly suspicious!

While the police, assisted by experts, conducted their on-site investigation, the detectives inquired right and left about the credibility of the suppliers, all of whom turned out to be individuals of highly questionable reputation. Apparently, in recent weeks, they had all started printing letterheads with a company name

---

38 This old Dutch saying about starting a fire refers to the weathercock (or weather vane), an instrument (often shaped like a rooster) that was mounted on the roof of a building and that turned freely to show the direction of the wind.
39 A province in the south of the Netherlands.

and various other forms. Gradually, the scheme became clear. The suspect had devised a phenomenal plan. An accomplice had gone to Brabant to rent a substantial store in one of the larger cities. When the property owner asked for references, the prospective tenant claimed to have recently returned from Indonesia,[40] stating that obtaining information would take too much time. However, he suggested that the landlord wouldn't mind signing a rental contract if the rent for the first three months was paid "upfront and directly." No, then there would certainly be no objections. Such generosity was the best recommendation!

Further investigation revealed that after the fire at a large bicycle shop in the eastern part of the country, a purchaser had come to collect the sad remains of the bicycles. He had also made an offer for the iron wires from the bicycle tires, the weakened coil springs from the charred saddles, and the remnants of what had once been carbide lamps. No one understood what the man intended to do with them; it seemed like worthless junk. But the remains of the saddles were placed in large, brand-new wooden boxes, along with the remains of the lamps and other parts. These boxes were marked as soon as they reached a wholesaler in Utrecht, and these markings were noted on freshly printed invoices from this so-called fallen-from-the-sky wholesale business. The reader can sense how all these individuals were involved in the conspiracy concocted by the suspect. After the fire I mentioned at the beginning, charred boxes were found containing remnants of a hundred saddles, a hundred and fifty carbide lamps, two hundred outer tires, and four hundred inner tubes. The "expert" carefully noted all these details, which coincided precisely with the invoices that the "victim" had in his pocket and were fortunately not burned! And the insurance could once again compensate for the "damage"(?) caused by the fire!

About three decades passed since then, and although the fire insurance companies paid out large sums to arsonists who had "individually" arranged the affairs, it wasn't until around 1930 that the police began to suspect that a conspiring gang of arsonists was launching various attacks on the insurance companies' purses. Initially in the capital city,[41] but gradually in other municipalities, fires of unknown origin occurred. If each fire was considered individually, no conclusions could be drawn, although many policemen sniffed suspiciously, as if they wanted to suggest that something was amiss. But no evidence could be found! It took quite some time for the police to get hold of the threads.

The man pulling the strings was a certain person X, who called himself an "expert" and appeared each time after an insignificant man had experienced a fire. He promised these victims all sorts of wonderful things and had them sign

---

40 A Dutch colony until its independence in 1945.
41 Amsterdam.

an agreement specifying what percentage of the "insurance amount" (this is not money to be paid out by the insurance!) should be paid for his services! This sinister figure had devised a new system to extract large sums of money from the insurance companies. We gradually discovered this during the investigation. After numerous fires had occurred in different parts of the country, and many payouts had been made, the Justice Department, based on growing suspicions, thought it would be a good idea to gather all the relevant files for a closer look. I also had the opportunity to become acquainted with all these seemingly unrelated fires that appeared unrelated. However, it gradually became clear that all these "victims" had some connection—either through blood relations, marriage, or otherwise—with the suspect or one of his two associates. For example, his in-laws, a nephew and niece, various family members of his "partner," and some of his "friends" successively had fires in their homes.

As I studied the files and examined the statements provided by neighbors, first responders, police, and firefighters, I noticed certain points of similarity that could be found in all those fires. Almost always, a fire broke out in a "new residence," where the furniture had just been moved in due to relocation, and the occupants understandably hadn't stayed there overnight; everything was piled up in the front room. They planned to arrange everything neatly the next day themselves. And what kind of furniture did the movers bring there? In many cases, it was so old and damaged (chairs with three legs, etc.) that there was nothing to ruin; no decent person would accept such furniture in their home. An old skeleton of a typewriter from the time of the earliest models; a rusty sewing machine—in short, all sorts of junk salvaged from a scrapyard and then moved into the residence that would be devastated by fire that same night, allowing the "expert" to appear afterward and make a list of the "lost items"! The observations of the upstairs neighbors also matched perfectly in various instances. Almost twenty minutes after the departure of the new tenant, strange noises were heard downstairs, as if something fell down the stairs, and then suddenly, flames erupted from the ground floor windows!

On a certain day, there was another suspicious fire reported in a house on the Marnixstraat.[42] When I arrived there to conduct an investigation, at the request of the police commissioner, I noticed that it seemed that all sorts of old junk had been brought into the house to justify a claim for valuable ladies' hats! I felt as though "the gang" was involved again. I expressed my suspicion and mentioned the name of the suspect and his two regular associates, advising them to investigate whether there might be any connection between the resident whose house had almost completely burned down the previous night and one of these suspicious individuals. Well, that didn't turn out as straightforward as one might expect! Another day went by.

---

42 A street in the city center of Amsterdam.

The resident in question was detained at the police station based on suspicion. A lawyer appeared at the police station and expressed a wish to be allowed to see the arrested person, as he would provide legal assistance. The commissioner was surprised, as far as he knew, the detainee had not had any "contact" with the outside world, and thus, he could not have called a lawyer. So he asked, "Then who called you and asked you to come here?" The other then mentioned the name of one of the "associates"! The existence of a "relationship" had been established once again!

Shortly after, a fire broke out in a house in IJmuiden,[43] where a widow and her son lived. On that evening, they had taken an unplanned trip to Amsterdam and missed the last train to return home. So, they took a taxi and drove back to IJmuiden. Meanwhile, their house had burned down! The insurance covered the damages and paid out! The two were planning to move to Amsterdam. The "new" furniture—presumably supplemented with some items from a secondhand store and other necessities provided by the scrapyard—had been "moved in" late in the afternoon. The movers later told us that they had neglected to take the usual precautions with most of the furniture, such as wrapping them in blankets before tying them to the hoist, because such safety measures would have been ridiculous for that old stuff! The completely burned inventory was piled up again in one room; the upstairs neighbors knew that about twenty minutes had passed since the front door slammed shut when the last downstairs resident left, and then a commotion was heard as if something was falling down the stairs, and suddenly ... the fire blazed fiercely.

It is no wonder that I immediately thought of the connection with the "firm" of the suspect and his associates. But ... was it be possible to establish any link between that gang and these two people who had just come over from IJmuiden to Amsterdam? Every question about whether "madam" knew any of the said partners was answered in the negative. In an extensive interrogation, it was revealed that the son from IJmuiden had sent a letter to the insurance company, informing them of the impending move to the specified property in Amsterdam, and requesting a note on the policy. That letter was claimed by the insurance company and temporarily added to the dossier, where I found it during my study. It caught my attention that it was typed on a specific typewriter, and I remembered that among the remains of the widow's burned furniture, the skeleton of an old typewriter was found. I managed to trace it, and though it was naturally impossible to operate it normally, I could still take good note of the typefaces. Soon, I determined that the specific letter sent to the insurance company was not typed on this machine. So, which typewriter was used? The court had in the meantime ordered a search of the residence of the suspect and the room that was grandiosely named the "office." Stacks of papers

---

43 A port city on the North Sea coast in the northwest of the Netherlands.

were seized, including lists of inventories, typewritten. By comparing the typefaces, I established that the letter sent by the widow (or her son) to the fire insurance company was typed on the suspect's machine! And thus, the following was achieved: the lady could no longer deny that she had connections with the firm of the suspect, which she had initially stubbornly denied. This didn't help her case!

Recalling the numerous arson investigations I had conducted for the criminal justice system, one case came to mind that took place in an tall, old building owned by a notorious slumlord. He had rented out the small apartments on different floors to numerous impoverished families. Until one day, the building inspectors ordered that the well-known sign "Declared uninhabitable" should be nailed to the front door. The man lacked the funds to carry out the required renovations on the property, and without those renovations, he would not be able to collect a single cent of rent. In desperation, he decided to set it on fire. First, he removed all the wallpaper from the walls of the front room and made a large ball of it, placing it in the center of the room. Then he visited the room above, removed a plank out of the floor, placed it slanted over the ball of wallpaper, and through the opening, he did the same in the upper rooms. The floorboards placed diagonally in the openings would later easily direct the fire to the attic and the roof. Now all he needed was to introduce a significant flame, and the entire property would burn down in no time! Using a can of gasoline he had brought along, he poured a considerable amount over the mass of wallpaper in the front room. However, the thought occurred to him that he could also pour gasoline and set it alight in the back room where he had a kind of carpenter's workshop with lots of wood shavings on the floor and various pieces of short wood stacked against the wall in a corner.

He immediately ignited the gasoline he had poured there, but the consequences were quite different from the back room! In the moments that had passed since pouring the gasoline, a large amount of it had vaporized. The resulting gasoline fumes had quickly mixed with the air, creating an extremely explosive mixture, comparable to the fuel in our car engines! Barely had he struck his match when a massive explosion occurred, smashing the windows along with the window frames, pushing the door outward, and dislodging the walls. The short-lived explosion engulfed the man entirely, resulting in his hair on his head, mustache, eyebrows, and eyelashes being severely burned. His shock was so great that, without further thought, he put on his hat, grabbed the gasoline can, and fled into the street ... right into the arms of a police officer who had rushed to the scene! He couldn't remember that he had grabbed his hat and put it on at the last moment, but the fact that the hair on the top of his head was also scorched indicated that he had been standing bareheaded during the explosion. We could still see the arrangement of all the items when the fire department had soon managed to extinguish the fire in the back of the house. Needless to say, he was caught red-handed!

In some cases, the fire can rapidly spread, causing complete destruction, leaving only debris and ashes. But don't expect, dear Reader, that there's nothing left for the investigator to find! Let me share the following case: In the western part of Amsterdam, a fire broke out years ago in a shop where everything was prepared for the festive opening of a ladies' hat store. The owner seemed very "desperate and theatrical," which only fueled suspicion against him. The fire was intense, and the next day, we found a completely burned-out ground floor. From the street to the back of the house, one could see a mass of debris, with the half-charred beams of the upper floor seemingly hanging threateningly over it. In that debris, sporadically, we found charred pieces of wood that could be identified with certainty. Among them were several stands used to display ladies' hats. Near those stands, we found bent "skeletons" of thin iron wire that, when covered, are concealed in many ladies' hats to keep them in shape. We didn't suspect then that these remains of stands and "hat skeletons" had been left behind from a previous fire and were now being used to justify a claim for so many expensive ladies' hats once again!

As I said, very little remained of what could be consumed by the fire. There was nothing left of the cupboards and sliding doors between the rooms! Under these circumstances, it seemed truly desperate to search for the cause of the fire successfully. The nervous resident had initially uttered incoherent words. Later, when a more coherent story came from his lips, we heard how, with no electricity yet in the property, after darkness had fallen, he had gone to write a letter to his girl, sitting at a small round table by the light of a small oil lamp. Suddenly, the cat jumped onto his table, startling him, and he gave the cat a swipe, hitting the wick of the lamp. As a result, the lamp fell to the ground, and the spilled oil caught fire, engulfing everything in flames. It seemed plausible; even very plausible, I would say, but … verification is always useful!

So, through a combined effort, we thoroughly searched through all the debris, charred bits of wood, and other remnants, so that everything whose origin could be distinguished would be gathered in one place for further investigation…. You never know! I should also mention that during the questioning of the resident, I had asked him with interest about the type of lamp he had used. He explained how it was such a "simple" oil lamp with a glass reservoir, broader at the bottom and gradually narrowing to the point where the burner was mounted. I thus expected to find something from that lamp. And my expectation was met; in the indicated place in the front room, I found the broken reservoir with the burner ring on it, but … the burner had been unscrewed! It lay, along with the charred wick, four meters away, under the debris in the back room space! Since it was difficult to imagine that a cat jumping off a table would cause the burner to make the necessary rotations to end up with the burner, wick and all, four meters away from the reservoir … we got the first trump card to play against the shopkeeper.

He had also boasted loudly about the beautiful, valuable paintings that had hung on the walls of his newly opened store. When he was understandably asked where these paintings had come from (to verify his claim), he replied that he had purchased them from his brother. In doing so, he deprived us of the opportunity to obtain sworn testimony since the brother, as a blood relative, would invoke the right to refuse to testify. Consequently, the man could comfortably conceal the truth. Nevertheless, this information also needed to be verified. Inquiring about the approximate dimensions of the various paintings—of which he mentioned a whole series!—he also informed us that most of them were framed in expensive gilded profiles. That was fortunate, I thought. It is important to remember that all those thick, heavy gilded frames are cast in plaster, with a layer of gilding applied on top. This plaster can never completely disappear since it is noncombustible. Those remains could be found again!

A floor plan of the room was presented to him, with a request to mark on it the locations where the various paintings, large and small, had been hung, along this wall and that wall, and he accurately marked everything as requested. Now, the wallpaper was completely burned away from the walls, revealing the smooth masonry, which had been neatly plastered. In that plaster, there were still two iron nails, and one nail was present in the charred upper slat. However, there were no loose nails to be found at the foot of that wall, even though the debris from the collapsed plaster from the ceiling was thoroughly searched. So, the justified question was: What did all those paintings hang from? The heat was getting to him. The story about the remains of the oil lamp and our findings regarding the missing nails and painting frames ultimately led him to ... a confession!

Epilogue by Arian van Asten

Arson, i.e., deliberately starting a fire with criminal intent, seems to occur in all ages. It can be financially motivated, for instance, to commit insurance fraud, as seems to be the lead motive for many of the cases that Co van Ledden Hulsebosch discusses. However, fire can also be used for extortion purposes (for instance, to send a message to someone not to talk to the police) or to damage the property of adversaries. It can even be an instrument to deliberately harm or kill people. Nowadays, ironically, fire is also used by criminals to hamper forensic investigation and to destroy any biological and other incriminating traces they might have left at the scene. In the Netherlands, it is not uncommon to find a fully burnt getaway car after an assassination or violent robbery.

The maestro gives an overview of infamous arson cases and the forensic investigation he conducted to support law enforcement. In my humble opinion, this chapter starts "on the wrong foot" when van Ledden Hulsebosch quotes a court president who states that "when no plausible cause for the fire is found, I always consider it a case of intentional arson!" This, of course, is a questionable if not dangerous statement for someone who needs to uphold the law. Clearly any suspect is innocent until proven guilty. The burden of proof is with the prosecution; it is not up to the defendant to proof his innocence (in the absence of clear signs that a fire was accidental). This is fundamental to criminal law in all civilized societies! Van Ledden Hulsebosch tends to support the point of view of the president, but in his carefully chosen words it is clear that he realizes that he is treading in dangerous territory.

So, how did he provide forensic evidence to solve these arson cases from the first half of the previous century? As he states vividly and rightly, investigating a fire scene is extremely challenging because of the damaging effect of the fire itself. This results in the destruction of the "silent witnesses" (physical evidence) that show the criminal action. In addition, an active fire first needs to be extinguished by fire fighters to create a safe situation and protect nearby buildings. This mandatory action leads to further destruction of crime-related evidence and severely hampers the forensic investigation as traces are literally "washed away."

What van Ledden Hulsebosch describes is a process where detailed statements of the suspects (or are they actually victims?) are convincingly debunked by his forensic findings. Being presented with such a wealth of evidence, the suspects then "break" and admit their foul play, a situation that is also not uncommon in episodes of the popular CSI TV series in modern times. It is for this reason that lawyers typically advise suspects to exercise their Miranda rights (i.e., the fundamental right of every defendant to refuse to make any statement that could potentially incriminate them). In the absence of any defendant response, the tactical (motive, witness statements) and forensic investigation must yield sufficient evidence to convince triers of fact that there is no reasonable doubt that the suspect committed the criminal actions as laid down in the indictment. Convincing and incriminating evidence can also be a trigger for suspects to "start talking".

Nowadays, two forensic expertise areas are dedicated to the investigation of potential arson cases: technical fire investigation and fire debris analysis. A technical investigation is typically conducted at the scene and often this expertise is embedded within the police force. Despite the destruction and the chaotic nature of a fire, indications may be found that the fire was deliberately set. Finding multiple locations where a fire started might, for instance, point to arson although flashovers during a fire might create a similar pattern. At these spots officers might take samples of the fire debris and bring those samples to the forensic laboratory. Forensic analytical chemists can study the head space of the fire debris to scan for the presence of compounds that originate from an ignitable liquid that was used to start the fire. Typically, fire accelerants are used that are widely and easily available, such as gasoline or white spirit. If these materials are not fully consumed during the fire, traces can be detected and identified using a technique called gas chromatography-mass spectrometry.

Interpreting the data is complex and to date still is a task for the forensic expert. The fire debris itself is a complex sample of unknown composition that can lead to a complex head space composition. It is known that the thermal degradation of certain substrates can lead to the formation of compounds that are also found in flammable liquids. The expert must rely on his/her expertise and training to prevent such pitfalls. Finally, showing the presence of an ignitable liquid does not necessarily prove that the fire was intentional. This strongly depends on the context of the case! But hopefully the reader will agree that finding gasoline residues in the fire debris of what once was a living room is not something you would expect if the fire was fully accidental. At this stage, a suspect might make a statement that he was storing a jerrican of gasoline in his house at the time of the fire. However, such a statement after the evidence is presented might not seem very plausible nor convincing to a judge or jury.

See Figure 11 (in the insert section) for a photograph of a typical GC-MS setup as used in forensic laboratories to screen fire debris samples for the presence of ignitable liquids.

39. To Whom Does This Pocketknife Belong? Whose Key Chain Is This?

Behold, Reader, questions, quite simple, as they may arise daily in practice during a police investigation. In the good old days when the Amsterdam Police had the canine wonder—named Albert—at their disposal, they would have let this four-legged detective easily answer these questions, although it still had to be seen whether the judge would have included these performances on the list of "evidence"! Working with dogs, especially their "sorting" of objects to demonstrate a certain "scent affinity" between various objects or between those objects and a sought-after person, did not always receive unanimous appreciation everywhere. Why was that? Simply because "they" dared to doubt the accuracy of the indications given by the dogs, claiming that in some particular case these dogs had given "incorrect indications." That I will always contradict. No creature is more honest than a dog—it never pretends, and one dog has more truthfulness than ten people together!

I want to start by telling you a case of "wrong indication" by the dog. At noon, some police officers are indoors at their office, having their lunch. One of them enjoys a deliciously fatty English bloaters. Due to the lack of other "tools," he uses his fingers to dissect the fatty smoked delicacy, leaving his hands oily and fishy in scent. Then the phone rings: in a warehouse, it has just been discovered that burglars must have been there last night; maybe they are still in the extensive building.... Some officers rush there. They don't allow themselves much time to wait before going out, and the fish lover is satisfied with his handkerchief to wipe off the worst grease from his hands. But the fishy smell lingers.

In the warehouse, one of the nocturnal visitors has lost a handkerchief, and with the still fish-scented hand, it is triumphantly picked up, then wrapped in a piece of paper that—just like the handkerchief—bravely absorbs the fishy odor, sufficiently strong to be later recognized by the noses of tracking dogs. An hour later, a report comes in that—a few streets away—three strange guys have hidden themselves in a shed on a property. The team rushes out again and arrests the three "suspects," with the one who still has the fish smell on his hands—albeit faintly but quite perceptible to the noses of the tracking dogs!—holding one of the detainees firmly by the collar. One can understand how inevitably the fish smell attaches itself to that jacket! If the help of police dogs is now invoked to determine if the found handkerchief possibly belongs to one of the three detainees, the four-legged officer will undoubtedly indicate with decisive certainty that handkerchief 191 and the clothing of that one detainee exhibit the same scent.

If he could speak,... he would tell us it was the smell of smoked fish. However, since he remains silent—or, barking, expresses himself in a language we cannot quite understand—his barking, indicating the observation of the mentioned scent affinity, is misinterpreted, and it is concluded that the "body odor" of that detainee is what the dog recognized as a "common scent"! And this while the man may be innocent! Would anyone dare to claim in such a case that this faithful helper had given "false testimony" and want to derive from that the right to disqualify the significance of canine assistance? It was a human who made mistakes here; mistakes that led to a wrong conclusion, but the dog was honest and true in its expressions and "statements."

What can be learned from this? Firstly, that abandoned objects to which one wants to give dogs a "scent" should not be touched with one's own hands—not even if one has recently washed them. It is necessary to place a clean piece of paper—for example, the middle sheet from a section of clean writing paper—on it, and when picking up a handkerchief or key chain, place that paper between the object and one's own skin. Then the body odor of the police officer is less likely to transfer to the object of the unknown person.

But I have completely strayed from the topic I wanted to address; I wanted to teach you another method to trace the owner of an abandoned pocketknife, key chain, or other object commonly carried in the pocket. Undoubtedly, each of you has, at some point, "cleaned" the handle of his pocketknife to remove the accumulation of lint that gradually collected in the slot where the folding blade rests. Let's examine the formation of that lint mass: most pockets of our suits consist of lining, woven from strong cotton; through the constant rubbing of a pocketknife, key chain, and other items carried, that fabric gradually wears away—sometimes so much that a hole forms in the pocket, posing a risk of losing one's belongings. This wear and tear lint primarily consists of cotton fibers from the lining material from which the pockets are sewn. But alongside these lint particles, wool fibers from the fabric of the costume are always present in the lint. When searching for the opening in which one puts away a pocketknife or key chain, one usually seeks the entrance near the pocket ... before pocketing. In that search, and by sliding along the costume fabric, those objects always pick up some wool fibers from the costume fabric, which then mix with the mentioned cotton fibers.

If one wears several costumes next to each other (a casual one, a Sunday one, and so forth), it is inevitable that each costume contains wear-and-tear lint of a different composition because wool fibers from that suit are mixed in each time. Let us now return to the objects (pocketknife, key chain, etc.) that are repeatedly transferred to another suit while changing clothes. A few lint particles, along with the characteristic hairs for that costume, get lost from each costume in the grooves where the knives lie, causing the knife (as well as the cavities in the pipe keys of the key chain) to receive that mishmash of colored hairs—mixed with the main course, the cotton fibers of the lining fabric—characteristic for the owner of the costumes he wears. We have conducted several experiments, with my student N. van Driest diligently assisting me. Objects (pocketknives and key chains) were examined for various people, and it was striking how easy it was, during microscopic examination of the harvested lint from those articles, to determine which objects belonged together, i.e., came from the same owner. If the work is done well and the various fabric hairs are correctly identified (if necessary, with comparative examination of the fixed dyes), mistakes are virtually excluded!

Epilogue by Jos Brouwers

In this chapter, Co van Ledden Hulsebosch addresses two issues that have not lost their relevance to this day, although the context may have changed. Van Ledden Hulsebosch, clearly a dog lover, begins with a small tribute to the reliability and loyalty of the sniffer dog and illustrates how contaminated input (retrieved object) can lead to seemingly incorrect output (match with a suspect). The rightful conclusion is that this cannot be attributed to the dog's performance because the errors are made on the human side. Here, the analogy with modern "artificial intelligence" imposes itself, where the dog is replaced by a neural network or another form of machine learning. Just like with the dog, input and output are linked without it being transparent to humans how or why they are connected. In both cases, it is important to consider that reliable output depends on reliable input and that there is always room for errors, not only in the model or dog being used but equally in preparing the input or assessing the output.

In the second part, van Ledden Hulsebosch provides an excellent example of what we would now classify as "fingerprinting." Just as in dactyloscopy the loops, whorls, and arches form a unique pattern without being unique in themselves, we now use the term fingerprinting for the identification of mobile phones, computers, or batches of raw materials based on similar grounds of hardware components, protocols, chemical contaminants, or other combinations of properties that are not unique in themselves. It is the combination that makes a particular object unique. Of course, van Ledden Hulsebosch, who passed away in 1952, twenty years before the introduction of the microchip, could not conceive of digital fingerprinting. But here, he teaches us about the same principle, using fibers from the wardrobe of the owner of the examined object. Although the key chain is on the decline due to the introduction of keycards, and a pocketknife is no longer part of the average citizen's standard equipment, the underlying principle in his lesson remains equally important.

40. The Pickpocket

The school day had ended, and satisfied with her work, one of the teachers from the Industrial School for Young Women (on the Weteringschans, next to the Gymnasium in Amsterdam) walked home. Then, suddenly, she made a terrible discovery: From the pocket of her raincoat, four ten-guilder notes had disappeared, which she had received during the lunch break and temporarily stashed there. The money—a small fortune to her!—had undoubtedly been stolen in the afternoon by someone who had gone to the teachers' room to search the clothing hung there. The following morning she informed her principal and colleagues at the school about this horrible incident, and—strangely enough—the person of one of the girls came to many of their minds. She could have easily done it, but no one dared to mention her name out loud. However, when one dared to voice her suspicion, the others nodded in agreement and declared they had thought of the same girl.

The janitor—the only man in the building—was called in. Had he seen any of the students in the teachers' room? Yes, wait a minute.... He had a faint memory of it. As he walked down the hall, he had briefly seen a back and still remembered a red blouse with a white X over the back from the apron strings. Again, the initial suspicion was reinforced: that particular girl had worn a red blouse and a white apron with cross-straps yesterday! The principal called her out of class—at least intended to, but soon learned that Marietje "was not there today." A friend from her neighborhood had brought the message that Marietje was not feeling well and had stayed home! Oh well, it was the last school day before the Easter holiday, so she wasn't missing much. The janitor was sent to her home but returned with the message that Marietje was not sick at home but had gone on a trip to Rotterdam, to spend the Easter holiday with an aunt!

Since no one dared to openly accuse or charge that girl, they thought it best to wait calmly until after the holiday, which would last fourteen days. When lessons resumed, and all the girls were back in school, two detectives also arrived, who took the girl aside to question her. She was a brazen and cunning creature from a bad environment. Her father was a casual laborer in the boating industry and a sister was already placed in a state institution. Thanks only to her cute face, Marie attracted the attention of a wealthy lady who funded her lessons at the Industrial School. Undoubtedly, the Easter holiday had given her ample opportunity to plan her strategy and consider how to answer the various questions. No matter how hard the detectives pressed, they couldn't get a confession, and—even though they left with the firm belief that this naughty child had committed the theft—there was no proof, so there wasn't much more to do than let the matter rest. This did not sit well with the principal. If the student had committed the theft, it was necessary that she be expelled from the school, but—before taking such a drastic measure and sending her home, they wanted more "conviction."

So the principal called me, briefly explained the situation, and urged me to help find the culprit. My answer was brief: "Since this case has already been thoroughly investigated and questioned by the detectives, I prefer not to offer my help because"—I noted—"I don't like leftovers!" However, a strong appeal was made for my assistance, and I finally relented but set the following conditions: I will try to find the culprit. However, beforehand, I must not be given the name or any indication of who is suspected. I didn't even want to know which class the person was in! And then I requested that they prepare a U-shaped table in the large hall that afternoon, where all the students would be seated, equipped with pen, ink, and paper. Upon arriving at the school, I was shown the hall where everything was prepared according to my wishes. The principal and teachers—probably very skeptical—stayed in the corridor. They might have found my methods a bit "creepy."

When I entered the hall where all the girls were seated at the large table. I noticed giggling, stemming from curiosity about who this strange person was and what kind of performance would take place.... Soon I explained to the crowd that I had come to conduct some tests to gather data on how quickly the students could produce good, legible handwriting. "So please," I said, "hold your pen ready and quickly, but legibly, write down everything I dictate. When a sentence or a group of words is finished, raise your finger." Then I very pompously took out a stopwatch as if I intended to record the times down to the second, and then I dictated: "January, February, etc." A scratching of more than a hundred pens, which seemed to die out at some point and—after a first, second, third finger was raised, all the others followed within a few seconds. In terms of speed, they didn't differ much from each other! Then followed the seasons: "Spring, Summer, etc." and the seven days of the week, and each time it was again clear that within very narrow time limits, all fingers went up. Everyone could write quite quickly!

For variation, I dictated a few proverbs, whose text was likely known, so I only had to say the text once. Finally, a sentence that the students could not know and therefore was dictated slowly, so that the writing hands could just keep up. Then came the big moment. In the same slow manner, I then dictated as follows: "Whoever secretly enters a room where he has no business must consider that a single fingerprint left behind can tell the police expert who has been in that room." Meanwhile, I had opened my briefcase and pulled out a strongly enlarged photographic image of a fingerprint ... without saying another word!

My eyes were on the crowd. There rose the first finger, the second, third.... Then, like a flock of birds taking off, the rest of the hands ... except for one! Yes, really, one of the girls did not raise her finger; she was not yet finished writing. I approached her and immediately saw how the last sentence had affected her nerves. For none of the others had writing the last words taken more time than the previous ones, and—this girl, who initially showed herself to be as fast and swift a writer as the others, hardly had that fatal sentence about secretly entering a room and leaving a fingerprint been spoken, or she alone, and no one else, was suddenly intensely pondering the question of where on earth that fingerprint might have been left and that pondering simply prevented her from continuing to write. It was absolutely impossible for her to write further, the sentence did not get on paper and thus her finger did not go up!

I asked her to come with me to the teachers' room. Crossing the corridor, where the principal and other ladies were talking, I noticed how surprised they were that I had identified "Marietje" within a few minutes, for she was the one they all suspected and distrusted of the theft. Marietje—a fundamentally malicious creature—did not confess to me any more than to the detectives; but with the writing tests in hand, I had the firm conviction that she must have committed the theft. The suspicions the teachers had were brilliantly confirmed! When the principal wanted to expel Marietje from school, it turned out to be unnecessary. She had already "disappeared" on her own!

Epilogue by Maarten Blom

At first sight, this chapter seems not to offer much for those with an interest in forensic evidence evaluation. There simply is no physical forensic evidence to discuss, and this is not surprising. What traces do we expect to arise from slipping your hand into the pocket of a raincoat and take out a few banknotes? I don't think even the most sophisticated forensic technique would have been of any help to Co van Ledden Hulsebosch. This is an act that will leave a trace only in the mind of the perpetrator. Therefore, I think the themes of this chapter are the following: lie detection and the (mis)representation of forensic evidence during questioning.

While reading the story, an academic newsflash from some time ago came to my mind. Researchers from the "LieLab" in the University of Amsterdam had tested an alternative approach to lie detection, which traditionally is based upon the idea that lying is associated with stress. In short, the new method tests the details of deceptive story itself, rather than the stressful condition of the storyteller.[44] According to the newsflash we should also forget body language or how convincing the message is,

---

44 "LieLab: The Devil Is in the Details," press release, University of Amsterdam, March 20, 2023, https://www.uva.nl/shared-content/uva/en/news/press-releases/2023/03/lielab-the-devil-is-in-the-details.html. The original research was published in B. Verschuere et al., "The Use-the-Best Heuristic Facilitates Deception Detection," *Nature Human Behaviour* 7 (2023), 718–728, https://doi.org/10.1038/s41562-023-01556-2.

we only have to note how detailed and rich the story is. It is obvious that neither the two detectives that tried to solve the case in vain, nor van Ledden Hulsebosch had this tool at their disposal. This may explain why van Ledden Hulsebosch tries an original and dangerous approach: to force a confession by suggesting the presence of very powerful incriminating evidence. However unconventional and questionable this approach is, the latter issue is still relevant today. If a forensic examination has revealed the presence of probative traces, in what manner should police officers and prosecutors present this during interrogation?

A good example can be found in the documentary *De jacht op de match* (The hunt for the match) in which the case against a serial rapist in the Dutch town of Utrecht is reconstructed.[45] It has a small scene in which we witness the struggle of the prosecutor to adequately formulate the findings and the evidential strength of a Y-chromosomal match with the (later convicted) suspect. Just like van Ledden Hulsebosch, his aim is to obtain a confession, but unlike van Ledden Hulsebosch he does not want to bluff or exaggerate the power of the evidence. This is a very high-profile case that he cannot risk blowing. So, he probes his words carefully. Can we say. "We strongly believe your DNA has been found?," the prosecutors ask the forensic DNA experts. As you may imagine, a vivid discussion on what may be concluded from a scientific and from a legal standpoint ensues.

---

45 The documentary is in Dutch and can be found on YouTube at https://www.youtube.com/watch?v=UyD4Yo4ixEo&t=4178s. The Y chromosomal discussion scene takes place from 1:05 until 1:11.

41. He Had It in Writing

A kind, lively maiden serving a family that lived in a grand house in the Amsterdam Concertgebouw neighborhood encountered a charming young man one day. At first, he cast a smile upon her in passing, and on a subsequent occasion, when their paths converged again, had addressed her. It seemed to be quite a coincidence. Might it be, as they say, mutual love at first sight? On the evenings when she was free, he would come to collect her for a nice stroll, a movie, or an hour of music with a drink. But the most delightful were the enjoyable walks through the Vondelpark on the Amstelveen side on beautiful summer evenings! If only their interactions had remained confined to walks, conversations, and shared drinks. Alas, the forbidden fruit tree played its role and, unfortunately, the consequences followed!

When he came to pick her up for another walk, she had to confide in him the secret she had discovered in the past few days. Yes, then trouble arose, for the "suitor" who had painted her the sweetest dreams of matrimonial bliss, now revealed himself as a married man and father of three young children! However, he would help her. He had no intention of leaving her "just like that" and he knew of a place where, so to speak, everything could be undone. The honorable lady who ran the establishment in question was an acquaintance of his, and, undoubtedly, she would be willing to assist in this matter. He would talk to her tonight....

The next evening, he reappeared at her residence, where he informed the worried maid that the "lady" was willing to help her, but ... she wanted a written statement beforehand, "expressing her explicit wish ... etc."—because, as she was told, this was mandated by the police, so it was a legal requirement! To make it easy for her, he held out a folded sheet of paper, with the lower right corner exposed on top, and asked her to sign her name there, and then he, the gentleman, could write the required statement above it as soon as he had learned the prescribed text. The poor girl fetched a pen and ink from her kitchen and ... signed her name in the indicated place! Then he said goodbye and never visited her again!

This "knight of the rueful countenance" didn't even contact her anymore. She could write, but her letters would never reach him, because she didn't know the man's real name or his exact address! Understandably, she went through incredibly difficult times. These begun when she, speaking openly to her madam, received a lot of advice, but also the advice to leave her job in short order. Once the time had come to leave the maternity home with her baby, she followed the director's advice and turned to the authorities that provided support to abandoned unmarried mothers, by—amongst other actions—claiming child support from the father. It didn't take long to find out who and what the man was—an architectural draftsman at an architect's firm.

He received a summons and complied. After the purpose of his visit had been explained to him, he vehemently denied being the father of the child … even though "that girl" claimed so much! But the simple soul, who had explained everything that had happened not once, but several times, enjoyed everyone's trust, so harsh words disapproving of the man's most feeble attitude were articulated. However, he could prove(!) that he was not the father. Yes, he had received it "in writing" from that girl … a declaration signed by her stating that he was not the father! And, if the gentleman didn't believe him,… well, he could show him that statement! And—putting his words into action—he pulled out a folded piece of paper from his pocket, which had the young mother's signature in the lower right corner, and above it, the scoundrel had inscribed the statement as mentioned. The official who had summoned him was taken aback and … relegated the document immediately to the drawer of his writing desk.

No, the visitor didn't agree with that. He had to and would have that paper back, as it was evidence for him! The official remarked dryly, "I can assure you that I am also not the father of that child, but I have no desire whatsoever to carry such an attestation with me! Where would we end up if we had to carry statements about all children of unmarried mothers with us to absolve ourselves?" The gentleman could go home without the document. However, the story didn't end there! As soon as the prosecutor learned of this story, he pursued the man, charging him with "forgery of a document"—which he believed was a particularly unique case.

The examining magistrate took up the case and requested me to assist him in the investigation. I attended the first interrogation of the suspect. After discussing at length how long the "relationship" had lasted, the beautiful document finally came up. Yes, she had indeed knowingly signed it after he had written the text. And immediately, I asked him where all of this had been written. "In the hallway, where she spoke to me." "What did you use to write that statement?" "My fountain pen." At that point, I thought I had him, since I had long discovered that the signature was made with a different ink on the paper than the text lines, and I asked why the girl had gone to her kitchen to get a pen and ink! "Because my fountain pen had just run dry; and so, in order to sign the document, she used her own pen with ink!" Next, I pointed out that there was no writing desk or table in that hallway, and I asked how he had managed to write that multiline text on the paper. "Against the wall; as an architectural draftsman, I often have to write on various structures, sometimes a progress note, sometimes something else, and so, I can easily rest my sheet of paper against a vertical wall and write on it like that. I don't need a table for that."

I couldn't quite believe this last claim. The smooth, normal handwriting of the text made me strongly doubt whether it could have been produced against a vertical support. But … maybe the man was extraordinarily skilled in that aspect!? And on a piece of note paper that I slid to the examining magistrate, I suggested that he ask the suspect to write a dictated piece of text in that manner "against the wall" as a test. But no, he wanted nothing to do with that! "I wouldn't be able to do it now; I'm far too nervous because of everything that's happening here. I wouldn't be able to do it now!" And the examining magistrate found it much more practical that the expert dealt with the problem. Thus, a "deputation" was drawn up for the latter, with a mandate to conduct an examination on the aforementioned document regarding whether the written text on it was produced while the paper was resting against a vertical support or on a normal horizontal support, with instructions to provide a written report on this matter! As I mentioned before, the writing of the text lines seemed outwardly unremarkable, but I would have to prove how this writing had been produced!

There is nothing in the literature about this point, and evidently, no one ever faced such a puzzle before; at least, there is no published information about it. Therefore, I had no choice but to search myself for characteristics that could distinguish between the two groups of writing. So, I started collecting material in order to search for different characteristics amongst it. I put my assistants "up against the wall" to write dictated text on a sheet of paper with ink. Many sighs were released during this process. I continued the test until signs of fatigue became also evident in the writing, and after a few moments of rest, I asked them to write the same text while sitting calmly at a table. While there was certainly a lot of difference between the writing produced "against the wall" and the writing produced sitting at a table ... mostly a consequence of the unusual posture ... the question constantly arose: What about someone who writes against a wall every day and has acquired a high degree of skill in it?

Gradually, I became convinced that I would never arrive at an answer based on graphological handwriting characteristics, as the comment kept coming up: "Yes, it's all well and good that these people can't do it, but what about the suspect, with all his skill, who is used to writing like this?" After much searching, however, I was fortunate enough to find a way to answer the question presented to me with definitive certainty. During a rain shower, I observed the raindrops running down my windowpane and noticed how, in each wet streak on my window, the majority of water molecules obeyed the Law of Gravity, causing the water layer at the base of such a wet streak to be much thicker than at the top. It stood to reason that this would also apply to the thicker ink strokes of writing produced "against the wall."

However, this was not visible without further examination, as the larger, thicker strokes (such as those found in the letters b, f, g, h, j, k, l, p) had dried out from top to bottom and were solid black. Considering that thickness differences were not observable, since a thinner layer could appear just as black as a thicker one, I decided to look for a way to reveal any potential thickness differences in those large downward strokes of writing. I placed the paper between two glass panes, which

I positioned vertically; a very powerful light source was placed behind it, and in front of it was the camera, which was set to capture a group of thick downward strokes. With a short exposure time, the result was a razor-sharp photograph in which the lines of writing appeared pitch black against the brightly illuminated background. By extending the exposure time, however, I reached a point at which the thinner layers of ink proved to allow some light through after a while, before the thicker ink layers were willing to do so. This resulted in a photo where the light clearly shone through the tops of the large downward strokes, while the base points of those strokes remained pitch black; those were thicker!

As one might expect, this phenomenon hardly occurred with writing that was produced on a horizontal surface while sitting at a table! (I will not explain the technical details here on how to create these photographs, as I have published them elsewhere for scientific researchers.) Armed with this fresh new knowledge, I now turned to the disputed document. In it, however, the ink layers of all the thick downward strokes turned out to be equally thick at the top as they were at their base; when this writing was produced, gravity could not pull the ink into the strokes' feet ... which meant that the paper was not supported against a vertical surface, but rather on a horizontal support. The many photos I included as evidence in my report proved effective. They also fully convinced the legal authorities of the accuracy of my conclusion, and the suspect was convicted of document forgery and was also required to pay child support for the child, of which he was identified as the father.

Epilogue by Titia Sijen: Forensic Kinship Analysis

The story clearly takes place in a bygone era: nowadays we hardly write with fountain pens, contraceptives are commonplace, society no longer shuns unmarried mothers. And DNA-based paternity testing is well-known, making appearances even on television shows to unravel family mysteries. In this particular case, a simple swab of the baby's and the alleged father's saliva could have swiftly resolved the central question: Was the draftsman truly the father?

In the domain of criminal forensics, kinship testing is generally a second resort. Initial efforts focus on matching the DNA profile from the crime scene evidence to references within the case, like suspects, or to profiles stored within the DNA database. When no such match arises, attention may shift to seeking a close relative of the DNA contributor. The closest relatives are parent-child relatives, who share 50% of their genetic material—a result of each child inheriting half of their DNA from each parent. Similarly, sibling share, on average, half their genetic makeup.

So, we search the DNA database for entries that align with this degree of genetic sharing, followed by a more comprehensive analysis of these candidates. This could entail an extended DNA profile with more markers, the inclusion of Y-chromosomal markers (passed largely unchanged from father to son, forming the paternal lineage), or even the incorporation of mitochondrial DNA markers (inherited unchanged from mother to child). Subsequently, it's the duty of law enforcement to pursue leads coming from such a familial match. This strategy of familial searching within the DNA database, occurs within the bounds of legal constraints.

In cases where a close relative remains elusive, one may extend the search to more distantly related individuals. This involves two primary strategies. The first strategy centers on identifying men of the same paternal lineage meaning that they bear the same (or highly similar) Y-chromosomes. This tactic is employed in large-scale DNA testing initiatives, where men fitting certain criteria—such as residing in a specific area at the time of the crime—are tested to match the Y-chromosome of the perpetrator. Matches can range from close to far relatives, necessitating extensive family tree analysis.

The second approach involves genealogy databases. These databases reside with DNA testing companies, where individuals have submitted their samples. These databases facilitate predictions about ancestry, physical traits, and even genetic risk factors for certain health conditions. Some also use these databases to reconnect with long-lost family members. Using these databases for forensic purposes is known as investigative genetic genealogy. However, ethical debates persist about repurposing samples for forensics. Different countries adopt varying stances, but more than 400 cases have demonstrated success in identifying culprits through distant relatives—sometimes as distant as third cousins, sharing a common great-great-grandparent, a link spanning four generations, and averaging around 175 potential cousins, far beyond personal acquaintance. Such an approach demands meticulous family tree exploration.

The technique of DNA profiling owes its development to British geneticist Sir Alec Jeffreys, who pioneered it in 1984 at the University of Leicester. This advancement emerged well after the above "he had it in writing" case. Interestingly, principles of liquid physics that helped analyzing the evidence in this story find their forensic application in bloodstain pattern analysis—an entirely distinct field of study.

42. A Burglar with ... a Brain

The inhabitant of one of the most beautiful houses in the famous bend of the Heerengracht had a friend over in his drawing room on a winter afternoon—a man from Zaandam. When the latter concluded his visit and entered the hallway to fetch his beautiful fur coat from the coat rack, he was shocked to find it missing. None of the household members could offer any explanation; the coat must have been stolen in the meantime. Just as the homeowner was about to express his condolences, he was struck by panic as his own fur coat had also disappeared from the coat rack! "Well, you see," said the man from Zaandam, "it's dreadful that they stole my beautiful fur coat, but that's not the worst part. What I regret the most is the fact that my notebook, in which I recorded the results of my two-week business trip along with all the orders I collected along the way, is also gone. I'm completely at a loss!"

The police soon received a report about this supposed theft, which was clearly the work of a burglar, and they filed an official report. That was the extent of their action for the time being. Descriptions of the two stolen coats were included in the detective lists that were usually sent to numerous buyers and other interested parties, but there was nothing more they could do at that moment. Two days later, a railway official appeared at the home of the man from Zaandam to deliver a package: "a booklet that you left behind in a third-class compartment on the train between The Hague and Delft yesterday!" The joy of the man from Zaandam cannot be described when he confirmed that his notebook, containing all his notes and orders, was indeed in the package. No wonder the delivery person had a "good day!" The businessman happily walked into his living room to share his joy with his partner, triumphantly holding up the returned booklet. Then something fell out. It turned out to be a detached section. Strange ... the book had been securely bound together, and according to the page numbers, one page was missing from the section. Apparently, someone had made a note on it, but he was not interested in that. His notebook with all the notes had been returned!

In the afternoon, the man from Zaandam had to be in town for a while and considered it his duty to inform the police, who had been notified of the theft, about the return of his notebook. Perhaps they could derive some useful information from it. He was soon made aware that it was necessary to hand over the booklet to the police expert for a few hours—a condition he reluctantly accepted. And so, the booklet with the detached section was handed over to my laboratory for examination. On the top page of the detached section, impressions were clearly visible, obviously made when pencil notes were written on the sheet of paper that lay on top of it. I conducted further investigations and managed to capture the entire text of that note in a photograph. It read roughly as follows:

Mr. Trensen,
Could you please be so kind as to give my brother Jan half of what I am owed.
Piet R.

This Piet R. was a notorious burglar well known to the police, so it was no wonder that he was quickly taken into custody! I submitted my report, along with the accompanying photos, to the examining magistrate the next day. It happened that he was about to call in the suspect for his initial questioning, which is why I was asked to remain present. Piet entered, self-assured, looking defiantly and boldly as if to say, "What's all the fuss about? ... You've got nothing on me!" After the usual questions about his name, age, and so on, the examining magistrate asked him if he admitted to stealing the coats. Great surprise and immense astonishment were evident on the other side of the railing where the suspect stood. No, he absolutely didn't understand any of that. But could he please come closer and take a look at the photograph on the table next to the detached section from the booklet?

I will never forget the short moment that followed for the rest of my life! After studying the photo with the aforementioned text on it, in comparison to the sheet of white paper, he nodded approvingly, brought his lips forward, and, with a highly serious look, uttered the following words: "Impressive work! Neatly captured ... excellently done, undoubtedly!"

Never before had a compliment on my work created such a mix of impressions in me! It truly took an effort not to burst out laughing. "But don't you understand what clues this piece of paper provides?" "Not at all, Your Honor! I literally don't get it. How can that prove anything? Let me tell you exactly what happened and why a photo of an invisible note I wrote is being used against me. Last Wednesday, I traveled to Rotterdam with my brother, Jan. My brother asked me if I had some money left that he could borrow for his business. Well, I was completely broke and said no. And when he asked me if Trensen had already paid me, I had to answer no to that, too. Then my brother asked if he could borrow half of what Trensen owed me if he managed to get it from him. I said yes to that. My brother pointed out that he would need authorization, so Trensen could give him half of what I was owed. I checked my pockets to see if I had a decent piece of paper with me, but I didn't. So, I asked a guy sitting across from me in the compartment if he could lend me a piece of paper. That lad took out that booklet from his pocket and tore out a section; I wrote the note on the top page, which you already know, and I gave him back the rest of the paper with my thanks. Can I help it if that fool left the booklet on the train? So, what exactly do you want from me?" The trump card he had played on the table was magnificent! An hour later, he was a free man again!

Epilogue by Bas Kokshoorn: Principles of Interpretation

Forensic scientists are frequently confronted with multiple scenarios. In this chapter the suspect presented an alternative scenario to the crime scenario that the police were investigating. Today forensic scientists will evaluate their observations (be it for instance the results of handwriting examination, DNA analysis, or the analysis of gunshot residue) given the scenarios that are relevant in a case. They do this by adhering to the three principles of interpretation of forensic observations:

1. All observations should be evaluated within a framework of circumstances.
2. Observations should be evaluated with respect to at least two competing propositions.
3. The role of the expert should be to consider the probability of the observations given the propositions and not the probability of the propositions themselves.

The first principle guides the scientist to consider all information that is relevant to the evaluation that they are performing. The issue that is being considered will determine what information about the case circumstances is relevant. Here we recognize the fact that the forensic issue could be about the source of the material (e.g., Whose DNA is it? Which garment shed these fibers?), or about the manner or time at which traces were deposited (How was the DNA transferred to the handle of the knife? When were the fibers from the sweater of the suspect deposited on the car seat?). These issues have been framed in the hierarchy of issues, which distinguishes these source level and activity level issues, as well as offense level issues. The latter (and highest) level deals with the ultimate issue of guilt or innocence, an issue not commonly addressed by scientists, but rather by a judge or jury.

The second principle ensures balance in the evaluation performed by the scientist. They need to consider the observation under two alternative scenarios to be able to determine the strength of the evidence. To this end the scientist will calculate a ratio of likelihoods; the probability of their observations given one scenario, divided by the probability of these observation given the alternative scenario. This likelihood ratio reflects the strength of the evidence, either being neutral or providing support for one scenario over the other.

The third principle clearly defines the role of the scientist with respect to those of other parties in the criminal justice system. While it is the role of the scientist to calculate the strength of the evidence, determination of the relative probability of the scenarios themselves, and thereby considering the strength of the evidence presented by the scientist, is left to the fact finder—the judge or jury. These different roles are reflected in Bayes' theorem, the statistical framework that is increasingly being used in the interpretation of forensic evidence.

43. The Evidence-Providing Phonograph Cylinder

It was the summer of 1922. That is the time of year when many venues that are planning evening programs with a diverse set of lecturers for the following winter start contacting potential speakers. So I was asked by the union of young police officials in Amsterdam to give a lecture about the newest developments from the field of detective science.

Before I knew it, I had already approved the request, and I began to wonder what kind of "novelties" I could present. The reader needs to know that I, an educator of detective science for multiple types of police officials, had the custom to serve the latest novelties as an appetizer in my lessons. I had been doing that since January 1914, when I started giving those police courses; much alike the "world news" short feature in the cinema preceding the main event. I always remained faithful to that habit, much to the liking of all my students, the number of which by then reached almost 4,000. I was committed. I had promised a lecture but ... I had no new developments in scientific policing to offer. Every time I heard of something I would use in the courses with my students they would talk about them and it was safe to assume that the majority of the audience would already know about the novelties in the field. What to do?

After ample consideration I decided upon making an autumn trip through Central Europe to visit my colleagues. I would bring a notepad to write everything down that I could about new methods and special cases. Many of those colleagues I already knew through mail correspondence. Soon I would have the pleasure of meeting them personally when I visited them in their workplaces. My tour ticket listed Karlsruhe, Leipzig, Jena, Munich, Vienna, Graz, Zürich, Lausanne, Lyon, Paris, and Brussels. The trip would last twenty days, which isn't much time for such an extensive itinerary. For that reason, I decided to travel by night train, giving me time during the day to make my visits. It seemed a bit tiring, but I could make up for the fatigue when I returned home.

This is not the place to expand on all the interesting matters that came up during this trip. I will only tell you about what I jotted down in the last place I visited: Brussels. There I visited among others the retired police official Goddefroy, whose ingenuity had already aroused my admiration several times. During the lengthy visit he again shared with me some examples of his fine work, one of which I found so remarkable that I'd like to recount it here for my readers.

Not far from Brussels, completely outside the city and surrounded by a lovely park lay a small chateau. A wealthy dowager lived there with her confidante, a maid who had already served her for many years. The old lady, however, did not know just how mean and malicious her servant was, and how she had secret dealing with a bunch of "tough" guys. The former had already persuaded the maid to disclose details about her patroness's habits. So they knew how the very precious prizes—including a diadem with large brilliants and a pearl necklace of high value—often were kept in the safe in a bank. But they also knew how those valuables, when the owner had worn them at a party evening at the court, were kept in the house the following night, since the bank did not offer the opportunity to store them there in the evening. The old lady would return them quickly to their safe place the next day. Soon, an evil plan was hatched. On such a night, following a soiree in the court, the bunch would come to the castle to steal the treasures ... and even kill the owner, if necessary.

The "good" maid had her friends already provided with wax prints of the house keys from the front door and the back door. She had also received a bowl of poison, which would be administered to the lady's favorite dog—a fine watchdog!—on the day preceding the night of the crime. There were many points to be discussed and many hours had been spent discussing how it all should be arranged. However, the group of "friends" was a bit large and one day a difference of opinion arose that led to one of the boys leaving the group.

He went to Goddefroy and asked him if there was a chance to receive a reward for important news. The clever detective replied to him: "Of course! When there are persons whose interests are served by your information, then I promise you hereby to arrange a reward for you!" And there the boy told the detective the whole history, down to the smallest detail. He further added that the leader of the group had contacted Susanne—that was the name of that good, faithful one maid!—by telephone to obtain further information or to give instructions for the night of the action. But they had to avoid getting the lady on the phone! Hence the leader always started with a question as a pass phrase: "Am I speaking to the military hospital?" If the lady answered the phone, her answer would immediately be: "You have the wrong number!"—but if Susanne had answered the telephone, she would immediately respond to that password with: "Yes, dear, Susanne is here!"

In two weeks there would be a party evening at the court, and the following night would be "the" night for the robbery. Before that they might speak to each other by telephone, to give the group of friends the certainty that there was no spanner in the works ... that the lady had really left for the court ball, etc., etc. Goddefroy soon made his plan of campaign. He arranged to have an interview with the dowager outside her house, and shared with her all his proposed measures. After the court ball Goddefroy would enter her house with her keys, go to the bedroom, accompanied by some alert police officers.

But in the next few days Goddefroy took some more remarkable measures that I want to tell you about. In advance I will remind you at what time this case took place: it was in the autumn of 1922, when Goddefroy told me the story, and this history had taken place in the winter of 1921/22. You should consider this, in order to be able to feel more appreciation for the man's work. Back then, radio technology was still in its infancy; the first audio equipment had come out and only a few knew how to operate these miracles. There was hardly any music from pickups and gramophone records, nor was there the ability to "write down on a record" the news that radio or phone may bring. Almost no one knew anything about that. But Goddefroy was thinking about ways to record those phone calls between the leader and Susanne, so that the voices could be heard again later.

What did he do? He was familiar with the importer of the Dictaphone, an American device that some large offices use. The boss can speak to the Dictaphone using a horn, recording the dictation of his letter onto a cylinder of wax, to give the typist the opportunity, outside his presence, to listen to spoken words and type them on paper. Goddefroy asked if he was able to borrow such a Dictaphone and then went with conductor wires, amplification lamps, and all kinds of other self-invented tools to build an installation that gave him the opportunity to record every voice from the telephone onto the wax cylinder. When he had that ingenious device ready and functioning properly, he took it to an attic room of the telephone service building, where it was set up. Wires were branched to that same room and connected to the wires of the dowager's castle and to the one of the Kraaiende Haantje, the inn where the bad guys used to meet to call Susanne. Goddefroy sat there for hours, patiently waiting for the moment when a red light would announce that there is a "connection" between the stations mentioned and, once that happened, he immediately switched on his ingenious device. The wax cylinder turned quietly, the needle dug itself in it and it captured the entire conversation flawlessly in the layer of wax, while the detective listened with headphones checking everything. His only fear was this: that the conversation would take so long that it would take more than a single wax cylinder to record, and installing a new cylinder would obviously entail the loss of part of the dialogue. But ... it all was recorded on one cylinder—thankfully!

In this way, Goddefroy recorded two conversations between the leader and the servant; and the second was precisely the conversation which served to give the men the assurance that the "fun could go on," as they put it. Goddefroy's strategic measures were brilliantly taken. Towards midnight he got out of the car, imitating the walk of the lady; behind him, on thick felt slippers, the detectives, who would assist him, followed silently. They expected that more than one bandit would wait for "the moment" in the kitchen with Susanne. She had promised, by the way, to make sure there was something to drink and had kept her word!

When Goddefroy started to get bored of waiting, he pressed a bell button. From the kitchen came the words, "Why are you making a fuss in the middle of the night, madam?" But—instead of the servant, who was used to responding to that signal, the guys came up the stairs ... into the bedroom, where, one after the other, they were told, looking down the barrel of a revolver, to hold their hands above their head so that handcuffs could be put on them. The maid was, of course, also arrested, even though she wanted to convince the whole world of her innocence. She did express her regret about being not alert, and that she didn't know in what "bad company" she had fallen into. But her mistress had always her allowed to receive a few visitors in the kitchen, etc., etc.

The court hearing came. There too, everyone pretended to be innocent as a newborn child; not in the least Susanne, who persistently insisted how she was a gentle, well-behaved, and faithful example of a maid. Until... the president ordered the playback device of the Dictaphone to be switched on, for which Goddefroy used a home-built device which was in the fullest sense of the word was a precursor of the later loudspeakers—again brave, ingenious work! In the silence of the courtroom came the words: "Hello, am I speaking to the military hospital?" and a female voice replied neatly, "Yes, darling, Susanne is here!" where the president, pointing with his finger, first to the man and then to Susanne, added: "That's your voice!" And so the entire dialogue came out clearly, understandable to everyone from the loudspeaker. The voices were without a doubt easily recognizable, because they were presented in the correct tone. And at the end of the trial they all received their punishment!

This story—more detailed than I can reproduce it here—was told to me by Goddefroy during my visit. No wonder I enjoyed the story and had to search for words to express my full admiration for him. Finally I had the opportunity to hear what was left to decipher on the wax cylinder. It should be remembered that the wax of those cylinders is intended to return the spoken word only a few occasions; it's too weak to be able to be played frequently and are of a different composition than the current gramophone records, which are much harder and produced in a different way! Based on a piece of paper given to me, on which the "text" was written, I could still understand quite well what was written down in the cylinder and was ecstatic about this brave piece of technical work!

I expressed my intention to Goddefroy to use this case in my presentation to the Amsterdam Police, to which he assured me that I would be happy to provide the cylinder for that purpose. Well, that wasn't too bad. When I returned from my great trip, I naturally had a lot to do first, to finish overdue work that was waiting for me. Then I went to organize everything what I had brought with me from my study trip and to make a schedule for my talk. The Dutch importer of Dictaphone equipment was pleased to lend me a complete device (a recording device, a device for playback, and a third device for cleaning the wax layer) and on the same day he made this promise to me the devices were delivered to my home! Now I could familiarize myself with it. Beautiful equipment ... but too expensive for my purse. I always typed my own letters, so that purchasing such a device used in big business would be nonsensical.

Six days before the evening of my lecture, a postal package was delivered from Brussels. I cannot describe to you the fear I felt at that time, when receiving the postal shipment, a rattling sound made it clear to me, that inside there was a wax cylinder in pieces! And so it was! What a shame ... now that everything was so finely prepared and I had imagined that this point of my lecture would have such a great effect. Something had to be done! I went—with "special intentions"—to discuss this with Willem Royaard, whom I was occasionally able to assist in devising new tricks to achieve certain theater effects with lighting and otherwise. He would think about this and message me as soon as he had found a solution.

At half past nine in the evening I received a phone call, reporting that Mrs. Magda Janssens and Hubert Laroche would be with me in about fifteen minutes to record a new wax cylinder, using the text, which was neatly written on the paper that was sent with the original cylinder. That could be a killer effect! My actors had already prepared themselves beforehand. Again, I tell you that in those days it was an almost unprecedented thing: capturing your own voice in wax, and then letting it sound loudly through the room. After a "dry rehearsal" had first been held, during which the dialogue was heard without the Dictaphone running, the recording was made. I will never forget the fun these two actors had a little later when the device returned their pleasant conversation beautifully! I was saved!

The large upstairs room of the Heystee Building was full. Apart from senior police officials there were also numerous members of the group from the Court of Appeals and from the District Court who were interested. There was hardly a seat left unoccupied. The many new methods that I had brought with me from abroad captivated everyone present. Numerous new light image plates were able to illustrate the spoken words. After the break I would discuss the Brussels case. I related everything as I just told it to my readers above, and continued my story until I reached the point of the court hearing, where Susanne and her accomplices were surprised by the Dictaphone. At that moment I signaled to my assistant, requested deathly silence, and then, the dialogue echoed clearly throughout the room. Everyone thought this recording was the original, because I had decided not to confess until the end of the evening, how I was forced to have a new cylinder fabricated, after the unhappy journey of the original. So everyone was expecting to hear the voices of the Brussels villains. Suddenly ... there was a listener who could no longer hold back any longer, and had to speak, and ... the voice of one of the seniors from the Amsterdam Palace of Justice said: "You can clearly hear that that woman is nervous!"

It is understandable what Homeric laughter resounded in the hall, when a few moments later I told how Mrs. Magda Janssens and Hubert Laroche had helped me out and—for achieving the effect that now crowned my evening lecture as the highlight—had prepared a new recording!

Epilogue by David van der Vloed

In this story, we encounter one of the earliest instances of telephone interception, where the recorded conversation is later employed for speaker recognition. Over time, telephone interception has evolved into a crucial tool for law enforcement, providing invaluable insights into criminal investigations. Some recorded conversations carry exceptional significance and may serve as crucial evidence in court cases. Often, a written statement regarding voice recognition by a police official is presented, following a process akin to the one depicted in the story: the recognition of a familiar voice by the listener.

In contemporary times, when disputes arise over the identity of the speaker, an additional tool is employed: forensic voice comparison or forensic speaker comparison. This field gained prominence as audio recordings became more prevalent. It has developed as a specialized discipline within phonetics, where linguists describe and analyze voices in linguistic terms. More recently, with advancements in speech technology, software-based methods (artificial intelligence) have emerged as a means of comparison. Furthermore, the field of forensic voice comparison is increasingly recognizing the importance of addressing cognitive bias.

Forensic speaker comparison is a dynamic field that has seen early calls for a transition to a likelihood ratio framework. It has also witnessed the growing use of automatic methods alongside human analysis. Today, a forensic scientist will conduct a comparison between the disputed recording and a reference recording using an auditory-acoustic method, artificial intelligence, or a combination of both.

Another intriguing aspect of the story involves voice disguise, where individuals attempt to present their voices as someone else's. Deception of this nature adds complexity to voice forensics, especially in cases where wrongdoers impersonate bank employees and adopt disguised voices. The impact of technological voice disguise methods, such as those utilizing deepfake technology, on the field of voice forensics remains an area to be closely monitored. The advent of deepfake technology has introduced new challenges and possibilities for voice analysis experts, raising questions about how these developments will shape the future of the field.

44. Restoration and Reconstruction of Documents

Among the many branches of criminalistics, the examination of documents—in the widest sense of the word—gradually become my hobby, and also earned me a reputation in certain circles at the stock exchange as a specialist in the cleaning of securities. For those who do not know, a dealer is not allowed to sell securities on which a name or anything else has been written in ink, or which have grease stains. There are fathers who write the name of their children in the upper corner of securities bought for Jan or Marietje. As long as they do this with a soft pencil, a piece of eraser is able to wipe away the writing; however, if they accidentally use ink, it becomes problematic!

There are erasing liquids to make ink stains or bits of writing (when one has made a mistake) disappear, but these liquids almost always contain chlorine, which is very harmful for paper. That is also taboo at the stock exchange! No security may be traded which has been tampered with using chlorine. The new buyer who unwittingly receives the document may later experience the destructive effect of the chlorine when the paper becomes brittle at the treated spot.

I had found a method to remove ink stains or ink writing from paper without using that dangerous bleach. (I apologize to the reader for not publishing this method; it would encourage tampering and I do not wish to be an accomplice to it!) Thus, for some dealers, occasionally securities on which a name was written in ink were freed from this.

One day—in the advanced afternoon, after trading hours—a phone call came in: "Sir, I had been busy at my writing desk before trading hours, taking stock of a batch of funds, when my servants alerted me that I had to hurry for the stock exchange. I rolled the lid of my writing desk closed with a thud and went to the stock exchange. On my return I made the terrible discovery—from under the edge of the desk lid a small stream of ink emerged … and I soon discovered that—by slamming the desk shut too violently—my inkwell (which had just been filled!) had somersaulted, its contents splashing all over the securities there. It's a terrible situation, sir.… What should I do?"

I had to imagine the man's situation in order to understand his fear. But that made me sound even more delighted when I gave him this advice over the phone: "Quickly get a bucket. Fill it three-quarters full with water and immerse all ink-stained documents in it as quickly as possible. Then get a car, get into it with your bucket, and bring it to me here at the laboratory!" Just over fifteen minutes later, the securities man got out of a car with his bucket of water and placed his precious cargo in my office. I immediately identified the type of the ink that had caused the inundation, which gave the deliverer some reassurance. I also promised to call him as soon as I had finished my work, but noted that I wanted to take an inventory first, in order to determine in duplicate what he had brought me. I was very touched when the reply was that this was not necessary ... because he was absolutely certain that, after cleaning, I would return all the documents to him!

They were all cleaned and smoothed to remove any wrinkles. Some documents required extra attention as they had strips of paper glued to them as backing and the paste had dissolved, of course. Returning them to their former state gave me some concern, too. The gentleman received a phone call and came, full of expectations, to my office, where the entire set of cleaned documents was displayed like a Saint Nicholas's Day shopping window. For a moment he looked suspiciously and thought for sure that I had laid out new replacement documents, but then immediately thought to himself ... surely that can't be, because obtaining duplicates requires a lot of writing and patience! There was not a speck of ink left on them, and with the best will in the world nothing of the catastrophe could be discerned on the documents themselves!

As I learned, this stockbroker has been singing the praises of my "chemical laundry" right and left on the stock exchange and, since then, securities came to me on occasion with ink writing or stains on them that have to be removed—especially "without chlorine," about which I always had to attach a statement to the piece! It also happened more than once that grease stains had to be removed from such documents; after all, with those stains they were untradeable on the exchange.

This occasionally caused great trouble and concern, especially when a painter had allowed linseed oil stains to get onto his documents. If linseed oil stains had completely "dried up" (chemically speaking, were completely oxidized), the stains could sometimes not be removed without severely damaging the documents. Why was this? Bear in mind, Reader, that the various inks used in the printing of these securities are, in fact, linseed oil paints; thus, in a chemical sense, after drying, they are on a par with the unwelcome linseed oil stains, which the owner had allowed to get onto them. If I dissolved the stains ... then I ran a great risk of dissolving the dried linseed oil parts of the printing ink as well ... and I would end up with a piece of white paper. In this type of rare case, my advice was to apply for a duplicate at the office of the company which had issued the document, in exchange for the contaminated one.

I would like to tell you about another peculiar case. From a bank in this town I received a security, which had been folded countless times, until finally a small parcel was formed as the end result. This parcel had a sticky, greasy appearance, as if it had been permeated with some oily substance. An accompanying letter asked me to remove the oily substance—presumably it was a type of oil!— from the valuable document. I went to work on it, but did not have much success. Together with my assistants we tried "organoleptically" (i.e., by smelling it) to find out what kind of fatty substance had penetrated the paper of this object so strongly, but no one could reconcile the smell with any fatty matter. And so I preferred not to experiment any further with such a valuable item—there is always the risk of encountering undesirable complications—but instead to ask my client to be frank and tell me what kind of substance had gotten onto the item. Then it would be easier to find the means to remove the substance!

It took some days before I received an answer—and it sounded rather mysterious. However, let me first point out to you that this case took place in 1918, when World War I was coming to an end. The information I received in answer to my question went something like this: "Our client reports that as soon as he was called to arms as a *landstormer*,[46] his wife—not knowing where she was going to store their only security (a government loan of a thousand guilders)—folded the precious paper several times and then hid it between her breasts under her clothes. There it remained for many months ... so that it can be assumed that no fatty matter but sweat was absorbed here." With this information we got there quickly. I put the item in lukewarm water, which removed a lot of the "foreign matter," and then freshened it up a bit, so that the last traces of the stains disappeared. We ended up by smoothing and shining the paper. They got the item back "like new"!

In the boardroom of an ancient foundation in Old Amsterdam, the board members met one day. As they discussed the present and the immediate future, one of the board members showed a keen interest in the foundation's past and inquired where the old papers relating to its founding, donations of buildings, etc., were to be found. Oh, those were downstairs in a safe in the basement. But after the death of the former curator, his heirs had been unable to find the key, and since then the safe had remained locked ... also because they never actually needed one! Everyone then became interested in the contents of the safe and it was unanimously decided to have it opened by a blacksmith. What was given the grand name of "safe" was in fact nothing more or less than an old privy in the back of the basement, the window of which had been bricked up, as well as the essential part of this room, after which the old wooden door had been removed to make room—in a brick frame—for a heavy iron safe door. In this vault they had stored the entire archive, at which the present administrators had hitherto never given a single glance, but in which they had suddenly—after the inspiration of one of their own—become interested.

When the blacksmith appeared with his drills, crowbars, and master keys, the board members attended in great excitement. Although the iron door was not very heavy, the lock was uncooperative, but within a relatively short time the blacksmith

---

46   Dutch military reserve unit consisting of older men.

RESTORATION AND RECONSTRUCTION OF DOCUMENTS

gracefully opened the door. Then the board members jumped backwards.... Although this "establishment" was given a completely different purpose than it originally had, like a fox that loses its hair but not its tricks, one could almost say that this place had not denied its original character either! The air of this room was indescribable, so that everyone was led to believe that the cardinal part of the original "convenience" had not been removed. However, the cause of this horrible stench was different: the seal on the vault had been so airtight that the abundance of moisture rising from the bottom of the cellar had accumulated in the pile of documents, encouraging the development of countless bacterial colonies, which had chosen the animal glue of the handmade paper of the most ancient documents (including piles of notarial acts!) as a highly desirable nutrient! Thick packets of folio acts bound together lay there like mushy soft lumps, into which their fingertips sank, like pudding, as soon as one attempted to grasp something. It was, in a word, a terrible sight, and one was convinced that the entire archive had been destroyed forever.

Most of the parcels of documents lay in large drums with lids, some of which were made of zinc, others of heavy tin; the latter, however, had been largely consumed by rust. With the greatest caution, the drums with their unpleasantly smelling contents of slimy masses of paper were brought into a dry room, so they could deliberate in the meantime about what to do. One of the board members came to consult me and asked whether there was any chance that the papers, which were of historical value to the foundation, might be saved from total ruin and restored. The drum containing the very oldest documents had already been brought to my home. I promised to try to save what could be saved.

Since the glue on the papers had been digested by the rotting bacteria, and the paper was wet through and through, the stack of documents seemed to consist of a single mushy mass of paper. It was impossible to get a grip on the individual sheets. I carefully put the whole packet in water and using a very fine nozzle I squirted a jet of water into it from the side. Then—if the jet was well directed—the top sheet would detach itself from the underlying sheets, in a similar way to how one can turn the pages of an open book by blowing on the pages from the side with a little blast of wind through a nozzle. The loose mushy sheet was then carefully scooped up and placed on fine metal mesh to dry.

After all the moisture had disappeared from it, there was apparently a little bit of cohesion in it, but it was still not great! Therefore, the next step was this: with the help of a paint sprayer, which was fed by an air pump with an electric motor, I sprayed a fine dew of zapon varnish over the sheets. When the zapon varnish had dried, the documents felt like solid paper again; a serial number could even be written on them with pencil or ink. Those who knew nothing of the processing that had taken place took the documents for "authentic," firm Old Dutch paper! It goes without saying that the documents which could still be carefully separated "on dry land" were immediately laid on the screens and—after drying—were "zaponized" (i.e., sprayed with zapon varnish). In this way I succeeded in completely restoring almost all the historical papers, such as the founding act, some copies of it—equally old—and the oldest real estate transfer papers and many other important documents. Nobody could see that they had been through so much! Many copies of notarial acts from later years, which belonged to this archive, and whose originals could in any case be found in the archives of the notaries involved, or in the general notarial archives next to the House of Detention, did not undergo this extensive artistic treatment; they were of no importance from a historical point of view. But often there was another reason why no further effort was made: along with the disappearance of the glue, the ink had completely disappeared from many of these documents, so that nothing at all could be found of what had been written! One notarial act was very remarkable; the ink with which the text was written had absolutely disappeared; but the ink with which the notary himself had signed the act, after having made a few annotations while reading it and having added here and there the line in the letter T or closed an open O from above ... that ink had stood its ground against the destructive elements which had been at work in that beautiful vault.

This fact again confirms that today's "inks" are by no means resistant to influences like the above, while the writing of the oldest historical documents from that vault, even if appearing reddish-brown, was still brilliantly readable. What a contrast! How so? Well, Reader, let me tell you. Our ancestors made reliable ink from the gall nuts of trees and iron salts. People today can still find similarly reliable inks here and there with which to obtain writing of high durability but too often prefer "inks" that do not really deserve the name ink—they are usually colored watery suds, in which there is too little iron. The durability of a document written with them cannot be high. As far as I'm concerned, such writing liquids are for schoolchildren doing their homework; there are no durability requirements for that at all. But wherever it is desired that writing remain clearly legible, i.e., imperishable, after many years, one should not use colored waters as "inks" which give the writing a colored appearance for a few days. Good inks give writing that turns jet black after a few days (although I do not mean to say that all inks that dry jet black belong to the first-class inks), but all inks, whose writing remains beautifully blue or green or purple, fall outside the class of the normal inks, that is, those, which reach the minimum of four grams of iron per liter and are prepared accordingly with enough gall nut parts.

I once received a letter from someone who had a special fondness for a grass-green writing ink. I covered the signature of that writing with a strip of black paper and exposed the text to the summer sun for several weeks, with the result that the sun's rays made the green writing disappear completely from the paper. I then typed some lines above that signature, which I sent to the person concerned, which he did not immediately understand. I presume that he has been cured for good and now uses only a more reliable normal ink, which looks nice and blue when writing, but jet black after a few days.

In Friesland, "somewhere" in the countryside, in a farmhouse, a farmer was dying. His loving children, who saw the moment approaching with fear and trepidation, did not in fact have their greatest fear about the father's passing; no, it came from something else. The father had always kept silent about his finances, and now the children did not know where "the money" was. They had already searched through all the drawers and cupboards—the sick man didn't notice anything anyway, not even that his keys were taken from his pocket and his papers were being rummaged through!—but they still couldn't find a clue as to where father's money was invested. The sick man was once more grabbed by the shoulders and shaken, to become properly "awake and fresh" to answer that one question, but he went into eternity without providing any clarification.

The doctor came to help with the deposition of the dead man. In the process, a cotton pouch was found on the chest of the deceased, hanging from a strap around the neck. Its contents—the size of a matchbox—seemed to be a cheesy mass, but on closer inspection revealed itself to be a folded up piece of large-format paper, steeped with sweat of however many years, the sweat having rendered all the ink of the writing illegible! The notary of the village was called in; he immediately took the document out of their hands and promised to enlist the help of someone who had examined all kinds of papers for the court, and sent me the faded, not-so-fresh-smelling document.

Yes, one could see that there was a text of more or less twenty-five lines written on it, but it was impossible to decipher a single letter of the writing! Then the ultraviolet lamp with its mysterious short wavelength rays helped. While the document was exposed to the action of those rays in the dark room, a camera was simultaneously pointed at it. The latter provided me with an image showing the entire text attesting to a debt with a signature. A brother of the deceased, who had soon learned of the discovery of an illegible document, had not found it necessary to point out to his nieces and nephews that this could well be the promissory note he had given their father when the latter helped him obtain capital for a business. You will understand, Reader, how that good uncle looked up when the notary held my picture under his nose and forced him to settle the matter!

I still remember the following case as if it happened yesterday: There was a crook who bought a check for thirty-seven guilders—payable to the Amsterdam branch of the Deutsche Bank—at a bank in Crefeld and as soon as he had it in his hands he altered it to make it a check for 2,830 guilders. He also changed the name which he had written on the check to another name, quickly crossed the Dutch border and—now as an "interested party"—went to a banker in Nijmegen to cash the check. And please do it very quickly, because he was very much in need of the cash! The banker sent the document by express letter to a friendly banking house in Amsterdam—a big one!—from where they immediately went to the Deutsche Bank to collect the money. Knowing the messenger who came with the request, they did not hesitate for a moment—even though the advice letter from Crefeld had not yet arrived—to pay out the money.

A few hours later came the advice letter, which said that the check with that number, issued to such-and-such a person, amounted to thirty-seven guilders. Immediately Crefeld was called. Surely this had to be an error? Surely they were mistaken, because this was a check for 2,830 guilders! But Crefeld insisted that the check was for thirty-seven guilders and only that amount should have been paid. Then the fun began! The clever fraudster had run off and nobody ever managed to track him down, but the Deutsche Bank claimed the difference of 2,793 guilders from the Nijmegen banker, because he had started it all by sending the forged document to Amsterdam for collection. The Nijmegen man did not care much for this and asked if the check—which had not looked suspicious to him!—could be returned to him. It was sent to him, and soon the check was in the hands of an "expert" who was to give his opinion of the document.

After some time, a weighty report appeared, which, in brief, amounted to this: "The check looks perfectly normal. Had anything been removed from it with eraser gum, knife or otherwise—that is, mechanically—I would be able to see it with my microscope from the roughened surface of the paper. But there is nothing of that nature to be discovered! If any chemical agent had been used to remove writing, I would be sure of that by discoloration of the surface of the paper. But nothing of that nature can be detected! Therefore, this check is perfectly "sound." It was originally made out to the amount of 2,830 guilders in the name of P. B. Previously there was no other amount or name on it!"

The check came back from Nijmegen with the expert's report, which understandably reassured the Nijmegen banker completely. But the Deutsche Bank in Amsterdam handed the matter over to its lawyer, Mr. Sibbe—the dean of the bar association in the capital—who in turn instructed me to examine the check thoroughly. Which I did! Hardly had I photographed the check—following Professor Kögel's method and using a special apparatus which Carl Zeiss had made for me (on Kögel's instructions), the only apparatus of its kind in all the country!—when I discovered in the photos all the original writing, which the bank in Crefeld had written on it and which the fraudster had so skillfully removed. Even the name for which the check was originally issued was clearly visible in the photo. I felt sorry for the Nijmegen expert. I wrote to him that he had made a bad mistake and advised him, before his client showed him my report, to ask for his own report back and declare that he had made an honest mistake. But he was not interested in that at all. He came to Amsterdam all upset, and wanted to know from me what right I thought

I had to criticize an older colleague in this way! Not much persuasion was needed. I merely presented him with the pictures I had taken with my expensive setup and he was soon convinced. "I was wrong, yes, but I do not have such equipment," he said, whereupon I politely advised him not to indulge in investigations such as these!

Since then, using the above-mentioned device, which contains lenses and prisms cut from quartz crystal (glass does not allow ultraviolet rays to pass through!), I have on several occasions taken photographs of removed writing, including that of a forged passport of an Italian, who had erased the original name written in it, to put his *nom de guerre* in its place. The setup cost me just under two thousand guilders at the time. I felt it as a part of my duty to buy that device; how else could I declare under oath, when accepting an assignment, to do my work "to the best of my knowledge"? But there were years when I could not even earn the interest from the aforementioned capital with that apparatus. It was always considered scandalous when I dared to charge an apparently high amount for a certain photograph, taken with that apparatus … and judged that a photograph was a photograph and should never cost that much! Honestly, it was often "provoking!"

Epilogue by Charles Berger

The work described in this chapter sometimes requires physical restoration of the actual document itself, and sometimes only the restoration of the information contained in it. These days, forensic document restoration will usually concentrate on the information in a document and how and by whom a document was produced. Using UV light is still a good way of making visible some of the things that the naked eye can't see. I remember a case in which UV light was the only way to make anything visible on a receipt in a container in which chemicals were illegally dumped. The information on the receipt finally led to a picture and the bank account of the person buying the container. But UV light is not the only wavelength that can reveal information. In hyperspectral imaging the full spectrum of wavelengths from infrared to ultraviolet can be used. Perhaps the biggest difference is the use of computers to process images and make the invisible visible. Color deconvolution[47] is one of those processing methods and can be used on normal, visible light images, too. It can exploit very small color differences to separate colors that are very close, or to remove colors that are obscuring important features. This helps, for example, in making text readable that has faded or been obscured.

---

47   Color deconvolution plug-in, 4N6site.com, https://4n6site.com/improc/decoplugin/webapp. This link allows interested readers to actively use color deconvolution themselves to restore and reconstruct digital pictures on their phone, tablet, or PC.

45. Charred Papers

In most attempts to "burn" papers, one usually fails to completely reduce them to ash. Typically, a charred mass is produced, which can only be burned after prolonged heating with sufficient oxygen supply, after which only the mineral components of the paper remain. In many cases, during the charring process, the mass twists into the most erratic shapes, and it is almost impossible to flatten the carbon mass again when it comes to investigating what was previously written on the paper. In such attempts, the mass generally crumbles into various small pieces, which can hardly be pieced together like a "puzzle" ... a hopeless endeavor!

Yet, occasionally, I have succeeded, through technical manipulations, in getting larger coherent portions of such carbonized scraps flat and determining what was previously written on them, whether printed or as handwritten text. This largely depends on the material with which the said text was applied. Certain types of printing ink remain very visible even after the paper is charred, and the numbers on charred banknotes are particularly decipherable, thanks to a precaution taken by our Nederlandsche Bank to print those numbers with a special ink that—due to its unique composition—clearly "speaks" on the charred paper. Pencil writing also shines conspicuously on top of the usually dull remnants of charred paper. Graphite, namely, burns very slowly, and pencil writing hardly changes even when the paper mass is charred. Printing inks also generally remain decipherable on charred paper with technical aids. This was evident in the following case, where the deputy judge of the Dordrecht Court called upon my assistance.

Somewhere in the countryside, clouds of smoke rose between the roof tiles of a small laborer's cottage. Several villagers hurried to the house upon seeing this smoke, where they found the occupant in the front room engaged in her daily work. "Mrs. Pieters, there's a fire upstairs!" to which the woman—apparently unpleasantly surprised—replied, "Well, don't go upstairs, or you'll suffocate!" The people ascended the attic stairs anyway and found some smoldering rubbish, which they quickly extinguished in a matter of minutes with a few buckets of water passed between them. Then the occupant came upstairs. Suddenly, she pulled out a tin presentation box from a baby carriage containing some rubbish that had not yet burned, opened it, and shuffled with her hand through the contents, consisting of charred paper, and, acting comically nervous, indicated several times that the cash inside—which the landlord was supposed to receive the next day—had been burned. The onlookers—who did not immediately realize that the contents of the baby carriage had not been affected by the fire and yet a tin box had been retrieved from it whose contents turned out to be completely charred—became concerned about the banknotes. They snatched the tin box with its contents out of the hands of the overwrought(?) woman, and one of them made the correct observation that, if, indeed, these were charred banknotes, new notes would undoubtedly be obtained in exchange for them. Meanwhile, a policeman appeared on the scene. He naturally was also extremely interested in the remains of the banknotes and confiscated the tin box. That box was then handed over to me for examination with the task of determining whether charred banknotes or other valuable papers were found in it or worthless paper remnants. My investigation revealed that we were not dealing with charred banknotes here, but with pieces of charred newspaper ... from the "shipping news" section! The police investigation revealed even more, and the lady was convicted of intentionally setting the fire.

In 1940, many Rotterdam businessmen brought me the charred remnants of valuable papers that had been excavated from the ruins after the bombing and subsequent fires. There was one wholesaler who kept all his accounting records on a card system, so he found metal drawers containing charred packs of cards. There was nothing to be found on these cards, which meant a gigantic loss. The accounts receivable information could not be read!!!! Here we had a case where my assistance unfortunately could not help, solely due to the fact that they had made all the entries with a blue-colored ink instead of proper ink. Even just separating the extremely fragile carbonized layers from the cards, which were twisted into numerous curves, was a slow task that required a lot of time because—no matter how carefully and cautiously one worked—portions of the sheets kept crumbling! But, gradually, we mastered small tricks that opened up the possibility of dissecting thicker, fused bundles of remnants without damaging them, in order to then photograph them in the most advantageous way. In this way the majority of the most important information in the securities was retrieved successfully.

Large drums containing charred documents, which lay together as a single piece of carbonized paper, were thus dissected in all their parts, and photographs were taken of everything, which then revealed a series of letters and numbers, all neatly displayed. I have a special memory of one share from the Nederlandsche Handel-Maatschappij,[48] issued at its founding. It featured numbers made with the help of pen and ink (there were no numbering machines then!), while the name of the first holder was also written on it: "King Willem II of the Netherlands." Thanks to the fact that a good writing ink had been used, I was also able to make that writing "speak" very clearly in my photo. But wherever the people of Rotterdam had used inferior ink, the writing had been completely consumed by the fire.

Isn't it high time that the government concerned itself more with ink as a product and issued regulations and requirements that good writing ink should meet???

---

48   The Nederlandsche Handel-Maatschappij (NHM, Netherlands Trading Company) was based in Amsterdam.

I thus saved securities worth about three hundred thousand. My photos, duly certified by me, and accompanied by a statement from me, were recognized by the companies concerned, and on that basis, the interested parties received new documents with the same numbers that the burned ones originally had. The demand that the government ensure the use of good ink was greatly recognized by a victim of the Rotterdam fires, a businessman who brought me a charred leather briefcase, in which a handwritten promissory note for six thousand guilders had been kept. This, too, had turned into an extremely thin sheet of shriveled carbonized paper. Here, too, unfortunately, I did not succeed in revealing the text of the document photographically, solely because an inferior ink had been used to write the promissory note. Had that ink contained more iron, the writing would have been recognizable even after charring!

Something very extraordinary also happened. Along with the charred papers from Rotterdam, I was handed a flat box containing an incredibly thin sheet of charred tissue paper, a remnant of a carbon copy made on very thin tissue paper. The text that had been on it was of great importance to the interested parties. I succeeded in photographing that text in its entirety, so clearly, as if I had placed an original in front of the lens. Remarkably, with this method, the letters I always obtained were white characters on the black background of the charred material.

Epilogue by Maurice Aalders

Since the writing of the chapter on charred paper by Co van Ledden Hulsebosch, the study of partially burned papers has significantly evolved, driven by both scholarly curiosity and technological innovation. As we can read, researchers depended on manual transcription and meticulous observation and, in van Ledden Hulsebosch's case, basic photography to decipher texts obscured by fire damage. This process was labor intensive and prone to inaccuracies. Van Ledden Hulsebosch, being an inventor, started with more advanced fluorescence photography. Today, the field has transformed into an area of multidisciplinary research that incorporates principles from material science, digital imaging, forensic analysis, and artificial intelligence (AI). Advancements in technology have introduced a variety of sophisticated tools that have revolutionized how investigators approach these fragile relics which sometimes have great forensic value. Techniques such as multispectral imaging allow for the visualization of ink through layers, while X-ray fluorescence provides elemental analysis without damaging the substrate. Topological analysis offers detailed surface examinations, and computed tomography scanning reveals three-dimensional structures within layered papers. Complementing these methods, AI now plays a pivotal role by enabling more precise text recognition and interpretation.

Machine learning algorithms can analyze patterns in the data to predict obscured characters and reconstruct texts, significantly enhancing the accuracy and speed of recovery.

Despite these technological strides, challenges remain. The preservation of burned papers is fraught with difficulties, primarily due to their fragile nature. There is a constant risk of further deterioration during handling and analysis, posing a significant concern for conservators. Even so, the combination of old-school study methods, modern technology, and AI keeps giving us deep insights into texts we couldn't read before because they were burned. The study of these burned papers really shows how creative van Ledden Hulsebosch was. His creativity helped lay the foundation for this field, just like it did in many other areas.

46. Emergency Relief

This happened quite a few years ago, but the case remains vivid in my mind, as if it transpired just last month. The public prosecutor of the Utrecht Court tasked me on a certain spring day to go to a village in the province of Utrecht, where the police inspector would take me to a villa. There, a burglary occurred the previous night and around sixty thousand guilders' worth of securities had been stolen from a safe. The occupant, Mr. X. Y. Z, received us. He was home alone. His wife and two daughters had left the premises the previous evening, along with him, to spend a few days elsewhere—and locked it. He had informed the police about his vacation plans, so they had telegraphed him to come back immediately as there had been a break-in at his villa.

The robbed safe—an old, unreliable type—was lying forward in the middle of the room. It must have been dragged from the corner where it had always stood to the center of the room, where it was laid down forward. Then it was child's play to detach the back wall of the safe, which turned out to be made of a piece of sheet iron connected to the rest by a series of rivets. It was just as if a large piece of cardboard, pinned in place, had been worked loose with a dull knife!

What struck me the most at first glance was that such a shoddy safe would be entrusted with securities worth sixty thousand guilders, while in the opposite corner of the room stood a strong Lips safe that would have made such a trick impossible. When I pointed this out, X. Y. Z. shrugged, saying that he "hadn't seen it that way" and that he now regretted, in hindsight, having been so reckless. But ... it had happened ... it was quite unfortunate.... Thankfully, he was insured against theft with forced entry!

As often happens, the nocturnal visitor had shown a touch of criminal humor: inside the broken safe, which lay before us like an open box on the floor, we saw a floppy felt hat, which—X. Y. Z told us—belonged to him. It had been hanging in the hallway on the coat rack and had been placed in the safe by one of the culprits after using the hat as a toilet(!)

Needless to say, Reader, that I immediately took an interest in this "visiting card." I was also interested in what had been on the household's "menu" in recent days, so I went to the trash can to see what vegetable remnants were deposited there.

While examining fingerprints on the safe, I found several "grip marks" on the side surfaces in the far corners above, near the front of the safe, bearing witness to a very peculiar way of gripping the safe. These must have been left by the person who handled the safe in those places to remove it from its corner with overturning movements. You never find such groups of fingerprints on a robbed safe that remained in place during the operation. Therefore, I intended to take the fingerprints of the homeowner on paper before returning to Amsterdam, in order to determine whether he had prepared the safe "for the robbery." You never know! I spoke very little during my work, which was followed attentively and unceasingly by the resident, who seemed somewhat restless to me. He initiated a conversation a couple of times about the interesting nature of my work, about how he found it so fascinating....

Our stomachs gradually signaled that it was time to pay some attention to our hunger, but before we decided to do so, I had already spoken to the public prosecutor about my vague suspicion. I told him that I would not be going to lunch with the members of the court as usual, but that I would accept Mr. X. Y. Z.'s invitation to have lunch together in a nearby restaurant. This is what happened. He continuously probed me for information on whether I had any idea about this mysterious burglary, a question I consistently answered in the negative, saying that I couldn't solve all crimes. He seemed somewhat relieved by that. Then he brought up the meager way in which the government usually compensated "freelance work" and—I must admit—I somewhat agreed with him! I truthfully told him that even as a "freelancer," I worked *pro bono publico*. I only received compensation when I had something to work on and that I did not have a fixed income as an expert, even though I had high expenses to cover throughout the year for maintaining my equipment, buying new devices, keeping up with my library of the latest study materials—all expensive!—etc.

Before we got up from the table, X. Y. Z. paused for a moment until the waiter was outside the room—no one could spy on us then. He pulled out a bundle of banknotes from his inside pocket, totaling five hundred guilders, and put it in my hand, saying, "Let me give you the opportunity to buy a couple of desired instruments or nice books for your laboratory!" It wasn't bribery, but it sure seemed like it! I accepted the money, barely thanked him, and silently put it in my pocket. As soon as I returned to the crime scene, I saw the public prosecutor and took him aside to tell him what had happened at the *koffietafel*[49] and to ask how to handle it. "Very simple, Mr. Hulsebosch. You keep that money. Draw up a report about this "donation" and place it along with the banknotes in your safe for now. We might need it later!" And so, I carefully documented the banknotes' details, even noting their numbers, in my report, and then, as instructed, secured everything away!

Further investigation did not yield any "grandiose" results. The composition of the "visiting card" did not match the vegetable remnants from the trash can, so it was "from the outside" and not from a household member. The fingerprints on the safe all belonged to the owner. Although the their placement was highly suspicious, it couldn't be used as evidence of guilt. And so, X. Y. Z. stayed out of jail.

---

49 *Koffietafel* is a light lunch that generally consists of coffee, tea, chocolate, juices, different kinds of rolls and breads, meats, rissoles, cheeses, jams, etc., often with soup as a starter.

However, the insurance company raised various objections, and quite rightfully so! X. Y. Z. couldn't prove that he actually possessed securities worth sixty thousand guilders ... and so the insurance company "temporarily" refused payment. There was no lawsuit! Soon *schraalhans* was the *keukenmeester*[50] in the villa and X. Y. Z. couldn't give his wife her household allowance anymore! No one understood how the family was still managing....

A couple of months later, a fake check was presented to a bank in Amsterdam for payment. The bank employee who immediately detected fraud raised the alarm, preventing the presenter from escaping. He was a fourteen-year-old boy who told the police, who had been summoned by phone in the meantime, that he was to collect the money for an unknown man who had instructed him to do so and would be waiting for him in a certain tavern. The boy was sent in that direction, followed by two detectives. When they arrived at the designated place, the "man" was already reaching out his hand to receive the money (which, of course, had not been paid out!) when he himself was received by the police. It was Mr. X. Y. Z., who was now clearly "busted." He received a heavy sentence for forgery, etc., and spent a few years in prison. He was completely "down and out," as they say.

Shortly thereafter, I spoke to the police inspector of the village in question when he came to consult me about another case. He told me how X. Y. Z.'s entire family had been ruined due to his misconduct. His wife—a woman from a respectable background—now rented out rooms and the two daughters were employed. But the rooms were currently vacant and a few days a week there was no hot meal on the table! That's when I thought the right moment had come to retrieve the envelope with the five hundred guilders from my safe. I had the inspector read the attached report and sign it to confirm the details (in terms of numbers and values). In addition, a deed of transfer was drawn up, in which I handed him the five hundred guilders to be given to X. Y. Z.'s wife and children. I asked if he would be willing to deliver it. If someone asked him where the money came from, he should reply that it had come "from Papa"! Finally, I sent both documents to the public prosecutor, who acknowledged receipt and was pleased with the satisfactory resolution.

Epilogue by Titia Sijen: Fecal Matter Analysis

As a forensic geneticist, the most interesting evidentiary trace in the story above is the fecal matter that was deposited at the scene of crime (and as a person, I also find it intriguing: why does someone do this: stress can stimulate the intestines,

---

50   This is a reference to the Dutch saying "Schraalhans is er keukenmeester," meaning, literally, that a miser is in charge of the kitchen, or, generally, that there are very few resources here.

but why fetch the floppy felt hat, drop the fecal matter in it and put that inside the broken safe?). Co van Ledden Hulsebosch was on the hunt for undigested plant matter that matched the plant matter in the trash bin. Nowadays, we have improved ways for examining such fecal evidence: fecal matter primarily consists of bacteria that once inhabited the intestines, along with fragments of the intestinal lining that were sloughed off during digestion. This provides two avenues: first, extracting a human DNA profile from the shed intestinal cells or delving into the intricate microbial community embedded within the feces. Our bodies serve as habitats for an intricate ecosystem known as the microbiome. Strikingly, each individual harbors a distinctive combination of microorganisms, encompassing distinct proportions of species, including unique strains of specific bacteria, thus forming a personal microbiome signature. The microbiome enclave in the large intestine is largely secluded from external influences and retains a relatively stable makeup, even if there was an antibiotic treatment. Consequently, the microbial profile of fecal material can offer insights into its originator. Forensic fecal analysis mirrors forensic DNA profiling principles, where a comparative basis is essential for accurate identification. Thus, a reference sample is pivotal. With DNA profiling, all kinds of samples can be used as reference. Samplings that can be taken the least invasive and from an area not much exposed to the environment, that is saliva or buccal scrapings. However, with fecal analysis, another deposition of fecal material functions as the reference, necessitating the suspect to leave again a "visiting card."

47. Yellow Powder

Without the slightest doubt, I dare to state that many detectives, upon reading or hearing about my "yellow powder," will have a smile appear on their faces because it evokes memories of remarkable cases where that yellow powder often provided an unexpected solution to a problem, although it sometimes also confirmed suspicions that had taken root. After some searching among dyes, I found one that, more potent than any other, adheres to the skin and cannot be removed with the usual cleaning agents, a dye also of an unusual, uncommon color. I began early on, sprinkling traces of this dye in money drawers from which thefts occurred at night or in other places where some less socially inclined individual might reach for someone else's property. Then that wrongdoer would have the yellow dye on their hands, leaving unmistakable traces of contamination from the "yellow powder."

Why did I choose the color yellow? Well, simply because many other colors could too easily be explained with some excuse. If I gave them red spots ... how easily they could acquire a bottle of red ink, further stain themselves with it, and then delicately claim, "These are spots of red ink that happened to get on my hands. The bottle is at home!" And purple spots would be attributed to owning an aniline[51] pencil, and so on and so forth. But this orange-yellow, so intensely staining the skin, could never be "explained," even though occasionally a determined smoker tried to convince us that they were nicotine stains from their cigarettes. But that could easily be verified and proven false!

At a large bank in Amsterdam, valuable items kept disappearing repeatedly from the belongings of the staff members, which were stored in a special cloakroom for employees. Various items of greater or lesser value vanished from the pockets of coats and jackets, causing some unease among the staff. This unease was easy to explain: the thefts had to be the work of one of the employees; no one else could access that cloakroom. As the management made various futile attempts to discover the culprit, the aforementioned restless atmosphere grew, especially among the female employees.

One day, a young lady approached my office, asking if she could seek my advice in a delicate matter. It turned out to be a young lady from that bank, who told me about the thefts and added, "The thought that it must be one of our colleagues is driving us to despair!" I reassured her that within a week, we would know who the scoundrel was. However, I would need an old ladies' raincoat, one of whose pockets would receive an additional lining that could easily be removed later ... of course,

---

51 Aniline, also known as aminobenzene, is (a precursor of) a synthetic dye discovered and synthesized for the first time in 1826.

so as not to ruin the entire garment with the yellow powder but only to soil that inside pocket, which could later be taken out. She took care of that!

This coat was then hung in the cloakroom; an old wallet with some small change was placed in the prepared pocket, and a small piece of the yellow powder was sprinkled on the coins. From what I had been told, it could be expected that, as before, the wallet would be emptied the next day and the wallet itself would be placed back in the side pocket. "All the better," I said, "then I expect even more success!" I then advised her to occasionally check the cloakroom to see if the coins were still in the pocket, and as soon as she noticed that the money was gone, to walk through the office spaces because I was convinced that the thief would have yellow-stained hands. The young lady was grateful for my help. Following my advice, she occasionally checked ... until she discovered that the theft had occurred ... the money was gone!

Now, a new difficulty arose: employees were only allowed to enter offices in which they worked, and this prevented her from making the required rounds to look for the yellow-stained hand! She confidently approached her department head, asked him if she could immediately speak with him in one of the meeting rooms, and there she informed him about the secret with "Mr. v. L. H."[52] He found the situation amusing and immediately said, "Then it's best that we go and look together; so walk with me and keep a good lookout, too!" But even after making two rounds, they saw no yellow hand anywhere. Confidence in the effectiveness of the method was briefly lost.

While they were still discussing the mysterious case in one of the corridors, one of the loyal old cleaning ladies stepped forward. There was still a trash can there, and the room supervisor asked the cleaning lady, who was carefully hiding her right hand under her apron!—to take the trash can to the department where it belonged. Then both hands had to be revealed, and the two detectives discovered that the good cleaning lady had a large saffron-yellow stain in her palm. When questioned about it, she tried to lie, but ... when coins came out of her pocket with remnants of the yellow powder still on them, denial was no longer possible, and she was caught red-handed!

A café owner on Gelderschekade,[53] who used to store the small change he took home from his cash register each evening in a money box, noticed that the supply occasionally and mysteriously shrank. He lived alone with his wife, and only an old, trusted cleaning lady, who had enjoyed the family's full trust for many years, came upstairs during the day to perform her cleaning duties. When asked for her opinion,

---

52 The initials of the famous Dutch forensic detective and author of this book, Co van Ledden Hulsebosch.
53 A street and canal in the city center of Amsterdam at the border of the infamous red-light district (De Wallen) and Chinatown.

the wife declared that she couldn't understand it at all, for Mina was like a bank; there was no need to doubt her. But she also had no idea who should be suspected!

The café owner discussed the matter with a detective; the detective had an idea and came to me to get a bit of "yellow powder," which was carefully sprinkled over the money in the box, very finely, so that the uninitiated wouldn't notice its presence! The next day, after the cleaning lady had worked several hours in the house, it was easy for the detective to determine that someone had touched the contents of the money box. In the meantime, the woman in question had gone home; she lived far away in the eastern part of Amsterdam.

The detective immediately headed to the apartment in question, where he found her and her common-law husband—a brute. As a reason for his visit, he stated that money kept disappearing from the box at the café; immediately, the common-law husband shouted out angrily, "You're not suggesting that my wife has anything to do with that, are you?" To which the detective replied, "Of course not, but the commissioner, who wants to know which people have been upstairs today, would like your wife to come and provide him with some information later.... Would you come with me, miss?" But before they had walked far, the detective had already told her that the yellow stains on her hands revealed everything, and that she could "pack her bags"[54]! She was kept at the police station. Her husband received a message that she had to stay and stood just as perplexed as the café owner's wife, for she had always been such an honest, decent woman!

In the heart of the old city is a large fancy goods store where a dozen young ladies work as shop assistants. There, too, the owner had noticed that thefts were taking place; he was unable to express any suspicion about any member of his staff, but thefts were happening, that was certain. When consulted about this, the police thought it advisable to set a trap with the yellow powder and then wait quietly. So it was done. The next day everything went on as usual until some of the girls on the sales staff noticed that Fietje[55] had been away for a long time. She had gone to the restroom and hadn't returned yet! And when she finally returned—with a bright red face—she walked through the store and onto the street to run an errand on the other side. (Later, it turned out that she had bought a bar of Sunlight[56] soap!) After that, she had returned and again rushed to the restroom ... strange, isn't it? And fifteen minutes later, the others saw her leave with her hat on and her coat on, wearing her gloves neatly on her hands, saying that she "didn't feel well at all" and was going home, asking the others to "tell the boss"(!)

---

54 That is, she should prepare for incarceration.
55 An old-fashioned Dutch female first name.
56 The English company that in 1930 merged with the Dutch Margarine Union to form the well-known consumer product company Unilever.

The following day, exactly twenty-four hours after making preparations, the detective came to check the situation, and he heard all about Fietje; no wonder he felt compelled to go to her house to see how she was doing. What he saw then is almost indescribable in words. Children who indulge in nail-biting and bite off bits of skin along with their nails show a picture that is almost trivial compared to that of Fietje's hands. She had nibbled away nearly all the patches of yellow skin that the treacherous powder had given her, so her hands were full of wounds. Yet, the detective with his keen eyes still discovered yellow spots on her skin in numerous places. Needless to say, she was "caught in the act"!

So I could go on further by mentioning successful cases with the yellow powder, but it would be monotonous; it always comes down to the same thing: any contact of the hand with an object that has been endowed with the yellow powder results in yellow stains on the hand that cannot be removed. Especially when, as almost always happens!—attempts are made to wash the stains away vigorously with soap, the yellow dye clings even more stubbornly to the skin, and the stains spread. If ever, here it can be attested: *Probatum est*![57]

Epilogue by Arian van Asten

After reading this chapter, I was surprised and amazed that the "Dutch Sherlock Holmes" was already applying forensic marker and tracer technology as a tactical means to expose perpetrators and reveal their criminal activities. To this end Co van Ledden Hulsebosch is using a magical yellow powder that he applies to items that are carefully placed to tempt an unknown thief to make a move (a coat with a money-filled wallet, for instance). In the chapter he does not disclose the nature of the powder that apparently leaves intense yellow stains on human skin and that are not easily removed by using soap or other cleaning agents. I am not entirely sure but I suspect it to be picric acid (2,4,6-trinitrophenol). This compound, also known as high explosive of the nitro-aromate class, is known to react with skin to create yellow to brown stains that are almost impossible to remove. It is also highly acidic, causing skin irritation, and toxic, so it is not a very culprit-friendly tool to use. Using such a strategy is special in that it involves the incorporation of forensic techniques in a tactical setting to solve repetitive crimes committed by an unknown perpetrator.

Legal complications can exist in using evidence that is obtained in such a premeditative manner. The defense council might argue that the defendant would not have committed the crime if he or she was not so explicitly tempted. Nowadays,

---

57   Latin for "It has been tested/proven."

forensic traces and markers are still used and developed. Digital GPS devices can be used by the police to track and find a stolen car or a shipment of drugs or weapons. This can be an effective strategy when authorities intercept such illegal transports and want to arrest the perpetrators involved. Additionally, special fibers, e.g., flock fibers, can also be used to create evidence of contact. Such fibers have been specifically designed to be invisible to the human eye under normal conditions whereas they strongly "light up" under UV irradiation. Being invisible is an important feature because otherwise the criminals might detect the presence of the marker/tracer prematurely and become suspicious. In that sense, the magic yellow powder is less ideal in that it has to be applied in a delicate and hidden manner to prevent detection.

Another interesting feature of a marker/tracer technology is its selectivity. Van Ledden Hulsebosch is also referring to this when he states that a yellow stain is more difficult to "reason away," that is, to come with an explanation for the presence of the stain that is not crime related. It means that the technology used must transfer an artificial trace that is highly characteristic and as such making it highly improbable that the material is originating from another source. This also has led in the post-DNA profiling era to the introduction of artificial DNA with unique base pair coding that has been specifically designed for a given batch of tracer material. Sprays exist to mark valuable objects with a DNA taggant and such technology is often also used as a crime deterrent. Potential perpetrators are then deliberately warned beforehand that items or even entire areas (in shops or banks) are protected by DNA spray technology. This then hopefully prevents any attempt to break and enter and steal valuable items. Such technology is offered by commercial security companies (e.g., SelectaDNA).

See Figure 12 (in the insert section) for a photograph of a bottle with yellow picric acid powder.

See Figure 13 (in the insert section) for a photograph of a sign to warn potential thieves of the presence of DNA-marking technology in Wilmslow, Cheshire, in the UK.

48. "*Souches*," or Physical Fits

Reader, let me ask you a question. Have you ever had the misfortune of breaking a plate in half at your breakfast table? If so, I assume that after picking up the pieces, you briefly tried to fit them back together, perhaps jokingly making the stereotypical remark at the table: "Yes, that's how it happened!" However, you probably did not consider the deeper meaning inherent in that act of fitting the two pieces together. If I were to give you one of the halves and to store away the other, if I were to provide you with the necessary travel expenses and instruct you to travel the world, searching for a half of a plate that would perfectly match your half, I am absolutely certain that the journey would be in vain and you would not succeed in finding such a matching half plate. However, if I present the half that previously formed a whole, it will fit precisely!

In criminology, term we use to describe this type of exact fit is *souche*, or "physical fit." If I were to provide a definition of that word, it would be: "It is a separation of coherence that is irrefutably proven with solidarity." If all subscribers of a newspaper with a circulation of a hundred thousand copies were invited to tear off the lower-right corner of their evening newspaper in a random manner after reading it, the torn piece in their hand would only fit what remained of the newspaper on their table, and not a single other newspaper!

Where does the word *souche* come from? I will tell you. The individual tickets of the large French lottery are, similar to tram tickets, bound in booklets of a hundred pieces when they come from the printing house. However, they are not perforated. A narrow portion on the left, bearing the same number as the actual ticket printed to the right, is separated by a strip adorned with exquisite and colorful filigree printing in delicate patterns. Scissors must cut along that pattern—for each ticket individually!—each time creating a different, irregular, curved cut through that fine-line pattern—never the same twice! On each ticket, printed in small letters along one of the edges, it says: "Attention à la souche; n'y coupez pas!" ("Pay attention to the *souche*; do not cut it!").

The intention is easily understood. Let's imagine for a while that a few ticket books are secretly taken from the printing house where the tickets are manufactured before being numbered by the counter. Imagine for a moment that on a certain evening, the newspapers publish the number on which the jackpot has fallen, and the thief of the blank ticket books hastens to print the "lucky" number on one of the blank tickets with the genuine counter. Conceivably, he could try to unlawfully claim the jackpot with the forged ticket. In such a case, there would be a whole ordeal to determine which ticket was genuine if the rightful owner also showed up with their genuine ticket. You see, in that case, the physical fit helps. Because no prize is paid out on any ticket without first finding the corresponding strip in the *souche* booklet that was previously attached to the specific ticket, and the irregular cutting line of the scissors must align perfectly when the ticket and its stub are placed together. This provides the certainty that one is dealing with the genuine ticket, immediately exposing the forged ticket as such!

Not long ago, someone stole a loose distribution voucher that had been torn from the sheet and set aside for the butter supplier. When that voucher was taken out of the perpetrator's pocket, he insisted that he had purchased the piece of paper a few days earlier from an unknown person. However, with the help of a microscope and a camera, it was proven that this small piece of paper originated from the injured lady's card! (This was a case at the Amsterdam Police headquarters.)

Another time, a burglar had an unfortunate incident when attempting to open a door lock with a fake key: a piece of the key blade broke off and remained stuck in the lock. The man was careless and left the rest of the key on his key chain. That proved to be his downfall. The connection between that piece of metal and the fragment found in the lock was clearly established beyond doubt!

Near the Vondelpark area, a teenage boy attempted a burglary. He had set his mind on removing the putty from one of the French doors, thus removing the glass pane and loosening the espagnolette bolts. However, the putty was rock hard, and the tip of his pocketknife broke off. It remained stuck deep in the hardened putty, where I found it during my investigation and carefully removed it as evidence. Thanks to the tireless efforts of the then-chief of the central detective unit, Pateer, it was discovered that a fingerprint left by the perpetrator belonged to a seventeen-year-old boy from the neighborhood. He was brought to the police station. I happened to be present when the suspect arrived. He was searched, and a mother-of-pearl pocketknife was found. "Boy, what a nice knife you have," I casually remarked, to which the owner responded, "Yes, but the tip is broken," unaware that I would immediately follow up with, "But I believe I have it for you!" The fractured surfaces revealed a perfect match: in the magnified image, the "peaks and valleys" of one rough fracture surface of the steel corresponded beautifully with the "valleys and peaks" on the other side! The connection was proven, and the villain was punished.

Another case involved a cardboard stub. In a cupboard where office supplies were kept, there had been a small cash box in a corner of one of the shelves, containing a few ten guilder notes. One morning, the bookkeeper discovered evidence of a fire on that shelf. There were charred remains of the cigar box in which the money had been stored, as well as some papers that had been nearby. And, as expected, the money was missing! During my investigation, I discovered a partially burned "cardboard" match, which was carefully preserved as evidence. There was suspicion that the youngest clerk might know more about it, but he didn't have a book of cardboard matches with him. However, it was noted that the rainy weather of the previous day might have caused him to wear a raincoat, so a detective quickly went to the young man's home to investigate. He found a matchbook in a side pocket of the raincoat, and it still contained ... one match. It was not easy, but nevertheless successful, to determine the exact spot where the match, found at the "scene of the fire" in the cupboard, had been attached to the matchbook. The correspondence of the three dimensions of the stub could be clearly demonstrated! And thus, the connection was proven.

Many years ago, in the Driekoningenstraat in Amsterdam, the lifeless body of an elderly widow living alone was found in her home. She was a peculiar woman who, ironically, had connections with dangerous individuals who came to her to sell stolen goods. We found about twenty pairs of new women's shoes and numerous other merchandise in her house, including a rolled-up piece of lace curtain. That last item proved fatal for the culprits. After murdering the woman, they took part of their loot wrapped in a piece of the lace curtain, which they had cut from the larger piece. It was remarkable how the stub presented itself, not only due to the woven pattern but also because of the occasional "snags" present at certain locations, made by the scissors (which did not cut cleanly). Moreover, this distinctive "packaging," found at the thieves' place, when combined with the piece left at the murder scene, exactly totaled fifty yards, the original length of the fabric.

My late colleague Loock from Dusseldorf reported a case of murder involving a boy. A "noose" made of several knotted pieces of new rope or cord was found around his neck. This fact raised suspicion towards a warehouse assistant at a rope dealership. Now, coincidentally, rolls of the same types of rope used in that noose were found in that warehouse. The pieces had been cut off with a knife, sometimes at an angle and, in another instance, with the knife making two separate cuts. In short, even in these separations of connected material, beautiful stubs were present!

One can indeed observe in how many types of materials *souches* (physical fits) can be found. For instance, a postal clerk—a sorter at the main post office—was suspected as robberies of registered letters occurred frequently in his section. One day, another clerk noticed how his colleague—who had been "absent" for quite some time—took a letter with stamps out of his pocket and placed it back among the other items. The chief was alerted. The specific letter was removed from the stack, but the suspect denied any wrongdoing. Then the sender, who had been summoned to the post office, was able to briefly open his letter to confirm that the money was missing. However, the evidence of the culprit's guilt came from a small, fine stub: I had noticed that a corner piece was missing from one of the sealing wax stamps. During the search, I found a tiny fragment of sealing wax in the pocket fabric, which presented a beautiful stub that perfectly filled the gap on the perimeter of the wax seal on the letter. It also had the exact thickness to prove that this wax fragment had previously been part of that wax seal on that letter. The case was thus swiftly resolved!

Many still remember the murder case in Leidschendam. A pseudo-military man lured an unsuspecting cattle dealer, who often carried a substantial amount of money, out of his house—supposedly because the captain needed his help to appraise some livestock!—and then fatally assaulted the unfortunate victim in the car, later dropping the body on the side of a country road on a grassy verge. To avoid being recognized, he preferred to avoid densely populated areas and took a detour along narrow country roads. At one point, while trying to turn the car around (he had taken a wrong turn!), he encountered difficulties. In the process, his front wheel struck an iron peg sticking diagonally out of the ground, which was connected to a garden gate post to support it. On that occasion, the said iron peg had pushed a piece of rubber out of the left front tire—similar to how one would make a hole in a pudding with a spoon—resulting in a small piece of rubber being left behind on the ground. He continued driving with a front tire where a small section of rubber was missing, exposing the canvas layer. The connection could also be brilliantly demonstrated in this case!

A tailor from a large ready-to-wear store was suspected of secretly cutting and taking pieces of fabric needed for his oldest child's sailor jacket. He denied it. The police seized the finished garment from his house. I had it taken apart by an expert, and the individual pieces were pressed flat. Then it became a childishly simple game of fitting and measuring, like a jigsaw puzzle ... and the proof was provided! We could precisely determine where the collar, the front panels, etc., were cut from the large piece of fabric, as well as the location of the back panel.

I would like to conclude my discussion on physical fits with a case that led to a guilty verdict and a fifteen-year sentence. In Garderen, located in the Veluwe region, two elderly women living alone were murdered in a remote small house. It was evident that the motive behind the crime was robbery. One of the women had a large piece of cloth forcefully stuffed into her mouth to prevent her from screaming. It turned out that two men were responsible for the crime. One of them quickly confessed, providing a detailed account of the events. The other, however, adamantly maintained his innocence, hoping to evade conviction. Initially, there was not much evidence against him apart from the incriminating statements of his accomplice during the two months that followed the murder.

At that point, the public prosecutor in Zwolle wrote to me, requesting a meeting. Despite having initially sought "expert assistance" from other sources, they were interested in my involvement, hoping that I might shed some light on the case and provide additional evidence. I was given access to the case file to study it thoroughly. As I read through it, I came across the statement of the first suspect, mentioning that the men had traveled by train to Amersfoort, with their bicycles taken as luggage. From Amersfoort, they continued their journey by bike. Upon reading this, I thought it would be worthwhile to inquire with the railway company whether it was possible to trace the tickets used for transporting bicycles from Amsterdam to Amersfoort on that particular day. Fortunately, it was still possible, and among the retrieved tickets, I found two with consecutive numbers, both filled out by the same hand in ink. It was the handwriting of the second suspect, as later confirmed.

Further on in the file, I read about the cloth used to stuff the woman's mouth and a bundle of rags that had been found in the dwelling of the second suspect (a houseboat located north of Amsterdam in a small side canal), which were now deposited at the court registry. I traveled to Zwolle and requested to see those rags. It was then stated to me that they had already been examined by experts. However, I expressed doubts about this assertion. No, really, they had been expertly examined! Once again, I regretfully noted that they had not been examined thoroughly. Naturally, they asked me how I could assert this with such confidence, and my response was:

> When I have to determine whether there is any "stub connection" between two wads of newspaper, the first requirement is to unravel and completely smooth out those wads, making them flat. Only then can you start fitting them together. The rags from that basket are heavily crumpled, also somewhat resembling wads. To determine if there is a piece among them that was once part of the cloth stuffed in the victim's mouth, it is necessary to thoroughly flatten those fabric pieces as well, and only then can you properly fit and measure them. The condition of all these rags clearly shows me that they have not undergone the aforementioned process, indicating that they have not been examined properly. Please understand that I am taking them with me to my laboratory for further inspection of the aforementioned cloth.

And so it was done.

Upon arriving home, I hurried to connect the electric iron that belongs to my laboratory inventory, and shortly after, I started ironing the rags and larger pieces I had brought. Then I established that the wad found in the mouth of one victim had been one piece with a strip, which had a hem (likely from a pillowcase) found in the houseboat on the other side of the IJ. Anyone who might doubt the reliability of the slightly frayed stub was fully convinced of the accuracy of the conclusion when I pointed out the presence of three excessively thick weft threads—fabric defects—found in both the incriminated cloth and the adjacent fitting strip, at the same height and interval. The perfectly equal width of the hem on a hemmed piece at the bottom confirmed the uniformity of the sewing machine stitch. In short, there was not the slightest trace of doubt. The cohesion was proven … and this physical fit resulted in a fifteen-year prison sentence for the person involved!

Epilogue by Rick van Rijn

This chapter reminds me of a case one of my PhD students, H. M. de Bakker, told me about. The case dealt with a decapitated homicide victim who underwent forensic radiological examination at his workplace, the Department of Radiology at Groene Hart Hospital in Gouda. Nowadays forensic radiology plays a major role in nearly all medicolegal cases. Since R. Dirnofer coined the phrase "virtopsy" in 2001, the use of, especially, postmortem computed tomography (PMCT) has increasingly become an integral part of forensic medicine.[58] In the Netherlands, de Bakker, a radiologist in the Department of Radiology at Groene Hart Hospital, must be seen as the founding father of forensic radiology. Since 2000, his department worked closely with the Department of Forensic Pathology at the Netherlands Forensic Institute. P. A. M. Hofman, of the Department of Radiology at Maastricht University Hospital, started the Unit Forensic Radiology, which since 2009 has provided a service to the Dutch Police. In the Netherlands there currently are two professors in the field of forensic radiology: Prof. Dr. P. A. M. Hofman at the University of Maastricht and Prof. Dr. R. R. van Rijn at the University of Amsterdam, with a focus on pediatric forensic radiology.

In forensic death investigations PMCT (and, to a lesser extent, postmortem MRI) has become an integral part of the workup. By using PMCT the corpse can be visualized in three dimensions; the imaging data then can be used by the police and forensic investigators to support their working hypotheses or be used in 3D crime scene reconstructions (e.g., in the case of gunshot wounds). It is, however, also essential for the forensic pathologist, as the information obtained from the PMCT (e.g., fractures or retained foreign bodies such as bullets or parts of a knife) can be used to guide the autopsy or even lead to a limited autopsy.

There have been numerous studies that have shown the advantages and disadvantages of PMCT compared to the conventional autopsy. A systematic review by G. Ampanozi et al. included 4,213 cases.[59] This review showed that PMCT was especially sensitive to skeletal trauma and air collections, but it is relatively poor in the detection of soft tissue and parenchymatous organ injuries. As shown by the study of Grabherr et al., the addition of contrast (PMCT angiography, or PMCTA) is essential to detect soft tissue lesions and/or hemorrhages.[60] The addition of PMCTA

---

58   R. Dirnhofer, "Von der Autopsie zur Virtopsie," *Rechtsmedizin* 11(3–4) (2001), 137.
59   G. Ampanozi et al., "Postmortem Imaging Findings and Cause of Death Determination Compared with Autopsy: A Systematic Review of Diagnostic Test Accuracy and Meta-analysis," *International Journal of Legal Medicine* 134(1) (2020), 321–337, https://doi.org/10.1007/s00414-019-02140-y.
60   S. Grabherr et al., "Postmortem CT Angiography Compared with Autopsy: A Forensic Multicenter Study," *Radiology* 288(1) (2018), 270–276, http://dx.doi.org/10.1148/radiol.2018170559.

MISDAAD EN X-STRALEN.

Proeven van den heer Hulsebosch in de Philipsfabrieken.

Naar wij vernemen heeft de directie der Philipsfabrieken te Eindhoven aan den Amsterdamschen politiedeskundige en criminalist, den heer C. J. van Ledden Hulsebosch, de gelegenheid gegeven om met een volledig Röntgen-apparaat proeven te nemen bij zijn deskundige onderzoekingen. De heer Van Ledden Hulsebosch zal trachten na te gaan in hoeverre nieuwe wegen ingeslagen kunnen worden met X-stralen bij het opsporen en het tot klaarheid brengen van misdrijven.

Figure 14. A news article from the Dutch daily newspaper De Telegraaf of August 13, 1929, reporting on first tests by Co van Ledden Hulsebosch with a Philips X-ray system in forensic investigations.

increased the essential finding in all cases from 63% to 91%, and in all cases with a violent death from 70% to 92%.

Let's go back to the case mentioned at the beginning of this epilogue. The Netherlands Forensic Institute requested that the corpse of the beheaded victim undergo conventional radiological examination (this case precedes the introduction of PMCT). The radiographs showed that part of the cervical spine was still attached to the thorax. Several days later a head was found and here, also, radiographic examination was requested. The piece of the cervical spine attached to the skull matched perfectly with the piece attached to the thorax. A true radiological stub! Had Co van Ledden Hulsebosch lived today he would have been amazed to see what information noninvasive imaging could yield. It is of interest to note that in 1929 Philips donated a portable X-ray system that he then used for forensic research (Fig. 14). Again, he was leading the way in advancing forensic science and medicine.

49. What One Little Blood Spatter Proved

During World War I all sorts of unsavory characters tried to get the Dutch to part with their gold coins by offering them fifteen, sixteen, even seventeen guilders in return. It was rumored that these individuals were employed by Eastern European states that desperately needed gold. In a certain café on Rembrandtplein in Amsterdam, every evening until closing time, one could see a man sitting in a particular corner, usually at the same table, buying the gold coins. One person would recommend another and bring them to the merchant, who paid a significant amount for the gold. A few visitors noticed how much money this man always carried, and they came up with a plan to "lighten his load" at some point. First, they discreetly followed him on his way home (the café in question closed at one o'clock in the morning, and there were no trams running by then) and determined that he lived in an upstairs apartment on Marnixstraat, across from the Trade School.

The next evening, or rather night, they planned to wait for him in the dark in the portal behind the street door to rob him. As the resident crossed the threshold and attempted to close the street door, he received an incredibly hard blow to the head, causing him to lose consciousness momentarily and collapse, but not before letting out a loud scream that echoed throughout the house. The assailants, however, had not expected this at all! They waited completely still, anticipating the next few seconds, and suddenly it became clear to them that the staircase creaked as a ray of light revealed the arrival of help for the resident who had returned home. Without further ado, they pulled open the front door and quickly fled in different directions; one ran toward the Rozengracht intersection, while the other sprinted in the opposite direction toward Leidscheplein.

Every ten steps, the second individual glanced back to ensure that nobody was pursuing them and walked along the sidewalk, staying in the shadows of the buildings, without the faintest idea that a police officer was covertly positioned in one of the doorways of that row of pillars. At the right moment, the officer emerged from his hiding spot to apprehend the runner, who was so out of breath that he couldn't provide an immediate response to the questions posed to him. Of course, the first question was, "Why are you running so fast?" To this, the policeman received the answer, "Oh, just ... to get home quickly," accompanied by a shrug, undoubtedly emphasizing the insignificance of the act of running. When you have no other reasons to run away so fast, "then come with me for a moment," the officer suggested, and they walked together to the police station at Leidscheplein, where the arrestee—who had caught his breath a little by then!—assumed the posture of a completely innocent person who, apparently due to a misunderstanding, would have to stay at the station for the rest of the night.

An hour later, a doctor arrived to make a "preliminary report" to the duty officer about an assault on a resident of an upstairs apartment on Marnixstraat, whom he had just treated but was unable to appear in person at that moment. The doctor could provide some information since the victim had given him an account. The duty officer soon realized that there could be a connection between the previously brought in detainee—the runner—and this robbery, but he also understood that further evidence would be necessary for the reconstruction of that fact. In other words, the causal relationship needed to be properly demonstrated!

The night had passed; the night shift was replaced by the day shift, which was briefed on the ongoing cases and the persons under arrest. During the late morning, the commissioner arrived. He familiarized himself with what had been booked the previous night. He was informed about the detainee and mischievously asked, "So, was this guy arrested just because he was running fast, or do you have any indication or evidence that he was involved in the robbery?" It had been understood that at least two individuals were involved because, while the runner, wearing a floppy hat, had arrived at the police station, one of the residents of the victim brought in a fedora that was found in the vestibule.

The commissioner asked if there were any bloodstains on the clothing of the detainee; however, no one had discovered any. Just to be sure, the coat and hat were sent to the laboratory for examination. I received the clothing items with a request to check for bloodstains and report any conclusions that could be drawn from those stains. I knew nothing about the incident! It was a so-called demi-season coat, quite rough in texture, with a speckled greenish-gray color. After some searching, I did find one bloodstain, extremely small, but it revealed a lot to me. So, I reported: "The wearer of this coat was present during the administration of a very hard blow to someone's head last night; mind you, he was present but did not deliver the blow himself." As expected, I was asked to further explain how I could determine all of that, including the timing and the presence during the delivery of a blow by someone else. I then provided the following explanation:

> The bloodstain is an extremely small spatter stain. The color is still red, like fresh blood. When a small piece of moist paper is pressed against it, it immediately takes on a red color. Therefore, the stain is no older than a few hours, which means it must have landed on the coat during the previous night. The amount of blood represented by this stain is extremely small. Such tiny blood droplets are only projected when a forceful blow is struck on a highly blood-rich area of the skin. While a projected blood droplet can slide quite far

on smooth fabric, on rough fabric that provides resistance when the slanted droplet lands on it, it seldom travels over a significant distance. However, it struck me how far that small quantity of blood from that minuscule spatter stain had slid over the rough fabric. It must have had an enormous velocity, which can only be explained by the tremendously powerful blow that caused it. That's how I explain the hard blow. If I wonder where that bloodstain came from, I first establish that it landed on the fabric of the coat diagonally from above—undoubtedly originating from a head. And how could I explain that the owner of this coat was indeed present during the robbery but could not have delivered the blow himself? That was as "simple as ABC!" The spatter stain was on the back of the coat, so the wearer—assuming he wore the coat properly—could not have made the attack but must have been facing away from the "source" of the bloodstain.

Bloodstains are and remain the most important silent witnesses when it comes to unraveling how things unfold. Their color, solubility, size, shape, thickness, direction, location, and grouping (when multiple stains are present) are examined, and from all that data, a considerable amount of information can usually be deduced, as demonstrated by the above case.

In relation to a murder of a man living alone on the Drenthe heath, I received a military uniform from Assen, which had several bloodstains. I was asked to examine the costume because it was suspected that the owner might be the perpetrator of the murder. After inspecting the package, I immediately returned it to the policeman, with the message that the owner/wearer of this uniform had not committed the murder, even if those bloodstains turned out to be fresh human blood.

The victim had been bludgeoned to death in the bedstead with a hammer. Countless fine blood spatters, which flew in all directions, had adhered to the bedding, the walls of the bedstead, and the inside of the partially opened doors. The perpetrator had leaned inside through those partially opened doors and delivered the blows. Therefore, there was every reason to expect that on his clothing—as far as it was exposed to the "spray" of blood—only fine blood spatter stains would be present. However, the bloodstains on the military clothing clearly indicated to me that streams of blood had flowed from the perpetrator's nose or mouth (or from a head wound) onto the chest area of the tunic. There were no spatter stains like the ones found throughout that bedstead. It was later revealed that the guy had recently received a significant blow "to his face" during a serious brawl.

It always brings extraordinary satisfaction when studying the "traces" and interpreting the statements of those silent witnesses can help exonerate an innocent person who happened to come under suspicion. Being falsely accused of a serious crime is also extremely unjust!

Epilogue by Josita Limborgh

In this case, during World War I, Co van Ledden Hulsebosch used his knowledge of bloodstain patterns to solve the crime. Bloodstain pattern analysis is a relatively old field within forensic investigation, likely because bloodstains are usually highly visible to the naked eye and often directly related to the bloodshedding event. However, at that time, not much had been published in this field. The first scientific publication dates back to 1895 by Dr. Eduard Piotrowski of the University of Kraków. He conducted his first experiments on living rabbits, something what is unthinkable nowadays.

The way van Ledden Hulsebosch approaches this case is more or less the same as we would still do today. We examine and classify the bloodstain patterns at the crime scene and on the suspect's clothing, and then assess how likely the bloodstains on the suspect's clothing are under different scenarios. In this case, the victim was struck on the head, resulting in an impact pattern: blood droplets landed on surfaces around the victim's head making it more likely that multiple blood droplets would end up on the front side of the assailants coat instead of just one blood droplet on the back side. With the knowledge we have today, we could have precisely calculated where the impact occurred, whether the victim was lying down, sitting, or standing. This would be possible using specialized software and advanced forensic techniques.

Bloodstain pattern analysis (BPA) involves examining the location, distribution, size, and shape of bloodstains in order to derive underlying actions or activities. The results of a BPA are ideally suited for evaluations at both source as well as activity level. In the latter examination, results are considered under several mutually exclusive propositions often describing the actors and their proposed activities. Source level analysis, on the other hand, can be extremely informative in, for example, stabbing incidents, where there is a reasonable chance that the assailant is also injured. In such cases it is therefore important to search specifically for bloodstains that do not seem to fit the bloodstain patterns relating to the injuries sustained by the victim both at the crime scene as well as on an item examined in the laboratory. DNA analysis of such bloodstains may then yield information about the origin (source) of the bloodstain.

Bloodstain patterns can be classified into four main groups, each containing a number of subgroups. During a bloodstain pattern analysis the examiner first determines to which of the four main groups a bloodstain (or bloodstain pattern) should be allocated after which it is assessed if further classification into subgroups is possible. The groups and subgroups are shown in the table below.

Main group	Subgroup
1. Bloodstain patterns resulting from gravity	Drip stain, drip trail, drip pattern, splash pattern, flow, pool
2. Bloodstain patterns resulting from a force being exerted	Impact pattern, projected pattern, cast-off pattern, cessation pattern, expiration pattern
3. Transferred bloodstain patterns	Transfer stain, wipe, swipe
4. Other	Insect stain, diluted stain, void, saturation stain

See Figure 15 (in the insert section) for a photograph of a typical impact blood pattern: A bloodstain pattern resulting from an object striking liquid blood, such as stepping in blood, kicking or punching, and shooting or explosions.

See Figure 16 (in the insert section) for a photograph of a typical splash blood pattern: A bloodstain pattern resulting from a large volume of liquid blood falling onto a surface.

50. How the Stolen Jewels Were Recovered

On a peaceful Sunday morning, Police Commissioner Wesser from Leeuwarden received news that something must have happened at the residence of Mrs. B., the widow of a famous painter. Despite repeated ringing, no one answered the door, although it was reasonable to assume that both the resident and her faithful maid, Annetje, were at home.

With one of his detectives, the commissioner gained entry by going via the neighboring garden and then through the conservatory door of the concerned property, which turned out to be unlocked and thus could be directly slid open. There they found the maid, moaning and complaining, lying on a sofa, her wrists and ankles bound with ropes, while on the first floor, in her bedroom, Mrs. B., who was well over eighty years old, was also bound with ropes around her hands and feet, lying under the covers in her bed.

From the statements of these women, it appeared that the previous evening—a Saturday night—the bell had rung. Annetje went to see who was at the door. An unknown man stepped inside brazenly. He had a black cloth masking his face and a threatening revolver in his hand. He had ordered the women not to make a sound, otherwise he would shoot them. He had bound Annetje in the conservatory downstairs and the old lady upstairs in the bedroom. She had initially been lying on the floor in the middle of the room but she had been picked up at her insistent yet very polite request to "Mr. Burglar" and had been deposited in the bed, after which the bandit had pulled the covers over her head before stealing all the valuables from the antique secretary desk, and making them vanish into a burlap sack. There were very valuable pieces among them, as well as many of historical value, gifts that her late husband, a famous painter, had personally received from royal personalities. Collectively—according to a recent appraisal—they were worth fifty to sixty thousand guilders!

Commissioner Wesser—an upright police officer and someone of even higher standing as a person (as I had personally observed in one of his "big cases")—soon noticed how deep the grooves of the binding ropes had pressed into the old woman's flesh, while at the same time it struck him how loosely the ropes around the wrists and ankles of young Annetje were tied. He smelled a rat. He remarked that Annetje could very well have freed herself from such loosely fitting bindings (it seemed she hadn't even tried!) and he had her wait in another room. The old lady—despite her advanced age still robust and sharp—had luckily not suffered further harm from the onslaught other than feeling a bit stiff in her limbs, which, however, soon disappeared. Then, of course, she felt the anguish over the disappearance of her treasures, most of which she was so extraordinarily fond of because historical memories were attached to them! The commissioner brought in a doctor; it was established that Annetje was pregnant. Further investigation revealed that her fiancé—a painter's apprentice—didn't earn enough to be able to afford the now necessary wedding.

The detectives searched as much as they could that Sunday. The judiciary, informed of the facts, telegraphed me to come over immediately. At the first opportunity, I traveled via Enkhuizen-Stavoren to Leeuwarden, arriving in the evening. I found the examining magistrate at the police station with the public prosecutor and the clerk, as well as the police commissioner and the doctor. They had—very rightly!—not undone the ropes with which the old lady had been tied but had cut them between the knots, allowing the manner in which the knots were tied during the binding to be studied further. Those knots were of a peculiar construction, undoubtedly the work of someone used to tying many things and quickly.

I heard that not only Annetje but also her fiancé—the painter's apprentice—and his best friend, who was a packer in a large warehouse, had been detained because there were reasons to assume that this friend and the man-with-the-mask could be one and the same person. Mrs. B. had a clear memory of the man's stature, had closely observed his hands, and also believed she recognized his voice! But all three stubbornly denied having anything to do with the theft. As I entered the room, the examining magistrate was busy interrogating Annetje. She was very nervous and her consistent denials made a very suspicious impression—one could "taste" the lies!

The doctor had identified something else during his examination that cannot be extensively discussed here, but which indicated that the "burglar" had done more than just tie her up with ropes. Even about this, she denied everything, which was very foolish, as there was evidence supporting the doctor's statements! Annetje was persistent in her denials. Extensive minutes of her statements were taken, which she signed after reading. She was then allowed to go to the neighboring room, the commissioner's room. He sat at his desk filling in some forms and she sat a short distance from him, sighing and distressed.

No word was spoken. Nevertheless, I am sure that in the heart of the good Wesser—whom I, as I already said, held in high esteem—a lot was going on as he saw that girl sitting there, pondering what must be troubling her mind. Then suddenly, he shook his head compassionately and said, "Annetje, I deeply sympathize with you, child. You have acted damned foolishly, and my heart bleeds at the thought that perhaps your child will have to be born in prison!" Suddenly—it became too much for her—she slid from her chair onto her knees, laid her head on one knee of the commissioner and pleaded with him: "Tell me what I must do, it weighs so terribly on me!" And to the best of his judgment, the magistrate advised her to fully confess with remorse rather than persist in this inflexible attitude, which would not prevent the truth from coming out. Yes, she would be better off telling everything honestly.

The commissioner then went through the connecting door into the interrogation room. In the meantime, the interrogation of the fiancé had already begun. He interrupted this, saying: "Let him be taken outside for a moment, because Annetje wants to declare something more!" During the further interrogation, she confessed everything. It came down to this: Her circumstances had become such that her family was pressing for a speedy marriage—but the couple lacked the means to buy furniture, a trousseau, a crib, or other needed items. Then the plan had ripened to rob the old woman, who was "sitting pretty." Yet neither Annetje nor her fiancé had the courage to do so. Should the latter, masked, enter the house, the shrewd old lady would without a doubt have recognized him by his stature, hands, voice, and movements, so that was not doable. But as a "third party," his friend was included in the plot. Mrs. B. did not know him. He would ring the bell on Saturday night; Annetje would let him in; then he would immediately put on a mask and—with an old revolver in hand (unloaded!) go upstairs to tie the old soul with ropes and pack the valuables in a burlap sack. It had been executed just like that.

The old lady shaking with fear of death continuously addressed him as "Mr. Burglar," and said: "Rob whatever you want, but for God's sake, let me live!" (Later, that friend probably thought he had the "right" to take the treasures when he claimed at his defense before the court that the old woman had practically given him permission to take them!) After he had tied her hands—she was lying on the floor—she begged him not to just leave her there, but rather to put her in bed, a request to which the burly fellow graciously complied. She was picked up lightly and tucked under the covers! She had very politely said, "Thank you, Mr. Burglar!" Then the friend went down to tie up Annetje as well. Before that, however, those two had a "cozy moment" (of which the fiancé was, of course, not supposed to know) and the ropes were not to pinch her too tightly—that hurt her too much!

After that, he left with the burlap bag, in which all the valuables from the silver cabinet were stored, leaving the house, and upon exiting the door, immediately handed the haul to the fiancé, who was waiting outside. Should an alarm be raised and he be arrested, he would not be found with the loot. The statement, now given in an improved form by Annetje, was put on paper and signed by her; then she returned, relieved, to the other room and her fiancé was brought in. He assumed, as agreed, the adamantine attitude, vehemently denying everything. After it was pointed out that Annetje had meanwhile told the truth, he didn't believe it, considering it a trap, so Annetje was called in. Bursting into tears, she said to her fiancé: "Yes, I've confessed completely; it has truly relieved me.... You must do the same!" What the fiancé hissed between his teeth in response I cannot write down here. Of course, the fiancé had no choice but to admit the full truth, too, and after him, it was the friend's turn to confess!

The extensive statements, which had to be put down on paper, took a fair amount of time, so it was about half-past three in the morning before everything was properly recorded. The director of the house of detention had already received a telephone message that he would be getting more "guests," so he could take that into account in connection with his night's rest! The documents were completed and stored in the clerk's briefcase. The gentlemen from the court bid farewell and left.

I stayed behind to chat with Commissioner Wesser. He looked quite content and asked me if I, too, thought everything had gone beautifully, to which I replied that I would only be completely satisfied when I had found the precious items for the old lady. The fiancé who had carried them away was briefly called back in. When asked where he had left the burlap sack with valuables, he became enraged and shouted: "I'll tell no one where they are! They'll be mine when I've served my time and come out of prison!" We couldn't sacrifice the interests of the old lady for that! Suddenly, I decided to go search for the treasures with this thief, who would unwittingly lead me to where he had hidden them.

The commissioner assigned two young detectives—runners—at my disposal. I asked them to follow six meters behind me when I took a nocturnal walk through the totally unfamiliar Leeuwarden with the fiancé. I told the fiancé: "My fellow, you are so tremendously overwrought, come on. We'll take a breath of fresh air." We left the station, constantly keeping the image of the stolen treasures alive in his mind. I sensed immediately from his movements—I held onto him by his jacket sleeve—which way we should go. When we came to a side street or a fork in the road, I could clearly feel which route was the correct one. We thus arrived at a park where the night sky provided enough light to recognize rhododendron beds on the left and a pond to my right.

Following us silently were the two detectives. With the utmost concentration of thought, we continued to stroll. My companion was—understandably—constantly thinking of the stolen loot, while I had to pay full attention to his breathing and all his movements, even unconscious ones. But then I felt how—after a peak of tension—he suddenly felt relaxed, which led me to conclude that we had walked past the goods. So I turned around with my companion, saying: "We are here, by the loot!" Then he tore away, hurried to the water's edge where, next to a dead branch sticking out of the bank, he began to search under the water's surface. "Then I keep my damn ... honor," he roared, and within a few seconds lifted the sack with the jewels out of the water. I signaled to the detectives, handed over to them both the sack and the suspect, and walked back to the station calmly.

Commissioner Wesser was still waiting there, and he looked more than surprised when the bag with its precious contents was emptied on the table. We now had to take inventory. Dawn was already announcing itself in the sky, but I could still get a few hours of rest. I thus retired to my hotel, content that I could log another success in my book! That trick I had copied from the telepath Rubini, from when he held séances at the Concertgebouw in Amsterdam. I immediately thought: Couldn't I learn how to do that as well? And after some practice sessions in intimate circles, when we had a room full of guests, I had noticed that I was also capable of perceiving all sorts of fine, unconscious movements made by others! That was the entire affair!

The main thing was that Mrs. B. got all her treasures back!

Epilogue by Paul van den Hoven

They had—quite rightly!—not untied the ropes with which the old woman was bound, but had cut them between the knots, allowing for closer examination of how the knots were tied during binding. These knots were of peculiar construction, undoubtedly the work of someone accustomed to tying many knots quickly. It is commendable that the importance of analyzing the knots in this case was recognized and the proper "securing" of the bindings to allow for knot analysis was promoted. During the investigation, the researcher believes they recognize that the knots were of a "peculiar" construction, drawing a connection to someone accustomed to quickly tying many knots. Now, the suspect was a "packer" by profession, indirectly suggesting a link with this occupation, but a direct link between the manner of knotting and the skills of the suspect in tying knots with a "peculiar construction" is not substantiated.

Certainly, the knowledge and experience of the knot tier play an important role in which types of knots are tied. In daily life, knots are frequently used, and even after the introduction of duct tape and cable ties, knots are used in various professions and hobbies. Consider professions in shipping, recreational boating, sailing, rescue services, BDSM activities, camping, bushcrafting, and mountain climbing. Often, these disciplines have a preference for using certain types of knots. People tend to tie knots that, in their experience, yield the desired result and in a manner familiar to them. The tendency here is that people tie the same types of knots in their lives. Try tying shoelaces where you change the order; for example, the lace ends left over right instead of right over left, and likewise with the loop order. This proves surprisingly difficult!

In the Netherlands, forensic knot analysis has regularly played an important role in detection and/or evidence gathering. For example, in a notorious Rotterdam case from 2006, a significant link was established between a package containing a victim and the perpetrator. An analysis by the Netherlands Forensic Institute (NFI) of the knots on a package in which the "Maas girl" (as the then-unknown girl was called) was found revealed a peculiar way of tying knots that was also used by her father to tie a box of belongings in his attic. In the mentioned case, the evaluation of the type of knots seems to contribute to detection, directing the investigator toward the suspect. In addition to using the method of tying knots in this way, knowledge of the way knots are tied can also help in locating and selectively sampling contact traces such as DNA from the knot tier. Thus, nowadays, forensic knot analysis can also contribute to the unraveling of a case.

51. Counterfeiters

In the following sketch I give the reader an interesting case that took place in 1884. It is needless to point out that the expert who served the police and justice could not have been the writer, who was then a seven-year-old child. However, it is now his pleasure to include in his series of sketches one in which his unforgettable father, who taught him to take his first steps in criminal investigation, played a role. To compile it I used, firstly, the notes I made when my father told me of his important cases; secondly, I consulted the old file on the case, which happened to come into my hands recently.

It was the summer of 1884. It was late in the afternoon in the old Botermarkt—now called Rembrandtsplein—when, just as in later years, the terraces in front of the inns were buzzing with people, especially in front of Café Mast (also called Mille Colonnes). No table was unoccupied. As a result, a few people had to content themselves with sitting at tables where others were already seated. A certain J., a stockbroker, who wanted to enjoy a drink in the open air, happened to find a table at which two foreigners were seated. They spoke in Spanish, but when they ordered something, they used French. They did the same when the person sitting next to them was asked for some information about places of interest in the city. Afterwards, they chatted some more in French, during which it became clear to the strangers that this J. came to Café Mast often to have an aperitif. So it was by no means just a coincidence that a few days later the three of them were once again sitting at the same table on that terrace.

The conversation became livelier. They inquired mutually "whether they were also in business" and so J. had truthfully declared that he made his living in the stockbroking business. The two strangers told him, in a small lie, that they traveled "in wines." It took a few more days of socializing over drinks before their confidence in the Amsterdam man was sufficiently elevated to inform him, in complete confidence, that they had come to Europe from South America to find agents to exploit a great invention—a way to make counterfeit gold. J. laughed scornfully, but he was assured with even more emphasis that the peculiarity of their process lay in the fact that with the usual methods of examination, such as the touchstone, the best experts could not distinguish their product from real gold! That struck a chord with the man from Amsterdam, who became increasingly interested in the invention of his new acquaintances.

His interest soared when he heard that his newfound friends were able to produce coins directly from that special metal mixture, which were "accepted" everywhere, so as not to arouse any suspicion in any bank, much less be rejected! But it seemed too good for him … and he made no secret of the fact that he would have to see it before he could believe it. Yes, that was now the difficulty. Those two had trusted him enough, and had told him what it was all about ... but attending a demonstration to fully convince him of the correctness of their claim could only be allowed when they could be certain that he was serious about purchasing a license, which they had already "sold" in Madrid, Paris, and Brussels over the past few months. They told him the amount to be paid for both the rights and the instructions. J. was a bit shocked, because the amount was beyond his means! But ... maybe his brother would be interested and would lend him the "working capital"! Yes, no doubt his brother would! With this, J. was allowed to know more about it and to see more.

They were staying at the Oldewelt (once called the Vermunt), a well-known travelers' hotel on the Nieuwendijk (now gone for many years!) and at an appointed hour in the evening J. was allowed to visit them in Room 50. He was given a password without which he would have no chance of being let in and was not a little pleased to get a peek into that magical place a few hours after their drinks together!

With his heart beating with anticipation, he walked up the stairs of the Oldewelt Hotel to knock on the door of Room 50 on the second floor in the agreed manner and answer the password question that came from inside. Upon entering, he was struck by a stuffy, smelly atmosphere. Between the table and the window stood—on a piece of sheet iron—a pot of glowing charcoal, which seemed to have served as a brazier. The table was full of mysterious bottles, partly stored in an antique liqueur cabinet with doors and drawers that could be opened, in which stood various tools, a small balance, a crucible and then there was—no doubt as the pièce de résistance—two heavy iron molds, each consisting of two adjoining halves, fitted with handles on the outside, and on their inner surfaces the cavities for sovereigns with the image of Queen Victoria—splendidly beautiful and finely embossed.

While one friend was distracting the guest and keeping him talking, the other was handling one of the molds and performing invisible manipulations near the coal fire. At a certain moment he approached the table, on which stood a bowl of water and with the gestures of a magician who announces the moment of his action with a "hocus pocus," he opened the mold and dropped four gold coins into the bowl of water. J. was naturally very interested in these and looked at them, admiring their beautiful natural appearance. He now had the results in his hands, but understandably didn't understand or suspect the process itself!

They planned to meet again the next day at Café Mast. J. would—so it was agreed—exchange the four "English gold pounds" for Dutch money at a bank or exchange office in the course of the next day and see that they would be accepted without hesitation. After leaving the Oldewelt Hotel, J. went to his brothers' house to speak to him in private about a very important matter. The latter, to J.'s great disappointment, not only objected to lending even one penny for such a matter but insisted most strongly that J. should immediately inform the police ... otherwise he would do it! That was a blow to his plan, but he saw no way out and therefore went to the Oudebrug (the building in which the Trade Information Office is now located which was then home to the "sixth" section of the police, which later moved to a new building in Warmoesstraat, which is still the section office today). There he spoke, first with an inspector and later with Commissioner Stork himself. Before long a raid was planned to take place the next evening.

During that bitter hour, J. sat with his "friends" as usual, pretending that he would gather the money together to become an agent for the "big concern" in the Netherlands. He was to return to their hotel room in the evening to see a bit more behind the veil, but the instructions would, of course, not be revealed to him until later, when the license fee had been paid! A quarter of an hour before the agreed time that J. was to arrive at the door of Room 50, Commissioner Stork, an inspector, and three detectives of the Oudebrug office entered the neighboring room, no. 49, which had been made available for that purpose by the hotel management, to wait quietly for the moment of the raid. Leaning against the connecting door, they could hear strange sounds. Only Spanish was spoken in Room 50! Thus, they could not understand a syllable of the conversation in the adjoining room! A few minutes later, there was a knocking in a certain rhythm in Room 50, announcing J.'s arrival and letting him in at the agreed password. Then one could catch some sounds and words, uttered in French, through the connecting door.

As agreed, after about ten minutes, a servant of J. appeared in the corridor to bring a telegram that had just arrived. In the immediate vicinity of this messenger stood the policemen, who had meanwhile left Room 49 and were preparing for the raid. Then the messenger stepped forward, tapped several times on the door of Room 50, shouting at the same time: "Mr. J., I have a telegram here for you!" It took little effort for J., who was already slightly nervous in playing his role, to walk "nervously" to the door and open it to the shock of both Spaniards. This was done in a flash and the detectives took charge of the two strangers. They were searched and placed separately in the corners of the room. The commissioner, who had hurried to open the windows as the smoldering charcoal fire in the stove had created a stifling atmosphere in which the necessary poison of coal vapor was present, immediately began an interrogation, during which the foreigners suddenly had great difficulty with their French. An inventory was created in which all the pots, pans, bottles, small bags, etc. were listed. It was quite a list!

During the first interview that the commissioner conducted with the foreigners in French, he noticed how the one person who had apparently been working at the table on the production had peculiar colored stains on his hands. And what did Commissioner Stork do on that July evening of 1884? He consulted Mr. M. L. Q. van Ledden Hulsebosch, a young pharmacist at 17 Korten Nieuwedijk! The latter saw to it that two large beakers with the necessary distilled water were quickly delivered to the Oudebrug police station, with which the man's hands were washed, so that a chemical analysis of the nature of the dissolved substances could be carried out in the washing water. The next day, when the case was in the hands of the Justice Department, the examining magistrate, Mr. Elias, appointed my father—together with his colleague, L. C. W. Cocx (a pharmacist at Heerengracht 222)—as an expert. It gave me a peculiar sensation, when I recently found the old file and saw the document swearing in my father and seeing his signature under the accepted appointment! In accordance with the provisions of the act, all coins suspected of being counterfeit must be examined at the National Mint while the raw materials and all other seized substances and objects were given by the chief magistrate to an expert of his choice for examination. And so in this case, the experts were given all the vials, jars, and molds—in short, all the other items—to examine.

It did not take long before the gentlemen experts were in full agreement. The entire inventory could have nothing to do with counterfeiting. There were flasks with copper bronze powder, with shellac, and a multitude of substances, of which—as far as we know—no counterfeiter had ever made use of to counterfeit metal money! There was also a small bottle containing pieces of metallic sodium surrounded by paraffin oil. For those who don't know, I would just like to point out that sodium, when put on water, floats and causes an intense reaction—sometimes accompanied by fire!—sizzling and violently decomposing the water, at the sight of which the layman is strongly impressed. On one of his visits, when J. probably got to close to the operation, he was driven away when one of the men suddenly threw a piece of sodium into a bowl of water and warned J. to stay back!

All this information did not deliver anything incriminating ... even greater was the surprise when a report arrived from the master of the mint in Utrecht saying that the gold coins sent in were all real! And so it soon became clear to the Lords of the Court that the two foreigners under arrest had never been guilty of a mint offence, but had tried to cheat J. out of a large sum of money by means of a magic trick and then run off without a trace! The public prosecutor therefore had to withdraw his primary charge and both foreigners were expelled as undesirables!

Epilogue by Mattijs Koeberg: Fraud in the Digital Domain

Although this story of the suspected counterfeiters involves a lot of chemistry (alchemy?), the main theme is financial crime. In this story a "scheme" has been set up to cheat the victim out of his money. Although this probably still happens to people, nowadays we think of these kinds of schemes mainly in the digital/online domain. From the emails from a "Nigerian prince" asking to send money, to fake WhatsApp messages, to phishing mails that are very hard to distinguish from the real thing, and ransomware attacks. A whole new area of crime has emerged in the digital/online domain, including fraud, deception, extortion, theft, etc. This is often referred to as "cybercrime." Cybercrime is a challenging new area with its own dynamics and forensic challenges. Because of these challenges, cyberforensics has a clear presence in the Netherlands forensic research agenda for the coming decennium.

Current statistics show that phishing is the most common form of cybercrime: 3.4 billion (with a b!) spam emails are sent worldwide every day and the average cost of a data breach against a company is four million euros. There are estimates that worldwide the inflicted damages from cybercrime is six trillion US dollars. Serious business. Related to the area of online/digital fraud is (deep) fakes. Modern-day deep learning technology allows criminals to generate very realistic fake pictures, video, audio, and text. Forensics has been and will be investing in techniques to help detect these fakes. This is a welcome contribution from forensic science to creating and maintaining a safe and just society in this "post-truth" era.

Many challenges in cyberforensics are new but can mostly be boiled down to the general challenges in forensics, such as detection/finding traces, authenticity and integrity of traces, and presentation to court. The same challenges that Co van Ledden Hulsebosch had to deal with.

52. The Clever Swindler

It is only granted to a few to ever win big in the lottery, and yet—until the day of the draw—every participant is in suspense. His heart beats in anticipation—but if he is not the lucky one this time, then he will play just as happily in the next round and take his chances! One morning, the innkeeper of a quaint café in a small town in North Holland found himself in the cheerful disposition of someone who had unexpectedly received a windfall. At breakfast, he read the following letter, just delivered by the post:

Dear Cousin!

I doubt whether you can still quite remember me, but we are very distantly related. Listen, this is why I am writing to you. I have, so to speak, no family. My marriage was very unhappy and I was always in a bad mood as a result. I lost hope and had no job. I fell in with a bad crowd and started breaking into houses. We made a good score on the last job we did and shared out quite a bit of money. But later we were caught and now I am in Leeuwarden serving a five-year prison sentence.

I have a secret way to communicate with the outside world, which is why you are receiving this letter through the post. I wrote it on ordinary postal paper that I had smuggled into me here. I keep up with what is happening outside and I have been informed that my wife is diligently selling off all my belongings, so that when I return home in four years, I will likely find nothing left. I'll get her, don't worry!

But there's something else. She doesn't know what I did in our house in the last week I was there. And now—as I understand it—she has sold off six mahogany chairs that were in my front room. It seems they have ended up at a secondhand dealer's in the Kerkstraat, in your neighborhood. Well, I'll never see them again—that's less than ideal—but as my sole remaining family member, I feel compelled to share this with you. During that final week at home, I discreetly stashed a thousand bucks in each of the seats of those six chairs. Of course, nobody has any idea except for me and now you!

The fact that my wife sold my household goods doesn't bother me much, even though those chairs were exquisite—"period chairs"!—but that now that my six thousand bucks are involved, it is truly dreadful. I already told you that I have absolutely no family. I only know that you—although very distantly—are my second cousin, and that's why I am writing this to you. Retrieve that money at least. Consider half of it as your own property and give me the other half at the end of my sentence, and I will be satisfied. So, get your hands on those six chairs as soon as possible. They have a red floral seat.

Your Cousin

Below was a false name, one that stirred memories of distant family relations in our friend.

The innkeeper, who was more or less nervous about this windfall, took some money with him and immediately went to the indicated secondhand shop, where, to his delight, he saw the six chairs standing in the window display. They had to be the ones—there were no others. These were the "period chairs" with the specified upholstery on them! The shopkeeper asked an exorbitantly high price. They were such fine chairs, really stylishly built, and he wouldn't sell them for a penny less! The other was consumed with desire to claim those chairs as his own. He abandoned his efforts to negotiate a lower price and sealed the deal. Where they should be delivered? "No, just leave them. I happen to have a handcart parked around the corner. I'll transport them straight home myself."

At home, his wife greeted him with her eyes wide in mute amazement. What on earth did this mean? Why was he acting so oddly as to buy six chairs while all their rooms were chock-full of furniture? But, without saying a word, the husband swiftly took the chairs up to the attic, locked himself in, and took out his pocketknife to slice open the seats. His disappointment mirrored that of the man who had dissected the hen that laid the golden eggs. He found nothing!

Furious that he had been swindled so maliciously, he rushed to the police station, where he showed the letter and reported on his purchase and the subsequent discovery. Later, I heard that the police had a hard time keeping a "professional" demeanor upon hearing the story and refraining from bursting into laughter. It was, without any doubt, a brilliantly executed scam! But they realized the secondhand furniture dealer must have been involved in the plot! Analysis and correlations were conducted, leading to a significant suspicion directed at a "burly individual" who had recently served time in prison for a few serious offenses and had been released not long ago. Yes, it was really something for this crook to stage such a clever swindle. Now it was simply a matter of how swiftly they could get a handwriting sample from him.

One of the detectives knew what to do immediately. He was aware that the suspect, following his release from prison, had forged a relationship with a respectable widow, from whom he had rented a room. This relationship was conducted, however, under a false name. He understood all too well, that—if he had given his real name, it would have sent shivers down her spine and she would have been terrified to harbor a man in her house whose name was so notorious throughout the Netherlands. However, he had reconciled with his troubled past, eager to embark on a fresh start. He had selected an opportune moment to openly and honestly confess everything to his fiancée. After his confession, she expressed her profound appreciation and affirmed her enduring love for him despite it all, agreeing to marry him. ... as long as he would change his name. To be able to do that, he had written a petition to the Queen, outlining his sincere intentions for the future and pointing out the importance of beginning his fresh start under a new name, underscoring the necessity to avoid being ostracized everywhere he went. The police immediately inquired where this petition was currently being processed and requested it to conduct a comparative handwriting examination.

Thus, I received both the petition and the letter about the chair purchase and demonstrated clearly that the two pieces must have been written by the same person. It was an ugly smudge on his account and, of course, a delay for the start of the "new" life!

I have become familiar with another incident from the life of this same scoundrel that I want to tell the reader about. (Perhaps the readeress would prefer to turn the page immediately, to be spared from a case that she might call shocking!) My old friend Dr. van der Schatte Olivier, who was a doctor at the institution in Medemblik at the beginning of this century, told me this story. At that time, the main character in the aforementioned case was detained as a "patient" in the Medemblik insane asylum. After committing a few very serious offenses, he preferred to stay there rather than in a prison and so he pretended to be insane! Now, I assume that the physicians who had to report on him (based on which his stay at that institution was ordered) had good reasons for issuing such advice, but, on the other hand, I remain convinced that the guy wasn't that crazy at all ... as evidenced by the following incident!

A religious service had been held in the institution one evening for all the patients, after which they were supposed to be escorted back to their cells through the corridor by the guards. During the service a gas light was burning near a side window. Suddenly, our visitor forcefully pushed the half-opened window wide open, shattering the glass of the gaslight with a loud crash. Then—before the guards could stop him—he leaped out of the window. Although they tried to grab him by his collar, he immediately raised his arms above his head and slid out of his jacket so that the guard was left holding only the garment! A major alarm was immediately raised, and the institution's director, followed by the members of his family, came running out of their house, eager to know what exactly had happened. It was already getting quite dark. Nonetheless, they embarked on a search with ample manpower and tracking dogs, scouring every direction for the fugitive. But after a while, they all returned to the institution empty-handed.

What had our friend done? He had hurried to seek refuge in the empty residence of the director. He entered through the garden door and climbed up to the attic, where he watched all the search efforts with the greatest interest from behind the net curtain in a skylight window. He also noticed—after a considerable time of fruitless searching—that measures were ordered to keep watch on the roads in the area with groups of people. This was deemed necessary, as they were well aware that a dangerous individual had achieved his freedom. And thus, during the night, patrols comprised of three or four robust farmers armed with hayforks and other tools in place of weapons diligently patrolled all the roads in the vicinity. But nobody found him that night! He remained seated quietly in the attic, patiently waiting until the voices on the floors beneath him went silent and everyone had gone to sleep.

The stress of the ordeal naturally took a toll on the man's internal plumbing, and he soon felt a certain urgency. However, he found it impossible to follow the laws of nature in a conventional manner—which would have been to go downstairs and seek the smallest room on a lower floor. He preferred to relieve himself of both "one thing and another" right there in the attic. The "one thing" wouldn't betray him so quickly; but … that "another." He couldn't just let it run "like God's water over God's field." It might look like a leak and then someone would immediately come up to the attic.

In a corner of the attic space, behind a curtain, there stood a multitude of suitcases and boxes. There was also a large flag, rolled up, which was hung out on national holidays. He searched further and found in some cardboard boxes a large number of glass jars for lamps, which had contributed to the fine illumination of the director's residence during the coronation celebrations. Meanwhile, the urgency escalated…. Suddenly, a brilliant idea stuck him: he arranged a sufficient number of jars in a row along the edge of a folding table that stood there … and just like that, the tension disappeared and no spills occurred!

He ripped the red, white, and blue Dutch flag into three strips and tied them together carefully. This way he made a rope to lower himself down from the window in the dead of night. You see, Reader, this guy really wasn't that crazy! Once outside, he soon realized that, according to the orders given, the outer roads were under continuous patrol. Spotting a group of four men armed with hayforks approaching from a dark corner, he quickly crawled into a dry ditch that crossed the road and was covered beneath a large iron grating. He hid underneath it, and a few minutes later the men walked over it, talking loudly about the clever escapee! However, he couldn't remain hidden for long. Hunger drove him to seek refuge at a nearby farm, where he was promptly apprehended by the farmer and his farmhands and he was handed back to the police. Nonetheless, he later recounted his adventures on that fateful evening with a sense of pride!

Epilogue by Pernette Verschure

This chapter about the clever swindler illustrates the character of a man who is not afraid to manipulate the truth to his advantage. Claiming to be a family member, he deceives the victim with a calculated lie, exploiting their trust for his gain. Recognizing that invoking familial ties instills confidence, he orchestrates a win–win scenario crucial to the success of his scam. The narrative delves into the character traits of a scam artist. The story suggests that the crook attempted to rebuild his life after serving a lengthy prison sentence. However, it also reveals that the scammer has perpetrated numerous offences beyond the clever ploy involving the chairs supposedly concealing money. This implies that the adage "Once a crook always a crook" holds true in this case.

I am the chair of the Molecular and Cellular Epigenetics group at the Swammerdam Institute for Life Sciences within the Faculteit der Natuurwetenschappen, Wiskunde en Informatica (FNWI, Faculty of Science) at the University of Amsterdam (UvA). The group's interest lies in understanding the functional dynamics of the epigenome. The epigenome (derived from the Greek prefix "epi-" meaning "on top of") refers to a layer on top of the genome that regulates gene activity based on chemical modifications to DNA and histone DNA packaging proteins. These modifications, facilitated by epigenetic regulatory enzymes, serve as a bridge between our environment and our genetic material being influenced by external factors like diet, stress, exercise, and environmental conditions. Since epigenetic changes are reversible, our epigenetic profile and gene function evolve as we age.

The clever swindler story highlights how law enforcement can identify a culprit by comparing handwriting samples. It also explores the notion of trust among family members and how the scammer exploits this trust. This mirrors the understanding that our genetic material, inherited from our parents, contains similarities in personal traits among family members. This is interesting content from a genetic/epigenetics/forensics perspective. Nowadays, suspects can be identified using genetic markers. Moreover, human characteristics can be discerned with epigenetic markers, including chronological and biological age as well as biogeographic ancestry. For example, in my laboratory, we have pinpointed a set of fifteen epigenetic DNA methylation markers capable of predicting an individual's chronological age using a blood sample for forensic purposes.[61] Furthermore, in a proof-of-concept study, we have demonstrated that many of these markers also forecast chronological age in various tissue cells.[62]

---

61 J. Naue et al., "Chronological Age Prediction Based on DNA Methylation: Massive Parallel Sequencing and Random Forest Regression," *Forensic Science International: Genetics* 31 (2017), 19–28, http://dx.doi.org/10.1016/j.fsigen.2017.07.015.

62 J. Naue et al., "Proof of Concept Study of Age-Dependent DNA Methylation Markers across Different Tissues by Massive Parallel Sequencing," *Forensic Science International: Genetics* 36 (2018), 152–159, https://doi.org/10.1016/j.fsigen.2018.07.007.

53. Faked or Actual Theft of Mail

It will come as no surprise to anyone that lawyers who receive an incriminating expert report in the criminal proceedings they are dealing with—whose accuracy they cannot appreciate—often consult another expert to get his opinion on the report. Criminal lawyers often come to me, asking whether there was "something to be done" about this or that report. I never liked such requests. But I considered it my duty to check whether—as the "suspect" of course is quick to claim—the expert who had made his report for the examining magistrate had erred, or even whether there had been a proper investigation and an equally proper report. If everything had been above board, then the lawyer was knocking on a deaf man's door, and I soon declared I was not prepared to take apart a piece of work that did not deserve it.

It has also happened that after viewing a case I was unsatisfied with the "expert report" or that I found errors in the investigation or that, in my opinion, a too far-reaching conclusion had been drawn. In these instances I felt it was my duty to provide help and assistance to prevent at all costs the possibility that an innocent person should become the victim of an erroneous expert report!

So, a lawyer once visited me. He was acting for a gardener, a young fellow, who had recently sent a letter containing an amount of paper money by registered mail to Germany. Upon receipt, the addressee had made the sad discovery that the envelope contained not a single banknote, but pieces of scrap paper. The case was returned to the originating post office, following the necessary protocols, and the director of the post office in that small provincial town had immediately informed the police. The police gathered up the evidence and summoned the gardener.

Now, it should first be stated that the five seals on the envelope had a completely normal appearance—they were intact and undamaged—while the envelope itself showed no other "damage" than that which the addressee had applied to the top edge with his pocketknife to access the contents. It came as no surprise that the police soon got the feeling that the sender, by posting a thick letter as "registered mail of high value," had actually sent an envelope containing worthless paper, expecting that, once the recipient complained, the debt would be resolved by the postal service, which would pay out the full amount as compensation.

The manner in which this policeman began to interrogate the summoned gardener did not leave the slightest doubt as to his suspicions. The "suspect," however, vehemently objected and asserted that he had actually sent the stated amount of banknotes in the letter. But the policeman didn't want to hear it. Didn't the envelope with its intact seals tells a sufficiently clear story? It had not been opened and closed again in the meantime, so it was impossible to accept what our gardener was trying to tell him.

Added to this was the extreme nervousness of the suspect. But this had an explanation. He had been required to make the journey to the police barracks—but the stork was supposed to visit his home at any moment to deliver his first child. No wonder, then, that the gardener's thoughts lingered uninterruptedly at home, and he yearned for the end of this torment, which he did not conceal, but emphatically announced to the policeman. This policeman, however, had "lit the fuse" and gradually developed the "conviction" of his guilt. He said: "Look, little fellow. I am convinced you filled the letter with scrap paper. Deny it no longer, for it is vain effort. You are not going anywhere. However, if you confess to me, I will set you free for the time being and can you go straight to your wife!"

And so it came to pass that the gardener, desperate to run home, swore out a "confession" and signed it, after which he was allowed to go leave. But he had signed a false statement, a false confession, out of necessity! The case continued on its path. The official report of the police, who had so quickly "cleared up" this matter, was forwarded to the public prosecutor—perhaps this resulted in a small compliment to the good policeman. The public prosecutor passed the matter over to the examining magistrate. This magistrate began to hand over the various documents—including the incriminating envelope—to the expert appointed and sworn in by him, who was to conduct a scientific investigation into this silent witness and to issue a reasoned report thereon.

The gardener was summoned to his office and interrogated again. In doing so, the "delinquent" took a completely different course from that determined by the police. He denied in the most insistent manner that he had committed the offense with which he was charged, which seemed strange to the examining magistrate. "We'll just have to wait and see what the expert investigation reveals!" he said. And the report on the expert investigation came in. This was the conclusion: The expert carefully examined the wax seals, "even with a binocular microscope," and was fully convinced that the seals had been primarily attached, that is, they had not been "separated" in order to be reattached to the envelope a second time. That report closed the door, and the case was forwarded for consideration by the court.

The gardener, fully convinced of the wrongness of the accusation, awaited the course of events with resignation because he was indeed innocent. He was advised to hire a lawyer. He related in detail how everything had happened, and so the defender soon became convinced there must be a misunderstanding here. So he turned to me, assuring me that something was wrong, and asked for my help. I felt that I couldn't do much. Surely the expert report was based on grounds leading to the conclusion that had been drawn—but I needed a copy of it. Naturally, I did not get my hands on the envelope, which I deeply regretted. The report, however, contained little information. The expert had made sure—by visual means only—with his microscope (and moreover with his binocular microscope, that is, with a stereo microscope!) that the wax seals were completely normal and could never have been removed from the paper.

I immediately noted that no expert should leave it at that. He must also confirm whether the seals had been placed on the paper in the normal way or whether they were secondarily attached to it. The lawyer considered my remarks important and summoned me to repeat my objections to the expert report to the court. I found that a less pleasant prospect. Knowing how that expert was regarded there, I foresaw that I, as the odd man out, ran the risk of being looked at less kindly, since I challenged that expert's report and thus challenged the position of the prosecutor. So I attended, as expected.

I was the last witness to be called from the waiting room in front of the green table. All the judges looked at me somewhat sharply. After the president asked the lawyer why he had summoned me to appear, I was asked whether I had any comments on the expert report issued in this case, and also whether I had seen the envelope in question myself. I began to reply that—due to circumstances—I had not been given the opportunity to examine the envelope myself. However, if the examiner had not confined himself to looking at the wax seals exclusively, I would not have made such a serious objection, since a clever investigator must not leave any evidence unexamined. To answer the fundamental question of whether the seals of the letter had been removed and reaffixed again, more investigation should have been done.

The reply of the other expert was something like this: "Using my microscope to inspect the wax seals was enough for me, so I wish to maintain my conclusion." "You hear what your colleague says," the president said to me, and he gave me the opportunity to make one more comment. I said as follows: "Mr. President, please take note of my statement, which I would like to make: I am not so clever as to be able to completely solve a problem of such importance by sight alone. In a case like this, a more in-depth investigation must be conducted!" I was then free to return to Amsterdam.

The court sentenced the man. As expected, his lawyer lodged an appeal for his client, which resulted in the case being heard again before the Court of Appeals. The defense also summoned me to this court hearing. The attorney general, having reviewed report in the file and the course of the court hearing, understood that the defender would again bring along "that counter-expert"(!), who would again raise his objections to the report and would challenge his colleague. This could have been prevented.

He telephoned the expert and instructed him to expand his investigation into the incriminating envelope using the measures that the counter-expert deemed to be "so necessary," so that at the court hearing they could say: 'Well, Co van Ledden Hulsebosch, we have had the envelope examined according to the methods you have indicated, and they have fully confirmed the results of the first examination!" The attorney general looked surprised when, a few days later—just a day before the case was to come before the court—he received a note from the expert with the following simple message:

> I am sorry to inform you that, under the suggestion of the circumstances, my first inquiry was somewhat too superficial. Now that I have applied the methods indicated by colleague L. H., it appears the wax seals are indeed glued to the letter with gluton[63]. By applying a few drops of water they lifted themselves from the paper, so they must have been removed from it in the meantime and then put back in place with an adhesive.

This was not a pleasant message for that expert to write! The gardener, who had already been held in custody for a few months, was immediately released, the charge was dropped, and the court session canceled. That expert, having read how the "suspect" had already fully confessed to the police, had taken his task a little too easily. I couldn't help but be pleased that I had made my voice heard from the green table of the court. The correctness of *audiatur et altera pars* (may the other side also be heard) was again demonstrated.

I once also appeared—at the request of a defender—in a session of the Court of Appeals in Amsterdam, where I had given my advice for countless years as an expert summoned by the public prosecution service. It was an arson attack. According to a report from a village chief of the fire brigade, a paint can partly filled with petrol was found in the middle of a fire. That can was presented at the session as a *corpus delicti*. Now, I had good reasons to doubt the correctness of that statement. In the middle of a lake of fire, a can containing gasoline could not have survived. The gasoline would evaporate, the can would burst apart, and the solder on the tin can would melt. Last but not least, the paper label, which was glued to the can, did not show any brown scorch marks!

I was convinced there must be a misunderstanding here, and I wanted to point it out. No sooner had the president noticed my presence, than a sharp expression came over his face. "Well, are you here as an expert or a witness for the defense?" was the question. This annoyed me terribly, and I immediately replied: "Excuse me, Mr. President, you are mistaken. I appear before the table always in the same capacity as an independent expert. It makes no difference to me which side of Lady Justice's scales is tipped. As a neutral expert, I give my advice regarding the truth that I find, and never act for or against the accused!" Neither an answer nor a comment was heard!

---

63 A type of glue from the manufacturer Royal Talens.

Epilogue by Zeno Geradts

False confessions are a serious problem in the criminal justice system. They can happen to anyone, regardless of age, race, or socioeconomic status. There are many reasons why someone might confess to a crime they did not commit. Some people confess because they are afraid of the consequences of not confessing, such as being beaten or tortured by the police. Others confess because they are confused or disoriented, or because they believe that they will be better off if they confess. Still others confess because they are pressured by the police or other authorities.

In this case, the expert witness's testimony appeared to be biased towards the prosecution's theory. The witness did not consider the possibility of alternative explanations for the removal of the seals, and this led the judge to believe that the suspect was guilty. This is a common problem in cases where false confessions are involved. The prosecution often presents the evidence in a way that makes it seem like the suspect is guilty, and the defense often cannot present a strong enough case to counter this.

The important message provided here is that an expert should be neutral. Expert witnesses have a responsibility to be neutral and objective in their testimony. They should not let their personal opinions or biases influence their conclusions. In this case, the expert witness should have considered all of the possible explanations for the removal of the seals, even if they did not support the prosecution's theory. If an expert witness later learns of new evidence or new methods that could change their conclusion, they have a responsibility to report this to the court. This is important to ensure that the justice system is fair and impartial, and that innocent people are not convicted of crimes they did not commit.

Cases like this are becoming less common in the digital age. However, there are still some parallels that can be drawn. For example, in cybercrime cases, it is often possible to forge digital evidence. This means that experts must be even more careful to consider all of the possible explanations for the evidence, even if they are not the most likely. The use of new technology, such as deepfakes, also poses a challenge. Deepfakes are videos or audio recordings that have been manipulated to make it appear as if someone is saying or doing something they never actually said or did. This technology could be used to create false confessions or other evidence that could be used to convict innocent people. However, with cybercrime, similar crimes can happen, such as when someone steals bitcoins or is a victim of money stolen from a bank account. In these cases, there are often digital traces available that can provide an alternative explanation of the events.

In cybercrime cases, there is often more (digital) evidence available than in cases involving items sent through the post. This evidence can be used to corroborate or refute the suspect's confession. However, it is important to remember that digital evidence can also be forged, so it is important to carefully evaluate all the evidence before making a conclusion. Though even here it is possible to forge the digital traces, and one should be aware of the use of new technology, such as deepfakes, where someone can fake the identity of a person in a video and audio message based on newer technology. It is true that digital evidence can be forged, and that deepfakes can be used to create false evidence. However, there are also ways to detect forged digital evidence and deepfakes. It is important to know about these techniques, so that investigators are aware that evidence can be tampered with.

Epilogue

Having reached the end of my series of sketches, I hereby respond—at the request of Mr. K. H. Broekhoff—to three questions that arose during the preparation of my writings for the press.

> Question 1. "You mentioned the police dog Albert and his trainer Water a couple of times. I would like to know what you attribute to the fact that neither Water nor the tracking dog Albert ever had a good successor. I got the impression that this is your opinion."

My answer is as follows: The training of police dogs can be done in various directions, such as:

- To apprehend an arrestee attempting to escape
- To defend their handler against attackers
- To guard a bicycle or any other entrusted object
- To track a specific scent and indicate the "source"
- To perform proper "search and detection"
- To perform proper "sorting"

In these actions the canine should not be deterred by gunshots, high fences, or other obstacles. Outstanding tracking dogs that excel in all these aspects are as rare as skilled trainers who possess the patience of angels and the aptitude to teach the dogs. Albert was an extraordinary tracking dog, and Water an excellent trainer.

After Water, the leadership fell to individuals who still had to prove themselves, focusing primarily on the first five points of the program. It could also be that they were unsuccessful in teaching the dogs proper "sorting" or that Albert's successors proved to be "slow learners." While following a scent trail in rural areas can be successfully accomplished—due to the larger expanse of land with fewer or no disturbing human scents—in a large city, where every square foot of ground retains scent trails from countless passers-by, searching for and following a specific "trail of the perpetrator" becomes a hopeless task. Therefore, Water sought and found a powerful counterpart in the sorting problem. I witnessed multiple occasions where Water allowed his dogs to "sniff" a discarded item containing the scent of the suspect, and then commanded, "search!" The dog would accurately identify the objects (or the specific object) from a collection of hats, handkerchiefs, or jackets belonging to suspicious individuals, having previously detected the same scent … and almost always with success, without making any mistakes. After Water, more new trainers emerged, but their four-legged companions did not demonstrate the remarkable abilities Albert had displayed. Apparently, little attention was paid to sorting. In one serious case a trainer with a dog capable of proper sorting was asked for. The response was disappointing.

Although I was an "advisor" at the time, I was not asked for advice in this regard, even though I expressed, unsolicited, that in a large city, I considered "sorting" to be a much more important quality for a trained police dog to have than the ability to follow a scent trail on the road ... which rarely or never succeeded in the city anyway! Whether the later "trainers" were unable to teach their dogs to sort like Water did with his two dogs, or whether they considered this aspect of training to be of little importance and could be neglected, I do not know. But after Water, there were no more grand displays of skill, as frequently occurred during his time.

What brilliant successes did the later trainers achieve with their dogs? They could excel at chasing down fugitives, guarding their handler's bicycle, defending the handler against attackers, but for true detective work, they were virtually unusable in the big city. It must be acknowledged that the gradually formed habit of storming the crime scene with a massive number of "interested parties" (justice and police authorities, department heads with detectives, the central investigative unit with photographers, and personnel from the fingerprint department, the medical service, and sometimes even the police experts) did little to preserve any potential "scent of the perpetrator" at the crime scene for the canine nose! More than once, I regretted how such invasions made the investigation with the tracking dog impossible from the very beginning.

Without better trainers and if better dogs are not bred, there will never be another "Water" nor another "Albert." And even if the future were to bring such gifted specimens, I foresee only limited successes unless the habit of deploying the entire "investigative apparatus" at the crime scene is broken, allowing the detectives to first search for silent witnesses before they are hopelessly compromised during the typical "invasion."

> Question 2. "You mentioned several times the advantage that a crime investigation in rural areas has over one in the big city, at least for the criminal investigator. In fact, you seem to prefer the simple village policeman who leaves everything intact but guarded until the arrival of the detective, over the entire investigative apparatus that comes into play in the big city. Now, it is known that there is a tendency to also involve the entire metropolitan investigative apparatus in rural areas from now on. I would find it interesting to hear your opinion on this."

To this, I respond as follows: Hans Gross first spoke of "silent witnesses" who each speak a separate "silent language" to those who have studied this matter and know how to understand the "communication" of these silent witnesses and make deductions from it. Whoever understands this "silent language" gains valuable insights into the crime scene and the events that transpired. If someone is not proficient in the Chinese language, they must call an interpreter when interrogating a Chinese person. But it seems as if everyone who is enlisted in the modern "investigative apparatus" believes themselves capable of extracting the necessary information for a swift solution to the problem from a small piece of lint, or the location, direction, size, or color of a tiny bloodstain.

Each person in their own field, whether it be the skilled photographer or the fingerprint specialist, considers their own work to be the most important and the most urgent, while in reality, experience has clearly shown how the true investigator, who starts his search alone at the undisturbed crime scene, can more quickly lead the investigation in the right direction than the complex machinery of the modern "investigative apparatus" that is paraded around. The scientifically trained investigator, who must see everything and deduce from everything he observes (even the seemingly insignificant things) because of his specialized study of all types of traces, truly requires complete concentration of thought to ensure that nothing escapes him. He must take note of everything he sees—sometimes even things that are missing (and should be there)—and draw conclusions from them.

It is no coincidence that he has studied so many exact sciences: chemistry, physics, botany, zoology, bacteriology, etc., and trained his mind in logical thinking and deduction. However, for such a scientific investigator, it is completely impossible to achieve the necessary intense concentration of thought in a room where a dozen or so "interested parties" wander around, talking, touching various things, opening things, and so on, until the required level of concentration is reached. In such cases, it would have been better to leave him at home! The system followed by many judicial officials to "seal off" the crime scene by posting a guard with the message, "An expert is on the way; no one is allowed to enter the crime scene until their arrival!" is not widely appreciated or followed enough. Instead, they prefer to leave the door wide open and let dozens of people in, each one thinking they are the most important official present, collectively spoiling the investigation area for the true "scientific investigator."

I know from experience how detrimental that method (!?) is. Unless a miracle occurs or there is a betrayal, one can never reconstruct exactly how everything happened based solely on the "traces left behind." I already spoke about the destruction of scent trails and the damage to canine investigations in such invasion cases when answering the first of these three questions.

Question 3. "I would like to hear your opinion on why the combination of police expert and investigator has actually remained limited to the generation to which you belong. The current police experts are more focused on laboratory research."

To this, I respond: As you rightly point out, the current police experts indeed examine the substances and objects presented to them by the investigators, sometimes accompanied by unanswerable questions and requests for impractical investigations. I assume that the police experts are competent in examining the "traces" presented to them according to the rules of the art. However, their investigation is limited to what is brought to the laboratory. "Investigating at the crime scene" is something completely different! That requires years of study, including learning how to deduce from the found traces.

I was lucky to have a sharp-minded father who earned his reputation in certain areas of criminology in the last decade of the previous century. I eagerly watched my father's work as a young boy. He taught me various things from the relatively small domain he had mastered in "police scientifique," that is, scientific policing. The study of fingerprints was not yet on anyone's mind! Inspector Te Wechel from Rotterdam and I were the first in our country to conduct dactyloscopic examinations. The same went for several other types of silent witnesses that had previously gone unnoticed.

To further improve my skills as a scientific investigator, I not only studied every book I could get my hands on regarding the matter but also embarked on expensive study trips to foreign centers each year to gradually master the other aspects of criminology. I continuously practiced deducing from observed matters and built far-reaching final conclusions based on them. As far as my resources allowed, I purchased the necessary expensive instruments and books each year to perform my work in the field of investigation as well as possible. Some of these devices had prices with four digits before the decimal point! Fortunately, my work was appreciated and I knew that, when the occasion arose, investigations would be entrusted to my hands, enabling me to use those devices and prove that the money spent on them has been worthwhile.

Among those who observed my work from the sidelines were many who also wanted to venture in that direction. However, as soon as they realized they had to start by acquiring such specialized equipment and then patiently wait to see if an examining magistrate from some district would assign them an investigation (assuming they had completed years of study and preparation for their task), they quickly understood that it would be too risky to invest so much money in such specialized instruments and hope for the best! As a result, no "school" was formed. The voice of Prof. Mr. Van Dijck (formerly a member of the Supreme Court and a professor in Amsterdam), who emphasized that it was the responsibility of the state to establish a national institute for forensic investigation, headed by an experienced criminologist who could establish a "school" and train successors, sounded like a cry in the wilderness. Detecting, searching for traces, and deducing ... these skills are not learned solely from books; they require prolonged practice under the guidance of superiors, which I realized all too well during my visits to foreign centers and studying under my mentors there.

I already admitted to you that the current police experts, as laboratory workers, know in which direction the traces delivered to them should be examined, but the actual investigation at the crime scene remains foreign to them. This is because it must be learned differently than in the laboratory and because the search for traces, the actual investigation, becomes impossible once the aforementioned "invasion" of the "complete investigative apparatus" at the crime scene has occurred.

I have said before: the strength of the scientific investigator lies in their ability to find traces at the crime scene (provided it has been left undisturbed) that others overlook; they question silent witnesses who have something to tell them and provide material for deduction, but go unnoticed by others!

That, in short, is my answer to your last question.

I would like to add one more remark: I am currently in my forty-fourth year of service as a police expert (with the Amsterdam Police) *pro justitia* (for the sake of the law), and I have put in for retirement. When I see the direction in which changes are being implemented and think about the overwhelming presence of the modern "investigative apparatus" at the crime scene, I can only look back with gratitude on my years as an investigator when I could search for traces without any distractions. I am even more grateful that I will not be forced to seek contact with my "silent witnesses" amidst a dozen or more people at the crime scene in the future.

Translation by Rick van Rijn with the use of ChatGPT.

For Product Safety Concerns and Information please contact our EU
representative GPSR@taylorandfrancis.com
Taylor & Francis Verlag GmbH, Kaufingerstraße 24, 80331 München, Germany

www.ingramcontent.com/pod-product-compliance
Lightning Source LLC
Chambersburg PA
CBHW080934300426
44115CB00017B/2819